THE ENCYCLOPEDIA OF
TRUE
CRIME

BLITZ EDITIONS

Published by Blitz Editions
an imprint of Bookmart Ltd
Registered Number 2372865
Trading as Bookmart Ltd
Desford Road
Enderby
Leicester LE9 5AD

ISBN 1 85605 146 3

Every effort has been made to contact the copyright holders for the pictures.
In some cases they have been untraceable, for which we offer our apologies.
Special thanks to the Hulton-Deutsch Collection, who supplied the majority of pictures,
and thanks also to the following libraries and picture agencies:
Cassidy and Leigh, Mary Evans Photo Library, Express Newspapers, Robert Hunt, Imperial War Museum,
Marshall Cavendish, Midsummer Books, Peter Newark/Western Americana,
Popperfotos, Press Association, Rex Features, Frank Spooner Pictures,
Syndication International, Topham Picture Source.

The Authors
Allan Hall is the American correspondent for a major U.K. newspaper.
He has written several books on crime, the paranormal and the unexplained.

J. Anderson Black wrote the chapter 'Assassination'.
He has been a professional writer for more than twenty-five years,
and his published work covers a wide range of topics from art to crime,
as well as three novels and several screenplays for feature films.

Designed by COOPER WILSON DESIGN

THE ENCYCLOPEDIA OF
TRUE
CRIME

TRUE CRIMES

Every society has its misfits; those who cannot, or will not, comply with the social consensus of behaviour. Most of these restless souls are harmless, petty villains, but every now and again there emerges a truly criminal type. And there are other – more horrifying – periods when a group, or even a nation, loses its head to commit hideous acts within and against itself.

True Crimes catalogues the full range of human frailty and weakness – and evil. Some misfits unconsciously seek each other out to form a strange partnership, a secret union of perversity and, as a couple, commit unthinkable acts. Others remain solitary: strange women who loosen the constraints of their sex to turn to murder, or the lonely men whose fantasies are dark dreams of power and strength. But these isolated cases of horror are but reflections of the madness that can overtake society itself – rounding up thousands of victims, imprisoning them, torturing and slaughtering in a mass blood lust. We need to understand what causes these outbursts of deviant behaviour, whether it is found in individuals or groups.

We need to absorb the facts, the dreadful details, because perhaps through knowledge we can stop the carnage, the exploitation of misery that criminals inflict on our societies. This volume chronicles the couples who join in crime, those whose mutual perversities unite in a life of evil. There are the stories of women who, to compensate for their inadequacies, will exploit and even kill to achieve money, power or love. And the men, who alone or in political and military groups, become bloodthirsty killers.

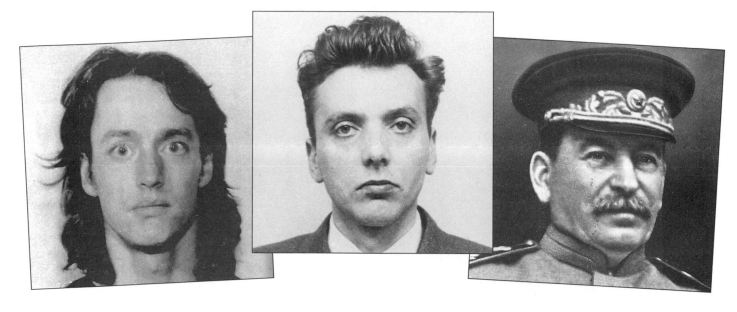

Contents

PARTNERS
IN CRIME

BONNIE & CLYDE
A Killing Love

The true story of Bonnie and Clyde is far more sinister than the movie. He was a homosexual and she a nymphomaniac, both were obsessed with guns and violent death and thrived on the publicity that surrounded them, even sending pictures of themselves to newspapers. Their small-time hold-ups were only an excuse for an orgy of killing.

Few villains achieve, in their own lifetime the status of folk hero. Robin Hood of Sherwood Forest was one who did, and in our own times, so has Ronnie Biggs, the Great Train Robber whose bravado and contempt for the law has earned him a certain popular respect. However, time adds lustre to even the most vicious criminals, and their evil is forgotten as myth gives them the glamour of brave individuals, outsiders who defy the constraints imposed by those in power.

Two such misplaced criminals are the professional thieves and murderers Bonnie Parker and Clyde Barrow, who went on the rampage during the Great Depression in America. Although they were ruthless killers, they have been immortalised in film, song and popular legend. They weren't very good robbers – most of their thefts were from gas stations, grocery stores and small-town diners. But they displayed a brutality and worked with a wild audacity that has earned them a place ias heroes in the myth of folk-lore.

Semi-literate and wholly without compassion, they roamed the Great Plains states of Missouri, Kansas and Oklahoma in their quest for easy cash. They loved their guns and their violent acts, cloaking themselves in the mystique of their 'mission' and recorded themselves for posterity in photographs.

With Buck Barrow, Clyde's brother, and other bandits, they formed the Barrow Gang, a nomadic outlaw tribe that criss-crossed state-lines, terrorising the small businessmen and farmers who were every bit as much victims of the Great Depression as themselves.

ALTHOUGH THEY WERE RUTHLESS KILLERS, THEY HAVE BEEN IMMORTALISED IN FILM, SONG AND POPULAR LEGEND.

Their relationship was an odd one, for Barrow was a homosexual, Parker virtually a nymphomaniac. Together they found a kind of love, a bond between misfits, focussed on firearms and violent death.

Clyde was born on 24 March, 1909 into extreme poverty in Teleco, Texas. One of eight children, his older brother Buck – who would later take orders from him – taught Clyde how to steal and hot-wire cars. After petty crime as a juvenile, and time spent in a boys' reform school, Clyde graduated to robbing roadside restaurants and small, country filling stations.

Often there was no more than a handful of dollars and some loose change to steal from these places but Clyde reasoned they were safer to rob than banks. His brother was sent to prison in 1928 after he was caught on a raid on a diner. With the heat

Above: *The shattered Ford V8 in which the gangster pair met their death.*

Opposite: *Bonnie Parker and Clyde Barrow have passed into folklore as glamorous outlaws but they were really vicious killers.*

on him Clyde drifted to Texas. In January 1930, feeling peckish while wandering around Dallas, he dropped into a cafe called Marco's and was served a hamburger by a vivacious and pretty waitress. Her name was Bonnie Parker.

Parker, born on 1 October, 1910, was the daughter of a bricklayer, a petite blonde package of boredom – 'bored crapless' as she confided to her diary at the time. She listened to the tall tales that the customer spun her about life on the road. Later that night she met him for a date, but there was no sexual interest on his part. Rather, they fuelled their friendship with each other through tales of robbery and mayhem. Parker, married to a convict serving ninety-nine years for murder, moved into a small furnished apartment in Dallas with Barrow.

Guns became the consuming passion of this strange pair. Parker was thrilled by the pistols that her beau wore holstered beneath his coat, and they took regular trips to the farmland outside Dallas for target practice with revolvers, rifles and sub-machine guns. Soon Parker was every bit as good a shot as he was. Parker undoubtedly saw in her trigger-happy new friend the means of escape from the life of menial work that bored her so much.

They soon took to robbery, she driving the getaway car – despite the fact that

Clyde was a much better driver – while Clyde ran into the stores and cleaned them out at gunpoint. He would then run back to the car, jump on the running board and cover them as the car raced away. The thrill of these escapades was almost sexual for Parker, who could never find satisfaction with Barrow. He had confessed that he became homosexual in the reform school and she satisfied her considerable sexual needs with a series of one-night stands and with the men who would later drift in and out of the Barrow Gang.

Three months after they teamed up Clyde was behind bars, having left his fingerprints all over the scene of a burglary in Waco, Texas. He was arrested at the Dallas apartment and sentenced to two years, but he didn't stay to complete his sentence. His brother Buck had broken out of jail and Clyde wrote a coded letter to Bonnie asking her to spring him. Together, she and Buck travelled to Waco, with

Parker wearing a .38 police issue revolver strapped to her thigh. She escaped the attentions of prison guards due to an incompetent search and contrived to slip the weapon to Clyde. He managed to break out that same night and rode freight trains across the plains states to Ohio.

Clyde Barrow stayed free for just a week before he was arrested again and this time sent to Eastham Jail, the tough Federal penitentiary from which his brother had

escaped. His mother Cummie Barrow deluged the state governor with pleas for leniency; pleas which were answered on 2 February, 1932, when he was released on parole. The prison was a crucial turning point in his life – after experiencing it he vowed to Parker, who waited to greet him at the gates, that he would rather die than ever go back inside. He had been tortured in the jail dubbed 'The Burning Hell',

Opposite, above: *This photo of Bonnie was to become a famous image of the wild outlaw girl – but she always regretted that the world saw her as an 'unlady-like' smoker.*

Opposite, below: *A police re-enactment of a Clyde Barrow store-stickup.*

Above: *Clyde cuddling his beloved firearms. The pair often sent photographs of themselves to the press for they delighted in their notorious fame.*

beaten with a whips and made to perform exercises until he dropped. He also killed a man, Ed Crowder, a cellblock informer, with a lead pipe, but authorities at the penitentiary did not credit him with the killing until after Clyde's death.

Parker was the next to go to prison after they stole a car and were pursued by police. Clyde escaped after crashing into a tree and running across fields, but Parker was caught and sentenced to two months. While she was inside, Clyde continued to rob the small-town stores and highway gas stations. In Hillsboro, Texas, he murdered sixty-five-year-old John Bucher in his jewellery store after taking just ten dollars from the till. It was when Bonnie was released that their wild and cold-blooded-killing spree began in earnest.

On 5 August, 1932, Clyde murdered two lawmen, Sherrif Charles Maxwell and his deputy Eugene Moore. He intended to rob the ticket seller at a barn dance in Atoka, Oklahoma, when the lawmen saw him loitering suspiciously. 'You better come out into the light boy, so I can see you better,' said Sherrif Maxwell, the last words he ever spoke. Clyde lifted up his overcoat and shot the two men at point-blank range with two automatic weapons.

A BUNCH OF NUTTY KILLERS

The bizarre couple then began their deadly odyssey across America. They robbed an armoury in Texas of an arsenal of sub-machine guns, ammunition, small arms and rifles. They fired indiscriminately into a dozen state troopers who had set up a road-block in Texas, wounding several. They held up liquor stores, gas stations and grocery outlets, all for a few dollars. They even kidnapped a sherrif, stripped him and dumped him on the roadside with the parting words: 'Tell your people that we ain't just a bunch of nutty killers. Just down home people trying to get through this damned Depression with a few bones.'

On the road they lived like old-fashioned outlaws, sleeping by camp fires, surviving on wild fowl they shot and peanut butter sandwiches. At night they would get drunk on bootlegged bourbon whiskey and Parker would write turgid romantic poetry that bemoaned their lot in life – that they were persecuted by the establishment and that in reality they were a new breed of hero. A sense of foreboding hung over the two of them; both sensed that they were not long for the world and that they would die young and die violently.

In the autumn of 1932, Bonnie and Clyde headed for New Mexico with gunslinger Roy Hamilton who joined them house in Dallas for another robber, were gunned down when Clyde turned up instead. And together they kidnapped gas station attendant turned apprentice-robber William Jones, who was to travel with them for the next eighteen months. This fellow traveller would later give lawmen many details of the criminals' life.

Above: *Those in authority were appalled by the public's interest in Bonnie and Clyde. The pair were written about in popular magazines, their images were in all the papers. Here, 'souvenirs' of their vagabond life are assembled – stolen car plates, clothing and baggage.*

but they decided that pickings were not as rich there as Texas, so headed back. Hamilton, an accomplished robber, was also as perverted as the duo he now allied himself with. He regularly slept with Bonnie... and with Clyde. This bizarre triangle seemed to suit them all.

They killed indiscriminately and often. Clyde murdered a butcher with eight bullets when the man lunged at him with a cleaver after Clyde had stolen $50 from his store. He murdered Doyle Johnson in Temple, Texas, when he tried to stop them stealing his car. Two lawmen, staking out a

Like gypsies, they criss-crossed the southwest, continuing to hold up shops and garages. They picked up brother Buck again, together with his wife Blanche, and the robberies increased. In Kansas they robbed a loan company office where Bonnie saw her wanted poster for the first time. She was so excited that she and Clyde were 'celebrities', she fired off a dozen letters to prominent newspaper editors complete with snapshots of her and Clyde they had taken on the road. She perpetuated the myth that they were fighters against authority – authorities like the banks that were foreclosing on poor farmers and businessmen. She made no mention, of course, of the pathological delight they both took in killing.

At this time she was working on a turgid, autobiographical poem, 'The Story of Suicidal Sal' that would later reach the newspapers.

We, each of us, have a good alibi,
For being down here in the joint.
But few of them are really justified,
If you get right down to the point.
You have heard of a woman's glory,
Being spent on a downright cur,
Still you can't always judge the story,
As true being told by her.

As long as I stayed on the island,
And heard confidence tales from the gals,
There was only one interesting and truthful,
It was the story of Suicide Sal.

Now Sal was a girl of rare beauty,
Though her features were somewhat tough,
She never once faltered from duty,
To play on the up and up.

She told me this tale on the evening,
Before she was turned out free,
And I'll do my best to relate it,
Just as she told it to me.

I was born on a ranch in Wyoming,
Not treated like Helen of Troy,
Was taught that rods were rulers,
And ranked with greasy cowboys...

The poem was interrupted at this point due to a police raid on a hideout they used in Joplin, Missouri. Bonnie and Clyde, Buck and Blanche, fired more than one thousand machine gun bullets at the cops coming to get them, killing two of them. Later she finished the poem and mailed it.

Then I left my home for the city,
To play in its mad dizzy whirl,
Not knowing how little of pity,
It holds for a country girl.
You have heard the story of Jesse James,
Of how he lived and died,
If you are still in need of something to read,
Here's the story of Bonnie and Clyde.
Now Bonnie and Clyde are the

Barrow gang,
I'm sure you have all read
How they rob and steal
And how those who squeal
Are usually found dying or dead.

There are lots of untruths to
 their write-ups.
They are not so merciless as that;
They hate all the laws,
The stool pigeons, spotters and rats.
If a policeman is killed in Dallas,
And they have no clues to guide,
If they can't find a fiend,
They just wipe the slate clean,
And hang it on Bonnie and Clyde.

If they try to act like citizens,
And rent them a nice little flat,
About the third night they are invited
 to fight
By a sub-machine gun rat-tat-tat.

A newsboy once said to his buddy:
'I wish old Clyde would get jumped,
In these awful hard times,
We'd make a few dimes,
If five or six cops would get bumped.'

They class them as cold-blooded killers,
They say they are heartless and mean,
But I say this with pride,
That once I knew Clyde,
When he was honest and upright and clean.
But the law fooled around,

Above, left: W.D.Jones and Henry Methvin (above) were part of the Barrow Gang but both were to betray Bonnie and Clyde.

SHE WAS SO EXCITED THAT SHE AND CLYDE WERE 'CELEBRITIES', SHE FIRED OFF A DOZEN LETTERS TO NEWSPAPER EDITORS.

Kept tracking them down,
And locking them up in a cell.
Till he said to me
'I will never be free
So I will meet a few of them in hell.'

The road was so dimly lighted,
There were no highway signs to guide,
But they made up their minds,
If the roads were all blind,
They wouldn't give up till they died.
The road gets dimmer and dimmer,
Sometimes you can hardly see,
Still it's fight man to man,
And do all you can,
For they know they can never be free.

They don't think they are too tough or
* desperate,*
They know the law always wins,
They have been shot at before
But they do not ignore
That death is the wages of sin.

From heartbreaks some people have
* suffered,*
From weariness some people have died,
But take it all and all,
Our troubles are small,
Til we get like Bonnie and Clyde.

Some day they will go down together,
And they will bury them side by side,
To a few it means grief,
To the law it's relief,
But it's death to Bonnie and Clyde.

Below: *Relatives of the Barrow Gang on trial for harbouring the criminals. Bonnie's mother is third from left, Clyde's mother third from right. The rest are sisters or sisters-in-law.*

The robbing went on. They switched mostly to small banks, in the rural towns of Indiana, Minnesota and Texas. A marshall was killed in cold blood outside the town of Alma and a two-hundred-strong possee set off after the gang. They were holed up in a rented log cabins at a country park near Platte City in Missouri but the manager became suspicious when they paid the rental in small change – the loot from several of their nickel-and-dime gas station hold-ups. The manager of the Red Crown Cabin Camp alerted police who, upon hearing the description of the guests, assembled a small army to lay siege to the rented cabin. It was 24 July, 1933.

In the ensuing confusion they escaped, leaving three officers dead. But Blanche had taken a slug in her leg, Clyde was grazed on the head, Bonnie was grazed with a bullet on her ribs and Buck... Buck was dying from a rifle bullet in his head.

NO PLACE TO GO

They escaped to a woodland area between Dexter and Refield in the rural state of Iowa where they did their best for Buck. But because they were always on the road, and without a network of contacts like those used by contemporary gangsters such as Ma Barker and John Dillinger, there was no place to hole up and get the medical attention Buck badly needed.

Below: *Her family gave Bonnie a fine funeral ill-suited to a killer.*

They were debating how to leave the wounded Buck when Clyde intuitively sensed a movement in the trees. Suddenly bullets began to rain down on their campsite. They returned fire with rifles and machine guns, even the mortally wounded Buck fired more than one thousand rounds at the lawmen. Bonnie and Clyde managed to bolt into thick undergrowth and escape but Buck was riddled with bullets. The posse found Blanche prostrate across his corpse, weeping inconsolably.

With the heat on, the duo headed back to the north and Minnesota, reasoning that they do.' The following month Bonnie and Clyde drifted back to Texas for a meeting with his mother at a roadside picnic spot. But the pair barely escaped with their lives – his mother had been followed by a sherrif's posse who ringed the site. Once again alerted by some kind of sixth sense, Clyde drove straight past the rendezvous site. The back of the car was stuck by bullets and both he and Bonnie were wounded in the legs but not seriously.

After pulling off a few more small robberies, they teamed up again with Hamilton – after springing him from a jail

there would be less trouble in a state where they had committed relatively few crimes. They were practically bums now, stealing washing from clothes-lines and foraging for scraps of food. Jones, the kidnapped garage attendant, was with them and he later told police: 'This was not the life I expected when I joined up with them. We was nothing better than hobos.'

In October, fed up with his diet of raw vegetables stolen from fields, Jones hopped a freight train back to Texas, was arrested, and told police about the antics of the gang making sure he disassociated himself from the killings. 'It's them two,' he said. 'I ain't never seen anyone enjoy killin' as much as

with minor thugs Joe Palmer and Henry Methvin – and the Barrow Gang was back to strength once more. The FBI, because of the murders and the transportation of weapons and stolen cars across state lines, was now in on the hunt and the officers were instructed to shoot-to-kill and ask questions afterwards. J. Edgar Hoover, celebrated head of the FBI warned his G-men that Clyde was a 'psychopath – he should be killed like a rattlesnake'. Even other gangsters, knowing about their bloodlust, decided that there should be no honour among thieves. Charles Arthur 'Pretty Boy' Floyd, the gangster, was furious when he learned that the psycho-

Above: *Police hold a distraught Blanche Barrow after they shot dead her husband, Buck Barrow.*

pathic pair had entered territory that he regarded as his own in the Cookson Hills, northern Minnesota. 'Don't feed them and don't give them shelter,' he ordered his cohorts and criminal associates. 'Stick the law on them if you can. They are vermin and have nothing to do with our people.'

Public opinion was rapidly turning against them. The banks they robbed were forced to close because they were suffering in the hard times, as were the businesses they raided. Soon the newspaper readers who had adored her romantic poem realised that there was nothing Robin-Hood-like about their exploits. They were simply greedy and ruthless killers.

KNOW THINE ENEMY

Soon only Methvin was left with the gang. Hamilton had argued with Clyde and gone his own way, Palmer dropped out with chronic stomach ulcers. The heat was on like never before, particularly in Texas, where a lawman called Frank Hamer, who had gunned down sixty-five notorious criminals during his career, was given the task of hunting down Bonnie and Clyde.

Hamer analysed every move they made, drew up maps and charts of all their movements over the previous years and discerned a pattern of sorts in the type of places they hit and the routes they took. 'I wanted to get into their evil minds,' he said. 'Know thine enemy was my maxim and I learned it well.' Several times during the early months of 1934 Hamer and his men came upon campsites that the duo had abandoned just hours before, but he was determined to stay on their trail.

In April that year, after hiding out on a farm in Louisiana, they returned to Texas to see Bonnie's relatives and hopefully lie low. But, as they neared the outskirts of the town of Grapevine, motorcycle police Ernest Wheeler and Harold Murphy rode past them. When they crested a rise in the road in front, Clyde pulled the car over and stopped. The motorcycle cops, their suspicions aroused, turned around and came back towards them. As they drew level with the car Clyde murdered them both with both barrels of a shotgun. Two weeks later in Oklahmoa, when their car got stuck in mud, they were approached by two police officers. One died with a

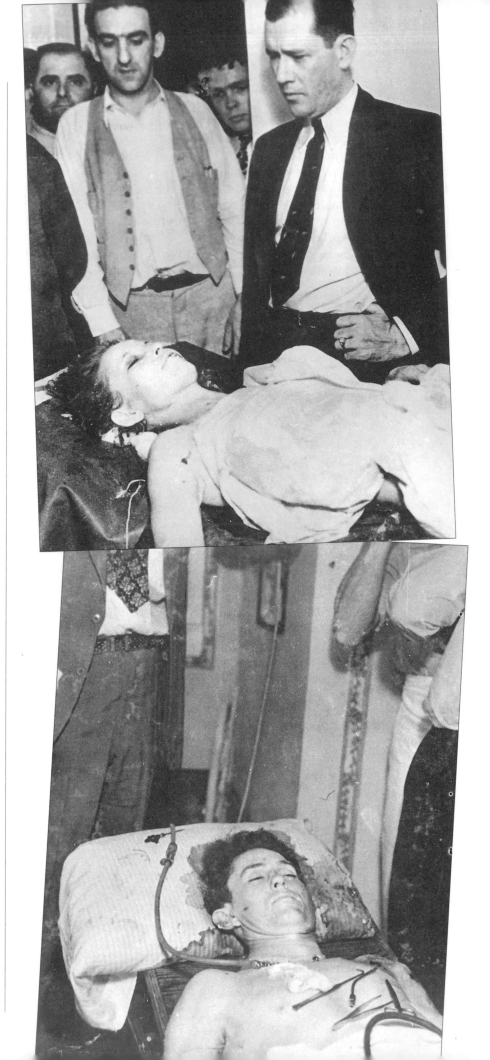

revolver bullet in the chest, the other was luckier - he was slightly wounded.

The key to capturing the outlaws lay with Methvin, who was still running with them. His father Ivan offered to help trap them if Hamer would agree to granting his son a pardon. Hamer, needing Bonnie and Clyde more than him, agreed to the deal. Henry Methvin, seeing a way out for himself, agreed to co-operate with his father when he next contacted him. Henry slipped away from a hideout shack in Shreveport, Louisiana, which was promptly surrounded by Hamer's armed Texas Rangers. Soon a posse had hidden themselves along the road leading to the shack; they were armed with Browning machine guns, high-powered rifles and numerous grenades and tear gas bombs.

At 9.15am on 23 May, 1934 the V8 Ford which the couple had been using for the past week – they changed licence plates every day – crested a rise in the road leading from the hideout. Clyde was at the wheel, his shoes off, driving with bare feet. He wore sunglasses against the strong spring sunshine. Next to him sat his deadly moll in a new red dress she had bought with stolen loot some weeks previously. Stashed in the car were two thousand bullets, three rifles, twelve pistols and two pump-action shotguns.

A FRIGHTENED DECOY

Methvin Snr has agreed to be a decoy. His truck was parked at the edge of the road and Clyde drew level with it. Clyde asked him if there had been any sight of his son. Methvin, almost quaking with fear, saw a truckful of black farm labourers coming down the road and he panicked, diving for cover beneath his own vehicle. A sherrif with the posse named Jordan suddenly yelled for the duo to surrender. But this was like a red rag to a bull for this homocidal pair. In one swift motion Clyde had his door open and a shotgun in his hand, Bonnie was equipped with a revolver.

This time there was no escape. A murderous rain of fire battered the car. More than five hundred bullets slammed into the bodies of the gangsters and they were literally ripped to pieces. Clyde was slumped backwards, his foot off the clutch pedal. The car was still in gear and it

Opposite: Pictures of the dead desperadoes were circulated all over the United States. The public could not get enough to read about the gruesome lives and bloody deaths of Bonnie and Clyde.

Below: Bonnie Parker at peace at last after a wild and dangerous life.

inched ahead, coming to a halt in a ditch. The posse of lawmen continued to pour fire into the wreck for four whole minutes after it had come to a stop.

As newspaper headlines around the world shouted the news of their deaths, local residents were charged a dollar a head to view the mangled corpses on a morgue slab. Thousands paid to look.

Ray Hamilton, the robber who ran with them, was eventually executed less than ten years later for other murders. Just before his death, he accurately described Bonnie and Clyde. 'They loved to kill people, see blood run. That's how they got their kicks.

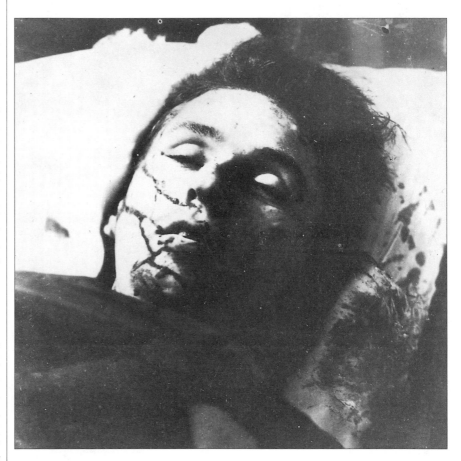

'THEY WERE DIRTY PEOPLE. HER BREATH SMELLED AWFUL AND HE NEVER TOOK A BATH. THEY SMELLED BAD ALL THE TIME. THEY WOULD STEAL THE PENNIES FROM A DEAD MAN'S EYES.'

There was many times when they didn't have to kill, but they did anyways. They were dirty people. Her breath smelled awful and he never took a bath. They smelled bad all the time. They would steal the pennies from a dead man's eyes.'

The Parker family tried its best to paint Bonnie in a different light. The horribly-inaccurate inscription on this murderer's tombstone reads thus: 'As the flowers are all made sweeter, by the sunshine and the dew, so this old world is made brighter, by the likes of folk like you.'

GOTTI & GRAVANO
A Broken Honour

John Gotti murdered and lied his way to the top of New York's Mafia empire yet the FBI could not make their charges stick to the 'Teflon Don'. That is until 1992 when 'Sammy the Bull' Gravano, the man who had killed nearly forty people in Gotti's name betrayed him in a spectacular courtroom drama.

J ohn Gotti, Capo di Tutti Cappi – Boss of Bosses of all the Mafia families in America – made just one mistake in his rise to the top of the $16 million per-year crime empire. He trusted Salvatore 'Sammy the Bull' Gravano and chose him to become his underboss. It was a mistaken decision that would send John Gotti to prison for the rest of his life.

Gotti's rule came to an end in 1992 when Sammy Gravano broke the code of *omerta*, the Mafia code of secrecy and silence, to betray the Godfather Gotti. Sammy's testimony also broke the power of the Gambino clan, Gotti's mob 'family'.

To his admirers, Gotti was a generous guy who wore $4,000 silk suits and kept the drug-dealing scum away from ordinary, decent folk. Every year, without fail,he held an annual fireworks display on America's 4 July Independence Day, releasing thousands of dollars worth of rockets to the delight of the neighbourhood.

On the street well-wishers tugged at his pure cashmere coat, others called out respectful greetings,as he made his way to the Ravenite Social Club – a nondescript tenement in the heart of Little Italy.

It was behind these doors – fitted with alarms, armoured and locked – that John Gotti, Capo di Tutti Cappi, held court. It was here that the veneer of philanthropist. was dropped. This was the office of the Dapper Don, as he was known. Gambling, corruption, liqour sales, prostitution, drugs and murder were his business and he did it well. So well, in fact, that he earned another title: the FBI called him the 'Teflon Don' as no indictment they threw at him ever stuck to this criminal.

That was hardly surprising as he had a finger in every illegal pie. And he was protected by witnesses and associates who

were too afraid of the consequences to tell the truth. These people believed that they would meet a horrible death if they testified against John Gotti, the ruthless and arrogant leader if the powerful Mafia.

THE NAUGHTY BUT NICE IMAGE

The FBI task force that concentrates solely on Gotti and his Gambino crime family, were determined his naughty-but-nice image would not save him from justice when he was seized in 1990. He is languishing now in jail.

TO HIS ADMIRERS, GOTTI WAS A GENEROUS GUY WHO WORE $4,000 SILK SUITS AND KEPT THE DRUG-DEALING SCUM AWAY FROM ORDINARY, DECENT FOLK.

Above: *The law came to take Gotti away, but he belived he was immune from the ordinary rules of society.*

Opposite: *John Gotti ruled a criminal empire based on fear and terror.*

Thanks to the testimony of his former sidekick Sammy the Bull, he was convicted of numerous murders, including the 1985 assasination of Paul 'Big Paulie' Castellano, the Gambino Godfather whose assassination he masterminded in order to take over the organisation. Even as the paramedics were trying to save Castellano's life after the shooting in 1985, John Gotti was being sworn in as the new Capo di Tutti Cappi in a ceremony that has all the solemnity of a Vatican mass. But in 1990 when he was arrested for the fourth and final time, the FBI were determined that it was time for the spell to be broken.

Gotti was born on 27 October, 1940, the fifth of thirteen children and their first son, to dirt-poor John and Fannie Gotti. The family were squashed into a townhouse in the South Bronx – then, as now, New York's toughest neighbourhood. Gotti came to despise the Bronx so much that when he was at the peak of his power, it was the one borough where he refused to do business.

He quickly decided that violence was more fun than studying. His father, who had come from Naples as a child, worked sixteen hours a day as a sanitation worker and John Gotti realised then that the work route to success was for schmucks – you had to take what you wanted.

GOTTI WAS KNOWN AS 'FAST FISTS'

When he was twelve, the clan moved to the Brownsville section of Brooklyn – still a predominantly Italian neighbourhood, but one that seethed with ethnic tension. There were dozens of white street gangs which clashed regularly with the black community on the fringes of Brownsville and the strapping, muscular Gotti was known as 'Fast Fists' to his admirers. By the time he was sixteen, he led the feared Fulton-Rockaway Boys Gang. .On 15 May, 1957 came Gotti's first arrest when he was nabbed for disorderly conduct but the charges were dropped.

Mostly, Gotti and his cronies were coffee bar thugs who inhabited the storefront clubs popular among the Italian immigrants. Gotti was a frequent visitor at a club run by Carmine Fatico, then a 'Capo', or captain, in the crime family headed by Albert Anastasia and nicknamed 'Murder Inc' by the Feds. Inside Fatico's

club, smug, hard men with ready cash and fancy clothes lounged around all day and were treated with the same brand of obsequious respect that Gotti would one day command on his own turf.

His formal schooling ended at sixteen when he dropped out of the Franklin K. Lane High School in Brooklyn and he drifted into dead-end jobs. He worked as a garment presser on Seventh Avenue, the city's fashion district, and as a trucker's helper. But his thrills came from hanging

Below: *This is the public face of John Gotti, the smiling, benevolent philanthropist.*

___

HE QUICKLY DECIDED THAT VIOLENCE WAS MORE FUN THAN STUDYING.

___

out with the tough guys at the storefront cafes where old men heard of his prowess with his fists and his quick-thinking mind.

Gotti became a numbers runner for the illegal bookmakers and performed small chores for the local hoods – running money to bent cops on the mob's payroll and stealing cars for heists. At seventeen he started his criminal record – a probation term for burglary. In 1959 he was working in the garment factory by day and running errands for the hard men at night. Around this time he met Victoria DiGiorgio, a petite woman with dark hair and classical Italian features and was won over by her serene charm and her quiet nature.

A SOLDIER IN CRIME

Over her parents' objections, she married him in April 1960 and they had their first

child, Angela, a year later. The year was significant too for another reason – Gotti had been accepted part-time into the ranks of the mob as a 'soldier' in the Gambino crime family. Here he was to meet Salvatore Gravano, nicknamed 'Sammy the Bull' because of his muscular frame which was always squeezed and closely-packed into too-tight suits.

Over the next three decades, John Gotti rose up the ranks; and with him he took along Sammy the Bull. Sammy came from the same background as himself and, lacking Gottis' ambition, was more than willing to be a loyal underboss. So blindly loyal to Gotti was he that he would later say at his boss' trial: 'John Gotti was my master and I was his dog. When he said "bite", I bit.' But the dog was to turn.

As Gotti rose in rank, the mobster king himself, Albert Anastasia, failed to read the

Above: John Gotti with his son, John Jnr. A devoted family man, Gotti was well regarded by his neighbours. They did not know how many men he had laid in unmarked graves.

writing on the wall. He surrounded himself with too many ambitious men and not enough loyal servants. By the time he was ready to change things just a little, it was too late. The head of Murder Inc was killed by Carlo Gambino's thugs. With Anastasia shot to death in a Manhattan barber shop, Gambino became the boss and demanded loyalty from the 'soldiers' who previously worked for Anastasia. Gotti, sensing the main chance, swore his allegiance to the Sicilian, now the powerful Godfather.

Gotti quit the garment factory and took another job with a trucking firm where he learned the rudiments of hijacking and warehouse raids. At night he and Sammy hung out in pool halls and bars, hustling for information on lucrative truck-loads that he could pass on to his 'crew' capo – the revered Carmine Fatico. The Capo in the Mafia hierachy commands a team of 'soldiers', around two hundred and fifty, who swear life-allegiance to the family under whom they operate.

Because of his loyalty to Gambino, he was singled out by Fatico – nicknamed 'Charley Wagons' because of his speciality of hijacking trucks – for a special task. He was sent with Sammy to rough up the proprietor of one of Fatico's 'chop shops' – garages where stolen cars were dismantled, reassembled in different combinations of parts and re-sold.

THE SLOW CLIMB TO POWER

His nocturnal activities put a heavy strain on his marriage and led to a short separation from Victoria, who by 1963 had given birth to two more children, daughter Victoria and John Jnr. Then Gotti went to prison for twenty days for stealing a car in 1963. In 1966 he was jailed again for four months for attempted theft and this time lost his job at the trucking company where he had been able to provide so much inside information for Gambino's hijacking crews. By 1969 he had become a full–time hijacker and had a flash car and house in the suburbs on Long Island. He was

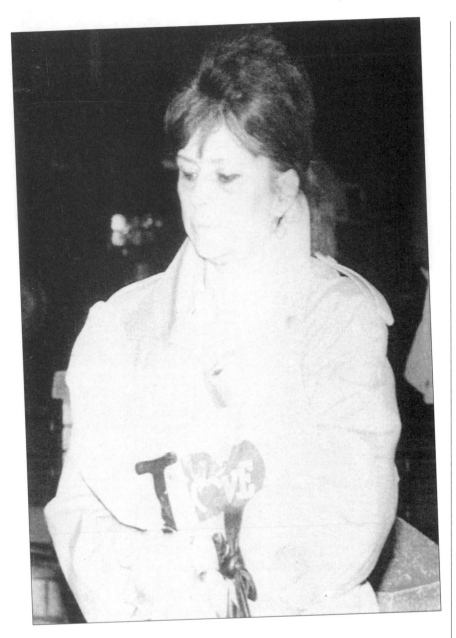

committed to the mob by this time and he dreamed of having the kind of ruthless power that Carmine Fatico wielded.

Salvatore was his closest pal now. Sammy was becoming something of a legend in mob ranks. He was completely dispassionate when ordered to 'whack' somebody – mob parlance for executing an enemy. One day he was sitting at home watching the movie M*A*S*H with his family when his dog came in with a human hand in its mouth – the hand belonged to a member of his own family who had crossed Gotti. And Sammy had whacked him as if he was of no more consequence than a fly, buried him on a local rubbish tip and thought no more of him until his dog, foraging for scraps, had had the good fortune to disinter his remains.

Above: *The faithful wife, Victoria Gotti, has always stood by her man and remains silent when asked what her husband does for a living. She says simply: 'He provides. He puts food on the table.'*

As Sammy became ever more enthusiastic about killing, so gambling became the chronic drug for Gotti. He had no weakness for wine or women and worked eighteen-hour days but he could never refuse a roll of the dice, a bet on a ball game or a long poker session. It left him forever chasing money which he made up for by taking on more and more dirty work for the mob. This also involved loansharking, and earning fat commissions from Gambino underbosses, to shake up businesses where the kickbacks were not fast enough coming through. Luck ran out, however, that same year when an FBI sting set up at New York's Kennedy Airport snared Gotti and several other Gambino associates as they robbed a warehouse on the airport complex of women's clothing worth $7,641. John Gotti was sentenced to three years in jail – and jail is the natural finishing school for any ambitious mobster.

When Gotti emerged from prison, the traditional order among the Mafia clans had not changed in New York. The city's rich pickings remained divided between his chosen tribe the Gambino family, and the Bonnano family, the Luchese family, the Genovese and the Colombo families. The structure of these criminal warlord societies was the same: the boss, followed by the underboss and then the *consiglieri*, or trusted counsellor, who relayed instructions to the capos in charge of the soldiers in their crews. The Gambino family had some twenty crews, each with their quota of 'made' men and numerous associates who shared their booty with the capos who, in turn, channelled profits to the top three leaders in the family.

While Gotti was in jail his capo, Carmine Fatico, moved the gang's HQ from East New York to a dismal storefront in the city borough of Queens at a club called The Bergin Hunt and Fish Social Club, which quickly became known to the underworld just as 'The Bergin'.

A TEST OF LOYALTY

In 1972, after three years inside, thirty-one-year-old John Gotti came out to a promotion. He had served his time 'honourably' inside, so the Gambino underboss Aniello Dellacroce gave the former hijacker and muscleman his capo's job, putting him in charge of the Bergin crew. Dellacroce had befriended Gotti before he went in to jail and was impressed with his cool, his intelligence and his deep respect for Cosa Nostra traditions.

In his new job, Gotti concentrated on organising and consolidating the Family's white-collar rackets – the pay-offs from rigging contracts, waste-disposal kickbacks, protection money from the entertainment industries. But it was the Don, Gambino himself, who set the ultimate test of John Gotti's loyalty and bravery. The ageing Godfather was stricken with grief a year after Gotti's release when his nephew Emmanuel was kidnapped and murdered. Gambino was beside himself with sorrow and pledged 'great things' for the *capo* John Gotti if he could track down the killer and revenge the boy's death.

GOTTI PULLED OUT A SNUB NOSED .38 REVOLVER

The word went out on the street immediately and the net was cast among hit men, five-and-dime killers and rival gangs, like the Irish Westies who often took on the contracts that the Mob refused to carry out. Gotti, with two others, was happy to learn that stick-up man turned contract killer, James McBratney, had been identified as the kidnapper and murderer.

On 22 May, 1973, Gotti went with his accomplices to Staten Island's Snoopes Bar and Grill where McBratney was drinking alone. Witnesses saw Gotti swagger up to him and pull out a card – it turned out later to be a fake ID for a New York police detective. There was a scuffle as McBratney realised the trouble he was in. He was reaching into his inside pocket when Gotti reached into his own shoulder holster and pulled out a snub nosed .38 police issue revolver and opened fire.

A dozen bullets from Gotti's gun and those of his accomplices made sure that the job was done. However, it was a sloppy 'hit' and too many people got too good a look at Gotti and his sidekicks. Gotti and one other, his old friend Angelo Ruggiero, were arrested within seventy-two hours to face charges of murder.

A grateful Gambino made certain that money bought the best lawyer in the shape of John Cohn for Gotti and his accomplice.

Hottest of New York's hotshot lawyers, he negotiated a remarkable deal with the Staten Island district attorney's office. In exchange for reduced charges of attempted manslaughter, they both pleaded guilty and each received maximum terms of four years at state penitentiaries.

The tentacles of the mob reached far into the jail. Although apparently in good health, he was taken on three, one-hundred-and-twenty mile round trips from his cell at the Greenhaven Correctional facility in upstate New York to Brooklyn – allegedly for examinations by a private physician. In reality, Gotti had bribed guards to take him to his home for meetings with his wife Victoria and to restaurants where he ate hearty Italian meals with his cronies before being transported back to jail.

Carlo Gambino died in 1976 while Gotti was still inside. By normal rights of succession the underboss – and mentor to Gotti – Dellacroce should have moved into the top slot. But before his death Gambino eschewed mob protocol and appointed his brother-in-law Paul Castellano as the boss. Castellano handed Dellacroce the consolation prize by allowing him to remain the underboss in charge of ten of the family's twenty-three crews. Observers of organised

> HOWEVER, IT WAS A SLOPPY 'HIT' AND TOO MANY PEOPLE GOT TOO GOOD A LOOK AT GOTTI AND HIS SIDEKICKS.

Above: *The house where John Gotti played the role of quiet family man.*

crime say this was the worst thing the dying Castellano could have done. By allowing a rival to wield such vast power within the empire, he had created two opposing and deadly factions. Paul Castellano had an image of himself as a corporate executive rather than a gun-toting Al Capone. He liked the loyal capo Gotti and displayed his affection for him.

In March 1980, however, Gotti's life took a tragic turn. A devoted family man, he was nevertheless especially fond of his

PAUL CASTELLANO KEPT AWAY FROM NARCOTICS BELIEVING ITWAS A TRADE FIT ONLY FOR 'THE COLOURDS'.

Above: *Gotti takes a stroll outside his home and shrugs off press questions about his alleged criminal activities.*

Opposite: *The 'Dapper Don' as well dressed as ever enters court to face numerous counts of racketeering and murder. John Gotti faced a long prison term.*

second youngest child Frank, then aged twelve. When this son was killed in a cycling accident Gotti was beside himself with grief. It didn't matter that it was the child's fault, which it was. Frank had ridden straight into the path of the car driven by neighbour John Favara.

Favara began receiving anonymous death threats and began to make plans to move with his family to another part of the state, away from John Gotti who cocked his finger at him in a gun symbol every time he drove past his house. Four months later – while Gotti and his wife Victoria were in Florida on holiday – furniture

salesman Favara vanished forever. He had parked his van in a parking lot near his home when witnesses claimed that they saw a burly figure emerge from the shadows and club him over the head. Favara, fifty-one, was bundled into the back of his van which was then driven away and he was never seen again.

Gotti never got over the death of 'Young Frankie' and he paid a monthly lone vigil to his grave. The front room of his home was turned into a shrine to his dead son, the boy's picture flanked by heavy velvet drapes that fell in folds round the gilded photo frame. However, Gotti continued to prosper as mobsters of the other families were falling like nine-pins to the prosecutions brought by the Feds.

GOTTI ESCAPES JAIL

An FBI wiretap placed inside the Bergin in 1981 (the first of many) gave agents their first glimpse of what made Gotti tick. They were seeking evidence to convict Gotti and his cohorts with running an illegal gambling operation on the premises. The taps paid off and several Bergin underlings were jailed but Gotti escaped.

By this time – July 1981 – other members of his crew were worried by his appalling gambling losses, rumoured to be up to $50,000 a month. More worrying for the crews than his gambling, however, was the new sharp turn the Gambino mob had taken in dealing with drugs. 'Big Paulie' Castellano, the Godfather, had run an organisation that kept away from narcotics, believeing it was a trade fit only for 'the coloureds'. An educated, meticulous man who studied the Wall Street Journal every day from cover to cover, he was furious when the heroin trafficking indictments landed on his doormat one day. Behind his back Gotti, using contacts established by Sammy the Bull in the drug underworld, had been dealing big-time. Gene Gotti was arrested, his old pal Angelo Ruggiero, a lawyer from the Bergin and a director of the Arc Plumbing Company – for twenty years Gotti's 'front' where the books claimed he was a salesman.

A police detective says: 'When we hit those guys back in '82 with indictments for trafficking Big Paulie was beside himself with rage. He screamed at Gotti: "Listen

Johnny, you had better prove you were not involved with this''.' But Gotti was involved and had pushed for drug distribution because he saw the massive profits and the potential power that the narcotics trade could bring to the family.

Castellano himself was indicted and it was the beginning of the end for Gotti under his reign. He let it be known that John Gotti had no future in his organisation. He had let drugs in, carelessly allowed an FBI informer into the ranks, and now he, the boss, was indicted on charges that could put him away for life. Now both men plotted the demise of each other.

The Mafia has a 'Commission' – the mob term for the committee composed of representatives from all five Mafia families that carved up the city.

The Commission met in 1957 at a now historic parley called the Apalachin Conference at which they decided to steer clear of drug dealing. The Mafia hierachy, determined to preserve their image as family men with a concern for the morals of society, decided to leave it to the blacks. The four other clans in New York flagrantly broke the treaty but Big Paulie made his crews stick by it. It enraged him that it was John Gotti's Bergin Crew that flouted his orders. Word was out after the heroin trafficking indictments that there was no place in the hierachy any longer for the upstart capo, John Gotti.

BILOTI NAMED AS SUCCESSOR

It is widely believed that Castellano was planning a hit on Gotti when he was swept along in the drug indictments. Rudolph Giuliani, the new, squeaky clean district attorney, hit him and the four other leaders under the powerful new RICO act which was eventually to lead to the downfall of all the Mafia families save one – the Gambino clan under Gotti himself. Dellacroce, his sponsor and mentor within the family, died from natural causes in December 1985. With him died any further hope Gotti may have had of sticking around in the clan. Thomas Biloti had already been named by Castellano as the successor to the top post – making it clear that Gotti's drug trafficking was the reason for the snub.

On 16 December that same year – according to testimony he has repeatedly

given to federal agents – John Gotti was nowhere near the fashionable Sparks Steak House in Midtown Manhattan. Sparks was Big Paulie's favourite restaurant and he had gone there that day with his chosen successor to discuss family tactics when he was put away on the heroin indictment.

At precisely 5.16pm on that evening Paul Castellano's limousine turned into East 46th Street and purred to a halt at the awnings outside Sparks. Big Paulie was halfway out of the passenger door when the first shots hit him. Thomas Biloti sat behind the steering wheel and the first of five bullets tore into his body and skull. The gunman ran to the corner where a waiting car sped off. Two streets away John Gotti and Salvatore Gravano were toasting each other with expensive champagne in the back of a limousine.

Federal agents say that it was later that night, at an unknown spot in the sprawling city, that Gotti re-swore the omerta and became the Godfather. Reno Franceschini, the New York police expert on the Mafia, said: 'I was in London and as soon as I heard about Paulie getting whacked I said Gotti is the next Godfather.'

Above: *Victoria Gotti enjoys her husband's wealth as she glides round New York with him in a large, armour-plated limousine.*

HE SWITCHED FROM WHITE-COLLAR MONEY LAUNDERING SCHEMES TO THE TRADITIONAL MOB SCHEMES BACKED UP BY VIOLENCE.

It was after the assassination that prosecutors believe that Gotti formally opened the heroin and cocaine pipeline to the Gambino family. He also switched from the white-collar money laundering schemes favoured by Castellano back to more traditional mob schemes backed up by violence.

TRIALS PUT AWAY MOST OF MAFIA HIERACHY

Police say he became Capo di Tutti Capi by dint of staying out of jail rather than by consent. A series of trials in the early Eighties put away most of the Mafia hierachy for life in New York – all except Gotti. His scare tactics, public image, a brilliant lawyer in the shape of Bruce Cutler, ensured that he earned the nickname 'The Teflon Don'.

John Gotti never forgets a double-cross and one of those doomed to find it out the hard way was Willie Boy Johnson. Willy Boy was Wahoo to the FBI, a low-level soldier in Gotti's crew when he was a capo and the one who gave details to the Feds of his boss's moves to begin dealing in heroin and cocaine. Willie Boy had been living under an assumed name in Brooklyn ever since his testimony led to the convictions of several mob figures – not least among them Gotti's brother Gene, who is currently serving a twenty-year sentence for heroin smuggling. On 29 August, 1988, at 6.20am Willie Boy left home to go to work on a construction site. He didn't see the three men stepping out of the stolen car parked opposite, nor their automatic pistols. When the shooting had stopped there were fourteen bullet holes between Willie Boy's head and his toes. The triggerman was Sammy the Bull.

In 1985 Gotti was accused of assaulting a repairman and robbing him of $325 in an arguement over a parking space. The repair-

'IT WAS A CLASSIC
DOUBLE ACT THAT
ENDED IN BETRAYAL AND
TREACHERY.'

murders he actually forgot many of them. Salvatore was arrested with Gotti.

This time the Feds thought they had a cast iron case. There were dozens of wiretaps and two low level informants willing to testify against them. But they couldn't believe their luck when Sammy, who had only served time in the past for low-level offences like hijacking and theft, offered to become the highest ranking mob informer in criminal history. It turned out that Sammy – who was tipped to be the heir apparent to the Gambino family leadership – had a terrible fear of ending his days in prison. So in a spectacular trial in March and April 1992 he took the stand to testify against John Gotti and his Mafia empire of evil and corruption.

A MARKED MAN FOR EVER

Methodically confessing to all the murders requested by John Gotti, he squirmed under the gaze of the Godfather's steely eyes and knew that he would be a marked man for ever. In return for his testimony Sammy knew he could expect leniency for his own crimes – he has yet to be judged on them – and a life spent looking over his shoulder. On 23 June, 1992, Gotti was sporting his full mob plumage – handmade silk suit and yellow silk tie – for the last time. He was sentenced to life in prison without parole for ordering at least five murders, and on forty-nine counts of racketeering. Going down with him on the one way trip was another underboss, Frank 'Frankie Loc' Locascio, a fifty-nine-year-old henchman also nailed by Sammy's testimony.

Gotti's empire is currently being run by John Jnr, his muscular son. One lawman described him as closer to John Gotti than the stubble on his chin and he's responsible for the day-to-day organisation of the empire. Crime busters predict that the fallout between Sammy and Gotti could lead to a bloody war as the gangsters fight for the right of succession. There is no end, it seems, to Mafia violence despite a keen effort from US law enforcement agencies.

'It would never have happened if they hadn't been friends that became enemies,' said gangland expert George Carmenza. 'It was a classic double act that ended in betrayal and treachery. A fitting end for two guys like that – almost poetic justice.'

men learned who Gotti was, checked into a hospital where he said he had developed amnesia and the charges were dropped.

A year later Gotti was accused of running a racketeering enterprise and hit with three charges, including murder. He beat the rap. In 1992 he made it a hat-trick when jurors ruled he did not order the bungled contract-killing of a union official who wasn't paying his dues. But it was the loyal, psychotic lieutenant Salvatore who did most of the dirty work. By his admission he became crazier in the second half of the 1980s and committed so many

Below: Bruce Cotler on the left gives an impassioned speech in defence of his client, John Gotti. Cotler was barred from defending Gotti in the crook's last trial. The lawyer's integrity was under question because of his intimacy with the mobs.

JUAN & EVITA
The Corruptible Perons

Proud dictator Juan Peron and his nightclub singer Evita presided over an evil and repressive regime. They brought their country to the verge of bankruptcy as they looted millions from charities and the state to fill their Swiss bank accounts. And they did it all in the name of the Argentinian people they claimed to love.

They were a most unlikely double act, this notorious nightclub singer and the ambitious army colonel but together they shaped the course of South American politics and still enjoy near-mythological status to this day.

Andrew Lloyd Weber's musical 'Evita' was not the only reason that Eva Duarte, mistress of Juan Peron, became a household name. In the southern hemipshere, in the land of the pampas, Peronism has become more than a political movement; it is almost a religious affirmation and to those who supported them; Juan and Evita were the demi-gods who put Argentina on the world stage.

However, it was, mostly, a clever show without real substance, for while the illusion created by this glittering twosome was lapped up by the masses, they used the peoples' ill-judged support to mask their own corruption – a corruption which channelled untold millions from the national coffers into Swiss bank accounts. They also supported the Fascist movements in Europe during wartime, clamped down on the press which opposed them, and even launched an anti-church campaign aimed at those ministers within the Catholic hierachy that they regarded as enemies.

While Peronism may still make the gauchos and the housewives of Buenos Aries misty-eyed for 'the good old days' it was in reality nothing more than a cover for a well-ordered fleecing of the state. It is an indisputable fact that before their rule Argentina was one of the wealthiest nations in the world; afterwards, the nation was ruined and bankrupt.

Before there was an Evita for the crowds in Argentina to cheer there was Colonel Juan Domingo Peron. Born in Lobos in 1895 to poor immigrant stock, he rose through the army ranks thanks to dilligence and ability. Equipped with charm, athleticism and that essential Argentinian characteristic, machismo, he was destined to go far. But he was also a moral and physical coward, a man who shunned reality if he thought confronting it would be unpleasant. He could not endure being unpopular and many of his ludicrous economic policies were pursued so he could enjoy the applause of the mob while he followed them through.

In 1943 Argentina was under the rule of President Ramon Castillo – at least until June that year, when the military decided to stage a coup. It was led by colonels calling themselves the Young Turks, Peron among them. The colonels claimed that the Ramon government was supporting the Allies in the war. This was alien to the Fascist-temperament of the officer corps, many of whom were of Italian extraction and saw

WHILE THE ILLUSION CREATED BY THIS GLITTERING TWOSOME WAS LAPPED UP BY THE MASSES, THEY USED THE PEOPLES' ILL-JUDGED SUPPORT TO MASK THEIR OWN CORRUPTION.

Opposite: *The glittering Eva and her husband Juan Peron managed to keep the adoration of the masses even as they stole from the nation's coffers.*

Below: *The successful politicians who promisd to turn Argentina into a paradise for the workers. But Eva and Jaun fulfilled little of their socialist programme.*

Mussolini in Italy as their kind of leader. At the time of the coup Peron was one of the keenest pro-Fascist officers among the colonels and worked in the Ministry of War, but by the end of October he was promoted when he was granted the critical job of running the Labour Department in the new military junta.

The labour movement in Argentina was split between trades unions and those workers on the ranches and in the slaughterhouses who had no organisation. Peron set out to mould the workers into a single, military-like unit, with the discipline and style of the black shirts he admired at rallies in Nazi Germany and Fascist Italy. Many workers' leaders had suffered cruelly under previous regimes, while the men they represented were mercilessly gunned down in the streets if they dared to strike.

Peron used his considerable charm to become the friend of the unions, the affable big brother who would ease their economic and social woes. Months earlier these same men had been called Communist scum and filth by the military but Peron believed flattery was a better way of attaining what he wanted from them.

What he wanted from them was subservience to the government. He made it, for instance, mandatory for wage negotiations between workers and bosses to go through his office. Kickbacks from the unions and the bosses were discreetly channelled into the seven-figure bank account he held in Switzerland. The more astute union leaders realised what he was up to but he outflanked the old guard. He

ordered free paid holidays, a month's bonus at Christmas for the meat packers and other fringe benefits. While the workers cheered at this short-term philanthropy, the bosses bemoaned the loss of their managerial rights, and the unions felt emasculated. They were both victims of Juan Peron's attempt to create a permanent Argentinian military dictatorship based on the solid support of the masses.

As the dictatorships which the Argentinian military so admired crumbled in Europe, so the movement for freedom and openness in Argentina grew. In August 1945, the military lifted a state of emergency that had existed throughout the war years – causing a half-a-million strong demonstration the following month on the streets of the capital from a populace seeking greater freedom and human rights. It was a frightening display of people-

Below, left: *A young admirer approaches a delighted Eva and Juan in their presidential box at a social event on the River Plate.*

Below, right: *The Perons, while promising a socialist regime, brought expensive glamour into their own lives.*

mistress Eva Duarte. Fierce and brave, she yelled abuse at the soldiers, while reliable sources have it that her colonel fell to his knees and begged for mercy. Eva, the nightclub singer who literally slept her way to the top, rallied support for Peron among the unions that he had helped so much and rioting broke out in the streets. For forty-eight hours, Buenos Aries was paralysed until the military backed down and Peron was released, his stature greater than ever.

power and sparked a Draconian response from Peron who ordered waves of arrests. But when disputes arose within the ranks of the military themselves (the air force officers standing with the workers while the army were against them), Peron played a gambling rusethat he was doomed to lose. He went on radio urging workers to 'rise up' and follow his path of liberation. It was a valiant but vain plea which ended with his own arrest and imprisonment.

With him when he was arrested in his apartment in the Calle Posadas was his

Opposite, above: *Eva uses the state radio to thank the nation for electing her husband as president. He stands on the left, while the Interior Minister, Angel Borlenghi sits to the right.*

Opposite, below: *Eva loved the glamour of state occasions. The Perons step out at an Independence Ball.*

With the adulation of the workers ringing in his ears, Juan Peron realised that his dreams of a neo-Fascist worker's militia had evaporated; instead he saw in the cheering *descamisados* – the shirtless ones – the roots of a new worker's revolution. So, believing this to be his chance, he resigned from the army and offered himself up as the leader of a new labour party.

His first step towaards domination of the workers was to ruin the unions of the shoemakers and the textile workers, two proud and disciplined welfare groups who

Above: *Eva Peron could rally the crowds, while winning over the army and the church.*

were not convinced by his scheme to bond workers to his state. Within six months they were finished, their leaders driven into poverty and exile. To gain credence for the free elections which were to be held in 1946, Peron also had to win over the Catholic church hierachy, especially because of his relationship with Eva Duarte – 'This woman Duarte' – as the newspaper *La Prensa* called her. Eva, born in 1919 into great poverty, was his real love and several years earlier he had divorced his wife, hoping to marry his 'Evita'. He peruaded the church to recognize his marriage to her in 1945, to view it as reparation for his sin of keeping her as a mistress. The church gave its blessings to the man who would soon be ruler.

'THE PURPOSE WAS NOT TO GIVE POWER TO THE WORKING CLASS, BUT TO ENCOURAGE THE WORKING CLASS TO GIVE POWER TO JUAN PERON.'

Below: *The Perons in Brazil (left) and in London the Worshipful Company of Butchers, pleased with the Argentinian beef trade, welcomed them (right).*

establishing the priorities which are necessary for the operation of any economic system. He taught the community to believe in the instantaneous and total pay-off, so that no one had any order of expectation.' Another study of Argentina, 'The Mothers of the Plaza', by John Simpson and Jana Bennett, says: 'It was all, essentially, a form of charity with Peron. Peron made working-class people feel they had dignity and an importance in the national life of Argentina. The purpose was not to give power to the working class, but to encourage the working class to give power to Juan Peron.'

His brand of socialism bound the workers and the bosses to the state as never before, while he wasted vast quantities of the nation's money by nationalising the run-down railways at super-inflated prices. He became a master of the pay-off, offering kickbacks to critics and bosses, while he remained the darling of workers who had never had it so good. But they never had it so good at the expense of a government that was rapidly paying out more than it was taking in. Peron's largesse in handing out holidays, pensions and bonuses was laying the foundations for Argentina's eight hundred per cent inflation rates of the 1970s and 1980s.

By 1949 his plans were badly adrift; inflation and unrest followed as a government of bribes and torture was exposed. Peron reacted harshly, arresting dissidents, purging churchmen and formulating a law which made it a serious offence to insult

In 1946 he attained his dream in one of the few fair elections ever held in Argentina. He gained the backing of the workers to take over the Casa Rosada, the pink palace of the national leaders, with Eva at his side; the country was his for the taking. Peron came to power with great expectations placed in him. The country was rich, it had been spared the war which had torn apart the Old World, business was booming and there was plenty of money in the bank. What went wrong?

'Indisputably, Peron operated his system extremely badly,' said historian H.S.Ferns in his authoritatve study 'Argentina'. 'Like a spoiled child he wanted everything and he wanted it at once. He revealed himself totally incapable of making choices and

the president or any of his public servants. He milked the agricultural aid programme for his own benefit and left the grain farmers and the beef herders increasingly impoverished. Newspapers that criticised him and Evita were closed down – like the honourable and influential *La Prensa*, which was seized and turned into a pro-government trade union sheet.

Evita, during these years, manipulated businessmen and landowners to contribute tinto what has been called the biggest political slush fund in history. The Eva Peron Foundation did indeed build schools, educate children, feed the hungry and shelter the homeless. However, the enormous amount of money that rolled in was administered by people who had to answer to no one but her. Her emissaries travelled to every factory, every workshop, every building site to take the tribute demanded by their new Cleopatra. Those who didn't 'contribute' voluntarily soon found their premises judged unfit by factory inspectors and were closed down.

Experts estimate that Evita stashed away as much as $100 million in hard cash into secret Swiss bank accounts from this fund, flown out twice a month to Geneva in suitcases. Gwyneth Dunwoody, the British MP said: 'With the euphemistically- titled Foundation behind her, Eva Peron handed out Christmas gifts for needy children to

Above: *Eva and Juan pose before their sumptuous country estate, paid for by funds siphoned from Eva's charity organization.*

Right: *Rapt attention on the faces of the leaders as they watch a boxing match.*

hospitals and schools, while ceaselessly driving home the message that it was because of the Peronistas that these remarkable benefits were available.

'What she omitted to say was that the Foundation, which had initially been billed as a society to be be supported by voluntary contributions, was rapidly taking on the air of a Godfather organisation. She did not hesitate to demand payment from every worker that obtained a rise and from every business that claimed that it needed the government's assistance.

'Every possible source of finance was milked so that this myth of Eva caring for the workers could be promoted. She was not a gentle and gracious woman – she relied on her own regime and army and police power to keep her where she wanted to be. In an organisation with astonishingly few accounts, the amounts of money that were spent were directly connected with what was useful for the Peronista regime. She was no Joan of Arc.'

MORE MONEY LESS LOVE

John Barnes, author of the book 'Eva Peron', says that after her death, investigators of defunct bank accounts traced to her found an estimated $14 million worth of money and jewels that she had literally forgotten she had. No doubt, much of this was stolen from the contributions to the Eva Peron Foundation.

'The love of the people feeds me,' Evita gushed, as large amounts of this unchecked and uncounted money were creamed off into her secret bank accounts. Whole government departments were taken over by her, many of them running twenty-four hours a day, to keep the Foundation supplied with untraceable money. On the government front, Colonel Peron bought off politicians to vote through legislation diverting $5 million worth of public funds into her Foundation. To this day, no one knows exactly how much was stolen from Argentina by the Perons, but it ran into the hundreds of millions of dollars.

She was as vain as she was greedy. Newspapers that did not print mentions of her glittering balls and glittering guests suddenly found that their supplies of newsprint had dried up. Although the workers cheered her and were solidly

behind her, as they were behind her husband, she never gained the acceptance she craved from the upper classes. She knew the whispers surrounding her rise from the streets, the 'favours' she paid to men who helped her singing career.

Her revenge against the snobbish elite knew no bounds – once she paid a fish monger and gave him the necessary permits

Below: *General Peron, Eva and General Dutra of Brazil meet at the opening of a new bridge connecting the two vast countries.*

to sell fish outside the snooty Jockey Club in Buenos Aries for a whole long, hot summer. She saw conspirators everywhere and, when a union boss had the temerity to tell her that she would be better off at home in the kitchen than meddling in politics, she had him arrested and tortured with electric cattle prods. Another man, Victor Belardo, was arrested because he answered correctly the jackpot question on a radio quiz show – and then announced that he would give his money, a large amount, to a charity that

'THE LOVE OF THE PEOPLE FEEDS ME,' EVITA GUSHED, AS LARGE AMOUNTS OF THIS UNCHECKED AND UNCOUNTED MONEY WERE CREAMED OFF INTO HER SECRET BANK ACCOUNTS.

was not affiliated with or overseen by her omnipotent Foundation.

The Perons accumulated further millions from kickbacks they received for import-export permits. Traders literally had to grease their palms with millions of pesos – and do so willingly – in order to trade with the outside world.

Evita became a master of stage-managed rallies, copycat versions of those which the deposed dictators of Europe used to hold so regularly. Weeks before one particular event she invited Argentinian women from

Below: *Eva Peron died a young woman. This photograph was taken shortly after she had undergone surgery.*

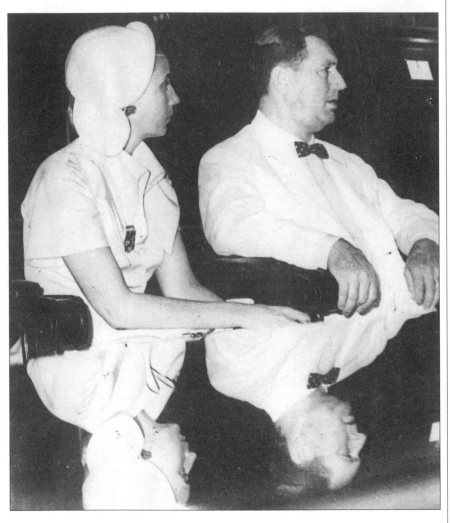

all over the country to bring their children to her to receive bicycles and dolls, a symbolic gesture to show that she cared for them, and that as the 'mother of the country' so all the children were her's to love and treat. It was a scene of chaos when they arrived outside the palace, so much so that police had to break up the crowds and at least two mothers went home without their offpsring – the children had been trampled to death by the mob.

In 1951 Peron's grip on polical power was faltering but his live-now-pay-later generosity with the workers still earned them both enormous support. He nearly lost this, however, in the 1951 elections by offering up his wife as the vice-president on his ticket. Much as the people adored Evita, this was still the land of machismo. The thought of Vice President Evita sent a shiver through the ranks of the military, upon whom Peron relied so much, and also troubled the workers deeply. A new slogan appeared on city walls – 'Long Live Peron – As A Widower!' Other graffiti depicted Evita naked, walking like a giant over masses of Lilliputian men. Juan Peron bowed to the pressure of the church and the military and his beloved Evita did not appear on his election ticket.

Shortly before the elections, which Peron was in danger of losing, there was another attempt at a military coup, this time put down by Peron and by the workers who idolised him. It ensured his victory in the October polling, giving him sixty-two per cent of the vote, ten per cent more than he had gained in 1946. And this, despite the falttering economy, the looted millions and the alienation of the ruling class.

But the following year one half of the double act was gone – Evita died from cancer. Juan Peron used her demise to canonise her in the eyes of an adoring people. She was only thirty-three and had recently toured the world, capturing hearts and minds for her country. Nevertheless, her death averted the fall from grace and power that would ultimately have been her lot. By dying, she became to her impoverished admirers a memory of diamonds and furs, not a woman who left her nation stripped of its wealth and teetering on the brink of bankruptcy while her detractors screamed under torture in filthy jails.

Economic conditions deteriorated after the death of Evita. The emperor was beginning to be seen without his clothes by the adoring masses burdened under hyper-inflation and suffering increasing harassment from his secret police and torturers. Moreover, the Catholic church, long the traditional dispenser of charity in the country, was beginning to feel aggrieved at having lost its place in society to the Foundation. The universities had been wrecked by semi-literate oafs who were given their posts by corrupt officials in return for kickbacks. Peron's goon-squads burned down the Jockey Club, which had spurned his late wife in the past, and he robbed the magnificent library and art gallery for his own pleasure.

In 1955 it all literally came crashing down when the air force bombed the Casa Rosada – missing him, but killing hundreds of civilians in the process – and armed gangs took to the streets, ransacking shops, businesses and even churches. The army garrison at Cordoba rose against him and there were no workers who believed in his Utopia anymore to save him. He went into exile aboard a Paraguayan gunboat.

A DAZZLING ALADDIN'S CAVE

In much the same way as the mob was allowed to look over the spoils of office of dictator Ferdinand Marcos in the Philippines years later, the poor of Argentina were given a glimpse of how their Evita had really lived when the portals of her stupendous palace were opened to the public after Peron's flight.

'It was a show which would outdazzle Aladdin's cave,' wrote Daily Express correspondent Jack Comben when he gazed at her riches. 'Glass shelves laid tier upon tier in the chandelliered brilliance of Peron's palace displayed gems which are estimated to be worth two million pounds. Diamonds almost as big as pigeons' eggs glittered and flashed. There was a two-inch thick collar encrusted with diamonds.

'I saw at least four hundred dresses – all perfect of their type and all expensive. And experts calculated that Evita owned enough shoes to last her for four hundred years. But all the treasures, the clothes, the pictures, are supposed to be only a fraction of what Peron and his wife acquired during nine years of power. The government believes he sent most of his fortune out of the country to Switzerland. And Peron was once quouted as saying: "The only jewellery I ever gave to my wife was a wedding ring".'

These event, had they occured in any other part of the world other than South America, would have been ended then. In 1973, however, after almost twenty years exile in Spain, Peron returned to power in Argentina with his third wife. Nostalgic,

perhaps, for the good old days that never really existed, the people embraced the man who threw his lot in with the workers,. They forgot all his sins, the massive amounts of money and assets that he looted from them in the past.

He died in 1974, the reins of power passing to Isabelita Peron, whom he had married in 1961. She excelled both her husband and his previous wife in the corruption stakes. Arrested in 1976, after she was deposed as president, she was charged with stealing $1 million intended for charity, convicted of embezzelling cash from a charity and for using government buildings for her own ends and was jailed. She was released in 1981 after serving two-thirds of her prison sentences.

Despite all this, the name Peron can still elicit nostalgia in Argentina – a land where 'strong' evokes a response than 'just'.

Above: *An Italian admirer sent this stone statue of Eva to the people of Argentina. It arouses mixed feeling among the citizens: some adore her memory, others despise her greed.*

EXPERTS CALCULATED THAT EVITA OWNED ENOUGH SHOES TO LAST HER FOR FOUR HUNDRED YEARS.

LOEB & LEOPOLD
The Perfect Murder

It took two Chicago teenagers to invent a new category of murder – 'thrill-killing'. Loeb and Leopold picked their innocent fourteen-year-old victim at random and brutally murdered him for kicks, all the time convinced that they were some sort of 'supermen', above the law.

The term 'thrill killing' is a relatively new one in the lexicon of crime. From time immemorial, men and women have killed for love, for hate, for money, for revenge, and for dark sexual urges beyond their control. But in 1924 in America, the frontiers of murder were pushed back even further and the phrase 'thrill-killing' was then coined to describe the deeds of an arrogant and evil duo who killed a fourteen-year-old boy merely for the intellectual satisfaction of doing so.

Richard Loeb, seventeen, and Nathan Leopold, eighteen, believed themselves to be so superior to ordinary mortals that they decided to end the life of a schoolboy. They were convinced that detectives would be baffled – no motive, no clues, no suspects – and they would bask in the glory of their secret crime for ever. That they were caught for the simplest of mistakes is testimony to their foolishness – and the end of their theory that applied intelligence was capable of devising the perfect crime.

This loathsome pair grew up together in Chicago and wanted for nothing. Both boys had rich parents who doted on them. Loeb's father Albert was vice-president of the Sears Roebuck chain of department stores. Nathan F. Leopold Snr was a shipping magnate, one of the wealthiest men in Chicago and, like Loeb's father, lavished money on his son.

Strong, athletic, handsome, Loeb – nicknamed 'Babe' by family and friends – was a raffish but clever young man. He was, like his partner-in-crime, a near genius and, at seventeen, the youngest graduate of the University of Michigan. Unlike most other students, he was never short of cash. When he needed more money, the family chauffeur took him from their home in the exclusive Kenwood district of the city to his father's offices, where he would demand $2,000 in cash – and get it. But he soon yearned for something more... something more exciting.

The excitement of murder.

The boy he grew up with was just as clever but less athletically inclined . Leopold had an overactive thyroid gland,

was undersized, round shouldered and, when he was fourteen, began to display homosexual leanings. He was, however, a true genius. He could speak ten languages and had an intellect that was well beyond his years – an IQ of two hundred by the time he was eighteen and was the youngest graduate with a Bachelor of Philosophy degree from the University of Chicago. Psychiatrists later said that Leopold was led by Loeb; he looked up to him, admired him, yearned to be strong like him. Historian Irving Stone wrote that he devoured the works of German philosopher Friedrich Nietzsche and longed to be a

Above: *Richard Loeb helps police search for clues in the murder hunt. Despite his helpful attitude, some policemen were not fooled by his manner.*

Opposite: *The teenage 'supermen' who planned the perfect murder, Richard Loeb on the left, and Nathan Leopold sit in court on trial for murder.*

was Leopold who suggested that they should ask for money for the return of the boy – even though the lad they intended to ransom would be already dead. In further letters to each other, they discussed the minutae of the murder. Often the letters were filled with violent, threatening tones as the plotters themselves argued about what they were going to do. But the agreement was reached and the victim chosen; fourteen-year-old Robert 'Bobby' Franks was to die for no reason whatsoever exept as a spawn in a game.

Loeb, a good tennis player, had known Bobby for some time. He had even played tennis with him and classified the boy as a 'friend' – certainly someone who trusted him enough to accompany him and Leopold on a short drive. Bobby was also from a good family and attended a private school in the neighbourhood where his future killers lived.

The date chosen for the murder was 24 May. The first step involved Leopold checking into the downtown Morrison Hotel under the name Morton D. Ballard,

'superman'. When he realised that his stunted form made that impossible, said Stone, 'he longed to be a superwoman, a female slave to some big, handsome, powerful king'. So, when homosexual Loeb sketched out details of his ghastly scheme, it was inevitable that Leopold would be an all-too-willing accomplice.

Loeb's fanatical dream of the perfect crime appealed to Leopold's dark 'superman' urges and he joined in the fantasy. In a letter he wrote to Leopold before they killed, Loeb said: 'The superman is not liable for anything he may do, except for the one crime it is impossible for him to commit – make a mistake.' Another said: 'We are supermen! Nothing can stand in our way.'

The plot was hatched in January 1924 but not carried out until May. Loeb was the brains, Leopold the partner necessary to enable him to execute it. Both polished every detail and added another lurid element to their 'perfect' crime: kidnap. It

listing himself in the register as a salesman from Peoria in Illinois. Next, using the same false name, he rented a car from a downtown agency where the president of the company, Joseph Jacobs, asked for a reference. Leopold was happy to give him the name and number of one Mr Louis Mason – in fact, Loeb. Jacobs made the call and heard a glowing reference as to the would-be renter's fiscal and moral fibre. After leaving a deposit of $50 on the rental of a luxury sedan, Leopald drove the car around for two hours, returned it to Jacobs and informed him he would be around to collect it later in the day.

Back in his hotel suite, he went over the finer points of the murder plan in his head. He checked with a local bank to make sure an acount he had opened in the name of Ballard was active – ready, in fact, to receive the ransom money.

Later that day the twisted 'supermen' drove around to the front gates of the academy at 4pm as the children were filing out for the day. From a local hardware store they had purchased a murder kit consisting

Above: *Lawmen sift through evidence relating to the crime. They are studying shoes and socks belonging to the victim and guns belonging to Loeb and Leopold.*

Left: *A detective with a section of the floorboard from the murder car. He is examining bloodstains.*

Opposite: *Richard Loeb (top) and Nathan Leopold shortly after their arrest.*

of a home-made garrotte, a chisel, rope and hydrochloric acid. They intended to pour the acid on to the young man's features to obliterate them. Two loaded pistols, taken from the collection belonging to Leopold's father, completed the kit.

'THE SUPERMAN IS NOT LIABLE FOR ANYTHING HE MAY DO, EXCEPT FOR THE ONE CRIME IT IS IMPOSSIBLE FOR HIM TO COMMIT — MAKE A MISTAKE.'

Leopold was at the wheel of the car as they spotted Franks coming out. 'Hey Bobby, want a ride?' yelled Loeb, who had concealed in his University of Chicago handgrip, in the back of the car, the heavy-handled chisel that he had wrapped in adhesive tape for a better grip. Bobby, innocent and unsuspecting, bounced over to the car and eagerly got into the empty front seat. As Leopold drove north in heavy commuter traffic, Loeb lashed out viciously with the chisel, driving it down on the boy's head and he went down on to the floor of the limousine. Leopold, glancing in the rear-view mirror, was horrified when he saw the boy's wounds gushing blood and yelled: 'Oh my God! I didn't know it would be like this.'

As Leopold drove on, Loeb calmly stuffed Bobby's mouth with rags and wrapped him in a robe. He slowly bled to death on the floor of the car. Some miles out of town, they parked at a beauty spot overlooking Lake Michigan and calmly had sandwiches while they waited for dark.

As dusk fell they went for a meal in a German restaurant – 'to fortify us for what lay ahead,' Leopold would later say. After that he drove the car with its grim cargo to a culvert at 118th Street on the outskirts of town, near railway tracks spanning reclaimed swampland. Leopold slipped into fisherman's waders and carried Bobby

'HE IS SAFE AND UNHARMED. TELL THE POLICE AND HE WILL BE MURDERED AT ONCE. DON'T THINK THAT WE WON'T DO IT.'

Below: *The victim of an intellectual crime, Bobby Franks. His grieving father and brother can be seen in the picture right.*

through the mud. The boy had been stripped in the car and, once at the flooded culvert, Leopold struggled to shove the naked body into the pipe. Sweating from the exertion, he took off his coat.

It was to prove their undoing.

Gathering up his coat, looking around into the darkness, the two men were convinced that their tracks were covered. But one of little Bobby's feet was left sticking out of the pipe.

They dumped the car near a large apartment building close to Leopold's mansion home and embarked on stage two of the plan. This involved typing a ransom note on a machine Loeb had stolen from his university the previous year. The note read: 'Your boy has been kidnapped.' It went on to demand $10,000 in old, unmarked $20- and $50-bills, to be wrapped in an old cigar box, the box to be further packaged in white paper and sealed with sealing wax. The note was signed with the fictitious name George Johnson.

Three weeks prior to the kidnapping, the killers, each on alternate days, had boarded the 3pm train between Chicago and Michigan City, Indiana. It was their plan for the ransom money to be thrown from the moving train at a specific place, where they would be hiding in wait to collect it.

After posting the letter, the boys drove across the state line to Indiana and picked a solitary spot in a farmer's field where they buried Bobby's clothes. Shortly before

midnight Leopold was ordered by Loeb to telephone the Franks' home, which he did. He told the missing boy's terrified mother: 'He is safe and unharmed. Tell the police and he will be murdered at once. Don't think that we won't do it. You will receive a ransom note with instructions tommorrow.'

There is nothing to suggest that the killers enjoyed anything other than a sound night's sleep after their tiring day playing supermen while brutally murdering a child.

NO PUBLICITY

But, already as they slept, their plot was beginning to fall apart. Jacob Franks, Bobby's father, was, like their own, one of Chicago's richest men, having made a fortune from manufacturing boxes and packing cases. He immediately contacted his lawyer after the call to his wife and secured a pledge that there would be no publicity while they attempted to track down Bobby's abductors.

The next day the killers cleaned bloodstains from the car and drove it to an abandoned building site on the outskirts of the city where they burned the bloodstained robe in which they had wrapped young Bobby. They were methodical. The typewriter was broken up with a sledge-hammer – the keys and carriage hurled into one pond, the bodywork into another.

By midday, however, their chances of extorting money from the distraught father of Bobby were finished. A railway gang doing routine maintenance on the section of line that passed near to the culvert were horrified when they spotted Bobby Franks' foot sticking out of the pipe.

A second ransom note, which Loeb left on the Michigan City train with instructions for it to be handed over to Franks, arrived at roughly the same time as the news that his son was dead. His brother-in-law had identified his pathetic little body so there was no longer any need for secrecy. The silent hunt for a kidnapper became a full-blown manhunt for a murderer.

A SECOND RANSOM NOTE

When the killers read the headlines in the Chicago Tribune, they abandoned their plans to wait by a disused grain elevator near Englewood, on the rail line, for the ransom. The second ransom note was handed over to police. It read: 'Dear Sir, proceed immediately to the back platform of the train. Watch the east side of the track. Have your package ready. Look for the first LARGE RED BRICK factory situated immediately adjoining the tracks on the east. On top of this factory is a large black watertower, with the word CHAMPION written on it. Wait until you have completely passed the south end of the factory count five very rapidly and then IMMEDIATELY throw the package as far to the east as you can. Remember that this is the only chance to recover your son. Yours truly, George Johnston.'

The manhunt was the greatest Chicago had ever seen and, for the likes of gangsters like Al Capone, the source of great discomfort. While police turned over every warehouse and factory in Chicago looking for clues, they interfered so much with the business of organised crime that Capone and a consortium of other hoods offered to contribute cash to find the killers so they could get business back to normal.

Richard Loeb, the supreme hypocrite, joined the outraged citizens who answered police appeals for help in searching premises. He was overheard by one officer to say: 'It is the least any of us can do.' He did, however, betray his real personality to another policeman when he remarked of the dead boy: 'If I was going to pick out a boy to kidnap or murder, that's just the kind of

Above: **The drainpipe where the boy's body was hidden.**

Top: **Leopold on the left, and Loeb shortly after their arrest. The boys were stunned to realise the police were smarter than they, the criminals with high IQs.**

cocky little son-of-a-bitch I would pick.' This was part of the thrill for Loeb – seeing 'bumbling coppers' looking for clues in a crime committed by supermen. Pathetic!

In the course of the next few days the supermen realised that things were going badly awry in the smooth course of their masterplan. First, police found the typewriter keys and carcass in the shallow pools, tipped-off by someone who had seen them thrown in. The bloodied chisel was found near the culvert.

And the one clue, the one which would damn them, was found near to the body – the result of Leopold taking off his coat to get on with the grisly business of stuffing the boy's body into the pipe. Out of his pocket had tumbled his glasses – the glasses which belonged to him and which were one of only three pairs sold by a particular Chicago optician. One pair belonged to a woman, who was wearing them when police knocked on her door; the other pair to a wealthy lawyer who was in Europe. And so Nathan Leopold Jnr became the number-one suspect.

'WHAT MOTIVE WOULD I HAVE?'

Police confronting him were met with a flurry of lies. He had been on one of his beloved bird-watching expeditions a week earlier – yes, he must have lost them then. But it had rained hard in the past few days and the glasses were virtually spotless. As he confronted the hard stares of policemen who knew every trick in the book he grew nervous and blurted out: 'What motive would I have for killing him? I didn't need the money – my father is rich. Whenever I need money, all I have to do is ask for it.' He explained that he and Loeb had spent the evening of the murder 'riding around' in his family car and had picked up two girls, girls they knew only as Edna and Mary.

'IF I WAS GOING TO PICK OUT A BOY TO KIDNAP OR MURDER, THAT'S JUST THE KIND OF COCKY LITTLE SON-OF-A-BITCH I WOULD PICK.'

Both boys were taken to separate rooms of the luxurious LaSalle Hotel for further grilling under the orders of Richard Crowe, the district attorney. Although not officially under arrest, Crowe had a hunch that the boys were the ones he wanted. Leopold made a statement to a local newspaper in which he graciously understood the predicament he was in: 'I don't blame police for holding me. I was at the culvert before the glasses were found and it is quite possible I lost them there. I'm sorry this happened because it will worry my family. But I will certainly be glad to do what I can to help the police.'

'BY GOD, I THINK WE'VE GOT THEM!'

The police had no fingerprints to match on the typewriter, but the ransom note was definitely typed on it. Then came the final proof which tied Leopold and his friend Loeb to the murder. Some enterprising journalists had obtained letters which Loeb had written in the past for his legal study group at university on the typewriter. An independent expert confirmed this to Crowe, who punched the air in delight and said: 'By God, I think we've got them!' Leopold named a student friend who had given him the typewriter. The student was quickly found by police and declared innocent. Then Leopold said it was, in fact, yet another friend's machine, then that it was still somewhere in his house. Finally, as he squirmed, Englund, the chauffeur,

came forward to say that the car in which they had ostensibly been joy-riding with the mysterious Mary and Edna had not left the family garage that night.

Faced with the mounting evidence, Leopold was the first to crack, followed shortly afterwards by Loeb. Loeb astonished police with his confession: 'It was a lark, you see, we just wanted to commit the perfect crime. We haven't got anything against the boy. It's just that we thought we could get away with it. I'm sorry for what has happened.'

OBSCENE SEXUAL ACTS

Loeb testified that he was the car driver and that Leopold had killed the boy. He also threw in details of perverse sexual acts which Leopold enjoyed, as if such gossip would soften his own guilty role in the crime which he himself had conceived .

Chicago went wild. The clamour of the mob, upon hearing their confessions, was instant and frenzied and nothing less than their execution would do.

In jail, the thrill-killers who thought themselves supermen were the loneliest felons in the world. No lawyer would take their case – it would be enough to blight even the most distinguished career. It literally took Nathan Leopold Snr to get on his bended knees to famed civil rights lawyer Clarence Darrow to ask him to take the case. 'I knew there was not freedom in store for the boys,' Darrow said later. 'But I wanted to save them at least from the electric chair.' It proved a thankless task.

Darrow was one of the most brilliant lawyers of the time and a relentless pursuer of truth and justice. But he knew that no legal techniques, however smart, would ever result in the boys' freedom. At best he could hope to prove them insane for such a brutal and senseless slaying. He opted for a bench trial, a trial without a jury, before judge John Caverly with the words: 'While the state is trying Loeb and Leopold, I shall be trying capital punishment.'

His decision to defend them was not a popular one. Years later he would write: 'The public seemed to think that we were committing a crime in defending two boys, who probably needed it as much as any two defendants ever on trial for their lives. The most senseless and the most unreasonable

criticism was indulged in against the defendants and their attorneys because of the lengthy hearing of the case. The proceedings became front page matter in every hamlet of the country, and were closely followed in all parts of the world. I seldom went to my office in those troublesome days, and rarely read any of the letters that came in stacks. These were usually abusive and brutal to the highest degree.' But Darrow was not daunted.

His was a tireless assault on the taking of human life. While in no way defending or trying to mitigate what they had done in the

Above and centre: Leopold, in the murder car, describes the crime to a detective. When he believed that he faced execution, he wrote this letter. It shows his intellectual curiosity for it does not express fear but debates the possibility of an afterlife.

Left: Loeb as a child playing at cowboys.

Opposite: Nathan Leopold grew up in the mansion pictured above. The lower picture shows Richard Loeb's childhood home.

'THE WORLD IS FULL OF EMINENT LAWYERS WHO WOULD HAVE PAID ME A FORTUNE TO DISTINGUISH THEMSELVES IN THIS CASE.'

Scenes from the trial: a friend, Lorraine Nathan (top right) testified that Loeb was not all bad. The murderers sit each side of defense attorney, Robert Clowe while Leopold's father and brother suffer as they listen to the evidence.

pursuit of fun his eleqouent plea for mercy is liberal, passionate and remains a classic of American bar history: 'I am pleading for the future... I am pleading for a time when hatred and cruelty will not control the hearts of men, when we can learn by reason and judgement and understanding and faith that all life is worth living and that mercy is the highest attribute of man... If I can succeed I have done something for the tens of thousands of other boys, for the countless unfortunates who must tread the same road in blind childhood.'

Darrow's eleqouence succeeded in persuading the judge that the 'incipient paranoia' in both boys had triggered temporary insanity. After a thirty-three-day trial, followed by a three-week period before sentencing, he came back to tell

Loeb and Leopold that they would serve life sentences for the killing of Bobby Franks, followed by ninety-nine-year sentences each for kidnapping.

His fee for the defence of the killers was rumoured to have been $1 million dollars – but years later Darrow stunned the legal world when he revealed what occurred when it came to the settlement of the account. In fact, he received only $30,000 dollars, paid over grudgingly by Nathan Leopold Snr, who displayed arrogance every bit as chilling as his son's. Handing over the cheque, the killer's father said: 'The world is full of eminent lawyers who would have paid me a fortune to distinguish themselves in this case.'

Loeb and Leopold were incarcerated in the Northern Illinois Penitentiary at

'IT WAS A LARK, YOU SEE, WE JUST WANTED TO COMMIT THE PERFECT CRIME. WE HAVEN'T GOT ANYTHING AGAINST THE BOY.'

Left: *A witness points at Nathan Leopold to confirm to the police that he thinks Leopold is the suspect.*

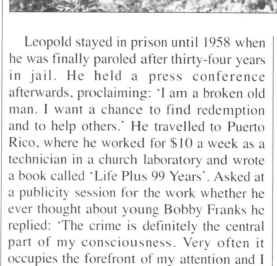

Statesville and, due to their incorrigible, doting fathers, were able to indulge themselves to the full. Although convicted killers, they had an enviable life behind bars, thanks to an ample supply of money.

They shared adjoining cells, complete with books, desks and filing cabinets. They were supplied with bootleg liqour from the guards and allowed to make lengthy telephone calls from one of the prison storerooms. Leopold kept a vegetable garden while Loeb sank further into depravity, stalking the young male prisoners to satisfy his sexual passions while paying off the guards to look the other way. But he went too far.

A GRUESOME FIGHT

In 1936 he set his sights upon James Day, accosting him in the library where he said, 'Be nice to me'. Day refused but Loeb followed him at every opportunity. On 28 January that year, Loeb entered the shower with a cuthroat razor and told Day to submit to him. He refused and there followed a gruesome fight. Day was cut – but he managed to get the razor and slash Loeb fifty-six times, including one stroke right across his jugular vein. Loeb staggered out, bleeding to death, and died hours later clutching Leopold's hand.

Leopold stayed in prison until 1958 when he was finally paroled after thirty-four years in jail. He held a press conference afterwards, proclaiming: 'I am a broken old man. I want a chance to find redemption and to help others.' He travelled to Puerto Rico, where he worked for $10 a week as a technician in a church laboratory and wrote a book called 'Life Plus 99 Years'. Asked at a publicity session for the work whether he ever thought about young Bobby Franks he replied: 'The crime is definitely the central part of my consciousness. Very often it occupies the forefront of my attention and I can think of nothing else.'

On 30 August, 1971 he died of heart failure in Puerto Rico.

Above: *The perfect crime was quickly solved by the police. Leopold left his spectacles at the scene of the crime, shown in this picture.*

PARKER & HULME
Their Secret World

Pauline Parker and Juliet Hulme were anything but normal schoolgirls. These teenage lesbian lovers bashed in the head of Pauline's mother who had tried to separate them. Were they criminally insane or just murderous little minxes?

The full extent of their wickedness and depravity revealed at the trial shocked this colonial outpost as nothing before or since.

It was on 22 June, 1954 that the two hysterical girls, covered in blood, shattered the tranquility of afternoon tea at a sedate Christchurch restaurant when they burst through the doors. 'Mummy's been hurt,' blurted out Pauline. 'She's hurt, covered with blood.' Tearfully they begged the manageress of the restaurant to phone for police while they gulped down sugared tea in an apparent attempt to ease their shock. Some of the customers went with police

Opposite: *Juliet Hulme, on the left, and Pauline Parker were so in love that they were prepared to murder anybody who threatened their relationship.*

Below: *The childish face of Juliet Hulme hid a passionate nature and a wilful nature.*

There is much in 'Partners in Crime' that dwells on the madness generated by two people that would not have have occured had the partnership never been formed. Normal lives and patterns of behaviour vanish as two personalities, each bland and safe on its own, ignite into intrigue and danger when combined.

Such was the madness that descended on two adolescent girls in New Zealand in the 1950s – girls who retreated into their own special world of aloofness, superiority and forbidden sex, a world that held murder.

When Juliet Marion Hulme and Pauline Yvonne Parker were brought before the Crown in Christchurch, New Zealand, in 1954 the case received worldwide attention because of its morbid themes. Like the case of Loeb and Leopold (Chapter xxx), psychologists were at pains to try to explain the fusion of two normal minds into a single entity bent on misery and death. For that is what happened to Juliet Hulme and Pauline Parker when their perfect world was threatened.

In order to prevent separation from one another, they plotted and carried out, the murder of Mrs Honora Mary Parker. Mrs Parker, forty-five, Pauline's mother, was bludgeoned to death by the two, who tried to cover their tracks by claiming she had fallen. But in the end their own inflated ideas of their intelligence and skill failed them badly and the most basic police methods proved that they were the killers.

and the girls to a beauty spot in a nearby park close to a small bridge over a stream. Lying in a pool of blood, her face unrecognisable, was Mrs Parker. Her head was brutally battered. It was a bad fall.

Initially the girls told police that Mrs Parker had fallen and slipped on a board. 'Her head just kept banging and banging,' blurted out Pauline to police, in a none-too-convincing explanation of why her mother came to have some forty-nine serious head wounds, any one of which would have been enough to render her unconscious. The

'HER HEAD JUST KEPT BANGING AND BANGING,' BLURTED OUT PAULINE TO POLICE.

officers knew that they were dealing with something far more sinister than an accident and both young girls – Pauline was sixteen and Juliet fifteen years and ten months – were taken into custody for further questioning.

As they were led away a sharp-eyed policeman found near the pathway, a few feet away from the body of Mrs Parker, a

> 'AFTER THE FIRST BLOW WAS STRUCK I KNEW IT WOULD BE NECESSARY FOR US TO KILL HER.'

brick wrapped in an old stocking. It was found to be covered in blood and great clumps of her hair were stuck to it. Clearly, this and not a board or a plank of wood had been the instrument which despatched the unfortunate woman. Later, a pathologist examined the corpse and said there was bruising around the throat consistent with her having been held down as blow after blow rained down on her head.

Above: *The distinguished father of Pauline, Dr H.R.Hulme, Rector of Canterbury University College, Christchurch. He intended to take his daughter away from her friend.*

Once in custody Pauline confessed almost immediately to the murder. She said she had 'made up my mind' a few days before the event to kill her mother during an outing in the park and that Juliet, who was walking with them, was not implicated in the crime. She told detectives: 'She knew nothing about it. As far as I know, she believed what I had told her, although she may have guessed what had happened but I doubt it as we were both so shaken that it probably did not occur to her.'

But while she was being questioned, one of the officers guarding her turned his back to her, and she tried to burn a piece of paper on which she had written: 'I am taking the blame for everything.' This was seen as a message that she intended to smuggle to Juliet – Juliet, who, on learning of the abortive bid to contact her, changed her story immediately and confessed to being a willing accomplice.

IT WAS TERRIBLE BUT INSANE?

'I took the stocking,' said Juliet, 'and hit her too. I was terrified. I wanted to help Pauline. It was terrible – she moved convulsively. We both held her. She was still when we left her. After the first blow was struck I knew it would be necessary for us to kill her.'

There would have been no need for a protracted criminal trial, along with all its publicity, had the pair pleaded Guilty to murder. Instead, they chose to plead Guilty of murder by insanity – something the Crown was not prepared to accept. While in custody they had both seemed perfectly aware of what they had done, had both shown little remorse and had both only wanted to return to their 'perfect world'. Their insistence on a plea of insanity meant that the spotlight would now be directed at their dark world.

In his opening speech the prosecutor Mr Anthony Brown ominously told the jury: 'I feel bound to tell you that the evidence will make it terribly clear that the two young accused conspired together to kill the mother of one of them and horribly carried their plan into effect. It was a plan designed solely so they could carry on being together in the most unwholesome manner.'

Brown went on to explain how something 'unhealthy' had developed

between the two girls; how they had met at school as friends but then their relationship had deepened and broadened into something much more than girlish camaraderie. He remarked that it was a relationship 'more commonly seen between members of the opposite sex, and of a more advanced age', than that seen between two schoolgirls. Unhappy when apart, disturbingly attached to each other when together, Mr Brown painted a portrait of two girls sharing an unnatural love.

Above: *Juliet Hulme photographed at the time she was involved with Pauline but before they turned into killers.*

Mrs Parker, not surprisingly, was most unhappy about the relationship and was doing her best to break it up when she met her end. She had been in touch with Juliet's father, Dr Hulme, a Rector of Canterbury University College, New Zealand. Earlier that year he had resigned his post with the intention of taking a new position in Cape Town, South Africa. He agreed to take Juliet with him, to get her away from Pauline. The date agreed for his departure was 3 July – and the two girls vowed to kill Mrs Parker before then, her punishment for engineering their separation.

All this was corroborated in a sensational diary kept by Pauline Parker and in notes passed between the two – correspondence which the Crown said was definitely the work of people who were quite aware of what they were doing.

'In it,' said Brown, waving Pauline's leather-bound diary before the jury, 'she reveals that she and Juliet Hulme have engaged in shoplifting, have toyed with blackmail and talked about and played around in matters of sex. There is clear evidence that as long ago as February she was anxious that her mother should die,

Above: *The girls ran to the Victoria Tearooms, crying that Mrs Parker had fallen and was badly hurt.*

'Their first idea was to carry out this crime in such a way so that it appeared that it was an accident which befell Mrs Parker,' said Brown. They persuaded Mrs Parker, having pretended for a couple of weeks prior to her death that they no longer cared about being separated, to take them on a picnic to the country. Juliet Hulme brought along the brick from the garden of her home and the deed was accomplished.

and during the few weeks before 22 June she was planning to kill her mother in the way in which she was eventually to be killed.' It was damning evidence.

On 14 February, he read: 'Why, oh why, could mother not die? Dozens of people, thousands of people, are dying every day. So why not mother and father too?' Later, in April, she wrote: 'Anger against mother boiled up inside me. It is she who is one of the main obstacles in my path. Suddenly a means of ridding myself of the obstacle occurred to me. I am trying to think of some way. I want it to appear either a natural or an accidental death.'

In June it continued: 'We discussed our plans for moidering [sic] mother and made them a little clearer. Peculiarly enought I have no qualms of conscience (or is it just peculiar we are so mad!)' On 22 June, the actual day of the crime, Pauline penned this entry: 'I am writing a little bit of this up in the morning before the death. I felt very excited like the night before Chrismassy last night. I did not have pleasant dreams, though.' She did not elaborate on these.

The reading of the diary caused a stunned shock to the court. The two looked for all the world like normal schoolgirls and yet they had plotted and committed murder. There was even more damning testimony about them which showed that they were sneering, arrogant vixens who enjoyed illicit adult pleasures wrapped up in a fantasy world of their own making. And much of this damaging testimony was delivered by Juliet's mother.

THE STRANGE DEBORAH AND LANCELOT

Mrs Hulme told the court how the girls were planning to publish a novel (although they hadn't yet written one) and practised writing in strange letters to each other using romantic pseudonyms. Juliet was often called Charles II, Emperor of Borovnia, then she changed to Deborah and then Bialbo. Pauline Parker, at the start of this bizarre correspondence, had called herself Lancelot Trelawney, a Cornish mercenary. Names of medieval drama.

The letters were initially full of romance as they created a fantasy world into which they escaped, but soon the tone changed to something far more sinister. They became violent, sadistic, with maidens raped and knights tortured as the girls' own lust for each other became ever more urgent. Soon they were sleeping together and even indulged in bondage. One said: 'I loved how we enacted how each saint might make love in bed. We have never felt so exhausted... but so satisfied!' It is no suprise that their parents wished to see the girls parted permanently.

Above: *Mrs Hulme broke down frequently during the trial of her daughter for murder. She refused to speak about the case for many years after the event.*

Further details emerged of how they spent their days when they were supposed to be in school. They often slipped away to a country barn where they frolicked in the hayloft as lovers, finishing their day by washing each other in a country stream. They talked of going to America, of becoming rich and famous and buying a house together where they would have eunuchs as servants.

Juliet said she wanted to be 'safe' with Pauline – as a child she was brought up in the East End of London at the time of the London Blitz, something which traumatised her deeply. One of their 'games' involved Pauline cradling her as she made noises like bombs exploding around her. And all the while they played out this weird relationship, all schoolfriends and other playmates were excluded; it was, as described in one of Juliet's missives to Pauline, 'their perfect world', one to which no other was admitted.

Initially, Mrs Hulme, who had emigrated with her husband and Juliet when the child

'I LOVED HOW WE ENACTED HOW EACH SAINT MIGHT MAKE LOVE IN BED. WE HAVE NEVER FELT SO EXHAUSTED... BUT SO SATISFIED!'

was five years old, welcomed her friendship with Pauline because it seemed to bring her out of her shell. 'Had I known where this would lead, I would have killed it stone dead there and then,' she sobbed.

Another entry in Pauline's diary, and one which was instrumental in proving their sanity, was the one which read: 'Prostitution sounds a good idea to make money and what fun we would have in doing it! We are so brilliantly clever, there probably isn't anything we couldn't do.' Was this, said the prosecution, the words of a pair who claimed they did not know what they were doing? Further, when Pauline was called to testify, her own arrogance virtually broke their defence. When asked if she knew that it was wrong to murder she sneered: 'I knew it was wrong to murder and I knew at the time that I was murdering somebody that it was wrong. You would have to be an absolute moron not to know that something was wrong.'

Lawyers for the two girls said there was no question that they were the killers but

> 'I KNEW AT THE TIME THAT I WAS MURDERING SOMEBODY THAT IT WAS WRONG. YOU WOULD HAVE TO BE AN ABSOLUTE MORON NOT TO KNOW THAT SOMETHING WAS WRONG.'

Below: *It was on this pathway, near the planking, that the two girls bludgeoned the mother to death.*

that they should not hang – a possibility, despite their age because they were being judged as adults – because of the abnormality of their minds. One medical expert, a Dr Medlicott, pointed out that each of the girls had suffered bad physical health as toddlers and that their siblings were also prone to illnesses, suggesting somehow that this contributed to the unbalanced state of their young murderers' minds.

Discussing the bizarre relationship between them the doctor told the court : 'Juliet told me: "I do believe that we are indeed geniuses. I don't wish to place myself above the law – I am apart from it." And when I performed a medical examination upon Miss Parker she turned to me and said: "I hope you break your flaming neck." In my opinion they are aggressive, dangerous, but most certifiably insane.'

It was not an opinion shared by expert Dr Charles Bennett who told the court: 'I find that they probably, very probably, knew what they were doing and knew it was wrong in the eyes of society at large.

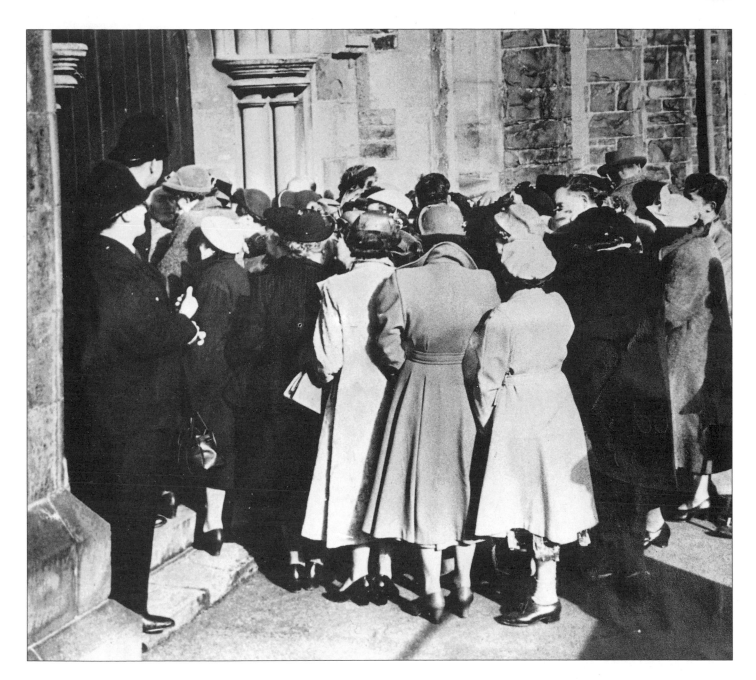

Above: *The trial aroused tremendous interest. Crowds clamoured outside the court for a glimpse of the young lesbian killers.*

But I doubt very much if they gave any consideration whatsoever to what society thought of them at all.'

In the end, after a careful summing up by the judge, it was left to the jury to decide whether the girls were mad or not. Mr Justice Adams said: 'The important word is the word "knowing". It has to be considered at the very moment of the commission of the crime. Were their minds so confused that they did not know this act was wrong? This is what you, ladies and gentlemen of the jury, have to consider.'

Consider it they did and in just two and a quarter hours returned a verdict of Guilty. There was a fleeting smile flashed between the two girls, these supreme egoists, when they were spared the rope by a merciful judge and ordered to be detained at Her Majesty's Pleasure – which meant indefinitely. But in a move which, to many, seemed to mock justice, they were freed just four years later after intense psychiatric counselling. They remained friends but the spark from that earlier relationship had been extinguished by the separation.

Herbert Rieper – he was with Pauline's mother for twenty-five years although he never married her – never recovered from her death. He never forgave the girl.and when his daughter was freed he said: 'It still doesn't make up for robbing a person of their life. It was evil between them that did it. Pure evil.'

'PROSTITUTION SOUNDS A GOOD IDEA TO MAKE MONEY AND WHAT FUN WE WOULD HAVE IN DOING IT!'

KARL & ILSA KOCH
Beasts Of Buchenwald

Even among the monstrous ranks of the sadistic killers of the Third Reich, Karl and Ilsa Koch stand out. Together they were the masters of the notorious Buchenwald concentration camp where their deeds even revolted their SS colleagues. When Frau Koch made a lampshade, it was from human skin.

T he vile racial politics of the Third Reich called for a brutal system of camps across the conquered lands to 'process' the enemies of Adolf Hitler. That these enemies included newborn babies, the crippled and the old, and just about every category of human being in between, was of no consequence to Hitler and the sadists of the SS. Auschwitz, Belsen, Treblinka, Dachau and Buchenwald have gone down in history as the true manifestations of hell on earth, for these were the death factories where some twelve million people, six million of them Jews, were systematically gassed, shot, starved, beaten and worked to death for the purification of the empire that Hitler proclaimed would last a thousand years.

Putting Hitler's warped gospel into practice required men and women so obviously without compassion and decency that it is hard, now, in the post-war years to envision what kind of country or system could ever have produced them. Some camp commanders, like Rudolf Hoess of Auschwitz, were clinically detached from the tortured souls they despatched in the camps' crematoria. Indeed Hoess, at his trial, boasted proudly of the Germanic efficiency that had been brought to bear on the running of the camps.

Karl and Ilsa Koch were a couple whose depravity knew no bounds; whose conduct was so shocking that even their SS masters were revolted. They ruled over Buchenwald concentration camp as supreme arbiters of life and death, reaching previously unplumbed depths of cruelty and evil. These two people personified the

Opposite: Ilsa Koch was tried after the war for her depraved behaviour towards prisoners in Buchenwald.

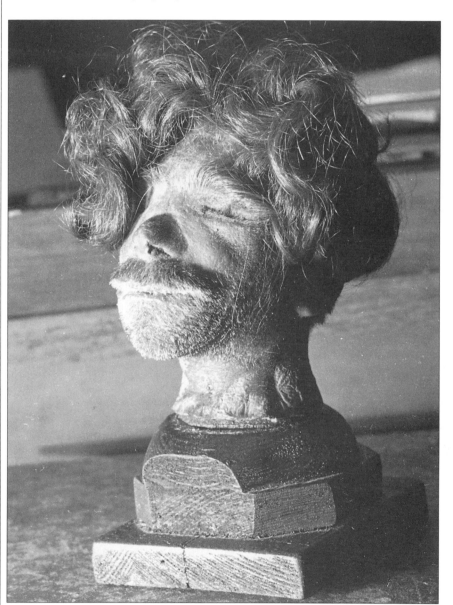

corruption of the Hitlerian ideal: the camp commandant and his wife Ilsa, a woman who spent her evenings making lampshades from the tattooed skins of innocent murdered men.

Ilsa Koch's journey from the rolling hills of Saxony, where she was born in 1906, to the abbatoir of Buchenwald, gives no clue to what turned the former librarian into the woman who sewed human skins together. The daughter of a labourer, she was a

Above: The shrunken head of a Pole hanged at Buchenwald was evidence of the barbarity of these camps.

diligent child at school, well loved and well cared for, and popular with village boys. Like so many individuals who descend into evil, it was only when she forged her relationship with ambitious SS man Karl Koch that her latent depravity was released.

When she met Karl in 1936, Hitler had already laid the foundations of the concentration camp network. Karl Koch was employed at the Sachsenhausen facility as a *Standartenfuehrer* (Colonel) and Ilsa became romantically linked with him when she became his secretary. Karl himself was born out of wedlock to his thirty-four-year-

Above: *Ilsa Koch talks to the German lawyer assigned to defend her in the trial before the Allied authorities.*

> HE WAS AN ADVOCATE OF THE THUMB SCREW AND THE BRANDING IRON.

old mother and a fifty-seven-year-old local government official in Darmstadt, central Germany; they married two months after the boy's birth. Karl's father died when the boy was eight. Never a good scholar, Karl left school at fifteen to work as an office boy at a local factory.

A few days after turning seventeen he tried to enlist in the army as the First World War raged across western Europe, but his mother intervened at the recruiting office and he was frogmarched home. In March 1916, when he was nearly nineteen, he managed to enlist as a rifleman and was rewarded with a tour of the trenches in some of the fiercest sectors of the Western Front before being captured in 1918 on a routine patrol in no-man's-land. He ended

the war in a POW camp and like so many other troops finally returned to a defeated, bitter Germany.

He managed to do quite well for himself at first, securing a position as a bank clerk, and in 1924 he married his first wife. However, two years later, after the birth of a son, the bank he worked for collapsed and he was out of work. In 1931, at the same time as his marriage collapsed, he was drawn to the Nazi movement and soon he was in the SS.

His destiny became intertwined with that of Theodor Eicke, head of the Death's Head units which founded the first concentration camps. Eicke had high regard for Koch, writing in 1936, as he set up the camp at Sachsenhausen: 'His achievements are higher than average. He does everything for the National Socialist ideal.' But at Sachsenhausen, among his peers, he quickly gained a reputation for being a sadistic bully. Soon these qualities were to influence and consume the previously gentle Ilsa and to change her personality.

SOME MEDIEVAL TORTURES

The good National Socialist Koch revelled in beating prisoners with a horse-whip that had razor-blade pieces embedded along it's length. He was an advocate of the thumb screw and the branding iron, inflicting these medieval tortures for the slightest infringement of camp rules.

His overlords in the Reich Main Security Office, that oversaw the administration of the burgeoning concentration camp network, singled him out for promotion. In 1939 he was moved to form the camp at Buchenwald, and took with him Ilsa, whom he had married at the end of 1936 in an SS ceremony at midnight in a grove of oak trees. Buchenwald was a 'correction' camp – as were all the original complexes – its purpose was to change in the middle of the war as Hitler's extermination programme was, at last, seriously planned and followed

Like Auschwitz, Buchenwald had a dual role. Those who were sick or too young to work were led to their deaths straight away. Those deemed fit enough to labour for the Reich were put to work under the most appalling conditions in an armaments factory adjacent to the main camp. Here the living dead toiled on starvation rations.

While Koch supervised the grim day to day destruction of those within his charge, his wife Ilsa became as feared as him. She took to walking with a whip across the camp compound, lashing out at any prisoner who displeased her. Sometimes she took her husband's dog with her and squealed with delight when she let it loose upon pregnant women and women carrying heavy loads. It was no wonder that soon she was known to all the inmates as the Bitch of Buchenwald.

Whenever exasperated prisoners felt sure that she was capable of no greater cruelties, Ilsa would dream up new ways to torment and hound them. Then she began to ask male prisoners to remove their shirts. Those without tattoos didn't interest her but when she saw a tattoo, she smiled a smirk that said: 'Those will be mine.'

For since the beginning of the previous year Ilsa Koch had become the lady of the lampshade, using the treated skins of murdered prisoners to make practical home accessories of which she was very proud. She particularly liked the skins of gypsies and Russian prisoners-of-war – men who had swirls of colour across their chests and backs that made very decorative lampshades. Ilsa liked lampshades.

Above: *Josef Mengele who practised bizarre medical experiments on camp inmates. He was known as the 'Angel of Death'.*

Left: *Sad evidence of thousands of lost lives in the camps were the great piles of victims' possessions like these watches.*

IT WAS NO WONDER THAT SOON SHE WAS KNOWN TO ALL THE INMATES AS THE BITCH OF BUCHENWALD.

Albert Grenowski, a Jew who was forced to work in the pathology laboratory at Buchenwald, told Allied judicial authorities after the war, about how those with tattoos were given orders to report to the dispensary. He said: 'After they were examined by her, those who were deemed to have the most artistically interesting specimens were killed by lethal injection. It was important that the skin of the victims was not damaged. There was one sure way to find yourself in a coffin and that was to damage the skin that the Hexe (witch) wanted for her lampshades.

'The bodies were taken to the pathology lab where they were treated with alcohol and the skins were removed with painstaking attention to detail so as not to split them or otherwise mark them. Then they were dried, often oiled afterwards, and taken in small packages to Ilsa Koch so

*Above: **The horrified American Army that liberated Buchenwald placed local German citizens under armed guard and forced them to walk round the camp to witness Nazi atrocities committed in the name of their nation.***

*Left: **A woman who survived the Dachau camp places her hand on a man who tortured the inmates. She was testifying at a war crimes trial.***

they could be made into lampshades and gloves. Once we saw her walking around the compound wearing a brightly patterned pair of summer gloves and just sexy underwear – you know, like she had forgotten to put a dress on. I particularly paid attention to the gloves. The last time I had seen their decoration was on the back of a gypsy prisoner in my block.'

'THE SKINS WERE REMOVED WITH PAINSTAKING ATTENTION TO DETAIL SO AS NOT TO SPLIT THEM OR OTHERWISE MARK THEM.'

Apparently Ilsa's lust for her lurid pastime became something of a fashion among her fellow tormentors in other concentration camps that had been spawned by the Nazi empire. She took pleasure in corresponding with the wives of other camp commanders and giving them full instructions on how to turn a human hide into a book cover, lampshade, gloves or a fine table covering.

These activities didn't go unnoticed by the authorities and at the end of 1941 the Kochs found themselves before an SS police court in Kassel on charges of 'gross brutality, corruption and dishonour'. For the SS, it was one thing to beat, torture and murder human beings. To be seen to derive pleasure from it, was quite another. In the organisation's loathsome logic, their mission was a crusade, not a means of satisfying sadists. The talk of the lampshades and the whippings had filtered out of the camps through dissatisfied guards and led Ilsa and Karl before Court XXII to answer the charges against them.

This time, the charges were dismissed. The court decided that they were the victims of rumour-mongers and trouble-makers. Koch spent some time at another concentration camp as an 'adviser' to new officers but he was soon back with Ilsa at Buchenwald. But in 1944 there came a second trial in which there would be no escape for the couple.

Commandant Koch was brought before a tribunal on charges that he had killed an SS man who complained about his blatant racketeering. It transpired that much of the loot taken from the victims at Buchenwald, intended for the coffers of the Reichsbank in Berlin to fuel the war effort, had found its way instead into a secret Swiss account that Karl had had the foresight to set up in neutral Switzerland.

Karl had been taking the gold teeth of dead inmates, the pathetic jewels and money they had tried to hide in their clothing, and wedding rings. He intended it to be his nest egg for himself and Ilsa at the end of the war. He was a devoted Nazi but he was even more devoted to the cause of Karl Koch, and realisd Germany was on the losing end of the war. He did not intend to go down with the Third Reich. Racketeering, over and above torture and

> KOCH PLEADED FOR A CHANCE TO REDEEM HIMSELF IN A PENAL BATTALLION FIGHTING THE ADVANCING RUSSIAN TROOPS IN EAST PRUSSIA.

Below: *This is the memorial to the dead of Buchenwald, where 250,000 Jews, gypsies, Russians and homosexuals died under Nazi rule. It is built where the camp once stood.*

murder was probably the most heinous crime in the eyes of his SS superiors.

A pastor whom the Nazis wanted kept alive, but imprisoned, was due to give evidence against him at the tribunal. Mysteriously, he was found dead in his cell the day before he was to give his evidence. From his stomach, traces of an almond-smelling compound were removed and mixed in with the food rations for that day for a dozen Soviet prisoners-of-war – a group who, like Jews, suffered dreadfully under the concentration camp system. All the Soviet prisoners died of cyanide poisoning but the deaths spelled the end of the camp's chief tormentor Karl Koch.

EVIDENCE OF CORRUPTION

A further charge of murder of the pastor was laid against him and he was found guilty and sentenced to death. A secret SS tribunal heard how SS magistrate Konrad Morgen was given Himmler's personal authority to travel to Buchenwald to find out the truth about the commandant's thefts. He found plenty of evidence of his corruption, including money stashed under his bed that had been taken from prisoners. Koch pleaded for a chance to redeem himself in a penal battalion fighting the advancing Russian troops in East Prussia but his request was turned down. IIis reputation for cruelty and evil had even stretched their limits of tolerance and so, on a chilly morning in April 1945, just days before the camp's liberation, Karl Koch was shot in the yard of the very camp he had commanded.

Ilsa, bereft at her husband's death, was equally as guilty as him. Indeed, many of the inmates in the camp felt that Koch was driven to commit his attrocities by the evil influence of his wife. But in the SS eyes she was innocent and acquitted.

However, Ilsa never returned to Buchenwald. She fled westwards in the closing months of the war with the tide of humanity seeking to escape the advancing Russians. By 10 April, 1945, the day that shocked American troops liberated the camp, she was on a farm with relatives outside Ludwigsburg, but her name had not been forgotten by the survivors of the camp. The great American radio broadcaster, Edward R. Murrow, moved his

Below: *Another infamous couple who festered in the camps. Irma Greese, the 'Blonde Beast of Belsen' and her Commandant Josef Kramer after their arrest in 1945. Both were executed for war crimes.*

THE BLOOD OF OVER FIFTY THOUSAND VICTIMS OF BUCHENWALD WAS ON HER HANDS, SAID HER PROSECUTORS.

'I PRAY FOR YOU TO BELIEVE WHAT I HAVE SAID ABOUT BUCHENWALD. I REPORTED WHAT I SAW AND HEARD, BUT ONLY PART OF IT. FOR MOST OF IT I HAVE NO WORDS.'

audience to tears the next day with his report of what those battle-hardened troops had seen there.

'We drove on, reached the main gate. The prisoners crowded up behind the wire. We entered.

'And now let me tell you this in the first person, for I was the least important person there, as you can hear. There surged around me an evil smelling crowd; men and boys reached out to touch me. They were in rags and the remnants of uniforms. Death had already marked many of them, but they were smiling under their eyes. I looked over that mass of men to the green hills where well-fed Germans were ploughing.

'As I walked down to the end of the barracks there was applause from men too weak to get out of bed. It sounded like the hand-clapping of babies. As I walked into the courtyard a man fell dead. Two others, they must have been over sixty, were crawling towards the latrine. I saw it, but I will not describe it. The children clung to my arms and stared. We crossed to the courtyard. Men kept coming up to speak to me, professors from Poland, doctors from Vienna, men from all of Europe. Most of the patients, though, could not move. I asked the cause of death and a doctor shrugged and said: "Tuberculosis, starvation, fatigue, and then there are those that have no desire to live."

I pray for you to believe what I have said about Buchenwald. I reported what I saw and heard, but only part of it. For most of it I have no words.'

A CAUSE TO FIGHT AGAINST

General Eisenhower ordered that all men of the 80th Division – men from the 80th had liberated Buchenwald – should be made to see it. 'They may not know what they are fighting for,' he remarked, 'but at least now they know what they are fighting against.'

Two names cropped up time and again in the days following liberation as the Americans tried to make some sense of the carnage that was Buchenwald. The names were Karl and Ilsa Koch.

In the days and months following the collapse of the Third Reich, Ilsa buried herself in anonymity, secure in the knowledge that the authorities had far bigger fish in the SS and Gestapo to fry than her. She remained free until 1947 when justice finally caught up with her.

Ilsa was forty and pregnant, by an inmate in the prison where she was held, before facing trial. In Munich she was brought before a US Military Tribunal to answer for her war crimes.

For several weeks a procession of wraith-eyed former inmates came in to testify of her sadism, of her love for the tattooed skins, of her wanton brutality. The blood of over fifty thousand victims of Buchenwald was on her hands, said prosecutors, and the fact that she was now a pregnant woman was no reason to show mercy towards her.

US Brigadier General Emil Kiel read her sentence in staccato tones: 'Ilsa Koch – life imprisonment.'

Ilsa went to jail after reading a statement in which she said she was merely a 'servant' of evil people. She denied manufacturing goods from human skin and said she was framed by enemies of the Reich seeking their own vengeance.

But there was a remarkable break for her in 1951 when an American General earned the scorn of both his nation and the new Federal Republic which had replaced

Hitler's fallen empire. General Lucius D. Clay, in charge of the US occupied zone of Germany, granted Isla Koch her freedom, saying there was 'insufficent evidence' that she had ever ordered anyone to be executed and that no articles of tattooed skin were found linked to her.

There was a worldwide gasp of disbelief when Ilsa was freed, the loudest of all coming from respected Washington lawyer William Dowdell Denson, who had prosecuted her. He spoke for the millions of dead as well as the living when he said: 'This is a gross miscarriage of justice. She was one of the most sadistic in the whole group of Nazi offenders. There was no way to compute the number of people that were willing to testify against her – because she was a depraved woman, because she was the commandant's wife – and because she was just so goddamned mean.

'If there is a cry being heard around the world it is for the souls of the tortured innocents who died in Buchenwald and places like it.'

Freedom, however, was fleeting for her. As soon as Ilsa Koch stepped from the US Military Prison in Munich she was arrested again and put behind the bars of a civilian jail by the German authorities.

Above: *Ilsa Koch enters court. She was pregnant by another inmate in the prison where she was held pending her trial.*

Left: *Gen. Patten's troops assembled this grisly collection of lamps and ornaments made from human skin and organs. Germans were obliged to view this display of barbarity when they were compelled by GIs to inspect the Buchenwald camp at the end of the War.*

ANOTHER TRIAL, ANOTHER SENTENCE

The new republic, mindful for its need to atone for the Holocaust and all of Nazism's terrible crimes, immediately re-arrested Ilsa and placed her on trial again. The Bavarian Justice Ministry scoured the country looking for survivors of Buchenwald, seeking new evidence that would commit her to incarceration for the rest of her days. Two hundred and forty witnesses stood in court and told again their stories of Ilsa's murderous actions and behaviour that defied belief. Second time around, she was tried by her own people in whose name she committed her foul deeds and she was sentenced again to life imprisonment. She was told this time to expect no parole of mercy. Life was life.

Above: *As the liberating American Army advanced towards Buchenwald, the guards started killing inmates but there was a revolt and the prisoners turned on the Nazi minions. This statue commemorates the bravery of these prisoners.*

SHE WAS ONE OF THE MOST SADISTIC IN THE WHOLE GROUP OF NAZI OFFENDERS.

In 1967, writing to her son Uwe, whom she had given birth to shortly after her first sentence, she complained bitterly that she was a scapegoat for the *prominenti* (the important ones), who had got away. There was no remorse from her, only recriminations and bitterness at what had happened.

In that year, on 1 September, at her jail in Aichach, Bavaria, she ate a final meal of schnitzel and potato salad before penning one last note to the son she loved. Then she knotted the bedsheets together, tied them to the lamp strung from the metal cage over her bed, and hanged herself. The Bitch of Buchenwald was dead.

It would be hard for anyone to find redemption for Ilsa and Karl Koch, but her son Uwe tried in 1971. Uwe Kohler – he took his mother's maiden name – made an unsuccessful attempt through the West German courts for the restoration of 'my mother's good name'. Insurance clerk Uwe also approached the New York Times newspaper to tell his story. He said: 'Since a revision of history was practically impossible in the West German courts I thought that the American people, since Americans had sentenced her to life imprisonment, should know her side of the story.'

Uwe was born on 29 October, 1947, the product of the liason between Ilsa and a German soldier inmate in Landsberg prison. The boy was removed almost immediately to a Bavarian foster home – the first of many that he was to grow up in, totally unaware of the identity of his parents or whether they were even alive.

'NO PARDON FOR ILSA KOCH'

At the age of eight he inadvertently saw his birth certificate with his mother's name on it and memorised it. Eleven years later he saw a newspaper with the headline: 'No pardon for Ilsa Koch'. He confirmed that the Koch in the story was his mother after confronting his state-appointed guardian.

At Christmas time in 1966, in a fairy tale setting of deep snow, he visited Landsberg to see his mother for the first time. 'To me she was not the Bitch of Buchenwald,' said Uwe. 'We had a joyous reunion.' He continued to visit her right up until the time she hanged herself the following year.

Uwe said: 'I always avoided talking with her about the war. She always denied her guilt and said she was the victim of libels, lies and perjuries. I didn't discuss it further with her because it was obviously painful for her. I wanted her to have hope that she would get out after two decades in prison. I wanted her to think other thoughts.

THE MADNESS OF THE TIMES

'I really cannot imagine what it was like for her in the War. I am not even convinced she was guiltless. But I feel that she just slithered into the concentration camp system like many others without being able to do much about it. I know that she will not be posthumously rehabilitated, but I do feel that she was not guilty of major crimes. She was caught up in the madness of the times, like so many others...'

Historians and psychiatrists alike have been keen over the years to return to the phenomenon that was Ilsa Koch, the corruption of a member of the 'fairer sex' into the embodiment of everything that is evil on this earth. Analysts decided she was probably a nymphomaniac, a meglomaniac and a sadist to boot.

But historical author Charles Leach said of Ilsa: 'Before Karl Koch and after Karl Koch, she displayed none of the cruelties with which she came be to associated. Her madness, if indeed that was what it was, seems to have been triggered solely by her association with this man. With his death, it seems the spell was broken. Maybe if they had never met, like so many evil partnerships, the murder and the mayhem would never have occurred.'

'MAYBE IF THEY HAD NEVER MET, LIKE SO MANY EVIL PARTNERSHIPS, THE MURDER AND THE MAYHEM WOULD NEVER HAVE OCCURRED.'

Below: *The end at Buchenwald and prisoners mill around in the courtyard after the entry of the American forces. The black flag was raised in mourning for President Roosevelt but it served also for the thousands of innocent people who died in the camp.*

BRADY & HINDLEY
The Moors Murders

Ian Brady and Myra Hindley arouse revulsion and hatred like no other murderers in British history. Together in an evil pact, they systematically tortured and killed more than six children. The real death toll is still unknown, forever locked up in the killers' deranged minds.

He was a twenty-seven-year-old stock clerk who idolised Hitler and sunk into horrible fantasies after drinking bottles of cheap German wine which transported him back in his imagination to the rallies and the marches of the Third Reich. Although the expression had not yet been coined in the Swinging Sixties, she would no doubt have been called a bimbo: a twenty-two-year-old peroxide-blonde typist who nurtured fantasies of eternal love. And, indeed, she did find immortality of a kind with the man with mesmeric eyes and quick temper. Together they have gone down in British criminal history as the most wicked of the wicked, for they are the child-killers, Ian Brady and Myra Hindley.

Even today, in a world hardened by violent crime, their vile acts set them apart as monsters of a very special breed. At 16 Wardle Brook Avenue, on the sprawling Hattersley council estate and on the wild Pennine Moors, children abducted by these two died a gruesome death before being buried in unmarked graves. But death was not all these perverts visited upon their innocent victims who should never have accepted the lifts home they offered.

They were sexually assaulted, they were photographed and, in the case of one victim, her screams were even tape recorded... screams that would later be heard in a criminal court, a shocking testament to evil.

Ian Brady and Myra Hindley are a classic case of partners in crime. Separate and alone, they were ordinary, if stunted, characters who might have lived their lives without ever plunging into the abyss of madness and depravity. Together, they fell prey to what the French call a *folie a deux* – the madness generated between two people. She was the girl he could impress; he was the errant knight for whom she would have sold her soul. In reality, they were bound by perversion and a taste for cruelty. Together they have left an imprint on Britain's national conscience that has not been faded or eroded by the passage of the years.

Brady and Hindley forged their relationship after meeting at work. He was a winkle-pickered youth with a fondness for crime B-movies and Nazi philosophy. An illegitimate child who had never known his father (widely believed to have been a reporter on a Glasgow evening newspaper),

> THEY FELL PREY TO WHAT THE FRENCH CALL A FOLIE A DEUX — THE MADNESS GENERATED BETWEEN TWO PEOPLE.

Opposite: *Ian Brady and Myra Hindley frolic for the camera during the thrilling days of their perverse passion.*

he was brought up in the Gorbals slums of the city. His mother, coping with both the stigma of being unmarried and the burden of being poor, put him in the care of a family called Sloan when he was small, during for the formative years of his life.

The kindness they lavished on him was misplaced; he became a cold, sneering, surly youth who shunned kindness as weakness, compassion as foolishness. Brick by brick, he built a wall around

Above: *Police search for clues in the garden of the Hindley-Brady residence.*

himself and convinced himself that he was better than everybody else and that society was against him.

After serving terms in Borstals as a teenager for housebreaking, he was finally given a chance to escape going to the 'big house' – adult prison – by a Glasgow judge who insisted that he live with his real mother. She, by the time he was a teenager, had moved back to Manchester with her new husband, an Irish labourer, but was willing to take a chance, putting her unhappy young son back on the straight and narrow. Here Brady's teenage rebelliousness metamorphosed into something altogether more sinister.

He began buying Nazi books like 'The Kiss of the Whip', which glorified the persecution of the Jews, and to drink heavily. Alternately in and out of work, in trouble with the law for drunkenness, he managed to land a job as a stock clerk at

Millwards Ltd, a chemical and soap company in Manchester. Here the partnership in evil would be irrevocably forged when Myra Hindley was introduced to him on 16 January, 1961.

Within weeks they had become lovers. Her diaries at the time show the student of crime as a pathetically ordinary, normal, unsophisticated suburban girl who confided to paper her childish hopes and fears: 'Not sure if he likes me. They say he gambles on horses. I love Ian all over and over again!'

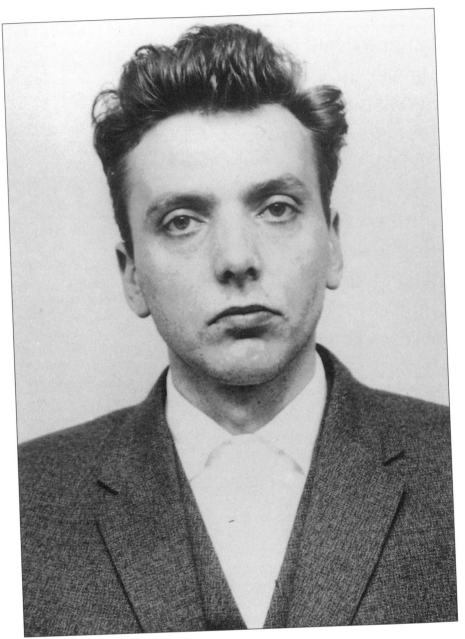

Above: *Ian Brady's image reveals an ill-tempered and defiant personality.*

Left: *The entrance to 18, Westmoreland Street, Manchester where Ian Brady used to live.*

Then: 'He has a cold and I would love to mother him.' Other times she is frustrated or cross with him, and determined to end their fledgling love affair.

Yet in the end he became her first lover, on a sofa-bed in the front room of the house she shared with her grandmother. It happened after they had seen one of his favourite films – 'Judgement at Nuremberg', a story of Nazi atrocities.

From these beginnings grew the seed of perversion and corruption. Brady's book collection of pornographic and sado-masochistic material had swelled now and his needs were more than conventional love-making. Soon he was taking lurid pictures of his girlfriend, complete with whips, a hood and even her pet dog. She

Above: *Myra Hindley shows a hard, grim vanity in this photograph taken while she was on trial for killing small children.*

HE WAS TAKING LURID
PICTURES OF HIS GIRL-
FRIEND, COMPLETE WITH
WHIPS, A HOOD AND EVEN
HER PET DOG.

over tea, as the buses taking their neighbours to work roared along outside? Or perhaps it happened on one of their weekend excursions to the wild and lonely moors that ring Manchester. But Ian and Myra, the loving couple did cross the line between perversion and murder on Friday, 12 July, when Pauline Reade, aged sixteen, accepted a lift from them on her way to a social-club dance in Gorton.

Then on 23 November, 1963, they crossed it again when little John Kilbride, aged twelve-and-a-half, accepted a lift from them at the marketplace in Ashton-under-Lyne. On Tuesday, 15 June, 1964 Keith Bennett, aged twelve, became their third victim when he took a ride on a busy Manchester road after setting out to buy some sweets. On 26 December, 1964, Leslie Ann Downey, born on 21 August, 1954, died at the age of ten years and four months after she climbed into their car parked at a fairground near Ancoats.

THE HOME OF MURDER

After the disappearances of these children, there were the usual appeals of help, the usual sad pictures of the missing were plastered all over their neighbourhoods and beyond. No clues linked ttheir disappearances to each other, there was no reason to believe an evil picd piper was claiming them one by one. It took the brutal murder of an innocent teenager in the front room of the home Brady shared with his accomplice, to lead the police to uncover the horrific crimes of this couple.

On the morning of 7 October, 1965, David Smith, married to Hindley's sister Maureen, made a frantic 999 telephone call at 6.07am from a coin box on the edge of the housing estate where Hindley and Brady lived. He was a young man with a stammer, who was already known to the police for a string of petty offences, and he blurted out a tale of murder perpetrated, he said, the previous evening in the living room of Brady's house.

Smith said the victim, later identified as seventeen-year-old Edward Evans, had been axed to death by Ian Brady to 'impress' Smith. Brady had often talked of robbery and murders with Smith but Smith had put it down to an overworked imagination fuelled by the wine. This time the

took pictures of him, too, surrounded by mirrors as he admired his body. But the thrill of this soon wore thin. Fuelled by the German wine he habitually drank, he drew her into his evil web of fantasy, when he talked of becoming a gangster and of her becoming his moll while they robbed and pillaged like latter-day Bonnie and Clyde.

They did not have the courage for this, however; it was only Dutch courage inspired by the wine. But they did find the courage to satisfy their expanding sexual perversions, if courage is what is needed for two adult people to lure, humiliate, abuse and then murder little children.

No one knows at what precise moment they slipped over the edge and fantasy became action. Did they decide about it fantasy became reality before his very eyes. Brady had murdered a boy and Smith was asked to help clean up the blood after witnessing the ghastly scene.

In a calm monotone, he described how the young man had been lured to the house by Hindley, was set upon by the axe-wielding Brady and was finally 'finished off' by a length of electrical flex with

Below, left: Ian Brady is driven in a police car to the court to answer murder charges.

Below, right: Hindley was hysterical at leaving her dog when police bundled her off in their barred van.

explain why he wouldn't be at work that day – he claimed he had hurt his ankle. In reality, he was planning an excursion to his private cemetery on the moors to make room for one more corpse.

Talbot, upon being greeted by Myra Hindley at the doorway, pushed past her into the house announcing that he was a police officer. Hindley tried to block his entrance to the bedroom but Brady, nonchalantly still lying on the divan, told her: 'Ye'd best give him the key.' Once inside the bedroom Superintendent Talbot discovered the corpse of the young man who died for their thrills.

With Brady in custody, charged with murder, the police re-interviewed Smith who told them that Brady had boasted of killing 'three or four others'. These others were allegedly buried on the bleak, beautiful Saddleworth Moor outside of Manchester. Talbot logged the number-scarefully in his orderly policeman's brain, for he believed he had seen in Brady's arrogant eyes and surly manner the mark of a very dangerous predator indeed.

Brady told police a bland story. He said he had met Edward Evans, the victim, in a

which Brady throttled him. Brady asked Smith to help him in his macabre clean-up afterwards, saying: 'This one's taking a time to go. Feel, Dave, feel the weight of that. That was the messiest yet.' Afterwards, with the glow of a sexual, murderous frenzy bathing them, Ian Brady and Myra Hindley made love as Edward Evans' mutilated body lay upstairs.

A FATAL DELIVERY OF BREAD

Police decided that there was more to Smith's tale than hysteria or mischief. The house in Wardle Brook Avenue was approached and police superintendent Bob Talbot put on the white coat of a local breadman, borrowed his loaves and knocked on the door of number sixteen. Hindley answered it; Brady was inside on a divan writing a letter to his bosses at Millwards. The letter was an excuse to

Manchester pub, the youngster had come to his house afterwards, they had rowed and, unfortunately, he had killed Evans with a hatchet. Talbot's superior officer, Arthur Benfield, Detective Chief Superintendent for the whole of Cheshire, was down at the police station by noon to investigate the drunken death but he was worried by the boast of 'three or four others'.

A search of the house revealed notebooks with ruled columns in which Brady had written down a series of what appeared to be coded instructions. There was 'meth' for method, 'stn' for station, 'bulls' for bullets, 'gn' for gun. After staring at it long and hard, Benfield realised he was looking at a shopping list for murder weapons. But whose murder?

Days later, as he sifted through the paraphernalia of Brady's bedroom, he came upon a tattered school exercise book filled with scribblings and graffiti. There was a list of names that apparently meant

nothing, jotted down by the day-dreaming clerk during moments of boredom. But Benfield read through all the names nonetheless – Christine Foster, Jean Simpson, Robert Uquart, James Richardson, Joan Crawford, Gilbert John, Ian Brady, John Sloan, Jim Idiot, John Birch, Frank Wilson, John Kilbride, Alec Guineas, Jack Polish, J. Thompson. John Kilbride... the name hit Talbot like a hammer blow and suddenly the feeling washed over him that he was on to a monsterous crime, something bigger than he had ever imagined.

The search of the house brought to light the pornographic photographs Brady and Hindley had taken of each other and the sado-masochistic and Nazi book collection. And there were other pictures too, of Hindly and Brady taken on the moors One in particular caught his eye, that of Myra sitting on the ground, looking wistfully at the gorse and peat beneath her, staring at

Above: *Myra Hindley's peroxide has faded, but her sneering defiance remains and can be discerned even in this partial view of her.*

'THIS ONE'S TAKING A TIME TO GO. FEEL, DAVE, FEEL THE WEIGHT OF THAT. THAT WAS THE MESSIEST YET.'

The police had two lucky breaks. Everyone was eager to help catch the murderers, and vital information from a neighbour's twelve-year-old daughter who accompanied Auntie Myra and Uncle Ian on excursions to the moors to 'help them dig for peat'. The second was from a car hire company that confirmed that they had rented a car to a Myra Hindley on 23 November, 1963, John Kilbride's last day alive. The police used photos removed from the couple's bedroom to locate the burial places of the murdered children. They were helped by the girl who, though she had been taken to the moors by the pair, had survived the trip.

A CASE OF LEFT-LUGGAGE

The body of Lesley Ann Downey was found by the police searchers on 16 October, ten days after the death of Edward Evans. Police thought that they would find the body of John Kilbride but they only found the little tartan skirt belonged to the trusting little girl. Two days later another

Above: *Mr David Lloyd Jones, in front, and Mr Philip Curtis counsel for Brady and Hindley respectively. The defence had an unenviable task.*

Right: *Scenes outside the courtroom as Lesley Anne Downey's uncle lunged at the man who murderd the child. Police restrained him but the public did not.*

nothing in particular except the ground as if... as if she were staring at a grave.

Brady played mind games with the police, claiming the stories he told to Smith were lies to build up an 'image'. He said there were no more bodies and that the name Kilbride in the exercise book was an old chum from Borstal days. Police made door-to-door inquiries in their neighbourhood.

policeman on the team made an even more startling discovery. Hidden in the spine of Myra Hindley's communion prayer book was a left-luggage ticket for two suitcases at Manchester Central Station. Once retrieved, they yielded up more pornographic books, small-arm ammunition, blackjacks, wigs, tapes and photos of moorland views.

And other pictures. Pictures of a little girl with her eyes bulging in terror, naked save for her socks and shoes, bound and gagged. Talbot felt the tears well up in his eyes as he looked into the helpless face of Lesley Ann Downey.

Later, the tapes were played. The first ones was a hotch-potch of Hitler marches and the BBC Goons show, interspersed with a documentary on Hitler's life. Then the second one was played – the tape that numbed the polcemen present, would later make hardened journalists weep and would finally nail Brady and Hindley for the cruel and evil monsters they were. 'Don't... please God help me. Don't undress me will you... I want me mam...'. Interspersed with screams, pleas and futile whimpers, against the barking commands of Hindley and Brady, these were the final words of Lesley Ann as she met her unspeakable end at the hands of the sinister people who gave her a lift at the fair.

Below, left: *Ian Brady takes a last look at the world where he behaved with such depravity.*

Below, right: *Patricia Cairns, second on the right, the lesbian warder who plotted to free her lover, Hindley.*

On 21 October the body of John Kilbride was found in the spot where Myra had been photographed with her beloved dog Puppet. John's underpants had been pulled down to below his thighs, knotted hard in the back to prevent him from moving his legs. He had been sexually assaulted and buried face down. Britain and the world were inflamed with anger at the killers now branded the

Moors Murderers. Myra Hindley was now under arrest to face charges of murder along with her lover, Ian Brady.

The trial gripped the public attention as no other had done when the pair came before Chester Assizes on 19 April, 1966. Both pleaded Not Guilty to murder and maintained an arrogance and swagger throughout that earned them the hatred of prosecutors, police, journalists, the judge and the parents of the dead.

In the Evans case, Brady maintained that it was Smith's idea to 'roll a queer' for money and that he had participated in the killing. In Lesley Ann's case, Brady gave the court a totally implausible story that he had taken photos of her after she had been driven to their home by men he didn't know and that he turned her over to them afterwards. In the case of John Kilbride, he denied murder and sexual assault.

It was the tape, however, which dominated the proceedings and for which they will always be damned. Emlyns Williams, in his authoritative chronicle of the crimes and aftermath 'Beyond Belief'

Opposite: *The pair had many snapshots of their excursions with dogs on the moors. Myra, particularly, was fond of animals. However, the police were able, with the help of these 'family' snaps, to locate the burial grounds of murder victims. The photos were grotesque 'souvenirs' of grotesque crimes.*

Right: *Hindley's sister, Maureen with her husband, David Smith. He was seduced by Brady's ideas on dangerous sexual thrills, but the reality disgusted him. Smith reported Brady and Hindley to the police after he witnessed them killing a young man.*

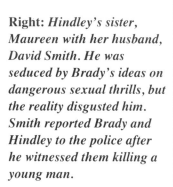

BRADY, WHEN ASKED WHY HE KEPT THE TAPE RECORDING, SAID IT WAS BECAUSE IT WAS 'UNUSUAL'.

wrote: 'This tape was to become the most scaring object ever to lie on the exhibits table below a judge at a murder trial... the tape began. And played for seventeen intolerable minutes. To listen to it was made doubly dreadful by the very nature of the invention which made the experience possible. In the course of murder trials, for centuries dreadful things have had to come to light, not only visually but mumbled by unwilling witnesses. Never before, however, has the modern phenomenon of preserved sound been put to such a grisly use as was the "the Moors tape".' The courtroom listened in shocked horror and disbelief to the pleading of the little girl as she begged for life and her mam, to the backdrop of Christmas carols and the barking commands of Brady for the child to pose in immodest positions.

Brady, when asked why he kept the tape recording, said it was because it was 'unusual'. It was a gross answer.

Hindley, in particular, became the focus of public curiousity. Men like Brady – well, there are many perverts and murderers down the ages, men who have killed to sate their demonic urges. But women were supposed to be the gentler sex, the givers of life, the nurturers of children. How could she have slipped into such an abyss? She gave little indication that she had a 'feminine' heart at her trial. Scrutiny of testimony during examination by the Attorney General Sir Elwyn Jones shows that she had little remorse for what had taken place, even though she pleaded Not Guilty to all charges. The following is an extract from the trial.

Attorney General: Time and again you were driving into this child's ears your orders, 'put it in'.

Hindley: I just wanted her to not make a noise.

Attorney General: Then you say, 'Will you stop it. Stop it'. Did you think there was the most terrible threatening note in the second order to stop it, Miss Hindley?

Hindley: No, it was a desparate tone.

Attorney General: Then one hears the poor little child making a retching noise. This thing was being pushed down her throat, was it not?

Hindley: No.

Attorney General: Who do you say undressed this child?

Hindley: Herself.

Attorney General: Can you therefore explain the child's saying: 'Don't undress me will you?' That was precisely what you were trying to do with the child?

Hindley: No, I was not.

Attorney General: A little further on Brady is saying: 'If you don't keep that hand down I'll slit your neck.' That is why you do not want to be landed with hearing that, is it not?

Hindley: No.

Attorney General: Then when the child was whining you say, 'Sh. Hush. Put that in your mouth again and...'. Then there follow the words 'packed more solid'. Why did you want the mouth to be packed more solid?

Hindley: Why more solid? I don't know.

Attorney General: That was preparatory to suffocating her in due course, was it not?

Hindley: No.

Above: *Police with long poles search near the site where they unearthed the body of Lesley Anne Downey. They were looking for other victims.*

THEY KILLED FOR SICK AND TWISTED KICKS. THEY ARE NOT FIT TO MIX WITH HUMANS.

But no one in the court believed they were innocent. On 6 May, 1966, both were found Guilty of murdering Edward Evans and Lesley Ann Downey, Brady further found Guilty of the murder of John Kilbride with Hindley being an accessory after the fact. Brady was jailed for life on each of the three murder charges, Hindley for life on the Downey and Evans murders with a further seven years for her part as an accesory to the Kilbride slaying.

They were driven off to separate prisons with the screams of the mob outside ringing in their ears, and the lovers were never to see each other again. Hindley appealed her conviction but three appeal judges ruled against her.

The grisly saga of the Moors Murders might have ended then but the disappearances of Pauline Reade and Keith Bennett remained unsolved. Police officers who had worked on the case felt in their bones, that these two monsters had something to do with the disappearances of these two but there were no photographs or tape recordings to link them with the youngsters.

These suspicions continued down the years as Myra Hindley became a model prisoner, then was involved in a lesbian love-affair that sparked a failed escape plot. She became an Open University graduate, converted to Christianity and established communication with Lord Longford, the prison reformer who is one of very few people who believe that Myra Hindley has been rehabilitated and now deserves to be released.

The correspondence between her and Brady was furious and passionate in the first months of separation, but time cooled the love while Brady slipped deeper into madness before he was finally moved, in November 1985, to a maximum-security hospital. But he was not so mad as to be incapable of thwarting the long-cherished dream that his former lover clung to throughout her long years of captivity.

A LOVER'S FURY

When Brady heard of Myra's attempts to be released, he broke his silence regarding the deaths of Reade and Bennett, prompting police to visit Myra Hindley in her jail cell. On 15 December, 1986, Myra Hindley returned to Saddleworth Moor, her first breath of the moors since the terrible events of more than two decades ago. Her memory, perhaps faded with time, perhaps by the enormity of what she had done, failed to pinpoint any graves, although she was sure she had the right area. But police searched diligently and in June the following year the body of Pauline Reade was discovered. Pathologists analysed that she had been sexually assaulted and her throat slashed from behind.

Her confession to the Reade and Bennett murders has effectively stifled any hope that Myra Hindley will ever be freed and she is said to have resigned herself to death in jail. It is highly unlikely that any prime minister would wish to be known as the premier who sanctioned her parole, even though she will be eligible to apply for release again in 1995.

Brady, meanwhile, continues in his mental degeneration. Now declared clinicaly insane, in the winter of 1987 he mailed a letter to the BBC containing sketchy information about five further murders, including unsuspected Moors victims, a man murdered in Manchester, a woman dumped in a canal and two victims gunned down in Scotland. Police are probing his alleged crimes but at the time of writing it is unclear if more prosecutions will follow.

Other victims of the killings are the families of the murdered children. Mrs Ann West, mother of Lesley Ann, is a vociferous campaigner for Hindley to stay behind bars. On the twenty-fifth anniversary of her child's death she wrote to Home Secretary Kenneth Baker, saying: 'Though a generation has passed since those evil monsters were put behind bars the horror of their crimes remains as fresh as ever. I beg you to turn a deaf ear to those well-meaning, but tragically misguided do-gooders who would now set them free on compassionate grounds. Ignore, at all costs, those who would forgive and forget. For just as there is no parole for we who still grieve, so must there be no parole for them.

'Every night I am haunted anew by the memory of that courtroom. I can still hear the taped screams of Lesley Ann begging for mercy...

'The enormity of those murders has not diminished. They killed for sick and twisted kicks, and showed no compassion. They are not fit to mix with humans. I implore you to make sure they do not.'

Below, left: *The bleak burial grounds of two murdered children.*

Below: *Ian Brady after years in prison. He has grown madder and madder and is in a psychiatric unit.*

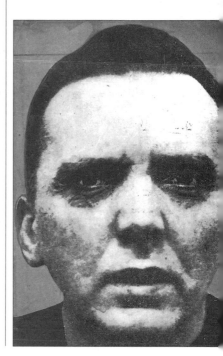

DOWNEY'S BODY FOUND OVER RIDGE

KILBRIDE'S BODY FOUND HERE

THE ROSENBERGS
The A-Bomb Spies

No-one ever thought there was anything special about Julius and Ethel Rosenberg, until they were tried and executed in the electric chair as spies. This ordinary couple were at the heart of a traitorous network which passed the secrets of America's first atomic bomb to the Soviet Union.

Julius and Ethel Rosenberg were the children of dispossessed Russian Jews who went to the New World determined to make a different and better life. Julius and Ethel were both born in the USA. Of course, as they matured they also nursed their hopes and their dreams. But their dream was not the same dream as that of their family and neighbours; it was one that could only be fulfilled by an alien creed hostile to their homeland, the government of the United States.

For Ethel and Julius Rosenberg were America's 'atomic spies', the suburban couple enmeshed in a plot to sell America's nuclear secrets to their Kremlin enemy. The Rosenbergs were the only Communist agents ever to be executed in peacetime and, while apologists and historical revisionists have argued down the years that the pair were the victims of a ghastly frame-up, experts conclude that the verdicts and sentences passed upon them have stood the test of time.

When the switch was thrown on them in the death chamber at Sing-Sing prison in New York on 19 June, 1953, it was the end of one of the grimmest chapters of international espionage. Many thronged the streets in the hours before they were executed, some protesting their innocence, others merely asking for clemency. The problem with both Julius and Ethel Rosenberg, for those who believed them innocent, was that they looked so damned ordinary. But that, say the counter-intelligence chiefs who trapped them, was precisely what made them so damn good.

Outwardly, there was nothing to distinguish this married couple from their fellow citizens. Ethel, whose maiden name was Greenglass, had graduated from high school on the lower east side of Manhattan – a neigbourhood that embraced most of the races on earth. She left school at sixteen, was employed in various clerical jobs and secretarial posts before becoming an active trade unionist.

Opposite: *Ethel and Julius Rosenberg who played no small part in the Cold War when they sold A-bomb secrets to the USSR.*

Above: *The A-bomb explosion over Japan in 1945.*

Julius, the bespectacled electrical engineer who once underwent religious training in the hope of becoming a rabbi, sprang from similar roots. A graduate of the same high school as his future wife, he studied the Torah for a year before abandoning his religious leanings in favour of a degree in electrical engineering from the City College of New York. He knew Ethel at school as a friend, but when he met her later at a dance, their friendship blossomed into love. In 1939, while the storm clouds of war were gathering over Europe, he married her shortly after his twenty-first birthday.

Below, left: *Given the innocuous name of 'Little Boy' this is an A-bomb, capable of a dreadful, long-term destruction of mankind.*

Below, right: *Dr.Enrico Fermi, the Italian who escaped Fascism in his own country, and worked in the USA. He was the scientist who first produced the chain-reacting fission that led to the A-bomb.*

expelled from the Army when his covert membership of the organisation was discovered by the FBI. America was yet to reach her peak of anti-Communist hysteria under the McCarthy hearings, but to be 'red' was still an alien and utterly distasteful concept to the majority of her citizens. Unemployed and with a family to feed, Julius launched his own business with capital from Ethel's brothers, David and Bernard.

David Greenglass was an integral part of the conspiracy to sell USA secrets to the USSR that Julius and Ethel Rosenberg had willingly joined several years previously. For Greenglass worked during the war at the Los Alamos research centre, the top-secret New Mexico site where Robert Oppenheimer and his scientists worked in a desperate race to build the first atomic bomb before the Axis powers did. This remote site, formerly the home of a boys school, was the centre for the greatest and most destructive scientific achievement of this or any age... and David Greenglass systematically stole its secrets for traitorous sale to the Russians.

Just like the British-born Soviet spies Burgess, Philby and Maclean, who were recruited as agents while at British universities, so Greenglass saw the Soviet Union

A SOCIALIST FAMILY MAN

After a year of odd-jobs Julius became a junior engineer for the Army Signal Corps. In the spring of 1942 he and Ethel, who had been living in cramped conditions with his mother, rented a small apartment in a housing development on the east side of Manhattan. Life was sweet for the Rosenbergs during the war years; he had a desk job which didn't require him to serve abroad, and there were few of the economic privations in America which tested British familes during the War. They had two sons, Michael and Robert and the young Rosenbergs doted on them.

But Julius was already a keeper of secrets. Years earlier he had joined the Communist Party, impressed by what he saw as the 'new order' shaping world events from Moscow. In 1945 he was

as the way of the future. But the FBI later maintained that it was his sister and Julius who had recruited him to the cause. And the Rosenbergs kept him sweet on the idea of world socialism with liberal handouts of money. With the family as his puppet-masters, he agreed to use his work position to deliver the stolen blueprints for the bomb to their Kremlin bosses. When Greenglass eventually came to trial, he turned on his family to save his own neck. By pinning the blame exclusively on the Rosenbergs, claiming their own fanatical Communist leanings were used to intimidate him, he saved himself.

It was the Rosenbergs who were the lynch-pin for the entire spying operation which began to unravel in 1950 with the arrest of thirty-nine-year-old Harry Gold, a bachelor employed as a chemist at a Philadelphia hospital. He was named by the

HE HAD JOINED THE COMMUNIST PARTY, IMPRESSED BY WHAT HE SAW AS THE 'NEW ORDER' SHAPING WORLD EVENTS FROM MOSCOW.

FBI and the US Attorney General as being the accomplice of the disgraced nuclear boffin Klaus Fuchs, who was behind bars in England after pleading guilty to selling nuclear secrets to Moscow.

REVELATIONS OF A BRITISH SPY

Fuchs, a brilliant physicist who had fled his native Germany when Hitler came to power, was part of the British mission that was given access to the highest security levels surrounding the development of the bomb. He received a fourteen-year sentence for his treachery. He admitted that he used Gold as the courier, although it is still unclear to this day whether Fuchs had any contact with the Rosenbergs.

He was indicted on wartime espionage charges that carried the death penalty, even though the War was over. Gold, who had been the contact in America for Fuchs, was a wretched little man who sang like a canary once he was in custody. His confession that David Greenglass, the Los Alamos worker, had fed him atomic bomb secrets throughout the War years, exploded like the bomb itself across the front pages of the nation's newspapers.

The FBI built up a dossier detailing Grennglass' spying activities inside the Los Alamos complex. Greenglass had frequent access to top secret material on the 'lenses' for atomic bombs – the detonators that released the plutonium and uranium to create the single critical mass. On 17 July, under intense pressure from his captors, Greenglass sold out his brother-in-law. His sister's arrest was to follow shortly. Anti-Communist hysteria was rising in America now and Americans were fighting once again, this time against the menace of Communism in Korea.

The Department of Justice press release on the arrest of Rosenberg proclaimed: 'J. Edgar Hoover, the director of the FBI, said that Julius Rosenberg is a most important link in the Soviet espionage apparatus.

'Rosenberg, in early 1945, made available to Greenglass while he was on leave in New York City one-half of an

irregularly cut jelly-box top, the other half of which was given to Greenglass by Gold in Albuquerque, New Mexico, as a means of identifying Gold to Greenglass. Rosenberg aggressively sought ways and means to secretly conspire with the Soviet government to the detriment of his own country. Investigation to date also reveals that Rosenberg made himself available to Soviet espionage agents so he might "do something directly to help Russia".' This was all denied by the Rosenbergs who said they were trapped in a nightmare of which they had no part.

But the FBI had indeed assembled a massive body of evidence which they would later use against the couple at their trial. Another member of the spy ring to be arrested was Morton Sobell, a friend of the Rosenbergs who had studied electrical engineering with Julius. He was charged on a separate indictment of passing to them the details and plans of America's latest radar on its ships and submarines. This too would be used against them when they came to trial in March 1951.

A MISTAKEN IDEALISM

The full weight of the US government's case had shifted from Gold and the other arrested spies to the Rosenbergs. The FBI evidence depicted them as the architects of the spy ring who forged the contacts with the Soviet diplomats and agents. J. Edgar Hoover said that American intelligence predicted that Russia would not have the atomic bomb until the 1960s. But thanks to the secrets passed along by the Rosenbergs, they exploded their first device in 1949, rocketing them into the nuclear age and laying the foundations of the Cold War. This, he said, was the end result of the American spies' 'misty eyed idealism'.

Irving Saypol, the government prosecutor at the trial, left no one in any doubt, when he rose to open the case, that he intended to go for the death penalty. He said: 'We will prove that the Rosenbergs devised and put into operation, with the aid of Soviet agents in this country, an elaborate scheme which allowed them to steal, through David Greenglass, this one weapon which might well hold the key to the survival of this nation and means the peace of the world, the atomic bomb. This

Below: *'Old Sparky' the electric chair that despatched many felons in Sing-Sing, the prison in New York State.*

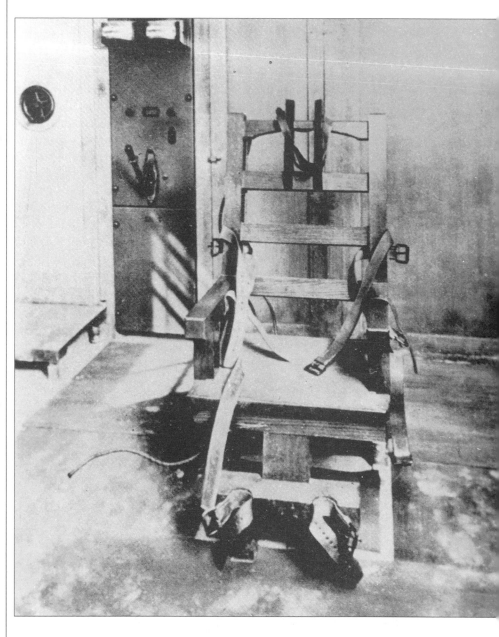

Opposite, above: *Enrico Fermi whose brilliant war effort was wasted by the treachery of the Rosenbergs.*

Opposite, below: *Sing-Sing prison where the traitors, Julius and Ethel Rosenberg, were executed.*

love of Communism and the Soviet Union led them into a Soviet espionage ring.'

The fifteen-day trial was a sensation, the more so because of the spectacle of a brother betraying his own sister. But there was a parade of witnesses who testified that the Rosenbergs had sold their souls to the beliefs of the hammer and sickle, not the stars and stripes. Max Elitcher, the first witness, testified that Julius Rosenberg had badgered him, asking him if his job in the Navy Department in Washington gave him access to secrets that he could pass on to the Soviets. Elizabeth Bentley, a Columbia University graduate, told how she was lured into the espionage web through a series of disasterous love affairs with Soviet agents. She testified that the bond was between the Rosenbergs and Moscow was unusually strong.

Undoubtedly, it was the evidence of David Greenglass which sealed their fates. He testified that he worked in Los Alamos and had access to the greatest secrets which he passed to his sister and brother-in-law. 'They preferred Russian socialism to our system of government,' he said. Greenglass said that he began passing on information, initially about the personnel at the closely-guarded complex, later on about the explosives used to trigger the detonator and the detonator mechanisms themselves. He detailed the jelly-box story that had been revealed by the Department of Justice press release at the time of the traitors' arrest. The words 'I come from Julius' displayed on the top of the box flashed by Gold, meant that the coast was clear and that the Rosenbergs required more information for their Russian bosses.

Greenglass passed on data and sketches and in one despatch, for which he received $200, he typed up twelve pages of notes about the mechanism of the bomb. He went on: 'Working in the Rosenberg's living-room Ethel did the typing and Julius, Ethel and my wife Ruth corrected the grammar. Julius told me he communicated with his Russian contacts by leaving microfilm in an alcove at a cinema. He said he had received an alcove table from the Russians as a reward – I saw this table at his apartment. It was used for microfilming.'

A BROTHER'S BETRAYAL

Greenglass said the spying operation was finished with the arrest of Fuchs in 1950. He said that Julius visited him, Greenglass, and said: 'You remember the man who came to see you in Albuquerque? Well, Fuchs was one of his contacts. Doubtless this man will be arrested soon and this might lead to you.' He was referring to Gold and he was correct on both counts. Greenglass said he offered money for him to go away to Mexico and later came back with $4,000 for the purpose. But the plot was already unravelling because, by then, Greenglass was under surveillance .

Ruth Greenglass stepped into the witness box to corroborate everything her husband

'THEY PREFERRED RUSSIAN SOCIALISM TO OUR SYSTEM OF GOVERNMENT.'

Below: *Hiroshima, Japan after the A-Bomb was dropped.*

had said. She produced bank deposit receipts that showed large amounts of cash being placed in their account – sums far larger than her husband's salary at Los Alamos could have provided. She also recalled the last visit Julius made to their apartment, when he said they would have to flee before the arrests began. 'I was worried about my baby,' she said, 'and he at first said we should go to the Soviet Union. When I said that I could not travel with an infant he said: "My doctor says that if you take enough canned milk and boil the water, everything will be all right." He said that they were closing the net, that we could expect arrests soon. But we never intended to go.'

THE MEANING OF TREASON

Harry Gold, the US contact to the now-imprisoned Fuchs, also delivered damning testimony. He said that Anatoli Yakolev, the Soviet Union's vice-consul in New York City, was the paymaster with the money man who controlled him and Rosenberg. He said: 'Yakolev reported that the information I had given him had been sent immediately to the Soviet Union. He said that the information I had received from Greenglass was extremely excellent and very valuable.' Yakolev had left America rather rapidly on a ship bound for Europe in 1946 and was never quizzed on his role in the atom spy ring.

Julius Rosenberg took the stand and answered every specific allegation of treachery with the three words: 'I did not.' He denied giving the Greenglasses any money other than some cash he owed David from the business that he helped finance. But he refused to say whether or not he was a member of the Communist Party – he was – although he admitted that he did have sympathy for the Soviet political system 'as it has done much to improve the lot of the underdog.'

Ethel, too, denied all allegations of espionage. She said she loved the brother who had branded her and her husband as traitors, but could offer no explanation why he had implicated them other than as a ploy to save himself. Observers at the time thought that she didn't help herself by refusing to explain why so often she had pleaded the Fifth Amendment – the right to

Above: *Julius Rosenberg*.

remain silent – during the grand jury hearings which led to her trial.

Morton Sobell refused to take the stand at the trial of the traitors.

In his summing up the prosecutor was emphatic that the accused were spies. Saypol said: 'This is one of most important cases ever submitted to a jury in this country. We know that these conspirators stole the most important scientific secrets ever known to mankind from this country and delivered them to the Soviet Union. David Greenglass' description of the atomic bomb was typed by Ethel

---

JULIUS TOLD ME HE COMMUNICATED WITH HIS RUSSIAN CONTACTS BY LEAVING MICROFILM IN AN ALCOVE AT A CINEMA.

Above: 'Save the Rosenbergs'. In Paris, certain groups decried the death sentence on the traitors.

'I BELIEVE YOUR CONDUCT IN PUTTING THE ATOM BOMB IN THE HANDS OF THE RUSSIANS... HAS CAUSED... CASUALTIES EXCEEDING FIFTY THOUSAND.'

Gold was involved with the Rosenbergs. They were all traitors.

On the morning of Tuesday, 29 March the jurors returned with Guilty verdicts on Julius, Ethel and Sobell. Judge Irving Kaufman told the Rosenbergs: 'The thought that citizens of our country would lend themselves to the destruction of our country by the most destructive weapons known to man is so shocking that I can't find words to describe this loathsome offence.' A week later, on 5 April, 1951, as they appeared for sentencing, he told them: 'I consider your crime worse than murder. Plain deliberate contemplated murder is dwarfed in magnitude by comparison with the crime you have committed. I believe your conduct in putting the atom bomb in the hands of the Russians has already caused the resultant aggression in Korea with casualties exceeding fifty thousand.

A CONTROVERSIAL VERDICT

'It is not in my power, Julius or Ethel Rosenberg, to forgive you. Only the Lord can find mercy for what you have done. You are hereby sentenced to the punishment of death, and it is ordered you shall be executed according to law.'

Morton Sobell got thirty years, of which he would serve sixteen. Later, Greenglass, who stole the secrets, got a remarkably light fifteen years, as did his wife Ruth Greenglass, who collapsed in the dock as the sentence was handed down.

There was to be no reprieve for the Rosenbergs, despite twenty-two appeals and numerous stays of execution. Julius, thirty-five, and Ethel, thirty-seven, died in the electric chair on the night of 19 June, 1953. Ever since then debate has raged about the possibility of their innocence, but top legal experts say their guilt is more than likely. Alexander Bickel, a Yale University law professor, said: 'It was a ghastly and shameful episode, but I believe they were guilty beyond a doubt.' And Roy Cohn, one of the prosecutors, added: 'I feel the guilt was overwhelming. Their apparent "ordinariness" made it possible for them to get away with it for so long.'

Only Cuba, satellite of the now-defunct Soviet Union for which they served, commemorated them as 'assassinated heroes' on a set of postage stamps.

Rosenberg, just so had she, on countless other occasions, sat at that typewriter and struck the keys, blow by blow, against her country in the interests of the Soviets.

'When Fuchs confessed, the Rosenbergs' position in the Soviet espionage hierachy in this country was jeaopardised. The evidence of the guilt of the Rosenbergs is incontrovertible. No defendants ever stood before the bar of American justice less deserving than them and Sobell.' Their defence lawyers tried to pin the guilt on Greenglass, but were unable to dismiss the fact that

EVIL WOMEN

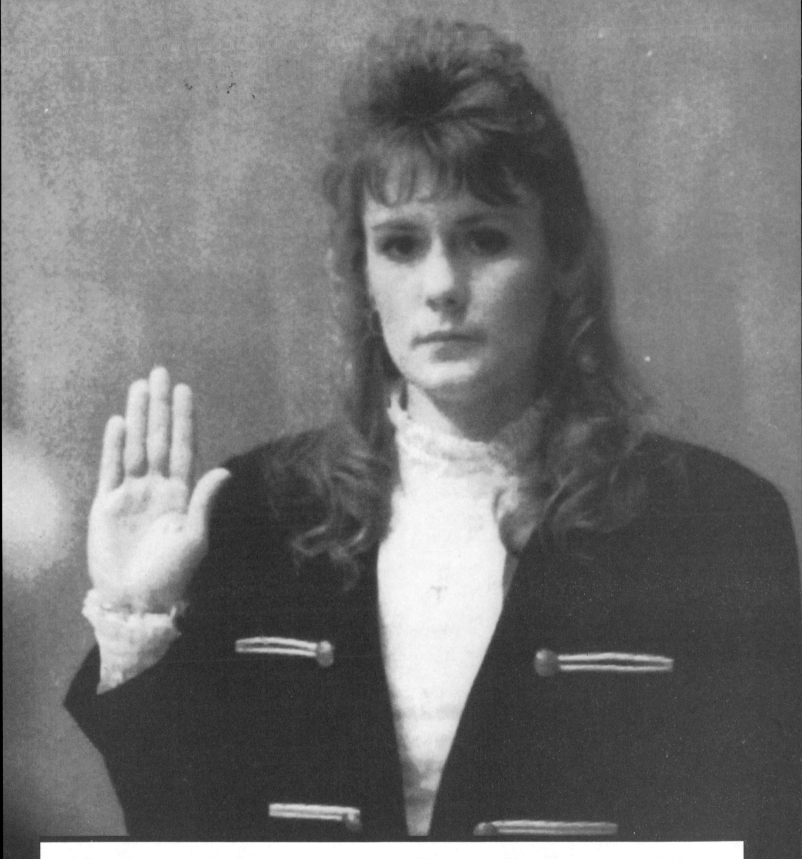

PAMELA SMART
Mistress of murder

She was a teacher, a person of some standing and authority. She was a wife. But Pamela Smart was also crazy for sex with a teenage boy, so maddened by lust that she was driven to commit a gross and ugly murder.

Pamela Smart was young, she was beautiful and she was ambitious. She lived in the small town of Derry, New Hampshire on America's eastern seaboard, and she was restless. Bored with her life as a teacher, bored and unhappy as a wife, she sought excitement in a love affair with an adolescent boy. But this illicit passion was to lead her and her young lover to disaster and tragedy.

Shortly after 10pm on 1 May, 1990, police patrolman, Gerald Scaccia, received an urgent call to investigate a crime at number 4E in Misty Morning Drive, Derry. Scaccia had been cruising for the usual drunks and speeders when his despatcher announced an emergency call at the address – something about a body. He found a sobbing Pamela Smart sitting on the stoop of a neighbour's house. Hysterical with grief, she pointed into the open doorway of her own home, saying: 'He's in there – my husband's in there.' Scaccia entered with his flashlight, saw a man lying face down, his heels toward him in the hallway of the residence. He turned the body over and was about to begin mouth-to-mouth resuscitation when he spotted the small circle in the man's temple, a wound caused by a bullet, fired at point-blank range from a snub-nosed .38 revolver.

Neighbourhood sympathy for the young widow was widespread. Friends appeared to comfort the popular and personable high school teacher whose husband, Greg, had been so cruelly murdered just six days before their first wedding anniversary.

Pamela, who was a director at a media studies' centre that managed a number of projects in local schools, was interviewed by the police. She explained that she had been at a school meeting that night. She and Greg had moved to Derry a few months ago. He worked as an insurance salesman with the Metropolitan Life Company and, no, she did not know why anyone would want to kill him. But a detective at the interview said: 'There was something strange about her. Her world had fallen apart and, well, she seemed very, very calm about it all. I thought it was a bit weird. Call it a cop's intuition. There was nothing I could put my finger on at the time.'

Above: *The doomed husband, Greg Smart, on his wedding day in 1989.*

Opposite: *Pamela Smart proved to be an accomplished liar, a philandering wife and a conspirator to murder.*

Smart described to reporters the crime scene. She revealed details that the police would have preferred to remain confidential as they tried to track the killer.

PAMELA'S VERY YOUNG VISITORS

Four days after the murder, Dan Pelletier, a detective on the homicide squad, took an anonymous phone call from a woman who claimed that a minor, named Cecelia Pierce, was the person the police should interview in connection with the killing. The caller then claimed that Pamela had confided, to Cecelia, her plot to kill Greg.

Captain Loring Jackson was the officer put in charge of the investigation. He was to uncover a story of manipulation, obsession, greed, sex and lust. Just as his detective had felt, so Jackson, too, was puzzled by the widow's apparent calm, and there were aspects of her husband's murder that did not fit the story she was telling, and neither was there was any sign of a burglary. A diamond ring had been left on the murdered man's hand. There was no cash in his wallet, but all his credit cards were there.

In the days following the killing, numerous rumours began to circulate about Pamela and Greg Smart, that the couple dabbled in drugs and held wild parties at the house. Pamela telephoned a local television station so that she could make a public statement, denying the truth of these rumours. She seemed very composed for one so recently, and tragically bereaved, thought Jackson. And he was very annoyed when, just two days after the murder, Mrs

Above and right:
Erotic poses from the sexually-bored Pamela Smart. She gave similar photographs to her student and lover, Billy Flynn. He kept them in his wallet.

The detective remembered that Pamela had supplied a list of the people who had been in her home a month prior to the murder. Cecelia Pierce was on that list, and the police were now interested to note how many other very young people visited the school teacher in her home. Billy Flynn, for instance, was a visitor.

Billy Flynn was fifteen when he met Pam Smart in her role as teacher, when she came to Winnacunnet High School to organise a series of lectures on the dangers of drug and alcohol abuse. A female friend recalled that the first time Billy saw Pamela, he turned and said: 'I'm in love.'

People noticed that Pamela enjoyed flirting with her students; and the police were to hear that she seemed to favour Billy Flynn.

Cecelia Pierce was also close to Pamela, pleased because the twenty-two-year-old woman did not treat her as a big child, as her mother and other teachers did. Cecelia worked with Smart on the drugs and alcohol project, and was soon confiding her romantic problems to the older woman. It seemed Pamela knew how to empathise with the adolescents she taught.

Pamela Smart began a love affair with Billy Flynn. Her marriage to Greg, the man she met when she was a college student, was volatile, and they had violent rows. Billy Flynn would never forget his first sexual experience with Pamela. He visited the older woman at her home when her husband was away. She put the steamy Kim Basinger film '9$^{1}/_{2}$ Weeks' on to her video recorder. Then, leading Billy to the bedroom, she mimicked the striptease act performed by the actress in the film. To the music of Van Halen's 'Black and Blue', they had sex. Later, again copying a scene from the film, Billy rubbed Pam's body with ice cubes before they made love again.

Later he would say: 'I was kind of shocked. It's not every day that a teenage kid gets to do this with an older woman who says she likes him a lot. I was totally infatuated with her. I was in love with her.'

BILLY'S JEALOUS HATRED

They made love in her Honda car, at her office in school and at her home. She was compiling an anti-drugs film for a Florida orange juice company, and as Billy was her student on this project, he was able to skip school. They spent a lot of time together. She gave him sexy pictures of herself in a bikini, that he kept in his wallet, and the boy began to develop a jealous hatred of his lover's husband, Greg. Pamela portrayed Greg as evil, a man who cheated on her, abused her. She wanted to get rid of him… have him killed. Soon, the idea of murder took root in Billy Flynn's mind. Pamela told him that, if she were free of her husband, she could be with Billy for ever.

Pamela Smart was not only persuading Billy Flynn to kill her husband. She influenced Cecelia Pierce, manipulating the girl into feeling a strong dislike of Greg Smart.

Above: *Pamela Smart tried to convince the police that her husband had been killed by burglars, but they arrested her for conspiracy to murder.*

'IT'S NOT EVERY DAY THAT A TEENAGE KID GETS TO DO THIS WITH AN OLDER WOMAN WHO SAYS SHE LIKES HIM A LOT. I WAS IN LOVE WITH HER.'

Billy told the police that it was Pam's idea to make the murder look like the act of a violent burglar. He said that Pam even revealed details of the plan to Cecelia Pierce, who treated such conversations as part of some sort of macabre game of love enjoyed by Pam and Billy.

Stephen Sawicki, in his book 'Teach me to Kill', a study of Smart, analysed the motives: 'Perhaps it had become something of a perverse game that had nothing to do with reality for Billy and Cecelia. Maybe it was the thrill of flirting with danger, a dance along the edge of a precipice. Or maybe it was simply the lack of a sound-minded adult that the kids felt comfortable with, someone who could point out just how crazy it had all become. Whatever the

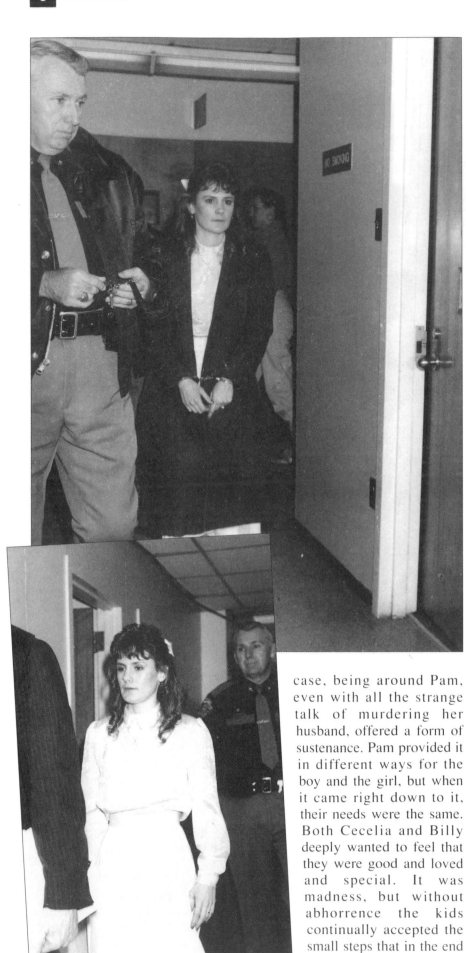

As Billy's infatuation for Pamela grew, so did his determination to kill her husband. He enlisted the aid of Patrick Randall, seventeen; Vance Lattime, eighteen, and Raymond Fowler, nineteen. All were promised a reward by Pam and Flynn, a little something for their trouble – a stereo, some cash or some other item of value from the house. Pam's only stipulation was that they hid her beloved Shih-tzu dog, Halen, away from the murder scene – she thought that witnessing the death of his master might disturb the animal.

A TOWEL WAS ALREADY SPREAD ON THE CARPET

The quartet's first attempt to kill Greg Smart failed when, travelling in Pam's Honda, they lost their way to the Smart's address. They planned to hide inside the house, waiting for Greg's return from work, killing him on arrival. However, when they finally arrived he was already at home.

On the second occasion there were to be no errors. This time, Flynn and Randall were dropped off near the house, and then changed into tracksuits they had bought for the occasion. As they started to move towards the home of Greg Smart, a couple appeared near the corner ahead of them. The two boys broke into a jog, pulling the tracksuit hoods over their faces. They broke into the house through the metal doors of the basement, and they began to vandalise the master bedroom, the bathroom and the lounge, hoping to create the scene of a frantic burglary. The other two accomplices, Lattime and Fowler, were waiting in a nearby plaza with a getaway car.

The killing took a few seconds. Greg was ambushed in the hallway of his own home. Grabbed violently by the hair and pummelled in the face by Randall, the man was brought to his knees. 'Don't hurt me dude,' pleaded Smart as Randall waved a long-bladed knife in front of his eyes. Randall told the police that he did not have the stomach to murder in cold blood. It was Flynn who pulled a gun out and shot Greg Smart, who dropped dead on to a towel that had been spread on the carpet. Pamela had made it quite clear she did not want blood on her precious hallway tiling and carpet.

The anonymous phone call that led the police to these confessions came from

case, being around Pam, even with all the strange talk of murdering her husband, offered a form of sustenance. Pam provided it in different ways for the boy and the girl, but when it came right down to it, their needs were the same. Both Cecelia and Billy deeply wanted to feel that they were good and loved and special. It was madness, but without abhorrence the kids continually accepted the small steps that in the end pointed to a death.'

Louise Coleman, a friend of Cecelia Pierce. Thirty-one and pregnant, Louise had been told by Cecelia that she knew of a woman planning to 'snuff' her husband for the insurance money. Louise thought at the time that Cecelia was acting out some kind of fantasy, or that her wires had become crossed. When Greg Smart was murdered, Louise felt it was her duty to tell the police about Cecelia's conversations.

A month after the murder, Captain Jackson was convinced that Pam was guilty. Her own behaviour combined with the gossip indicated that she was not innocent. She was, once again, hanging around with her adolescent friends – which, under the circumstances, smacked of impropriety. Captain Jackson decided to enlist the aid of Greg's father, Bill. Smart Snr was appalled by Pam's callous indifference to the murder of his son, her husband, and he realised that, probably, Pamela had killed his son. He would co-operate with the police in their investigations.

The police questioned Cecelia again and again. But the girl was loyal to Pamela Smart, and, although Cecelia had nothing to do with the murder, she refused to say anything against the woman whom she believed was her closest friend.

However, the young killers were unable to resist boasting of their exploit, and soon their school was abuzz with gossip. One of the students, Ralph Welch, did not view the adventure as part of a game, and after Randall and Fowler boasted to him of the murder, Welch told Vance Lattime's father that his gun had been used in a murder and that his son was invloved. Lattime checked his weapon and noticed it was dirty, although it was clean when he had put it away in his gun cabinet. He went straight to the police. Soon the four boys were rounded up for questioning.

CECELIA AGREES TO WEAR A 'WIRE'

Pam's wicked world was falling apart, but she was determined that she would not crumble. The boys gave their statements, in which Flynn admitted his role as killer, while the others claimed that they thought it was a game, that they had no idea they were part of a murder plan, but they all implicated Pam, insisting that she made Flynn kill her husband. But it was not enough to arrest Pamela Smart. The boys' claims needed to be supported by evidence of her part in the crime.

'We had to get some proof,' explained Captain Jackson after the investigation. 'We needed Pamela Smart to convict herself. Luckily, Cecelia Pierce came around for us after two more interviews. Like the rest she realised that what had happened was ugly and filthy and vile. She finally, finally helped us nail Pamela Smart.'

Cecelia agreed to wear a 'wire' to record her conversations with Pamela Smart in a bid to get her to implicate herself in the death of her husband. Cecelia was coached by lawmen to ask leading questions. Pamela Smart must have been very concerned that now her accomplices, the boys, were in custody, telling police her role in the drama, but she maintained a facade of calm composure. In the first few conversations with Cecelia she gave nothing away, and even denied that she was having an affair with Billy. But as the conversations proceeded, the police coached Cecelia and told her to mention to Pam that the district attorney wanted to interview her over a love note that she had written to Billy. This was the conversation between Pam and Cecelia:

Pam: All I can say is that no matter what they try and make you talk about, if I were you I didn't know a damn thing.

Cecelia: Well, all I know is that I had to come and talk to you because I... I mean I don't know what to do. I have to go talk to the district attorney. I'm just sick of lying, you know.

Above: *Throughout her trial, Pamela Smart tried to maintain a posture of wounded innocence. She did admit that the evidence seemed to be against her, but this, she said, was merely coincidence. These pictures were taken during the court case.*

A MONTH AFTER THE MURDER, CAPTAIN JACKSON WAS CONVINCED THAT PAM WAS GUILTY.

PAM'S WICKED WORLD WAS FALLING APART, BUT SHE WAS DETERMINED THAT SHE WOULD NOT CRUMBLE.

Above and opposite: These pictures reveal the cool detachment of the chief accused. Pamela Smart treated her court appearances as a fashion show and bemoaned the fact that there was so little time to fix her make-up. The court revelations of her sordid sex games with youngsters did not shake her demeanour and she maintained her plea of innocence to the end.

Pam: Well, you know, I'm just telling you that if you tell the truth, you're gonna be an accessory to murder.

Cecelia: Right.

Pam: So that's your choice. And not only that, but what is your family going to think? I mean, they're like, 'Cecelia, you knew about this.' You know?

Cecelia: Yeah.

Pam: Nothing was going wrong until they told Ralph.

Cecelia: No.

Pam: It's their stupid-ass faults that they told Ralph.

Cecelia: I can't even believe they told him.

In another conversation she tried to keep Cecelia on her side: 'I think I've been a very good friend to you and that's the thing, even if you send me to the f***ing slammer or you don't or if anybody sends me, it's gonna be you and that's the big thing, and that's what it comes down to. But what good is it gonna do you if you send me to the slammer? Because if you think that's gonna be the end of your problems… don't think it's the end of your problems. It's gonna be like your whole family going: "You knew about a murder, how could you have lived like that?" And the newspapers are gonna be all over you. And you're gonna be on the witness stand a million times, you know?'

THE GOOD NEWS – AND THE BAD NEWS

Pamela Smart began to incriminate herself in these conversations with her good friend – someone whose destiny was closely tied up with her own. In one of the final wiretaps Pamela said: 'Bill coulda told them all I'd pay them. I don't know what Bill told them to get them to go, and then that was just a lie. You know. They're not going to have any proof. There's no money. So they can't convict me 'cause of a sixteen-year-old's word in the slammer, facing the rest of his life. And me, with a professional reputation and a course that I teach. You know, that's the thing. They're going to believe me.'

Pamela Smart was taken by surprise when Detective Dan Pelletier entered her school on 1 August and confronted her in her office with the words: 'I have some good news for you and I have some bad news for you. The good news is that we have solved the murder of your husband. The bad news is that you are under arrest for first degree murder.'

When she was arrested, the boys admitted they had been involved in the murder plan and told the police that they did it because of Billy's love affair with Pam. But Pamela maintained that she was innocent, the victim of a teenager's infatuation. She said she had never encouraged Billy Flynn, had never slept with him and had not solicited any of them to commit murder. But it was clear in the first days of her trial in March, 1991, that her story was difficult to believe; she may have been adept at manipulating impressionable youngsters, but she did not impress the prosecutors or jurors given the task of weighing up the facts.

Pamela Smart could not believe it when the verdicts were read out. She turned to her attorney and said: 'First Billy took Greg's life, and now he's taking mine.' But Captain Loring Jackson, who has met a fair cross section of criminals in his twenty-five years service with the police, was not impressed. He said: 'She not only took Greg's life but she also took away the lives of these bright, impressionable young men when she enlisted them in her scheme of murder. She is cold, calculating, manipulative, self-centred, totally unfeeling for anybody but herself. I have never met such a cold person as her. I think life in prison is, for this young lady, very, very fitting.'

Billy Flynn gave damning witness when he was under oath. He told how he had loaded the weapon with hollow-point ammunition, bullets designed to cause maximum destruction to a human target. He said he held back a moment after aiming the gun at Greg's head. 'A hundred years it seemed like,' he sobbed. 'And I said: "God forgive me".' He paused before admitting: 'I pulled the trigger.'

SHE TOOK MORE THAN GREG'S LIFE

The recordings, made by Cecelia, were played in court. Pamela Smart did not sound like a grieving young widow. The court heard her boast that her position in the community would give her an edge over her accusers. Smart's lawyers denounced the state case against their client as 'toxic soup', claiming Flynn and his cohorts were no more than deranged thrill-killers who had murdered Greg Smart because he was a romantic rival. The jury of seven women and five men took just thirteen hours of deliberation to decide that Pamela Smart had set out to teach the boys the business of murder and that she was Guilty as charged. Judge Douglas R. Gray imposed the mandatory sentence of life, without the possibility of parole, on Pamela Smart; Billy Flynn and Patrick Randall received sentences of not less than twenty-eight years each, while Vance Lattime was given eighteen years. Raymond Fowler's case has yet to be tried.

ROSEMARY ABERDOUR
The Lady is a Thief

She was plump, generous and fun-loving. She was also a lonely little fraud. Rosemary Aberdour gave herself a grand title and stole a vast sum from a charity. She spent it on parties, inviting all the friends that money could buy, but the only return on this investment was a prison sentence.

There is no denying it – when Rosemary Aberdour lived it up, she did it in style. She bought herself a Bentley turbo car worth £50,000 and promptly hired a chauffeur to go with it. In the course of a few years, she splashed out an amazing £780,000 on parties, once setting up an entire funfair in London's docklands. She bought a string of luxury cars, including a Mercedes and five other smaller models for her staff at a cost of over £200,000. In one lavish week Rosemary poured two hundred and forty bottles of Dom Perignon champagne into a bathtub for a friend to bathe in.

SWINDLING IN STYLE

There were Caribbean yachting holidays, buying trips to London jewellers and clothes purchased from the best couturiers in London and Paris. Once in London, when her black labrador dog Jeeves was looking a little ill, she decided to take it for a walk… in the Scottish hills. So she hired a chauffeur-driven car to take the dog for walkies in Scotland. Excess was the motto of her life. But so was cheating, for 'Lady' Aberdour was nothing more than a swindler, a fake aristocrat who decieved many good and trusting people, so that she could use their money to finance her lifestyle. She fiddled almost £3 million from a hospital charity before she was

EXCESS WAS THE MOTTO OF HER LIFE. BUT SO WAS CHEATING, FOR 'LADY' ABERDOUR WAS NOTHING MORE THAN A SWINDLER.

Opposite: *Rosemary Aberdour was trusted with large sums of money. She used the funds to transform her own dull life.*

Below: *Flanked by family and legal men, Aberdour makes her way into court as a common criminal.*

Above: *Rosemary grew up in a semi-detached home in Worcester Park, Surrey (lower picture) but she wanted the secluded luxury of a house hidden in private gardens. She stole the money to pay for her dreams.*

detained as a guest of Her Majesty, in surroundings that bear little resemblance to those she left behind.

Her rise to riches was the result of a carefully orchestrated plot. Rosemary Aberdour was born in 1961, neither titled nor rich, but with lashings of that essential ingredient necessary for any good thief – greed. The daughter of Kenneth Aberdour, an Essex radiologist, and his wife Jean, once a secretary at the National Hospital, Rosemary was brought up at Witham, near Chelmsford, and had an ordinary education at a local school. She was a bright child who left school with several 'A' levels and then trained as an accountant with a city

firm. After working in various jobs, she landed the plum job of book keeper to the National Hospital Development Foundation in 1987. It was the beginning of her trek down the pathway of deceit.

During the first two years in this position, Rosemary worked exceedingly hard – and honestly – raising cash for a new wing and for medical equipment. The National Hospital, in London, is recognised internationally as centre for the treatment of multiple sclerosis, Parkinson's and Alzheimer's diseases, epilepsy and strokes. One of Rosemary's early successes came after she convinced the hospital trustees that the annual Queen's Square Ball, which got its name from the hospital's Bloomsbury address, could be promoted as a profitable fundraising event.

HAVING A BALL FOR CHARITY

The ball was little more than a staff party, but Rosemary knew that, if society folk and celebrities could be persuaded that this was a grand charity ball, worth the expense of the highly-priced tickets, the hospital would make a good deal of money. The Queen's Square Ball was so successful, that Rosemary organised three more similar occasions, as well as other fundraising events, some of which were attended by the Princess of Wales, the charity's patron.

Rosemary won the respect of the charity's bigwigs, who were impressed by her remarkable energy and genuine talent for persuading the rich and famous to donate large sums to the National Hospital Development Foundation. She was very persuasive, as her words in a society brochure reveal: 'I have gained great motivation from meeting patients who show immense courage in coping with their illnesses, often against incredible odds.' However, Rosemary was to lengthen those odds when she stole the money, that should have been used to treat these sickly patients, to top up her own income.

SHE BEGAN TO DOCTOR THE BOOKS

She crossed the line into criminality in 1988, when she began filching small amounts of the cash donated to the charity. Because she was held in such high esteem by the trustees of the charity, Aberdour had wide control of the charity's finances. There were several accounts in banks and building societies in which cheques, donated to the charity, were deposited. Aberdour became a signatory on these accounts when she organised the first re-vamped Queen's Square Ball. However, other signatures, like those of Richard Stevens, the charity director, were required on each cheque, and Rosemary began to forge these. Initially, she took enough money to pay for a car. She simply doctored the books so that the amounts she stole never appeared in the charity's legitimate accounts. She quickly realised that this was a very easy way to siphon off cash for her own purposes, and the horizons of her world were broadened considerably.

The bulk of the cash disappeared between April 1989 and 1991, when she was caught. And as the money flowed into special bank accounts she set up for herself, Rosemary Aberdour set about spinning a web of lies to give herself a completely new persona.

John Young, the chairman of the charity, recalls the day he became aware of her metamorphosis. He was used to seeing Rosemary arrive at work in her modest saloon, so he took a double-take when she

pulled up outside the offices in a gleaming Bentley, complete with chauffeur and bodyguard. 'We might have thought the queen was arriving,' he said to her jokingly at the time. Aberdour replied gravely: 'You must understand that I have inherited £20 million and I have to have a minder because I might be kidnapped.'

She informed anyone who cared to listen that her windfall also gave her the right to assume the title of 'Lady' Aberdour.

After her enormous inheritance, 'Lady' Aberdour began to collect the trimmings necessary for her new status in life. She moved to a Thameside penthouse, complete with indoor swimming pool that had an ivy-covered swing suspended from its atrium roof. There were maple wood doors,

> SHE STOLE THE MONEY, THAT SHOULD HAVE BEEN USED TO TREAT THESE PATIENTS, TO TOP UP HER OWN INCOME.

Below: *At the Red October Ball in 1990, Rosemary, third from right, waits eagerly in a line-up to shake the hand of Princess Michael of Kent.*

pink marble bathrooms, outstanding views of the Thames and celebrity neighbours like the actress Brigitte Neilsen. Her lavish bedroom was swathed in blood-red and gold silks, while a cushion, placed on an antique chair, had been embroidered in her own hand. It read: 'I love old money, young men and me.' The chandelier in the living room – in the corner of which nestled a baby grand piano – was worth £10,000. In a valuable antique cabinet in her bedroom she kept her supply of bargain-basement Marks and Spencer knickers. Careful to avoid old friends and family, who might blow the whistle on her, Rosemary Aberdour began to cultivate the 'right' people who would appreciate the finer things in life that she now enjoyed.

WILD TWO-WEEK PARTY

Rosemary Aberdour was a brilliant party hostess. At one, held in the thirteenth-century Thornton Watlass Hall, in North Yorkshire, the revels continued for two weeks, with new guests coming and going every two to three days. A fleet of rented cars ferried the guests to and from airports and railway stations, and bottles of vintage champagne were cracked open for every arrival. It took weeks to fix the ancient mansion after the Bacchanalia had ended.

Tim Mudd, who ran the estate, said: 'They damaged silver and furnishings and left, owing a great deal of money to local tradespeople. The saddest thing was that

> SHE HANDED OUT CARIBBEAN AND INDIAN OCEAN CRUISES, AND INVITATIONS TO THE BEST PARTIES IN LONDON.

> SHE HAD AN INCREDIBLE BEACH PARTY AT HER FLAT WHERE THE WHOLE PLACE WAS EMPTIED OF FURNITURE AND THE FLOORS WERE COVERED WITH SAND.

Below: *This note to the media reveals the love and support the sad little fraud received from her family.*

they put silver salvers worth thousands of pounds in the oven, melting the lead which secured the handles. Some became stained with carrot juice – so they cleaned the silver with scouring pads, totally ruining it. On Hallowe'en night she staged the biggest party of the lot and totally tore the place apart. One room was stripped of all its antique furniture and another was turned into a dance hall. There were imitation dead bodies everywhere and "live" bodies which jumped out of coffins. The bill for that one alone must have run to thousands a head.'

ROSEMARY AS QUEEN OF THE CASTLE

There were other memorable events. To mark the birthday of a girlfriend, Aberdour hired Conwy Castle in North Wales. To get there she rented a helicopter, and she planned an elaborate medieval-style pageant to greet it on arrival. The pampered labrador, Jeeves, was not allowed in the chopper but joined his mistress later… after a newly-hired flunkey drove him down the M4 in the Bentley. As the helicopter bearing Aberdour and her friend landed, minstrels, in elaborate costume, blew a triumphant fanfare on the battlements while a menacing black knight, replete with mock-armour, approached the giggling girls. They were saved by a dashing 'white' knight who fought his 'black' counterpart to a fake death. Rosemary was then playfully-crowned 'Queen of the Castle'.

Following this little display – estimated cost, £10,000 – she flew her friend on to another castle, where the reception committee consisted of a brass band and a full Welsh male voice choir. The whole day ended with bucketloads of champagne and elaborate food. The estimated cost of the fantasy jaunt was £40,000.

To her frequent hangers-on and staff, it soon became apparent that the plump charity queen was an unloved, lonely person who hoped to buy friendship with her lavish generosity. Rosemary handed out Caribbean and Indian Ocean cruises, and invitations to the best parties in London. She housed her London butler, Manuel Cabrera, a Filipino who worked for her for eighteen months, in a luxurious flat. He claimed, that although she had a fiancé, British Army Captain Michael Cubbins,

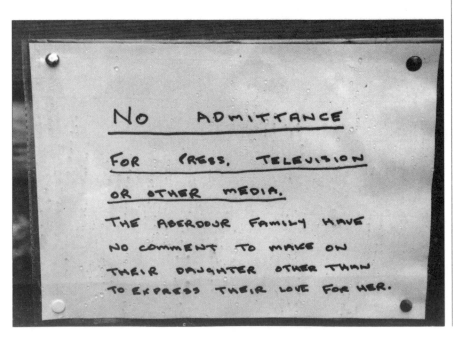

Rosemary also entertained a boyfriend. It was Cabrera's job to help her keep this secret, and to prevent the two men from bumping into each other.

A £60,000 VALENTINE'S PARTY

Cabrera described his employer: 'When Michael and Rosemary got engaged he gave her a fantastic diamond ring but she didn't like it, and bought herself another for over £8,000. She seemed to think money could always buy happiness. She meant to throw a hen party in the Grenadines but she didn't go because it would have meant leaving Michael – so she paid for all her girlfriends to go while she stayed home. Once she had an incredible beach party at her flat where the whole place was emptied of furniture and the floors were covered with sand. The bath was filled with bottles of Dom Perignon champagne that were just poured in one after the other. Another time she had a Valentine's party – and that was really one to remember.'

She called it the St Valentine's Day Massacre party and she spent £60,000 on it.

Top: *Mr and Mrs Aberdour outside the Old Bailey where their daughter stood trial.*

Above: *Her parents were driven away in shock after Rosemary was given a prison sentence.*

Guests were handed exotic cocktails as they entered her flat, then were led to tables groaning under the weight of fabulously cooked food. After the meal, guests went upstairs to her swimming pool where they were invited to change into costumes especially laid on for them. Pink heart-shaped balloons festooned the place and

Above: *Captain Michael Cubbins, Rosemary's fiance, who persuaded her to return to London for her trial.*

Below: *Her solicitor tried to justify Rosemary's crime when he claimed she lacked self-esteem and was immature.*

the fun began with a jolly water fight that ended in more champagne, more frolicking and more indulgence. It was a never-ending cycle of fun for 'Lady' Rosemary.

The National Hospital Development Foundation hoped to collect £10 million, intended to pay for a complete refurbishment of the hospital. So clever was Rosemary Aberdour at juggling figures in the foundation's accounts, that twice the accounts passed the scrutiny of top city

auditors and were declared to be perfectly in order. Nothing could have been farther from the truth. Aberdour used to give the auditors her accounts in sections, allowing herself time to move funds from one to the other, so that no discrepancies would show in the section she sent to the auditors. It seems foolish that the trustees of the charity allowed her this access to, and control over, their finances. But they trusted her and she abused their faith.

THE REAL LADY ABERDOUR

With such a successful system of fraud, greed grew fat and demanding. 'Lady A' became more and more extravagant, stealing £1 million in the first six months of 1991. In an ironic, some would say callous twist, she signed over a cheque for £100,000 from a personal account – money she had diddled from the charity – and 'donated' it to the hospital. It was an act of great magnanimity from the aristocrat who worked so hard for them and her generosity was not lost on the grateful trustees.

Such extensive embezzlement would not, of course, go unnoticed for ever. But long before the fraudster was rumbled by her bosses in London, there was, on a Scottish estate, a Lady Aberdour who was aware that something strange was afoot when her husband, Lord Stewart Aberdour, began receiving thank-you mail from guests who attended parties at strange venues, not in his home. Christmas cards, addressed to his wife, were signed by people neither the lord nor his wife had ever met.

'WHO WAS THIS WOMAN IMPERSONATING MY WIFE?'

'There was one incident,' said Lord Aberdour, 'when I was at a shooting weekend and this chap came up to me and said: "I met your wife recently – she's hosting the most amazing parties." He had never met my wife, Mady, so he just assumed she was this person. I was perplexed. I said: "My wife's up in Scotland having a baby so I don't see how you could have done." I told him he must have met someone who was pretending to be Lady Aberdour. I thought about turning up at one of her parties and exposing her as a fake. Another time I saw an article in a Sunday

newspaper describing this woman as my daughter. When letters started arriving I sent them back to the post office saying "person not known at this address". When you discover someone is an impostor there is not really very much that you can do.'

Two weeks before she was caught, Rosemary, a hopeless romantic, hired a grand hotel in Sussex, then rented the services of a professional video company. She dressed as Scarlett O'Hara, one of her favourite screen heroines, and kitted her friends out as other characters from 'Gone With The Wind' to create her own version of the screen classic. She spent £50,000 of charity funds on this little lark.

When her tissue of lies and deceit unravelled, it unravelled rapidly. One careless slip on her part caused her downfall – and saved the remaining cash in the bank accounts for the hospital. Rosemary Aberdour grew complacent, was less meticulous about covering her tracks. In June 1991, she left her office for a few days to take another of her fabulous holidays. But on her desk, she left, unhidden, a copy of a £120,000 cheque which had been drawn from one of the

Foundation's building society accounts. With this copy, was a letter authorising the transfer of the cash to a Barclays Bank account which was one of five used by Aberdour to 'launder' the charity cash. Both the letter and the cheque copy were found by Richard Stevens, the charity director. He knew that the building society account did not allow Aberdour as a signatory to it and realised with horror that the signatures on the cheques were crude forgeries of the legitimate signatories' writing.

TREASURES AND RARE WINE

The following day, 14 June, fraud squad officers visited Aberdour's apartment to take stock of the Aladdin's Cave of furnishings and fittings that graced Aberdour's home. Box after box of papers, and other evidence relating to her mammoth swindle, were removed from the flat as neighbours of the fake aristocrat stared. The police inventory of luxury goods found in the Battersea apartment ran to thirty-seven pages and included over three hundred bottles of old and rare wine.

Above: Michael Cubbins and Rosemary's vicar leave the Old Bailey. They both attended Rosemary's trial to give her some comfort and support.

THE SIGNATURES ON THE CHEQUES WERE CRUDE FORGERIES OF THE LEGITI-MATE SIGNATORIES' WRITING.

ALL THE SO-CALLED FRIENDS WHO HAD WINED AND DINED OFF HER HAD EVAPORATED LIKE SO MANY CHAMPAGNE BUBBLES.

THE MONEY SHE STOLE WAS USED TO BUY FRIENDSHIP.

Below: *Rosemary returned from her refuge in Brazil and was whisked off from the airport in a police car that took her to for questioning at the Fraud Squad headquarters.*

But there was no sign of the fraudster. She fled Britain after hearing that Fraud Squad officers had been to her apartment. In the footsteps of Great Train Robber Ronnie Biggs, she escaped to Rio de Janiero, as the horrified trustees of the charity began to realise the massive scale of her fiddling. From a rented flat near the Copacabana Beach, Aberdour contacted her parents and called her fiance Cubbins in Germany. There were numerous telephone conversations, over several days, during which they tried to persuade her to return to Britain. Finally the Ministry of Defence allowed Cubbins leave from his regiment to fly to Rio in a bid to bring her back to face the music. An old school-friend, called Sarah Boase, was also instrumental in trying to coax her back.

LAST FEAST BEFORE PRISON

Finally, Rosemary agreed but her journey back was in the high style that she had grown accustomed to. She forked out, presumably with charity money, for business-class seats for herself and her fiancé. On board she tucked into filets of beef and fine wine… the last meal before prison food faced this woman, ruined by her own greed. When the aircraft landed in

Britain, detectives and security men escorted the ashen-faced Rosemary to an ante-room in the terminal building. She was cautioned by Fraud Squad officers. Then the woman who was used to being chauffeured in a green Bentley limousine, was sandwiched between two burly detectives in the back of a Montego police car. She was driven off to face questioning at the Fraud Squad headquarters which are in Holborn, Central London.

There followed a drastic change in lifestyle for the bogus aristocrat. Stripped of her Hérmes and Chanel creations, it was strictly prison flannel for Rosemary when she was remanded without bail although she was allowed to visit home for Christmas.

SHE LIVED IN A FANTASY WORLD

Rosemary Aberdour came to settle her account – not with the charity, but with justice – in March 1992, when she appeared at the Old Bailey. She pleaded guilty to seventeen charges of fraud and remained motionless as a litany of her crimes was read out in court by the prosecution; a £65,000 surpise party for a friend, £80,000 for the rental of a yacht in the Caribbean, £780,000 in all on parties, £134,000 on personal staff and £280,000 on cars.

In her defence, Graham Boal said: 'She is not an ordinary criminal or a sophisticated fraudster, stashing away funds. She had absolutely nothing to show for her crimes, nothing except shame, remorse, poverty and the courage to answer the indictment.' He said all the so-called friends who had wined and dined off her had evaporated like so many champagne bubbles. Aberdour had poured money down other people's throats. He said that she suffered from an impenetrable lack of self-esteem, insecurity and immaturity. He said she was a victim of the hard-bitten and glossy world of high-society fund raising. 'Eventually,' he said, 'the fantasy world became reality. Self-deception started to take over.' He added: 'This binge, this gorging, became a disease.'

The prosecution painted a rather different picture. Brendan Finucane said: 'It is clear many people were taken in by her, close friends and even her boyfriend. Thousands of pounds was given away to hangers-on and spongers. She had started

humbly and then had grander designs. She was bound to be caught and fled to Brazil when the crime was discovered.'

Sentencing Aberdour to four years in jail, a sentence perceived as remarkably light by many at the charity, Mr Justice Leonard said: 'You spent the money on gross extravagance. It is said the motivation which brought you to these offences was complex or unusual. So it was, I am sure, but for two and-a-half years you went on milking this fund. You were trusted and you abused that trust.'

Rosemary Aberdour was certainly a rogue, and one of the greatest swindlers in British criminal history, but there is a certain sadness in her story, for the money she stole was used to buy friendship. Even as a schoolgirl, it is reported, she had used bribery to attract loyalty and company.

But there is one man who would like to befriend her. He has issued an invitation to 'show her the sights' of the Rio Janeiro she missed. Ronnie Biggs, who has holed up in the Brazilian sunspot for sixteen years ever since his jailbreak from a London prison, said: 'I could have given her so much pleasure around town before she went back. It's the perfect place for a girl who loves parties and she would never have had to flash that much cash.

Above: *As she was taken off to start her prison sentence, Rosemary Aberdour managed a smile for the press.*

Right: *The grand riverside block where Aberdour installed herself using money she swindled from charity funds.*

'I don't think she's mad to give herself up. In the circumstances I think she did the right thing. She is a young woman and has her whole life ahead of her. But you can be sure I will not be on the next plane. When she comes out I hope she comes to visit me – I'll show her what a true friend can be.'

IMELDA MARCOS
The Steel Butterfly

Imelda grew up in poverty, but her beauty lifted her out of the slums. A powerful politician wooed and married her. Imelda Marcos became a wildly greedy woman who robbed her own kind to pay for her extravagances.

The wife of the last of the great dictators walked free from court after a trial which ended in humiliating defeat for the American government. As Imelda Marcos emerged blinking into the Manhattan sunlight on 2 July, 1990, she carried in her heart a dark secret... the whereabouts of the missing millions she and her husband milked from his impoverished land. Ferdinand Marcos ruled the Philippines in the manner of a robber baron.

He used foreign aid and stole national treasures to finance a luxurious lifestyle. But he did not escape the consequences of his greed, for he died in exile and shame. His wife Imelda, dubbed the Steel Butterfly by peasants who gazed in awe at her extravagance and her ruthlessness, survived to face charges of fraud, grand larceny and racketeering. She had the dubious honour of being the first wife of a head of state to stand trial in the USA.

SHE HAD NO REGRETS

At her trial she gave no hint of the repentance that her accusers expected; rather they were subjected to Imelda's arrogant boasts about her lifestyle. From the first day she stepped into the dock in New York to face charges of racketeering, conspiracy and fraud and a possible sentence of fifty years in prison, she happily revealed the fabulous wealth she had enjoyed as wife of the president. Imelda and Ferdinand had viewed the Philippines as their personal fiefdom and appropriated, for their own use, bundles of aid-dollars donated by America. But their rule came to an end when Cory Aquino ousted the Marcos

Opposite: *Imelda, former beauty queen, who became more famous for her greed than her looks.*

Above: *Grace and corruption marked the Steel Butterfly.*

SHE HAD THE DUBIOUS HONOR OF BEING THE FIRST WIFE OF A HEAD OF STATE TO STAND TRIAL IN THE USA.

Below: *Ferdinand and Imelda Marcos with the Pope during his visit to the Philippines in the Eighties.*

couple from power and then pressed the US to put the pair on trial. But Imelda Marcos was moved neither by the accusations nor the anger of her people. She did not regret her old life. Instead of feeling shame over her wealth, Imelda flaunted it. 'I get so

in jeopardy if Imelda Marcos was not prosecuted by the US government.

But the Justice Department was hindered in its investigations by the Swiss banking system that prides itself on its total secrecy regarding clients' finances, while allowing

tired of listening to "one million dollars here, one million dollars there,"' she yawned in court. 'It is so petty.'

When Imelda Marcos was found Not Guilty of the charges brought against her, observers thought that heads would roll in the US Justice Department because, it was felt, they had not properly prepared the case against Marcos. The Justice Department spent £20 million preparing this case and they had all the resources of the State Department, the FBI and the CIA behind them. But they lost their case.

SACKS OF MONEY WERE DELIVERED TO HER HOTEL ROOM

The American government was under pressure from Marcos' successor, Cory Aquino, who hinted that the important US military bases in the Philippines might be

---

MARCOS AND IMELDA MAY HAVE SALTED AWAY AS MUCH AS £7 BILLION WORTH OF NATIONAL TREASURES, HARD CURRENCY AND BULLION.

---

the clients the same discretion – they do not have to reveal the source of their money. Vital documents relating to the Marcos' personal accounts were hidden in the vaults of banks in Geneva and Zurich and they were not released to the US prosecutors. Despite damning testimony from Phillipine National Bank officials who could show documents and who claimed that, although she had never earned a penny during her rule, Imelda had sacks of cash delivered to her hotel in New York every time she visited the city. But there was not enough evidence against the woman and she was found Not Guilty.

Despite her acquittal, the Phillipine government insists that Marcos and Imelda may have salted away as much as £7 billion worth of national treasures, hard currency and bullion in banks and investments around the world. The arrest of the billionaire arms dealer, Adnan Khashoggi, on charges that he 'laundered' the Marcos' fortune so that the US government would not be able to trace the money, were also dropped. His case only served to further the speculation that the Marcos couple were thieves on a fabulous scale.

In twenty years of power, initially as a democratically-elected politician but later as a despot who imposed martial law, Marcos and his Steel Butterfly drained the national economy. America supported his regime on the strategic Pacific islands because they saw the Philippines as a bulwark against Communism. They maintained important military bases in the country, and pumped in millions and millions of dollars intended to improve the economic growth of the sixty-two million inhabitants of the islands.

Instead, these funds fell into the personal piggy bank of the state leader and his wife.

Imelda, a former beauty queen, became a symbol of grotesque greed to her fellow Filipinos, most of whom lived in frugal poverty. At the height of her career as 'leader's wife', she was spending £300,000 a week on clothes. Designer gowns from

> AT THE HEIGHT OF HER CAREER AS 'LEADER'S WIFE', SHE WAS SPENDING £300,000 A WEEK ON CLOTHES.

Below: *Imelda Marcos playing stateswoman at her desk in the Plaza Hotel in the Philippines.*

Paris and Rome were jetted over to her and she spent weeks touring Europe on shopping expeditions. After one shopping trip, she filled three sea containers with goods. Shoes were her quirky addiction. Three thousand pairs of Gucci, Christian Dior and Karl Lagerfeld designs were found in her wardrobes.

While she spent, her husband – a wily, shrewd politician – was gradually dismantling the democratic state which the world believed he was protecting.

A PRESIDENT WITH A PAST

Marcos was born on 11 September, 1917, the son of a lawyer and schoolteacher, in a small town two hundred and fifty miles from the capital of Manila. He trained as a lawyer and qualified for his bar exam with flying colours. In 1939, he was arrested on charges of murdering his father's political rival, and was sentenced to life imprisonment. But in a re-trial, when he cleverly conducted his own defence, the charges were dropped. During the Second World War, he claimed that he led guerilla fighters

Above: *The Marcoses entertained the great and the good. Here, Princess Margaret is led aboard their private yacht.*

Opposite: *The former First Lady suffered the indignity of police fingerprinting sessions when she returned to her homeland. She was charged with tax fiddling, and later for keeping unauthorised foreign bank accounts.*

Rolls-Royces, channeled millions of aid dollars to secret bank accounts in Rome and Switzerland, while his financial advisers purchased, on his behalf, properties all over Europe and in New York. As his own greed increased, his patience with democracy wore ever thinner. He won re-election in 1969 in a campaign tainted by allegations that he had practised vote rigging, intimidation and corruption. Three years later, in 1972, Marcos dispensed with democracy in the Philippines and imposed martial law on the country.

HAND-MADE LAVATORY PAPER

The attempted assassination of a senior military figure was the excuse for suspending democracy, though it has been claimed that the assassination was only a pretence, something Marcos set up so that he could justify his political move. Under the new martial rules, thousands of political enemies and dissenting journalists were thrown into jail, tortured and murdered. Then Marcos lifted martial law in 1981 to hold another election. However, his political opponents boycotted these elections, saying that to participate in the farce would only give Marcos a credibility he did not deserve. So the man held on to his immense political power. His power was unchallenged but he became increasingly paranoid. His secret police continued to fill the prisons with rivals, while all political parties were kept under surveillance or infiltrated by Marcos informers.

During these dark days, the Steel Butterfly lived in bizarre luxury. Every detail of her style was richly excessive. Every roll of loo paper was hand-made, silk-screen printed in Thailand and cost seven pounds. There was a storeroom of them in Manila's Malacanang Palace, and each of the building's fourteen bathrooms was graced by two rolls of this exquisite tissue. When she fled her homeland in 1986, she took her collection of pearls that, when it was spread out, covered thirty-eight square feet. She even coined a word for her own excesses – 'Imeldific'.

Guests at the palace were treated lavishly. They got to keep the contents of the wardrobes in the rooms where they stayed as visitors. These wardrobes were stashed with furs, clothes and jewellery. In

against the Japanese conquerors, although this is disputed. Nevertheless, the story helped him become a representative in the Philippines Congress when he was only thirty-one years old, the youngest politician in the country. In 1954, after an eleven-day courtship, he married Imelda. Ferdinand Marcos said that her love for him 'drove me to the pinnacles of success'.

In 1965, after the general elections, he became the President of his country. Ironically, he won on an anti-corruption platform. Throughout his twenty years in office, his salary never varied. He received £3,300 a year, yet he lived in great opulence. He rode in armoured plated

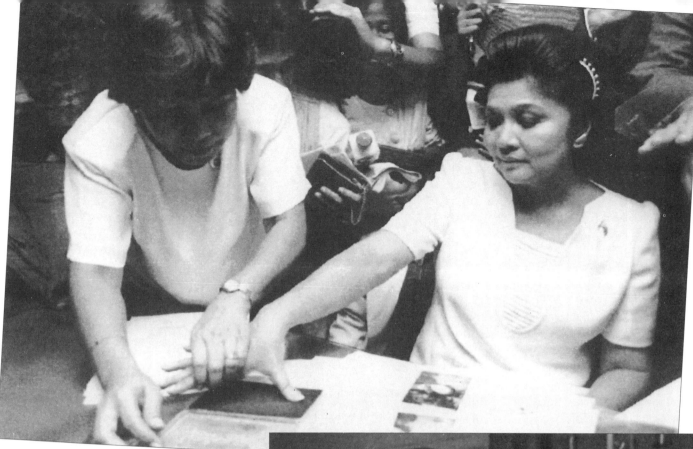

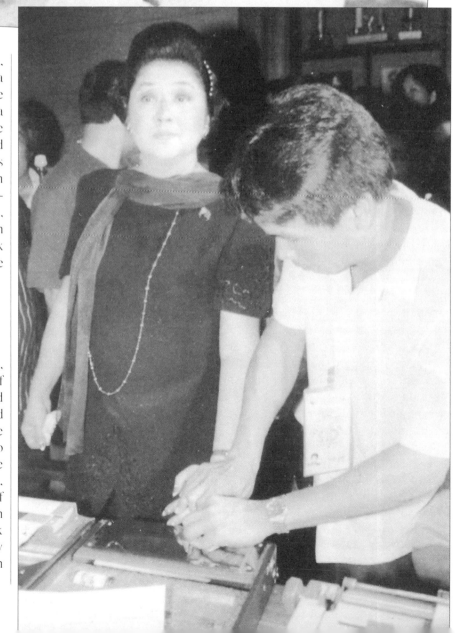

the main dining room, in a silver tureen, Imelda kept a great mound of Beluga caviar, renewed every day. And when she felt very generous, she would airlift a planeload of pals to New York for a little shopping. She could afford it. She headed thirty lucrative government corporations and she used the money for her own purposes. According to Filipino government investigators, Imelda, at one stage, was sending so many suitcases stuffed with cash to a bank in Geneva, that the bank cabled her and asked her to stop because she was overloading the staff with work.

THE YOUNG IMELDA SANG FOR CANDY

If Imelda ever noticed her fellow citizens, if she did take a trip to the seamy side of town, to the barrios where people lived next door to open sewerage ditches and had no running water, she behaved as if she were royalty and she expected people to bow. But Imelda understood poverty. She came from a poor family, and as a child, had sung to American GIs for gifts of candy. She earned a living as a singer when she was a young woman. Her big break came in 1954, when she won a beauty contest and was introduced to the politician who would make her his Pacific empress.

Imelda preferred – naturally – to forget her poor youth. She banned a book called 'The Untold Story of Imelda Marcos', written by Filipino journalist, Carmen Pedrosa. Pedrosa's book revealed that Imelda was once as poor as the people she now ruled over, and had been obliged to sleep on milk crates in the garage of a relative's house after her mother pushed her out of the family home. 'She did not want her poor origins ever to be known,' said Pedrosa. 'She conveyed a completely different image of herself, that she had been born with a silver spoon in her mouth. And that was important to them – because if the Marcoses had been born with wealth, there would be no questioning of that wealth. When she went into the barrio, she was regarded as a celebrity. She would wear a gown in places where people didn't even have a toilet. She was just living a fantasy life in a very poor country.'

THE CIA VERDICT

The fantasy was almost shattered in 1972, when an assassin stabbed her with a foot-long dagger as she was handing out awards at a beauty contest, but she only received a flesh wound. This incident re-inforced Imelda's strange belief that 'God has great things planned for me and is watching carefully over me at all times.'

The CIA had their own impressions of Imelda Marcos. During the Seventies, the agency prepared a character analysis of the woman that was not flattering, but accurate It read as follows: 'Mrs Marcos is ambitious and ruthless. Born a poor cousin of landed aristocracy, she has a thirst for wealth, power and public acclaim, and her boundless ego makes her easy prey for flatterers. Although she has little formal education, she is cunning.'

Imelda's relatives prospered with her. Her brother, Benjamin Romualdez, master-minded the take-over of the Manila Electric Company. Brother Alfredo ran the national government-controlled gambling industry. Initially Marcos outlawed gambling, but legalised it when he realised that huge profits could be made from this form of entertainment. William Sullivan, the US Ambassador to Manila from 1973 to 1977 said: 'When I was there foreign investors did not come into the Philippines without

> 'GOD HAS GREAT THINGS PLANNED FOR ME AND IS WATCHING CAREFULLY OVER ME AT ALL TIMES.'

distributing shares to Imelda or some of her cronies. That was the way business was done.' American officials described the country as being run by two factions – the FM factions loyal to Ferdinand Marcos and the FL faction, loyal to the first lady of excess, his wife, Imelda.

Imee, her beloved daughter, got in on the act too. A vice-chairman of a Filipino bank tells a story about four business people who had fallen behind with their kickbacks to the Marcos gang. The four were summoned to the palace in 1985, where they were

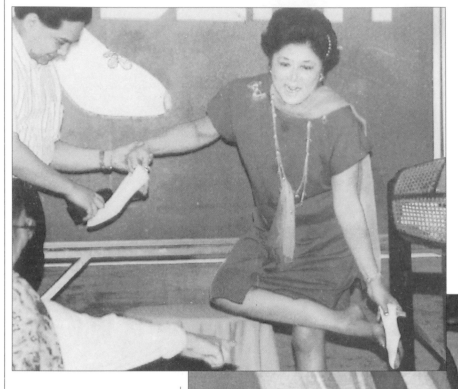

Above: *Imelda Marcos removes her shoes to offer them as a prize in a Filipino radio competition.*

Right and opposite: *Imelda was incredibly greedy. She became notorious for her huge shoe collection, but her numerous homes were filled with vast amounts of valuable objects and furnishings.*

confronted by Imee. She had become her mother's bookkeeper, and she sat in front of the four, with a notebook on her lap and armed secret servicemen at her side. Rather than face the niceties of a torture chamber, they promptly paid the illicit funds to Imee.

> IMELDA SPENT £9 MILLION DURING A SHOPPING SPREE ON DIAMONDS, RUBIES AND PEARLS.

The first lady preferred to spend her money on jewellery and clothes and she lavished gems and couture collections on herself whenever she felt depressed or sad. Documents drawn up by the Aquino government list some of Imelda's treasures: diamond bracelets, brooches and earrings valued at £1 million; one hundred and sixty-seven racks of designer dresses valued at £2 million; five fur coats, four hundred Gucci handbags and a mere sixty-eight pairs of handmade gloves.

But other documents were to make that lot seem like the remnants of a jumble sale.

MULTI-MILLION SPENDING SPREE

On one day in Switzerland in the late Seventies, Mrs Marcos spent £9 million during a shopping spree. She gobbled up diamonds, rubies and pearls, along with a diamond-and-garnet encrusted watch for her husband. Another US customs document proved that in seven days in May and the beginning of June, 1983, she squandered £4 million on a shopping orgy in New York. Imelda also spent a great deal of money on diamonds, shopping at Cartier, Van Clef & Arpels and Tiffany. She then splashed out a further £21,000 on towels and bedsheets. Finance for these spending sprees came from the New York

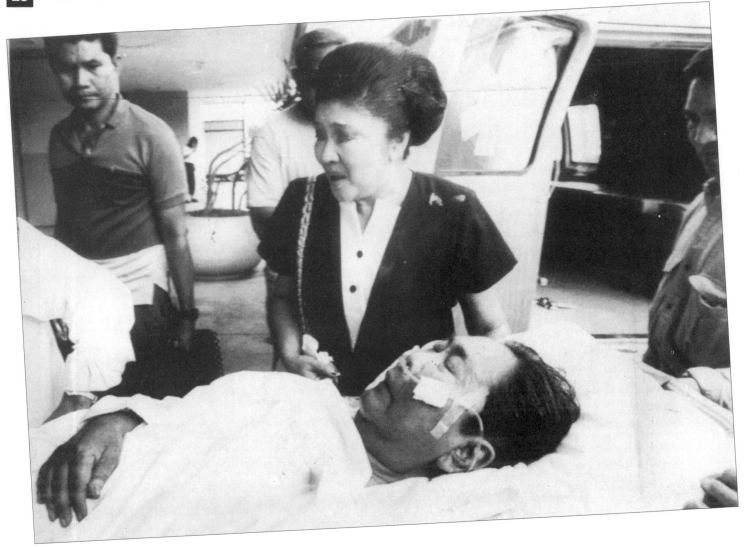

Above: *No one could doubt the very real love the Steel Butterfly felt for her husband. She was desolate when he died in exile and has campaigned ceaselessly to have his body flown home for burial.*

TWENTY-FOUR-CARAT GOLD-PLATED TAPS WERE TARNISHED AND DRIPPING IN EVERY BATHROOM.

---

branch of the Phillipine National Bank. Bank official, Willie Fernandez, testified at Imelda's trial that between 1973 and 1986 he personally authorised transactions of £24 million for Mrs Marcos.

'The call would come in: "Ma'am needs two hundred and fifty thousand cash,"' said a bank official who was granted anonymity at her trial. 'The money was carried to her in a big over-sized attaché case.' The prosecution called the bank: 'Mrs Marcos' private piggy bank.'

The goodies inside of her Manhattan townhouse made one angry customs official declare: 'Such opulence made me feel sick to the pit of my stomach.'

VALUABLE ITEMS JUST TOSSED ASIDE

Alan Ehrlichman, the auctioneer hired to sell the contents of this house for the Phillipine government, described valuable crystal glasses found hidden in an oven; rare Biblical manuscripts from the twelfth century were stuffed under an old boiler; two gilt mirrors which belonged to Marie Antoinette's husband, King Louis of France, were found broken and mysteriously lying in water in the bath; hand-embroidered bedlinen had been left lying in damp piles which attracted mildew; twenty-four-carat gold-plated taps were tarnished and dripping in every bathroom.

Ehrlichman said: 'It broke my heart. Many collectors aspire to work of that calibre but never attain it. Here's somebody who owned it who had no respect for it. It's a sacrilege. If two words summed up what I felt about it those words would be opulence and waste.' The house also had Jacuzzis in every bathroom and a discotheque where Imelda would gyrate while her bodyguards would sidle up to her to ask her for a dance.

A stitched pillow on one of the many sofas in the room bore the inscription: 'To be rich is no longer a sin. It's a miracle.' Another read: 'I love champagne, caviar and cash.' And then, there were also three baby grand pianos in her New York house.

Yet Imelda rarely stayed in this house, valued at £7 million. She preferred the comfort of a suite at New York's Waldorf-Astoria Hotel. But Ehrlichman said that while she wallowed in opulence, the servants were treated disdainfully, and lived, five beds to a room, in the basement.

Between 1980 and 1986, Imelda drew on another account in New York. This was held in the name of her secretary and was credited with a whopping £19 million. She also used her wealth to commission expensive portraits of herself and her family from New York artists. One of them is a version of the Renaissance artist Botticelli's 'Birth of Venus'. His painting shows the goddess rising from a shell. In her version, Imelda is shown rising from the shell with her arms extending to embrace the world. She commissioned portraits of Nancy and Ronald Reagan, her husband, Ferdinand Marcos and General MacArthur – the wartime leader who liberated the Philippines from the Japanese occupation.

THE TIDE TURNED AGAINST THE MARCOSES

But the politics of the Philippines were changing. On 21 August, 1983, Senator Begnigno Aquino, who had been imprisoned and then exiled by Marcos, returned to Manila. He was shot dead by a Marcos assassin as he stepped from the plane at the airport in Manila. Marcos claimed that the murderer was a Communist agitator, himself shot by government forces just after he had shot the returning exile. No one believed this story. Marcos sought to quieten the growing unrest of his people by calling for an election in 1986. After the votes were counted, Marcos declared himself the elected winner. However, Cory Aquino, the widow of the murdered exile, had won the support of the Phillipine army and had convinced the United States that Marcos was a corrupt and unworthy figure.

Finally, confident that she had the full support of the army, Aquino toppled the Marcos regime. The Marcoses, with their entourage, fled their homeland on 26 February, 1986, as, outside the palace gates, the mob bayed for their blood. Only hours after the deposed leader and his wife had left, this mob broke into the palace and were astonished by the excessive consumerism that they now confronted. The opulence which the Steel Butterfly and her husband had enjoyed was photographed for the world's amazement. Pictures of Imelda's shoe collection also showed closets the size of bungalows, built to hold her vast number of acquisitions.

The Filipino people wanted their money back and an international treasure hunt was launched. Jovito Salonga, the Filipino lawyer charged by his government to find the loot, said: 'They stole and stole and stole. And then they stole some more. Not only did they take what was not theirs, they also seized businesses and created monopolies, granted exclusive import licences and guaranteed bank loans for associates and relatives, loans that they never paid back. As new businesses rose the first payments were delivered to the boss, Marcos, and it got so crazy that I would estimate that even

'THEY STOLE AND STOLE AND STOLE. AND THEN THEY STOLE SOME MORE.'

Below: *Ferdinand Marcos died in Honolulu. His wife says her last farewells.*

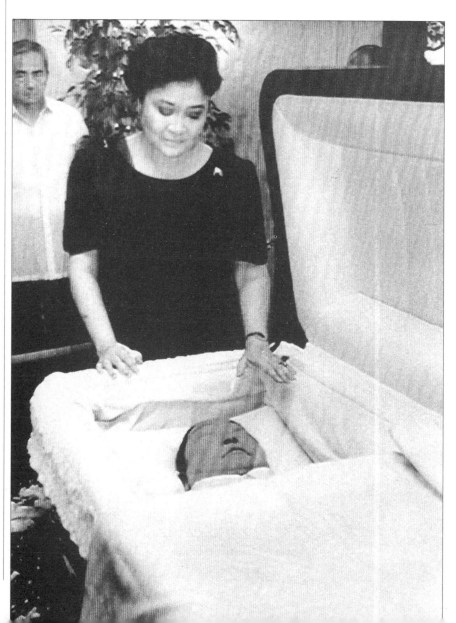

he doesn't know how much he was worth. The time has come to return their ill-gotten gains to the Filipino people.' Salonga maintained that between them, they ran off with something in the order of £7-9 billion.

Imelda remained proud and arrogant and revealed herself as rather stupid, if cunning. When she arrived in Hawaii, seeking a refuge after fleeing Manila, she declared shamelessly; 'They call me corrupt, frivolous. I am not at all privileged. Maybe the only privileged thing is my face. And corrupt? God! I would not look like this if I was corrupt. Some ugliness would settle down on my system. My people will judge me innocent.'

FAIRY-TALE OF JAPANESE TREASURE

The Marcoses called it a 'despicable act' when the USA government slapped racketeering charges on them. The CIA and FBI had built up an enourmous list of crimes with which to charge the pair. They were charged with, among other things, fraudulent use of foreign aid, with the connivance of members of their family who controlled major western-funded public works projects in the Philippines. 'There wasn't one pie, one cash register, one scam going that this duo didn't have their sticky fingers in,' said international money expert, John Stapleford. 'They were rotten to the core but blessed with a supreme arrogance which made them think that they really could get away with anything.'

Marcos was horrifed that America turned against him. Imelda said they had been 'shamed' by their old ally. Shortly before his death in September 1989, Marcos came up with a novel explanation for his wealth, 'I discovered the treasure of Yamashita,' he said. 'That is the key to it all.' Lt General Tomoyuki Yamashita was the Japanese commanding officer of the occupying forces in the Philippines during wartime. He is said to have stashed priceless works of art and gold bullion in secret caves. However, he was hanged in 1946 as a war criminal and he died without revealing the whereabouts of his hoard. But investigators on the trail of the treasure say it was just one more lie from Yamashita, a man who had spent his life evading the truth and destroying those who tried to tell

it. The treasure is as much myth as reality and there is nothing to prove that Ferdinand Marcos ever laid his hands on anything other than all the money he stole from his own impoverished countrymen.

In July 1987, two US lawyers posing as Marcos allies, telephoned the exiled despot and claimed to be interested in representing him. They taped a telephone conversation in which he claimed to have £7 billion worth of gold bullion lying in secret vaults on the island of Mindanao. He didn't make any claim at this time that this gold was part of the fabled wartime booty of the Japanese general, Yamashita.

THE AMERICANS ARE UNKIND

Before she stood trial, Imelda,whose tears flowed freely during numerous press conferences, said: 'I have only one dream now. I am not asking for justice anymore, I am asking for a divine human right to die, to be buried in my own country. I am shocked by all this inhumanity shown by America, they have not been nice to us – us

Above: *In 1991, Imelda and her son, Ferdinand Jnr., spoke at a political rally in Manila. There is bitter rivalry between the 'reformist' Aquino faction and those who favour the Marcos family.*

Opposite, top: *Attending church, Imelda Marcos is comforted by other church-goers. Despite her years of misrule, she has enthusiastic followers in the Philippines.*

Opposite, bottom: *Imelda Marcos with her attorney, Antonio Coronel, when she faced charges in a Manila court.*

who were such good friends to them.' She believed this statement.

Imelda was left alone to face the music when Marcos, suffering from a disease of the kidneys, died. 'He settled with a higher authority,' one embittered State Department official said. 'She faced earthly justice – and won.' The secrecy of banking laws protected her from detection, but there is no one in the Philippines or in the American intelligence agencies who believes that justice was done.

IMELDAS 'DIVINE' MISSION

The Steel Butterfly has returned to the land she looted, where she risks facing further criminal charges. She has lost none of the arrogance that was her chief characteristic. Recently she has taken to calling herself a goddess, a deity who has confronted mortal challenges and troubles and won. She explains: 'I must be a deity because I was given a divine mission, to return to my homeland, which I did. An ordinary mortal would not be able to stand what I did.'

TZU-HSI
China's Dragon Lady

A lowly concubine in the harem of the Chinese Emperor nursed grand ambitions. With sly cunning, combined with the luck of giving birth to a son and heir, she came to rule the great imperial nation. But Tzu-Hsi was so evil, so cruel, that she destroyed the very empire she fought to control.

The pages of history are filled with the exploits of bloodthirsty autocrats. Medieval Romania was led by Vlad the Impaler who liked to have his victims silenced by driving great stakes through their bodies. In Russia, Ivan the Terrible massacred entire communities, relishing the sight of pain and bloodshed, while twentieth-century Uganda produced Idi Amin who feasted on the flesh of his victims in horrifying cannibalistic rites. But as nature shows us in the black widow spider, the female of the species proves herself to be even deadlier than the male, as in the case of Tzu-Hsi, Dragon Empress of China. Compared to her deeds, the crimes of male tyrants pale into insignificance. She filled her jails with those who displeased her, sanctioned gross tortures and put to death thousands upon thousands whom she claimed had betrayed China to the West. Her cruelty reached its zenith during the Boxer rebellion in Peking, in 1900, when the Chinese declared war against the foreigners and Christians, who controlled the profitable opium trade.

THE EMPEROR'S CONCUBINE

Tzu-Hsi whipped the mob to heights of violence hitherto unseen in the Chinese capital. She ordered her troops to fire their artillery on the French Cathedral, in the centre of the city, killing hundreds of innocent men, women and children in the process. She ordered a cessation of the shelling when she could no longer stand the headache caused by the incessant booming of the guns. She gave an edict to her troops that no one was to escape alive from the massacre. 'My empire must be purged,' she said, 'and purged in blood.'

The bloodletting occurred just eight years before her death, yet it served, not to protect the feudal China she wished to preserve, but to hasten its demise.

The Dragon Empress ruled for fifty years as the last aristocratic ruler of the four hundred million people of China. She was a descendant of the great Manchu dynasty, established by the people of Manchuria after they captured Peking in 1644. Born in November 1835, to a Manchu mandarin, she was destined to become a concubine in the harem of the

Above: *The Empress can be seen waving a handkerchief at the camera. The robed attendants are the court eunuchs.*

Opposite: *Tzu-Hsi, the last Empress of China, widow of the last Manchu Emperor whose dynasty had led China for centuries.*

HER CRUELTY REACHED ITS ZENITH DURING THE BOXER REBELLION IN PEKING.

正大光明

弘敬五典無輕民事惟難

惟精惟一道積于厥躬

克寬克仁皇建其有極

表正萬邦慎厥身修思永

Emperor. At the age of sixteen, she entered the Forbidden City in Peking, home to the rulers of China. Inside this City, was a world of exquisite beauty and harmony, designed to fulfil the principles of a life devoted to pleasure. There were some three thousand concubines and some three thousand eunuchs living in the palace. The emperor, Hsien-Feng, was rumoured to take ten lovers a day to his bedchamber. However, his concubines were graded into ranks, and those in the lower ranks often lived their whole lives within the palace walls without even meeting the emperor. Tzu-Hsi was in the fifth and lowest rank when she first entered the court.

TZU-HSI'S RISE TO POWER

But the young girl was immensely ambitious, well-educated and intelligent. She set about making the most of her life in this gilded cage. She read voraciously, dipping into the great works on the Emperor's bookshelves and she persuaded

Above: *The Imperial Throne Room in the Forbidden City. This room and its artefacts were commissioned by a ruler five centuries before Tzu-Hsi came to power.*

IN APRIL, 1856, SHE GAVE BIRTH TO THE ONLY MALE CHILD THAT THE EMPEROR WAS TO HAVE.

the courtiers to hire tutors to further her education. While she became a learned member of the royal household, she also became a shrewd one. She made it her business to understand the protocol that operated within the palace walls, while she concentrated on working out ways to get close to the Emperor, Hsien-Feng.

Wisely, she befriended his wife, who was fifteen years older than her, and, as it turned out, barren. When the feckless Hsien-Feng decided he wanted to have a child, he asked his wife to select a concubine and she chose Tzu-Hsi. The girl had been in the palace for only three years, but she had achieved one ambition. She was now one of the Emperor's intimates. In April, 1856, she gave birth to the only male child that the Emperor was to have. Naturally, the birth of a son and heir to the Chinese throne brought immense staus to Tzu-Hsi. She became the centre of attention, the focus of all praise, but more significant than the respect of the courtiers, was the attention the Emperor bestowed

upon her. Hsien-Feng realised that this concubine was a very clever, capable woman. He gave her more and more power until Tzu-Hsi was the real ruler of China.

This was a period when China had lost her aloof privacy from the world. The French and British had come as traders, and brought their soldiers with them. They also brought new ideas to the country that provoked an anti-monarchy movement among some Chinese subjects. These rebels were most numerous in the city of Taipeng. In response to the foreign intrusions, Tzu-Hsi moved the court to Jehol in the mountains surrounding Peking. She ordered public decapitations of any rebel captured by her forces. And, in great secrecy, she organised a terror campaign against Westerners and Christian missionaries. Foreigners were harassed, their businesses burned and, if these tactics did not drive them out of China, they risked being murdered. The Dragon Empress was determined to maintain the ancient feudal traditions of China and, of course, the power and wealth of the monarchy. She knew that the presence of foreigners was dangerous to the stability of the Chinese social system, and she believed it was essential to chase them out of her land.

Top: *Peking in the late-nineteenth century. It was a rich trading centre.*

Bottom: *The Summer Palace in Peking, residence of the royal family.*

Prince Kung, brother of the emasculated Hsien-Feng, did not share the isolationist views of Tzu-Hsi. He believed in opening up China to trade and new ideas, and was appalled at the tactics used to chase foreigners out of China. He went over the head of the Dragon Empress and sued for peace with the English and French; an act that Tzu-Hsi was never to forgive or forget. When the Emperor died in 1861, Tzu-Hsi and his widow shared the title of Regent.

Although political power was to be shared equally between them, the Emperor's widow had little interest in politics, and was happy to let Tzu-Hsi cope with the demands of state. However, not everybody was pleased by this arrangement, and a there was a plot to assasinate the regent concubine. Tzu-Hsi was swift and brutal in her response to the rebels; she put to death an estimated five hunred people, including one wealthy feudal landowner, Su Shen, who, it was believed, was the brain behind the dissidents' plot to kill her.

HOW DID THE EMPEROR CATCH SMALLPOX?

Su Shen came from a family of ancient warlords, who owned vast estates and was immensely wealthy. On his death, his family were banished into the remote hinterland of China, and their property confiscated by the Dragon Empress.

Her son, destined to become Emperor when he turned seventeen, had a curious upbringing. Known as the Tung Chih Emperor, he was a healthy, lively boy who was left in the care of concubines and court eunuchs. It is said that, at an early age, he was introduced to orgies involving both men and women, taken to the stinking brothels in the backstreets of Peking and

AT AN EARLY AGE, HE WAS INTRODUCED TO ORGIES INVOLVING BOTH MEN AND WOMEN, TAKEN TO THE STINKING BROTHELS IN THE BACKSTREETS OF PEKING.

learned all the deviant practices which had helped speed the demise of his father. His mother was busy, consolidating her power, introducing severe taxes and fighting a bloody rebellion in the north of the country.

When her son reached the age of power on 15 November, 1874, Tzu-Hsi issued a Royal Decree that confirmed the end of her regency and the start of her son's reign as Emperor. The boy had taken a bride, Alute, but Tzu-Hsi regarded both with disfavour. She was not ready to relinquish her power to these two children. Less than two years after the decree, her son was dead – and it has long been rumoured that his mother was the architect of his demise, despite the fact that in December, 1874, the Emperor Tung Chih issued a decree which read: 'We have had the good fortune this month to contract smallpox.' This was not a bizarre act for a Chinese, for the national belief was that those who suffered this illness, and survived it, were somehow chosen by the gods. But, apparently, the Emperor had little resistance to disease. It has been claimed that his body was weakened by venereal disease, and, less than two weeks after his decree, the young man was dead.

Gossip at the time rumoured that Tzu-Hsi had killed her own son. It seemed likely, but Charlotte Haldane, in her authoritative book 'The Last Great Empress of

Below: *The prosperous port of Shangai where trade with foreigners thrived during Tzu-Hsi's reign.*

China', wrote: 'Tung Chih might easily have caught his smallpox in one of the brothels or opium dens he visited during his nocturnal escapades into Peking. This could be neither proved nor disproved. But the outward symptom of this virulent infection is an eruption of running pustules all over the sufferer's face and body.

A SIMPLE AND DEVILISH MEANS OF MURDER

'Table napkins were not used in China; instead, small square towels, sterilised in steam, were passed to the diners, who, between each course, wiped their faces as well as their lips with them. This was an agreeable, and normally, more hygenic practice than the use of a dry table napkin. But it could be, and on certain occasions was, turned to a deadly purpose. If the hot, steaming little towel were first rubbed on to the face of a smallpox sufferer, covered in highly infectious running pustules, and then passed over the features of an intended victim...? A master, and above all a son of heaven, would never himself wipe his face. This menial task would be performed by a reverential attendant eunuch under the supervision of the chief eunuch. It might be a simple and devilishly effective method of assasination.' Tsu-Hsi ruled the eunuchs.

Certainly, Tzu-Hsi quickly resumed the mantle of power and declared herself, once again, Regent of China.

When Tung Chih died, his wife was pregnant, a fact which infuriated Tzu-Hsi. If Alute gave birth to an heir he would have the right of accession to the throne. This did not suit Tzu-Hsi; she wanted to choose the heir to the throne, someone who would bend to her will. She ordered her eunuchs to beat the young widow, with the aim of causing a miscarriage. Three months later, Alute was dead, the victim of suicide – although there were those who wondered if the vengeful hand of Tzu-Hsi was not behind the tragedy. The Regent named her nephew, Tsai Tien, as Emperor. His royal name was to be Kuang Hsu, meaning 'Brilliant Succession'. As the boy was only four at the time of this announcement, Tzu-Hsi was not threatened by his presence.

BRAVE DISSENTING VOICES

Her choice of emperor was in breach of dynastic law, for there were others, who by right of blood ties and hereditary, had

Top: *These young warriors carry the circular shields and long machettes favoured by the Boxers.*

Bottom: *A Chinese caricature of a Westerner whom the natives called the 'Hairy Ones'. The Chinese were also fascinated by the smoking habits of the Europeans.*

stronger claim to the throne, and ten men of the royal court bravely expressed their anger at her decision. Tzu-hsi merely noted their disapproval, but was not persuaded to abandon her choice to satisfy protocol.

As the child grew he revelled in the affection of the Regent Niuhuru, the widow of the old Emperor, Hsien-Feng; the wife who had favoured the young, ambitious concubine, Tzu-Hsi, all those years ago. Niuhuru was a gentle soul who loved her role as surrogate grandmother and lavished affection on the boy. Tzu-Hsi was not pleased to see the child fall under the influence of another woman. When the old lady

died in bed, all at court believed she had been poisoned after consuming some rice cakes sent to her by Tzu-Hsi. The boy-Emperor was only eleven at the time, so he did not fall under suspicion.

The Dragon Empress now began to enjoy a reign of absolute power. She executed the ten men who had voted against her when she decreed that her sister's child was the future emperor. She consolidated her power base with further executions of her political foes. She moved members of her own family into positions of power within the court and, to ensure no dubious stranger entered the domestic power arrangements, she arranged the marriage of the Emperor to his cousin, her own niece, although neither party was happy with the partnership.

SHE WAS FIFTY-FIVE YEARS OLD, BUT SHE WAS NOT CONTENT TO LIVE OUT HER LIFE ON A COUNTRY ESTATE.

SHE WAS APPALLED AT THE NUMBER OF FOREIGN RESIDENTS THAT HER NEPHEW ALLOWED IN THE COUNTRY

Left: *A drawing of the young Tzu-Hsi, made some time after her nineteenth birthday. She rose rapidly from the lower echelons of concubines to become the Emperor's admired intimate.*

Opposite, above and below: *This was the kind of society that the Emperess Tzu-Hsi wanted to preserve. It was a formalised and rigid system. Clothes were both elaborate and symbolic, and in court, richly gorgeous. Aristocratic women had their feet bound to render them useless for any 'crude' physical labour.*

THE EMPEROR DECIDED TO LOCK HIS AUNT TZU-HSI AWAY FROM HER FRIENDS AND THUS, DEPRIVE HER OF INFLUENCE.

In 1889, Tzu-Hsi was compelled to relinquish her regency. The Emperor had already turned nineteen, but had delayed his ascendancy to the throne until after his marriage. Tzu-Hsi took up residence in a villa, just outside Peking. Her villa was a sumptuous affair of marble nestling in groves of trees among lakes covered with lotus blossom. Much of her exquisite furniture was covered in solid gold. The place took a fortune to build, and a fortune to maintain. It is alleged that Tzu-Hsi stole her money from the royal coffers, helped in her crime by her chief eunuch, Li Lien-ying, a cruel, crude man who had been instrumental in the corruption of her son.

THE WRATH OF THE DOWAGER EMPRESS

There are authenticated stories concerning Tzu-Hsi's behaviour at this time. It is said that she ordered eunuch-gardeners to be whipped – and on several occasions, beheaded – if she found, in her gardens, a wilting leaf or a petal that looked as if it had not been cared for properly. She was fifty-five years old, but she was not content to live out her life on a country estate, no matter what fun she devised for her gardeners. She hoped to rule through the emperor she had chosen, but a yawning gulf developed between aunt and nephew. He was a gentle, intelligent man, and he was 'progressive' in that he wanted to bring China out of the isolation that Tzu-Hsi hoped to enforce upon the country.

She was appalled at the number of foreign residents that her nephew allowed in the country, and was suspicious of the creeping encroachment of these colonial invaders. Then China threatened war against Japan after that country invaded the Liuchiu islands in 1874. Delicate negotiations staved off a military confrontation but in 1894, when Japan tried to invade Korea, the Chinese Emperor called up the Chinese navy. He found his navy depleted of funds and completely run down. The Emperor learnt that the money earmarked for his navy had been appropriated by the eunuch, Li Lien-ying, for Tzu-Hsi's villa. When quizzed by the Emperor, Li Lien-ying is supposed to have replied: 'Even if the money had been spent on the navy, the Japanese would have beaten us all the

same. As it is, at least the Dowager Empress has her glorious summer palace!' The war against Japan was a brief but it was a disaster to the Chinese.

In 1898, while the nation was trying to recover from the disgrace of the defeat by Japan, Tzu-Hsi was approached by fellow travellers, who also despised the foreigners and feared the threat they offered to the Chinese system. A continuous procession of these people to Tzu-Hsi's summer palace was perceived as a conspiracy to undermine the Emperor's authority. Kuang Hsu was aware that, without his aunt's support, he would find it difficult to wield power. He also knew he would never have her support for the reforms he wished to instigate. The Emperor decided to lock his aunt Tzu-Hsi away from her friends and thus, deprive her of influence. But the Emperor unwittingly confided his plan to reactionaries, loyal to the Dragon Empress, so his plot was doomed. When Tzu-Hsi was informed of her nephew's scheme 'her features froze into mask-like immobility, only her eyes expressing her fury and resolution.' Murder was in her heart.

She marched on the Forbidden City where she forced her nephew, the Emperor of China, to abdicate. His personal servants were beheaded. Tzu-Hsi watched the

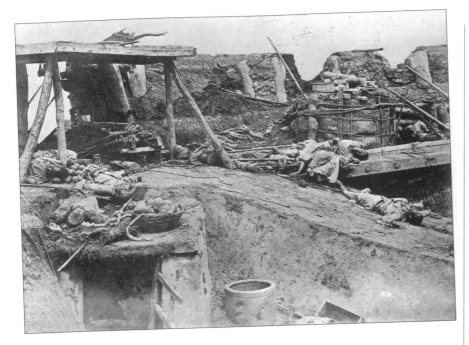

Above: *Chinese bodies, slaughtered by the English in 1860, line the walls of North Taku Fort . Such events fed the xenophobia of the militant group, the Boxers.*

executions as she sipped jasmine tea. The Emperor was imprisoned on a lake island guarded by eunuchs, and forced to live an impoverished life. Many court observers thought he would go the way of the old Emperor and his wife, but Tzu-Hsi kept him alive. It is thought that protests of several foreign ambassadors in Peking, among them the British, were probably instrumental in saving his life. After a year on his island prison, the ex-emperor, Kuang Hsu, was allowed to live under house arrest on a small estate outside Peking.

THE MASSACRE OF THE FOREIGN DEVILS

Six ringleaders in the Emperor's plot were arrested and executed, before Tzu-Hsi turned her attention to the foreign missionaries. All over China, she saw the presence, the insidious invasion of her country by the forces of France, Britain, Germany and Russia. On 21 November, 1899, after several missionaries had been brutally butchered, Tzu-Hsi issued a decree which left no one in any doubt that she would not tolerate the foreign devils in her country.

This decree was sent to all provincial governors, and it read: 'Never should the word peace fall from the mouths of our high officials, nor should they harbour it for a moment in their breasts. Let us not think of making peace, nor rely solely in diplomatic manouvres. Let each strive to preserve, from destruction and spoilation at

ALL OVER CHINA, SHE SAW THE PRESENCE, THE INSIDIOUS INVASION OF HER COUNTRY BY THE FORCES OF FRANCE, BRITAIN, GERMANY AND RUSSIA.

KILLINGS WERE SO NUMEROUS AND FREQUENT THAT FEW HAD TIME TO BURY THE CORPSES.

the hands of the invader, his ancestral home and graves. Let these our words be made known to each and all within our domain.' This decree delighted many conservative Chinese but none more so than the group known as 'the Boxers'.

The I Ho Chiuan, or Patriotic Peace Fists, were nicknamed the Boxers because of their skill in, and emphasis on, martial arts. They were patriotic and zenophobic. Their loyalty lay with the monarchy, and they feared, as did Tzu-Hsi, the corrosive effects of foreign thought on their society. When the Boxer Rebellion broke out out in 1900, their acts were endorsed by the state. Their first victim was a British missionary, murdered shortly before midnight on New Year's Eve, 1899. The dislike of foreigners was widely felt in China, and the Boxers easily organised support for their fight. Telegraph lines were cut, railway tracks dynamited and foreign factories set alight. Tzu-Hsi played a wily game: she pretended to protect the foreigners by dispatching troops against the rebels, while telling one of her army commanders to offer a large reward 'for the ears of every dead foreigner'.

THE EMPRESS FLED IN A HANDCART

She abandoned this game, however, and Chinese troops, under the orders from the Dragon Empress, joined the Boxers and soon every foreign legation was under siege. Killings were so numerous and frequent that few had time to bury the corpses. Disease swept through the city of Peking. When foreign ministers called for the intervention of the Emperor, Tzu-Hsi roared: 'How dare they question my authority – let us exterminate them!' The foreign powers then sent troops from Europe to rescue their threatened citizens.

On 14 August, an emissary rushed to Tzu-Hsi to warn her that 'The foreign devils have come!' The Dragon Empress had to flee the palace in a handcart. As she was leaving, she was approached by Chen Fei, a concubine of the Emperor. She flung herself at Tzu-Hsi's feet, begging her to let the Emperor stay in the palace. Tzu-Hsi ordered her eunuchs: 'Throw this wretched minion down the well. Let her die at once as a warning to all undutiful children.' The unfortunate concubine was hurled to her death down a deep well.

During her exile from Peking, the Dragon Empress lived in a humble, frugal way. Confusion and danger reigned in the countryside. Food was scarce, authority broken. But, within a year, the allies had quelled the Boxer Rebellion and Tzu-Hsi was allowed to return to Peking after peace terms were settled with the European Haldane wrote, in her study of the Empress, that it was a time of supreme hypocrisy for this woman. 'Her chief preoccupation was to protect herself from any attempt by the allies to deprive her of power. She saw that in order to retain it she must give herself a new image, and her future policies a new look. Therefore, by a stroke of superlative hypocrisy, Her Majesty ordered that all pro-Boxer decrees and edicts had to be expunged from the records of the Ching dynasty.'

In the final years of her life, Tzu-Hsi saw foreign-inspired reforms introduced to China. She was obliged, also, to bestow posthumous honours on the Emperor's ministers, whom she had executed – and even one on the concubine who had been flung so cruelly down the well.

In the summer of 1907, she suffered a stroke and her health deteriorated. As she worsened, so did the health of the Emperor. He did not regain power, but had won some respect, and the right to live in his palace. On the morning of 14 November, 1908, he

Above: *The last imperial event of the Manchu dynasty was the funeral of Tzu-Hsi. Her cortege stretched for six miles.*

Right: *Tzu-Hsi on the Peacock throne, after she had schemed and murdered for the immense privilige of ruling China.*

'HER CHIEF PREOCCUPA-
TION WAS TO PROTECT
HERSELF FROM ANY
ATTEMPT BY THE ALLIES TO
DEPRIVE HER OF POWER.

died, showing symptons of poisoning. Certainly his doctor could not diagnose what had killed him. Suspicion fell on Tzu-Hsi. It seems she conspired with her eunuch, Li Lien-ying, to poison the Emperor by giving him small doses over a long period. The eunuch feared that, if the Emperor outlived the Dragon Empress, he would order the execution of Li Lien-ying.

The Dragon Empress outlived her nephew by a mere twenty-four hours. She left a fortune of £16 million, testimony to her reign of plunder; and she left, also, an old, proud dynasty in tatters. Her reign was to open China to a system diametrically opposed to that of an hereditary monarchy.

MA BARKER
Machine-Gun Mama

She was a rare person – a woman who was a leader of men and dangerous gangs; a woman who bred criminals, deliberately teaching her sons to be wicked delinquents. Ma Barker has secured her place in the annals of crime, for her story is that of a truly evil person.

Ma Barker was a mother who taught her children the three 'Rs' – reading, writing and revolvers. She had been brought up in the same rural area that Jesse James used to roam, and she was steeped in criminal lore. She taught her four sons – who became, under her tutelage, one of the most feared and ruthless criminal gangs in American history – to despise authority and follow the maxim that all laws were made to be broken. Unlike their contemporaries such as Pretty Boy Floyd and John Dillinger, who, although notorious, did not make much money from their crimes, the Barker boys did steal vast amounts of money, and were very careful about publicity. They acted with stealth and skill, as they roamed across the United States, from the mid-west to Texas in the far south. And they had no qualms about killing. They were social misfits, encouraged by their own mother to live as habitual criminals.

Ma Barker was born Arizona Donnie Clark in Springfield, Missouri, in 1872, the daughter of a hard-drinking, illiterate ranch hand and a God-fearing mother who taught her to read the Bible and play the fiddle. She left school when she was ten, although she never abandoned her habit of reading lurid penny crime sheets which chronicled the exploits of the James gang and other villains of the Old West. Arrie, as she called herself, was particularly excited whenever she caught sight of Jesse, riding tall in his saddle at the head of his gang. In 1892, when she was twenty years old, she went into a kind of mourning when the evil Dalton Gang were riddled with police bullets during their last vicious bank robbery in Coffeyville, Kansas.

TRAINED IN VIOLENCE

By the end of the year, her grief was mitigated by her marriage to George Barker, a common labourer every bit as coarse as she was. Weak and ineffectual, he winced under the savagery of his wife's tongue – particularly vicious after she had been drinking whiskey. He was a hag-ridden husband, dominated by his wife. But they managed to produce four healthy sons – Herman in 1894, Lloyd two years later, Arthur in 1899 and Fred in 1902. Every single one of them was trained in violence... and they were all to die by the gun, just as their mother did. They started life in Aurora, Missouri, and were known as 'The Four Horsemen of the Apocalypse' by their Sunday school teachers.

In 1908, perhaps driven out by the neighbours who believed that she had given birth to sons of the Devil, Ma moved her brood and her milksop spouse to Webb City, Missouri.

Above: *Jesse James, the outlaw who was Ma Barker's girlhood hero.*

Opposite: *Kate 'Ma' Barker who was the leader of men, and hardened criminal.*

Below: *Another role model for the young Ma Barker was Pretty Boy Floyd.*

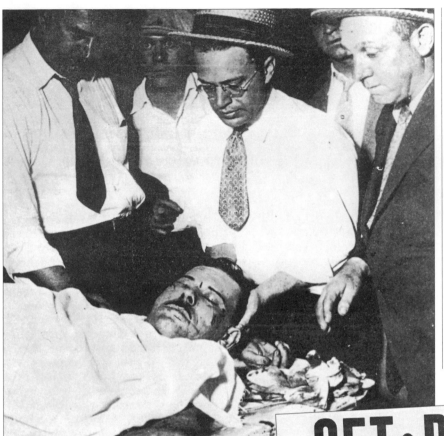

burn in hell before you lay another filthy pig hand on a Barker boy!'

In 1915, after more run-ins with the law, the family upped and left for Tulsa, Oklahoma, where her husband had found a job as a railway worker. They still lived in soul-destroying poverty, and her sons continued to confront the law. These boys went through the whole catalogue of juvenile crime – from breaking and entering, to stealing cars and mugging.

NEW AND DEADLY FRIENDS

Ma Barker herself developed friendships with a motley assortment of bums, heels, con-men, robbers and murderers. She became very attached to an ex-con, called Herb Farmer, who ran a hideout for villains on the run in nearby Joplin, Missouri, and she met many big-name criminals of her day, men like bank robber Al Spencer,

There was money in this town where recently gold had been discovered in the surrounding hills.

But Ma's dream of wealth was sadly at odds with the reality of their impoverished life; the Barkers continued to live in grinding poverty, in a shack made of tar and paper with no running water or electricity. It was the perfect breeding ground for the kind of resentment that turns a dissatisfied young person to crime.

'MY BOYS ARE MARKED'

Ma had a pathological hatred of authority and to those who proferred the slightest criticism of her crooked brood. Policemen, in particular, were regarded as prime suspects in a universal conspiracy against her sons. In 1910, when Herman Barker became her first son to get arrested for stealing, she astonished the neighbourhood policemen at the Webb City police station when, instead of berating her delinquent young son, she turned on the officers of the law with a tirade against them; 'My boys are marked,' she screamed at them. 'You'll

GET·DILLINGER!
$15,000 *Reward*

A PROCLAMATION

WHEREAS, One John Dillinger stands charged officially with numerous felonies including murder in several states and his banditry and depredation stamp him as an outlaw, a fugitive from justice and a vicious menace to life and property;

NOW, THEREFORE, We, Paul McNutt, Governor of Indiana; George White, Governor of Ohio; F. B. Olson, Governor of Minnesota; William A. Comstock, Governor of Michigan; and Henry Horner, Governor of Illinois, do hereby proclaim and offer a reward of Five Thousand Dollars ($5,000.00) to be paid to the person or persons who apprehend and deliver the said John Dillinger into the custody of any sheriff of any of the above-mentioned states or his duly authorized agent.

THIS IS IN ADDITION TO THE $10,000.00 OFFERED BY THE FEDERAL GOVERNMENT FOR THE ARREST OF JOHN DILLINGER.

HERE IS HIS FINGERPRINT CLASSIFICATION and DESCRIPTION. ————FILE THIS FOR IDENTIFICATION PURPOSES.

John Dillinger. (w) age 30 yrs., 5-8½. 170½ lbs., gray eyes, med. chest, hair, med. comp., med. build. Dayton. O., P. D. No. 10587. O. S. E. No. 559-646.

F.P.C. (12)

	M	9	R	O	O
	S	14	U	OO	8
13	10	0	0	0	
u	R	w	w	w	
5	11	15	I	8	
u	U	u	w	u	

FRONT VIEW

Be on the lookout for this desperado. He is heavily armed and usually is protected with bullet-proof vest. Take no unnecessary chances in getting this man. He is thoroughly prepared to shoot his way out of any situation.

GET HIM

DEAD

OR ALIVE

Notify any Sheriff or Chief of Police of Indiana, Ohio, Minnesota, Michigan, Illinois,

or THIS BUREAU

SIDE VIEW

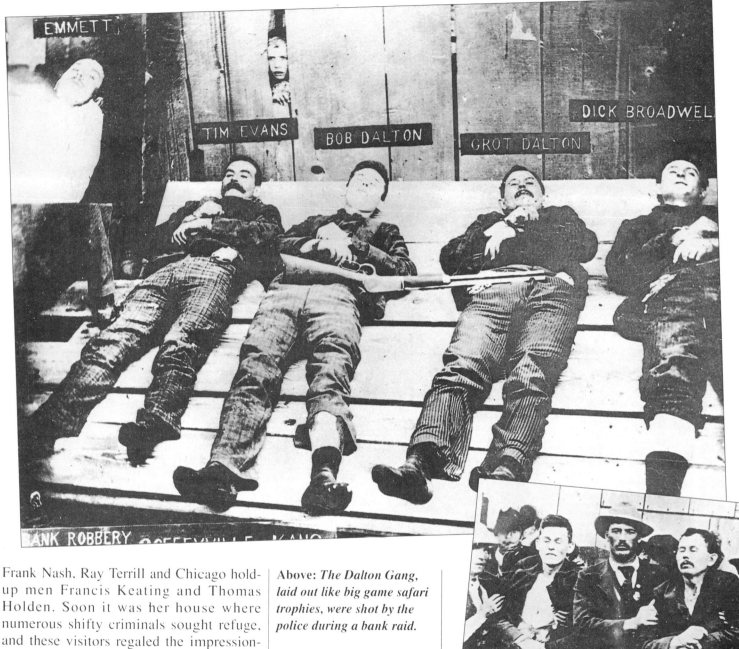

EMMETT — TIM EVANS — BOB DALTON — GROT DALTON — DICK BROADWEL

ANK ROBBERY GREENVILLE KANS

Frank Nash, Ray Terrill and Chicago hold-up men Francis Keating and Thomas Holden. Soon it was her house where numerous shifty criminals sought refuge, and these visitors regaled the impressionable boys with tales of murder, robbery and general mayhem. Psychiatrist James Allen, who has made a study of Ma Barker, said: 'This woman saw in the hoodlums and robbers that hung out at her home a re-incarnation of the bandits that she idolised as a child. She was incapable of instilling in her offspring a respect for the natural laws and rules of society; she portrayed the underside of life as a kind of romantic, Robin Hood affair, which of course, to wayward young boys with limited education and even shorter attention spans, was exactly what they wanted to hear.'

The Barker boys, by the time they reached adolesence, were carrying guns and were deeply involved in the under-

Above: *The Dalton Gang, laid out like big game safari trophies, were shot by the police during a bank raid.*

Right: *Brothers Bob and Grat Dalton held up, even as they are dying, for the benefit of photographers. Ma Barker mourned the passing of this notorious gang.*

Opposite: *Ma Barker copied the murderous methods of John Dillinger and taught her sons to do the same. The police eventually killed Dillinger on 22 July, 1934.*

world. Ma Barker took great delight in hearing of the boys' exploits at the family-dinner table, and was happy to dispense advice on how they could best become stick-up men or jewel-store robbers.

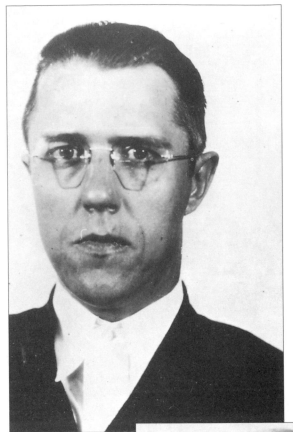

In 1917 the Barkers were members of the Tulsa Central Gang, a loose-knit consortium of teenage hoods who robbed banks, post offices and country gas stations. Ray Terrill, who spent many hours with Ma plotting bank raids, took Herman with him on a number of minor robberies. After these outings, Ma would turn her son's pockets out to make sure he was not holding back her share of the spoil. Once she found a fifty-dollar bill in the top of his sock, and laid into him with the butt-end of a .38 police issue revolver.

In 1922 she kissed goodbye to the first of her crooked brood when Lloyd was caught during a raid on a post office, when he shot and wounded a guard. Nothing she could say or do would persuade the court that her boy was innocent and she was inconsolable when he was sentenced to twenty-five years hard labour in Leavenworth Jail, the state's penitentiary. Arthur was next in line for justice when, in 1922, he was convicted of murdering a night watchman in a Tulsa hospital. Arthur was trying to steal a supply of drugs to satisfy his morphine addiction. He got twenty years in jail, despite an attempt by Ma Barker to bribe another man to plead guilty to Arthur's murder charge.

After Arthur went to jail, Ma Barker abandoned her husband, George, and descended into deviant sexual practices with young girls. 'Hell, when Freddie and the others weren't knocking off banks, they were running around trying to find young girls for Ma,' said James Audett, a reformed bank robber who had once been part of the Barker gang and was an expert on the family. 'The boys would bring the girls, all under-aged, to Ma and when the old lady was through with them, she would tell Freddie and Alvin Karpis, an associate of the gang, to get rid of them. Those two crackpots would just up and kill these poor girls and dump their bodies in lakes nearby. God, there were bodies of young girls floating all over those lakes because of crazy old Ma Barker. Disgusting. The whole bunch of them made me so sick that I only went on two jobs with them. They couldn't keep regulars in the gang because of the way they lived.

'THEY WERE ALL KILL-CRAZY LOVERS'

'That was the key to them. Ma became a lesbian, and all the boys – with the exception of Arthur – were homosexuals, and there ain't nothing worse than a homosexual bank robber and killer. You see, if one of them saw a cop coming at them with a weapon they would shoot to kill because they thought their lover might be bumped off. They were protecting their lovers as well as themselves. Freddie killed a lot of people to save his sweetheart Karpis. They were all kill-crazy lovers.'

In 1926, Freddie drew a fifteen-year sentence for the armed robbery of the main bank in Windfield, Kansas – a raid that had been organised by Ma. The only son not in jail was Herman. Ma, saddened by the loss of her sons, was never tempted to make

Herman go straight in order to keep him free; instead she encouraged him to join the Kimes-Terrill gang, a mid-western mob who specialised in stealing entire safes from banks. They would drag the safe out with a pulley and a truck, then blow it open. This method worked successfully on many raids but, in 1926, Herman was shot when a posse of policemen surrounded the gang during a raid on a Missouri bank. He scuttled home to Ma's hideout in Tulsa where, even as she tended to his wounds, she plotted new methods of robbing banks and stores. On 18 September, 1927, Herman held-up a grocery store in Newton, Kansas, before fleeing town at the wheel of his getaway car with an unknown accomplice. On the outskirts of town, SherifF John Marshall raised his gun to fire at the speeding vehicle, but was cut down by a hail of Thompson sub-machine-gun fire from Herman. Marshall died instantly.

The next day in Wichita, Herman was alone when he drove his car into a police trap. He emptied his machine gun and pistol at the law officers – then he withdrew a bullet he called his 'lucky piece' from his waistcoat pocket. It was his last round and, although he was wounded by return fire from his cop pursuers, he chose to blow his own brains out.

SHE DEVOTED HER LIFE TO FREEING HER SONS

Ma Barker was convinced that Herman had been executed by police, claiming: 'A Barker don't do things like that. Barkers weren't raised to kill themselves for pigs.' But an autopsy proved that he had, indeed, ended his short, violent life.

She maintained her lust for young girls, but knew that she needed a man to look after her while her boys were in jail. She took up with a penniless alcoholic, Arthur Dunlop, saying: 'A drinking man's better 'n no man at all.' Now, Ma Barker divided her time between writing petitions to governors and prison wardens, asking for clemency for her sons, and maintaining a safe haven for villains on the run. She also began 'fencing' – selling stolen goods – for the rabble who stayed with her. Edgar J. Hoover, the legendary head of the FBI, would later say of her: 'It was the suicide of Herman, and the imprisonment of her

other three sons, which changed her from an animal mother of the she-wolf variety to a veritable beast of prey. She slipped deeper into depravity and villainy.'

The money she received from the desperadoes she was hiding, plus her take from the sale of stolen gems and other valuables, soon meant that she no longer needed the spurious protection of Arthur Dunlop, although she continued to live with him. She ignored his presence, however, as she devoted her life to freeing her sons. Ma said: 'I gotta have at least one of my poor babies free. At least one... it's all I ask. Who would deny a poor woman at least one of her brood?' In 1931, her pleas for clemency finally paid off when Freddie was released from jail. He brought with him his cell-mate and partner-in-crime, Alvin Karpis, who, by a freak quirk, had also wangled his way out of hard time. It was about the worst mistake the authorities could have made.

Now admitted lovers, the duo embarked on a Ma-inspired wave of terror. Karpis later explained: 'What I wanted was big automobiles like rich people had and everything like that. I didn't see how I was going to get them by making a fool of myself and

Opposite: *The morose features of Alvin 'Creepy' Karpis with whom Ma threw in her lot. The lower picture reveals the scar left by a botched plastic surgery job. Karpis hoped to change his looks and evade the law.*

Below: *Fred Barker, the beloved son who died on 16 January, 1935, after a four-hour gun battle with FBI agents in Florida.*

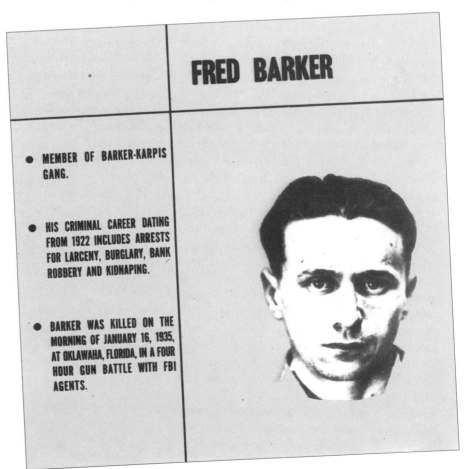

FRED BARKER

- MEMBER OF BARKER-KARPIS GANG.

- HIS CRIMINAL CAREER DATING FROM 1922 INCLUDES ARRESTS FOR LARCENY, BURGLARY, BANK ROBBERY AND KIDNAPING.

- BARKER WAS KILLED ON THE MORNING OF JANUARY 16, 1935, AT OKLAWAHA, FLORIDA, IN A FOUR HOUR GUN BATTLE WITH FBI AGENTS.

working all my life.' Such an attitude delighted Ma Barker, so it was no surprise that Karpis became a surrogate son, replacing Herman in her affections.

Freddie had fallen deeply in love with Karpis and, in jail, they made a pact that they would never bluff their way past lawmen after doing a job, nor risk a high speed chase. They would simply kill and take their chances.

In the summer of 1931, with the Great Depression ravaging the lives of millions of ordinary Americans, the pair embarked on a crime wave, robbing several jewellery and clothing stores. Captured twice and confined in small-town jails, they escaped easily and continued their spree. They often returned home to Ma with details of their exploits, and to give her a share of the spoils. They persuaded Ma to move with them from Tulsa to set up their crime HQ in a farmhouse in Koskonong, Missouri. Karpis – a skilled electrician, thanks to his years in the federal slammer – rigged the house with an elaborate alarm system to

Above: *J.Edgar Hoover, crime buster extraordinaire, who ruled the FBI with an iron fist for fifty years. He went to war against the mobsters with astonishing success.*

IT WAS TIME FOR THE BARKERS TO HIT THE ROAD, AND FIND SOMEPLACE SAFE UNTIL THE HEAT DIED DOWN.

---

keep cops at bay. Under the aliases of Dunn and Hamilton, the two lovers roamed the mid-west states. In July of that year they successfully held-up a hardware store and took $1000 before making their getaway. Two days later, however, Sheriff Charles Kelley spotted them sitting in a car, dividing up the loot. He pulled his gun to arrest them, but they fired first and he fell dead on the road. It was time for the Barkers to hit the road, and find someplace safe until the heat died down.

Ma cleared out of the Missouri farmhouse, and headed for St Paul, Minnesota, well-known as a place where gangsters could hide from the law. Once more, she set-up a refuge for gunmen, while she became closely associated with the well-known hi-jackers Jack Pfeifer and Harry Sawyer. Ma planned the hi-jackings of long distance trucks and Freddie and Karpis carried them out. The goods were fenced through Pfeifer and Sawyer, and Ma used her share to pay lawyers in her fight to free her other sons from prison.

Now poor Arthur Dunlop, overshadowed and detested by the criminal family into which he had married, was no longer wanted. His bullet-riddled body was found floating in the icy waters of Lake Freasted, in Wisconsin, towards the end of 1931. It was Freddie Barker who pulled the trigger on his own stepfather.

Freddie and Karpis had, by now, acquired some criminal clout of their own, and no longer relied on Pfeifer and Sawyer. Many hoodlums and gunslingers were prepared to work for Freddie and Karpis, and the pair began to run their own gang. Between 1931 and 1933, they knocked off dozens of banks, killing numerous people along the way, including a marshall called Manley Jackson. Several armed guards and policemen were also killed. Ma Barker and Freddie were now among the most-wanted criminals in America, for they had stolen an incredible $500,000 in cash and had murdered many people.

In October 1932, Arthur Barker was released after being paroled. Now Ma had two sons to run her business in crime. In May, 1933, Ma had a brainwave. She had tired of bank robberies and plotted a kidnapping. She reasoned in her warped brain that, just as she herself would pay any amount of money and pull any string to get a loved one out of jail, so a wealthy family would hand over any amount of cash to get one of their brood back. Teaming up with Fred Goetz, a member of the old Al Capone gang, wily Ma Barker hatched a plan to seize William Hamm, the head of a wealthy brewing dynasty.

MA'S FIRST KIDNAPPING

On 15 June, 1933, after Hamm left his brewery in St Paul, he was snatched by Freddie and Karpis. He was ordered to sign a ransom note, was fitted with a pair of goggles stuffed with cotton wool, and

MA BARKER AND FREDDIE WERE NOW AMONG THE MOST-WANTED CRIMINALS IN AMERICA.

Below: *The most famous inter-gang killing of them all – the St Valentine's Day Massacre, masterminded by Al Capone. But Fred Goetz, the close friend of Ma Barker, was rumoured to have played the role of executioner at this grisly event.*

driven for several hours to the Ma Barker hide-out, where he was placed under the machine-gun guard of Goetz. For three days the brewer's family consulted with police, and their own consciences, before deciding to pay the ransom. On 17 June, the ransom was thrown from a car speeding along a dark road on the outskirts of St Paul; the plot hatched by Ma Barker had worked perfectly and William Hamm was returned safely to his family.

Below: Sent by Ma to live in Chicago, Arthur Barker was arrested as he left his apartment. He was killed when he tried to escape from Alcatraz prison in California.

ARTHUR BARKER
ALIAS "DOC" BARKER

- MEMBER OF BARKER-KARPIS GANG.

- CRIMINAL CAREER DATING FROM 1918 INCLUDES ARRESTS FOR LARCENY, JAIL BREAKING, BANK ROBBERY, MURDER, AND KIDNAPING.

- APPREHENDED BY FBI AGENTS IN CHICAGO, ILLINOIS, ON JANUARY 8, 1935.

- CONVICTED AND SENTENCED TO LIFE IN PRISON.

- HE WAS KILLED IN AN ATTEMPT TO ESCAPE FROM ALCATRAZ PENITENTIARY ON JANUARY 13, 1939.

KARPIS AND FREDDIE BARKER, TOGETHER WITH MA, NOW CHOSE TO HAVE PLASTIC SURGERY TO ALTER THEIR APPEARANCES.

The Barker brothers, with Ma as the mastermind, then resumed their old trade of robbing banks. In August, 1933, they hit a payroll truck in St Paul, and stole $30,000. But in the subsequent shootout with cops, one policeman died and another was seriously wounded. Another cop was killed in a botched Chicago raid a month later.

MA AS MASTERMIND

Ma decided to go back to kidnapping, believing that the ease with which they ransomed Hamm was proof that this was a lucrative, and relatively safe, criminal pursuit. Feeling the heat after their numerous killings, with the Barker names on thousands of FBI wanted posters, Ma proposed the kidnapping of Edward Bremer, a wealthy Minneapolis banker.

Ma masterminded the snatch meticulously, spending several months on the crucial planning stages before unleashing her boys to do the dirty work on 17 January, 1934. Bremer dropped his eight-year-old girl off at school that morning and began driving to his office. He was ambushed at a traffic light by Arthur, who held a gun to the victim's head.

Bremer was forced to sign a ransom demand for $200,000. The Bremer family did not contact the police, but their attempts to pay the ransom were botched on several occasions. Meanwhile, the psychopathic Arthur Barker tried to kill Bremer but his brother Freddie stopped him with the words: 'Sure, blow his brains out, but you know what Ma will think about that!' The mere mention of the one and only person Arthur feared was enough to make him put his twin revolvers down. Edward Bremer lived to be re-united with his family after the ransom cash was delivered on 17 February, 1934.

PLASTIC SURGERY FOR MA BARKER AND HER BOYS

Karpis and Freddie Barker, together with Ma, now chose to have plastic surgery to alter their appearances and so elude the law. They selected a doctor called Joseph Moran, who was also an alcoholic. Moran drugged them with morphine before setting about his crude surgery. Ma was about to undergo her operation when she saw the results that Moran had achieved on Freddie. Moran was murdered by Freddie and Arthur on Ma's orders.

Ma insisted that the gang should split up, so she sent Arthur to live in Chicago. She rented a house in the rural backwater of Oklawaha, in Florida, where Karpis and other gang members were regular visitors. In 1935, following an underworld tip-off, Arthur was arrested outside his Chicago apartment by FBI agents. In normal circumstances he would have reached for his gun and started blasting away – but he had left his weapon indoors and was captured without a struggle.

A search of his apartment revealed a detailed map and directions to the hideout in Florida, used by Ma and Freddie. This was a welcome breakthrough for the police who alerted FBI agents. An armed siege of the hideout was carefully planned.

THE END OF MA BARKER AND HER SONS

On 16 January, 1935, agents surrounded the house and one inspector, wearing a bullet-proof jacket, drew the short straw; he actually had to approach the house and tell Ma to surrender. She opened the door the merest crack and hissed through yellowing teeth; 'To hell with you, all of you.' As she closed the door the quaking law enforcer heard her say: 'Let the damned Feds have it – shoot!' Ma, the cool brains behind the murderous brawn of her thieving sons, went to an upstairs window to begin firing a gas-powered automatic rifle at the men ringing her lair. While Freddie opened up with a sub-machine gun, the FBI returned automatic fire and poured tear gas shells into the house. For forty-five minutes, the air crackled and hissed with the sound of gunfire and splintering wood.

Finally, when the return fire from the house quietened and stopped, a handyman, who worked for the Barkers, volunteered to go check on the outlaws. He found Ma Barker with three bullets in her heart, Freddie dead from fourteen machine gun bullets. Ma Barker's reign as the berserk gangland matriarch was over.

Her two remaining sons were to die violently. Arthur was killed by guards in the Alcatraz fortress jail in San Francisco Bay on 13 June, 1939, when he tried to escape the prison. Lloyd served his full twenty-five-year stretch for murder and was freed in 1947. He married soon after his release and his wife stabbed him to death in 1949. It was a fitting end to the story of the Barker boys who did everything for a wicked woman, their own Ma.

SHE OPENED THE DOOR THE MEREST CRACK AND HISSED THROUGH YELLOW-ING TEETH; 'TO HELL WITH YOU, ALL OF YOU.'

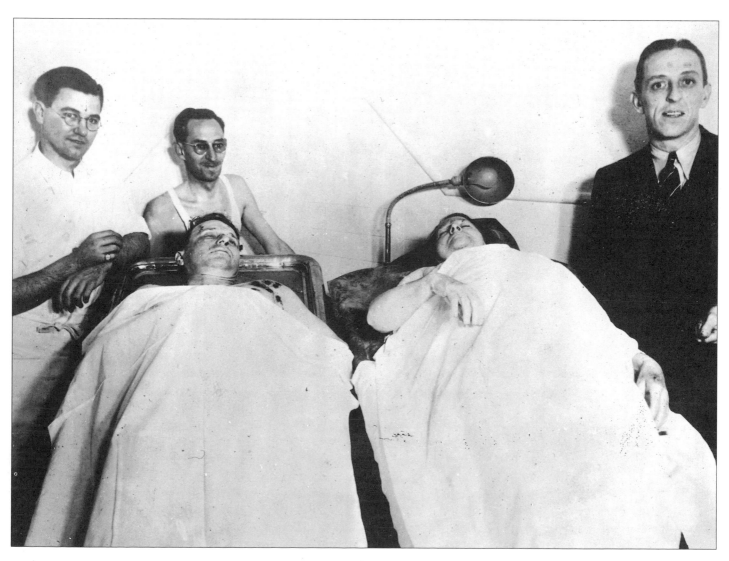

Below: *Side by side for all eternity – Ma Barker, right, and her son, Fred, after they died resisting FBI agents. Few mourned their passing.*

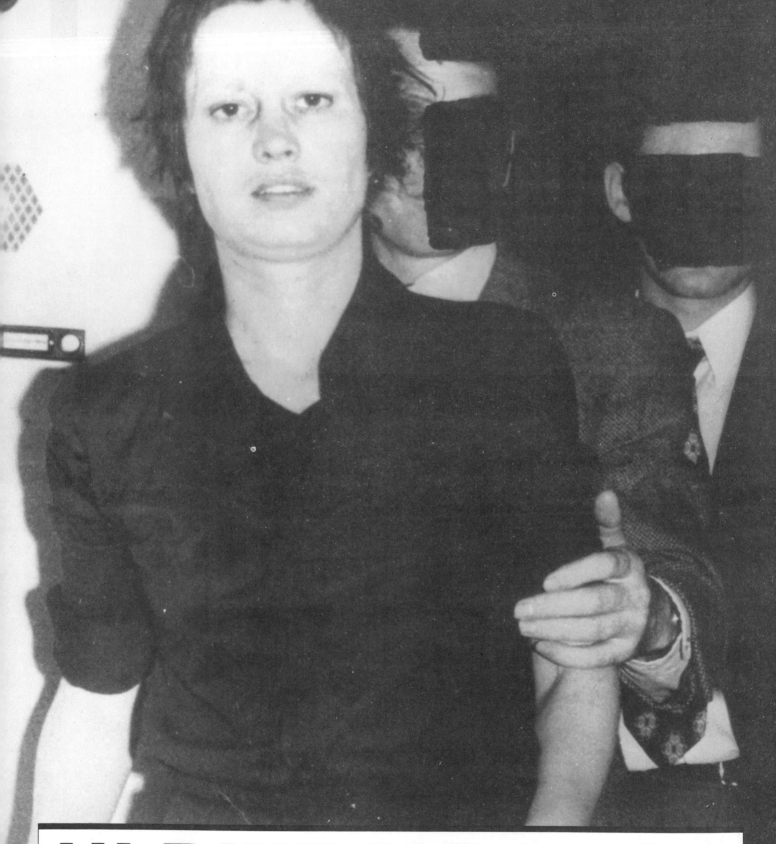

ULRIKE MEINHOF
Queen of Terror

This woman is one of the most enigmatic poltical figures of our time. Ulrike Meinhof was well-educated, bright and the radical darling of the national media. But she chose to become an outcast, a fanatic and a ruthless killer. Hers is a very mysterious tale.

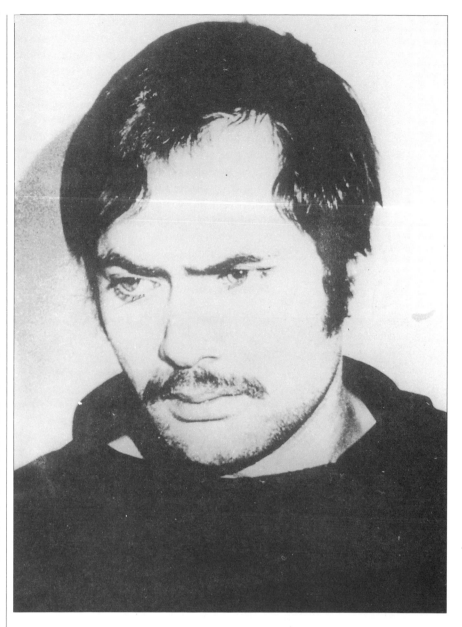

Not all of Germany's post-war children shared in the vision of the economic miracle, the rebuilding of their shattered industries and bombed-out cities to heights greater than that which the Third Reich achieved. Nestling in the schools and universities, in certain stratas of the intelligentsia and the academics, the seeds of a new revolution were being nurtured by a breed who looked to the east and, particularly, the German Democratic Republic, hiding behind its wall and its wire, as the model state of the future.

These coffee-bar radicals and middle-class Communists believed that capitalism was a dead concept and that the time for the true proletarian revolution had arrived. But their vision held no hope for such a Utopia to be achieved by peaceful means – the new Jerusalem was to be forged with guns and blood. Into such a maelstrom of fury and fire fell Ulrike Marie Meinhof to be indelibly linked in history with Andreas Baader when they formed the Baader-Meinhof gang which scorched its way across Germany to become one of the most successful terror groups the world has ever known.

A QUICK WIT AND READY CHARM

She was born in Lower Saxony on 7 October 1934, a child of the misfit generation called 'Hitler's Children'. Spawned in his rise to power, old enough to see him

bring her country to its knees, she lived through the conflagration and came out of it an orphan. Her father died from cancer at the outbreak of war and her mother in 1948. A foster mother took care of her during her high-school years – a period when she matured into an intelligent, thoughtful young woman, highly gifted in classes, polite to all she met and possessed of a quick wit and ready charm. She was also a pacifist who devoured works by Bertrand Russell and Vera Brittain. Her views were shaped by her mother; but also by the turbulence of the era which left its stamp on her young mind.

By the time she was twenty-three and studying for her post-graduate doctorate at the University of Münster she had embraced many ecological, left-wing and

Above: *The brooding good looks of Andreas Baarder helped attract many women to his violent cause.*

Opposite: *Ulrike Meinhof, darling of the left, brilliant scholar, gifted teacher, loving mother and urban terrorist par excellence.*

pacifist causes, including ban-the-bomb campaigns and calls for Germany to resist growing militarism from the right. It was mainstream stuff – even Willy Brandt, the anti-Nazi socialist who went on to become Chancellor of the Federal Republic, was a supporter of similar trends. In 1959, her reputation as a chic radical and avant garde academic was established. And Ulricke knew how to keep an audience interested, so she was asked to speak at an anti-bomb conference in the capital, Bonn. It was there that she met Klaus Rainer Rohl, the Marxist editor of the student newspaper 'Konkret'. They fell in love and were married in 1962, and Ulrike gave birth to twins the following year.

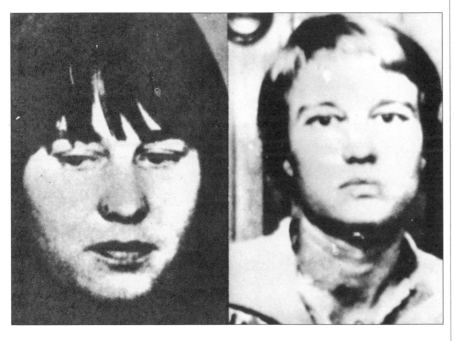

Above: *The changing of Ulrike. She became a master of disguise and this talent helped her evade the law for some time.*

> SHE DIVORCED HER HUSBAND – A COMMITTED WOMANISER WHO FINALLY INDULGED IN ONE AFFAIR TOO MANY.

> THE COMMITTED PACIFIST HAD TAKEN THE FIRST STEP TOWARDS BECOMING AN URBAN TERRORIST.

Although committed to her domestic life, her husband and family, Ulrike's infatuation with the politics of the Left began to deepen. In the permissive Sixties, as England swung to a beatnik sound and 'free love' were the two words on everyone's lips, the old order of capitalism and class seemed worthy to her of destruction. But even as she steeped herself more and more in left-wing ideology she prospered within the system she was one day to despise.

She and Rohl led comfortable lives. Rohl began to translate some pornographic Swedish books into German at a considerable profit while Ulrike's income expanded as she took on the editorship of 'Konret' and increased its sales. In their avant-garde world they attracted an eclectic mix of friends – some rich, some poor, but all imbued with a passion to change the world. She became a successful talk-show host and a radio personality, wheeled out to give the 'alternative' viewpoint whenever an issue of the day was being dissected by the media. And not once, during these years of comfortable affluence, with a white Mercedes parked outside her door and her cellar stocked with fine Rhine wine, did Ulrike Meinhof for a moment consider that violent upheaval was the only answer to all the ills of society.

Towards the end of the Sixties, two events occured which went a long way to derailing her peaceful and ordered world. The first occurred in 1968 when she divorced her husband – a committed womaniser who finally indulged in one affair too many. The second was the trial of a young revolutionary – Andreas Baader.

Baader, born in Munich on 6 May, 1943, was a believer in a violent solution to the class struggle which he saw confronting modern German society. Work-shy, handsome, appealing to women, he drifted in his twenties to Berlin where he was a regular in the agitprop demonstrations that happened daily in the old imperial capital against everything from squatters' rights to increased students' fees. In 1967 Gudrun Ennslin, a committed Communist, left her husband with her young child to live with Baader, whom she had met at a student demo. It was during this period that Andreas Baader began to evolve his philosophy of anger and class hatred, leading him to call for an armed guerilla war against the state – his so-called 'People's War'.

ULRIKE'S FIRST STEP TOWARDS TERRORISM

However, their very first act of armed resistance went badly wrong. He and Ennslin planted incendiary bombs in Frankfurt department stores in a protest at the Vietnam War. They were seen escaping, soon tracked down and put on trial. It was while the trial was going on that Ulrike Meinhof began to speak out for him and for the action he had taken. The committed pacifist had taken the first step towards becoming an urban terrorist – absorbing the atitudethat any human life is worth taking if the cause is worthy enough.

Baader, Ennslin and two other guerillas who were caught torching the department stores were sentenced to three years each for arson. In June 1969, after serving fourteen months each, they were released pending the outcome of an appeal, but Baader, his lover and one other militant fled to France. When they were re-captured on an Interpol warrant in 1970 and sent back to jail in Germany, the flame of righteous indignation burned deep within Ulrike Meinhof. Now living in Berlin and her credentials with the the Left firmly established, her apartment became a meeting place for political sympathisers. In 1970, Ulrike committed herself to the path of terrorism when she plotted with Baader cohorts to spring him from jail.

There was a group in sympathy with Baader and his cause. It was known as the Red Army Faction, a Marxist cadre founded by Horst Mahler, a lawyer who defended Baader at his trial, and was committed to the violent overthrow of the

MAHLER, A LAWYER WHO DEFENDED BAADER AT HIS TRIAL, AND WAS COMMITTED TO THE VIOLENT OVERTHROW OF THE WEST GERMAN STATE.

Below: *The scene of devastation at Frankfurt Airport after a bomb was planted by terrorists. Three people were killed and twenty-eight injured.*

West German state. Linked to an underground network of revolutionaries via university and Communist party contacts, the Red Army Faction also had contact with Middle Eastern terror groups.

On 14 May, 1970, Baader was freed in an audacious escape from the Institute of Social Studies in Dahlem. The prison authorities had allowed him to further his academic studies at the institute, although he was kept under guard. After the getaway Mahler, Meinhof, Baader and Ennslin fled to a terrorist training camp in Jordan where they hoped to learn advanced terrorism.

STUDYING WITH THE PLO

Under the tutelage of the Palestinian Popular Liberation, Meinhof was an adept pupil. She learned how to roll out of a fast-moving car without seriously injuring herself and how to aim accurately with a recoiless pistol. But the relationship between the Arab hosts and their German

the camp their mother had chosen as their new home was reduced to rubble in an air strike by King Hussein's forces.

Ensconced in their safe houses and apartments, Ulrike and her colleagues set about planning the 'People's War'. First, they needed that essential tool – money. Mahler co-ordinated a series of bank raids intended to provide the loot needed to buy explosives, false papers, arms and the places needed to store these goods. In one day, they hit three banks, but Ulrike was disappointed because she netted just £1,500. There were more robberies and a mixture of bravado with clinical planning ensured their repeated successes.

Karl-Heinz Ruhland, a working class car mechanic, was brought into the gang because he was able to supply them with a constant stream of getaway cars. The elitist, intellectual fighters looked down on this lowly working-class recruit, but he was to be the first of two lovers Ulrike chose from the men of the Red Army Faction. Gossips said her sexual choice demonstrated her belief that the class system was dying and that she did not recognise it anyway.

guests was a frosty one; each side accused the other of behaving arrogantly. Apparently the Arabs were particularly annoyed by Baader, who refused to take part in commando exercises saying they were 'unnecessary' for the kind of war he was planning back in Europe.

On 9 August, tension between the two groups reached breaking point and the Germans were asked to leave the training camp. Ulrike wanted to stay longer – she was particularly interested in bombs and how to fuse them correctly and she was reluctant to depart before she had completed her bomb-making course. But the Palestinians insisted and the gang slipped back into Germany, where they were hidden in the flats and houses of the radical friends whom Ulrike had cultivated during her political activities with the left.

ULRIKE SENT HER SONS TO THE TERRORIST CAMP

Ulrike was so convinced by the cause of the Red Army faction that she arranged for her seven-year-old twins to be packed off to the terror camp in Jordan that she had just left. She wanted them to become fighters in the Palestinian conflict with Israel. This ambition was, she explained, the ultimate expression of her love for them. The children travelled no further than Palermo, Sicily, on their journey to the Middle East when they were stopped by police who promptly arrested the terrorist who was acting as their escort. Weeks later

Top: *A bomb planted outside the gates of the Munich Oktoberfest in 1980 killed nine people. These random attacks on the public were a legacy of the Baader-Meinhof reign of terror.*

Klaus Croissant (above) and Christoph Hackernagel (right) are the terrorists suspected of the murder of industrialist, Hans Martin Schleyer.

However, Ruhland had his view. 'I am a worker she has studied,' he said later. 'But although she is intellectually far above me, she never reminded me of that.'

Ulrike became the quartermaster for the group, securing weapons from Palestinian contacts and planning raids on government offices for official paperwork and stamps. These latter were used to forge documents that would give the gang access to places like army camps and government research facilities. The raids on the banks continued and the money – some £100,000 in 1970 – mounted up. But while the institutions of capitalism were being hit, the pillars of the system were not. The People's War had yet to define its targets clearly .

In October of that year Mahler was arrested when he blundered into a police trap, and leadership of the gang fell to Baader. Slightly unbalanced, prone to erratic mood swings, Baader needed the intellectual and analytical mind of Ulrike to help him keep his guerilla army together.

THE CRAZY GANG JOINS THE RED ARMY FACTION

In 1971, after the gang robbed two banks in Kassel and escaped with £15,000, police pressure to capture them became intense. Germany's Kriminalpolizei – known as the Kripo and the equivalent to the CID – formed a task-force assigned to eradicate

Christian Stroebele (above right) Kurt Groenwald (centre) and Rolf Clemens Wagner (left) were drawn to the Baader-Meinhof cause. They deliberately cultivated an 'ordinary' appearance to avoid suspicion from both neighbours and police but Wagner is believed to have played a major role in the killing of Hans Schleyer.

them. One by one, the members of the Red Army Faction were arrested. At one stage just Baader, Meinhof and six others remained free, but there was no lack of willing recruits to their twisted cause. Some of these came from a revolutionary group calling itself the SPK. Soon the blood would start flowing, as the gang switched from knocking off banks to wiping out human lives.

The SPK – Socialist Patient's Collective – was the warped brainchild of Dr Wolfgang Huber of Heidelberg University, who taught that mental illness was created by the state; change the political system and psychiatric illnesses would disappear. He schooled his patients in explosives, in surveillance techniques, in judo and other forms of unarmed combat. His wife Ursula assisted him. By mid-1971 the SPK, a bunch of psycopathic killers, believed that they had found their spiritual home with the Red Army Faction. The Kripo gumshoes trailing this network of misfits called them the Crazy Gang.

On 22 October, 1971, a patrol car in Hamburg spotted Margrit Schiller, an SPK

member, walking out of a train station. She met two comrades. The patrol officers, Helmut Schmid and Heinrich Lemke, chased them into a park. But the trio were heavily armed, and the policemen presented just the kind of target these crazies favoured. Schmid died with six bullets in him, Lemke was lucky to escape with only a leg wound.

A NEW RECRUIT LIQUIDATED

The killing of the policeman gave added impetus to the police in the determination to capture the Red Army Faction. Margrit Schiller was arrested two days after the killings. She carried a considerable amount of weaponry and a book written by Meinhof called 'The Church Black Book Volume 1'. It contained a list of pastors, doctors, journalists and lawyers who could

be relied upon to give aid and succour to the Red Army. This book, with its damning list, caused an outrage in a Germany that was disgusted by the ruthless violence of these urban guerillas.

Nevertheless, the killing continued. On 22 December, 1971, Herbert Schoener, a policeman, was shot dead as the gang robbed a bank in the Rhineland town of Kaiserslautern. Aged thirty-two, with a wife and small children, Schoener was shot three times and was severely wounded by flying glass before he died. The robbers seized £33,000 in loot, but the bloodshed and the screams were too much for Ingeborg Barz, a nineteen-year-old girl who had recently joined the gang. She wanted to go home to her mother in Berlin, perhaps resume her job as a typist in a small clerical firm and try to forget her life as a revolutionary and forget the screams of the children frightened in that bank raid. But Meinhof decreed a policy of `liquidation` for any member of the Red Army who wanted to desert. Gerhart Muller, a gang member who would later turn state's evidence against his former comrades, said Meinhof flew into a rage when she heard Ingeborg say she wanted to leave. Muller said that Ulrike Meinhof drove Ingeborg to a remote gravel pit near Aachen, where Andreas Baader executed the girl.

ULRIKE'S 'BABY BOMB'

More policemen were killed – one of them with dum-dum bullets fired by a Crazy Gang member. Meinhof, meanwhile, perfected a series of pipe bombs, and a device called a 'baby bomb'. This consisted of an explosive device slung from shoulder straps, so that it lay on a woman's belly and gave her the appearance of being pregnant.

> BUT MEINHOF DECREED A POLICY OF 'LIQUIDATION' FOR ANY MEMBER OF THE RED ARMY WHO WANTED TO DESERT…ULRIKE DROVE INGEBORG TO A REMOTE GRAVEL PIT NEAR AACHEN, WHERE BAADER EXECUTED THE GIRL.

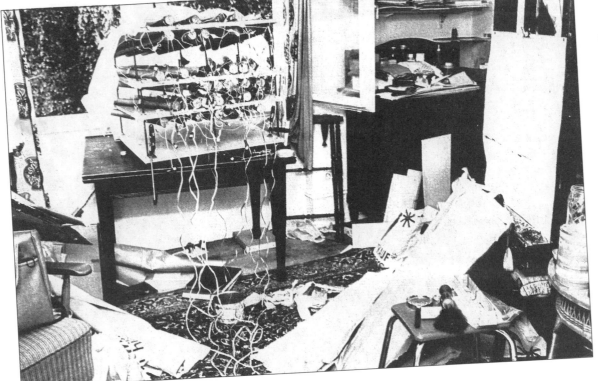

Left: *A 42 barrel home-made rocket launcher. The Red Army held a couple hostage in their own flat, then aimed this weapon across the street to the home of Germany's chief prosecutor but the police apprehended the gang before they launched the rocket.*

Meinhof, the brains of the bombing campaign, mapped out targets at government offices near Hamburg, Heidelberg, Augsburg, Munich and Frankfurt.

At Frankfurt, on 11 May, 1972, Jan-Carl Raspe, now Ulrike's lover and a leader in the group, Baader and Ennslin, planted several pipe bombs in the American Army's 5 Corps HQ. The explosion was devastating, killing a Lt Colonel and wounding thirteen other civilians and military personnel. The US army was deemed a target by Ulrike because she said America 'pulled the strings' in Europe, and also for its involvement in the Vietnam War, a conflict that the Red Army was opposed to for obvious idealogical reasons.

The following year the campaign was stepped up. Five policemen were injured in Munich's CID offices when time bombs left in suitcases exploded. In May, the wife of a judge who had signed arrest warrants for the terrorists, was seriously wounded by a bomb that went off as she turned the key in her car ignition. On 19 May, 1972, Ulrike personally planted the bombs which ripped through the offices of the right-wing publisher Axel Springer in Frankfurt. Three more Americans died a week later in a bombing at a barracks in Heidelberg. Ulrike's bombs were perfected in their design by Dierk Hoff, a mechanical genius who swopped his occupation as a sculptor to become a political terrorist. He manufactured timers so sensitive that armaments manufacturers would later ask for the

designs so that they could be applied to commercially-manufactured ordnance.

The police were frustrated that they could not find the core of the gang, even though several lesser members had been captured and several more killed in shoot-outs on motorways and outside banks. At the height of their terror campaign, the Red Army could still count on some thirty-five safe houses and a fleet of forty cars with false number plates to ferry them around Germany with ease and privacy.

THE DEADLY AMBUSH

The ease with which they operated and the carnage they left behind caused acute embarrassment and concern to the West German government. They knew that often Meinhof slipped across the border to East Germany to replenish arms supplies, but it was extremely difficult to trace her because of the multitude of aliases under which the gang-leaders operated. Ulrike Meinhof was the brains behind the entire operation, even though much of the blood was spilled by Baader and Raspe.

Seven days after the Red Army committed the murders in Heidelberg, people leaving their homes in a Frankfurt suburb to go to work, did not give a second glance to the corporation workers unloading turf outside a row of garages in a neat suburb. There was a patch of scrubland nearby and observers thought that the council labourers were at long last going to lay grass on it. In

Above: *The wife of Johann Heinrich von Rauch abuses a photographer outside the court where her husband, a Red Army member, was facing charges of murder.*

fact, the labourers were Kripo marksmen, and the turf was to be used as a barricade if they needed such protection. The Kripo had received a tip-off that in one of the garages was a Red Army weapons cache. After a lengthy wait, the police swooped on the site and found a formidable weapons dump – but none of the gang. They replaced the explosives and guns with harmless substitutes and waited for their quarry to show.

At 5.50am on 1 June, a Porsche drew up in the street where the police marksmen waited, and three men got out. Two walked to the garage while the third, Raspe, the lover of Ulrike Meinhof, waited nervously as he scanned the gardens nearby. Years as a criminal fugitive had taught him well; he smelled something was up and decided to flee. He let off a hail of bullets, but he was brought down by a rugby tackling lawman.

Andreas Baader and Holger Meins, were in the garage when tear gas bombs were hurled at them. The two terrorists fought back, but Baader took a bullet in his right leg. Eight minutes after the first tear gas bomb was released, Meins appeared with his arms in the air. Moments later, police stormed the garage where Baader lay with blood pumping from his wound.

THE LAST REFUGE

A week later, Gudrun Ennslin was seized in a Hamburg boutique. She was picking out sweaters to try on and carelessly threw her leather jacket on to a chair, while she went into the changing room. An assistant, who picked it up to fold it neatly, felt the unmistakeable coldness of a gun barrel. She told the manageress who feared that the woman might be a robber, and she in turn called the police. When they arrived Ennslin went for the weapon but after a fierce fight the female terrorist was overpowered.

Only Ulrike remained at large. And because she was the ideological force behind the Red Army Faction, she was the most wanted member of the group. Ulrike knew the organisation was badly-damaged by the police activity. Her lover was arrested, her co-leader arrested, her 'family' dead, dispersed or incarcerated. Even her friends in the political left had deserted her, for they were now thoroughly frightened and disgusted by the violence and robbery that she and her group had practised.

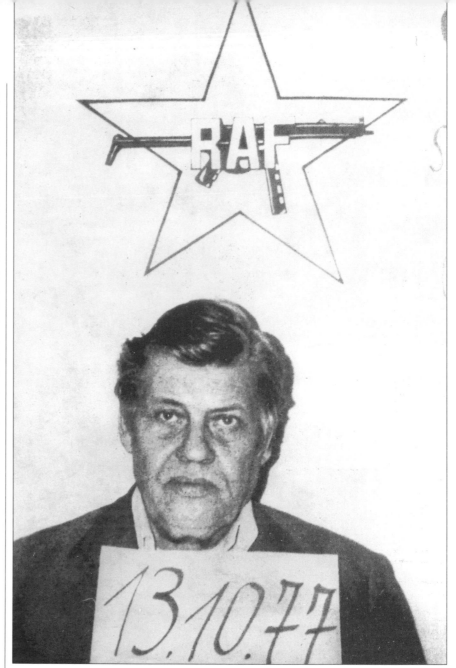

Above: *The industrialist, Hans Martin Schleyer, was kidnapped on 13 October, 1977. He was photographed beneath the Red Army emblem before the Baader-Meinhof gang killed him.*

YEARS AS A CRIMINAL FUGITIVE HAD TAUGHT HIM WELL; HE SMELLED SOMETHING WAS UP AND DECIDED TO FLEE.

Desperate for refuge, after a safe house in Berlin fell under police suspicion, Ulrike and Gerhard Muller turned up at the home of Fritz Rodewald, a left-wing schoolteacher who, initially, had been sympathetic to her cause. But Rodewald was a socialist, not a terrorist. He was a respected president of a teacher's union, a man with a family and a position in the society she wished to destroy. He took the advice of friends and called the police.

When Kripo squads swooped on the apartment, Ulrike was unpacking her luggage. Nestling among her clothes were three 9mm pistols, two hand grenades, one sub-machine gun and one of her beloved bombs. Gerhard Muller was to become the state's witness against her. But she struggled like a wildcat when the police seized her and eventually had to be sedated. Her face looked puffy when the mug-shots were taken at the police station but, in fact, life on the run had been unkind to her; Ulrike had lost three stone and now weighed less than seven stone.

The capture of Ulrike Meinhof was the final nail in the Red Army coffin. She had been the driving force behind the whole operation; she was much admired by her kind, and many guerilla groups sprang up to committ numerous terrorist acts, including bombing the West German embassy in Sweden in an effort to free her. On 21 May, 1975, in the ultra-secure £5 million Stammheim Prison, the trial of Meinhof, Baader, Ensslin and Raspe opened – Meins would have joined them but he had starved himself to death in captivity.

FOUR THOUSAND MARCHED AT HER FUNERAL

For a year the trial dragged on, a litany of bank robberies, murders, arsons and explosions. The defendants said nothing, save that they did not recognise the court. Finally, Ensslin broke in May 1976 and admitted that the gang had carried out a series of murder-bombings. Four days later Ulrike tore her yellow prison towel into strips, tied it to the bars of her cell, and slowly strangled herself to death.

The agit-prop brigades that she had once so proudly led poured into the streets of several European capitals, claiming that she had been murdered by her guards during the night, although independent examinations of her corpse proved that she had ended her own life. It was an unexpected end to the woman who intellectualised terrorism, who once wrote in a training manual for her fellow guerillas: 'We women can do many things better than the men. We are stronger and much less anxious. This is our People's War and we must all fight it alongside the men. Violent revolution is the only answer to society's ills.' When this misguided follower of the left was buried in Berlin, four thousand sympathisers, many of them masked, marched to her grave.

Her death unleashed new waves of terror, that, culminated in the murder of industrialist Hanns Martin Schleyer and the seizure of a Lufthansa airliner bound from Majorca to Frankfurt in October 1977.

Eventually the plane landed at Mogadishu after a five-day ordeal in which the captain was murdered and the eighty-six passengers terrorised. A German commando team, under the guidance of British SAS officers, stormed the plane. Three of the four terrorists were killed outright, one wounded, but no passengers were hurt.

The news caused Raspe, Baader and Ensslin, now all serving life sentences after being Found Guilty of the kidnappings and murder, to kill themselves – the men with smuggled pistols, Ensslin by hanging.

When police issued the list of wanted terrorists in connection with the killing of Schleyer – murdered in the hours after the failure of the Mogadishu hi-jacking – it was significant that half of them were women from the same background and class as Ulrike Meinhof.

> ULRIKE TORE HER YELLOW PRISON TOWEL INTO STRIPS, TIED IT TO THE BARS OF HER CELL, AND SLOWLY STRANGLED HERSELF TO DEATH.

Jillian Becker, who chronicled Meinhof's life, said: 'She was an ambitious love-hungry child. Her education bred both a puritan and a rebel in her, the one never reconciled to the other. She was drawn to Utopian Communism.'

But those who fought her would say that somewhere within her was a bitter hatred, and not a longing for love or the need for affection, that turned Ulrike into the terror queen of Europe.

Above: *A US Army personnel office after a Red Army firebomb attack in 1981.*

WANDA HOLLOWAY
Wicked Wanda

A madness grew in the quiet Texan town. Girls starved themselves, turned to drugs and a mother plotted murder. Wanda Holloway was arrested when she tried to hire a killer and her crime was to reveal the town's crazy obsession with the girls who were cheerleaders.

Not much happens in Channelview, Texas. It is a small town ignored by the motorists who bypass it on Interstate 10, and overlooked by the well-heeled residents of its brash, big neighbour Houston, thirty minutes away on the same highway. It fits neatly into that perfect - if contemptuous - description of Main Street America – 'Nowheresville'.

However, the residents of Channelview display a stoic civic pride in its few industries, its quiet solitude in a state that Texans regard as God's own backyard. During the Gulf War, yellow ribbons bedecked every street sign, every lampost and every front door knocker while the neon sign standing outside the local Baptist church flashed the message: 'God will be your patriot when the Scuds come flying in!' No, not since Santa Anna and his Mexican armies defeated, in 1836, the Yankees at the battle of San Jacinto, twenty miles away, has anything remotely of interest to the outside world taken place in Channelview. That is, not until 1991 and the sensational case of Wicked Wanda Holloway – the woman branded the 'ultimate stage mother'.

In a diabolical scheme Wicked Wanda hatched a plot to kill the mother of her daughter's best friend. Wanda figured that pretty Amber Heath, thirteen years old, would be so overcome with grief at the

Opposite: Wanda Holloway planned to orphan a little girl who was a cheerleader rival to Wanda's own daughter.

Below: Shanna Holloway (centre) leaves court with her mother who was charged with conspiring to murder. The girl walks hand-in-hand with the family attorney, Stanley Schneider.

seconds of venomous hatred poured out of her mouth. The recording made by her brother-in-law was enough to damn Wanda. The police arrested her and her bizarre motive to commit murder became public knowledge. Reporters from all over the world descended on the town to investigate a murder scheme, so wicked and so evil for a purpose so trivial. They came to check if the story was true – after all, would a woman kill another because of their daughters' rivalry over cheerleading? The newsmen who descended on Channelview found life in the town of seventeen thousand five hundred people far from simple 'Main Street' style.. especially where cheerleading was concerned.

DIET PILLS AND CHEERLEADING MANIA

They discovered that the schoolchildren of Channelview were the victims of a potty cheerleading mania that possessed their parents – and was exploited by drug pushers. The other adults were as fanatically eager as Wanda to see their daughters succeed in the cheerleading world.

These girls were willing to starve themselves, and many had become addicted to dangerous amphetamine diet pills in their desire to shed their puppy fat, because they longed for the glory of cheering for the football team. Wanda Holloway's arrest, and the craziness of her murderous ambitions, forced the police to investigate the apparently harmless world of high school sport. They uncovered a flourishing network of drug dealers selling drugs to desperate children, who longed to match a 'weight chart' provided by their school. This chart determined 'suitable' sizes for girls who wanted to be members of the cheerleading team. In this school, there was an inordinately large number of girls suffering anorexia, the dietary disease.

Mrs Barbara Blackstock, whose two daughters Laura and Loretta were on the Channelview High School cheerleading team, recalled: 'There were dozens of girls making themselves throw up after meals and taking laxatives and diuretics to drain the fluid from their bodies. Everywhere the talk was of prescription diet pills and where to get them from. The health hazards really were enormous.' Yet no one stopped it.

death of her mom that she would quit the school cheerleading team. Her departure, Wanda dreamed in her twisted mind, would pave the way for her own daughter Shanna, also thirteen, to squeeze into her slinky rah-rah skirt and to prance noisily on the sidelines of state football games as a 'Channelete Drill Team Cheerleader'.

And more than anything else, Wanda wanted her daughter to be the cheerleader.

After recruiting her former brother-in-law to kill Mrs Heath – and giving him diamonds as a down payment – Wanda told him: 'Make it quick. I want the bitch out the way before the weekend.' But her conspirator bolted with the diamond earrings and details of the evil plot to police. When he returned to Wanda to finalise details of the 'hit' he was wired – he had a tape recorder strapped to his stomach. And Wanda raved as she plotted the killing. Forty-seven minutes and thirty

Above: *Verna Heath, whose life was threatened by her neighbour Wanda, leaves the trial with her daughter, Amber Heath.*

Opposite, top: *Verna Heath giving evidence during Wanda's trial.*

Opposite, below: *Wanda is led away after being sentenced to fifteen years in prison.*

WANDA TOLD HIM: 'MAKE IT QUICK. I WANT THE BITCH OUT THE WAY BEFORE THE WEEKEND.'

Her own daughter, Laura, was a victim of this slimming madness. Laura was swallowing fifteen diet pills a day and running in two track suits every night, to sweat off fluids, before she collapsed and needed hospital treatment. After Wanda's arrest, a school teacher, Julia Dunsford, resigned from her job as a sponsor of the cheerleading competition, saying: 'The pressure on the kids to compete was enormous. The kids were so mercenary it was incredible. I actually heard a young girl say: "I would kill to get on the squad." It's sad that a young girl would feel that way. It's really, really sick that a mother would too. But taken in the light of what the kids would do to become cheerleaders, can we really blame anyone but ourselves if the mothers become equally obsessed – obsessed enough to kill?'

Assistant district attorney Joe Magliolo, who prepared the prosecution of Wanda Holloway, said: 'It is a diabolical story, but when you think that we have parents who slap teachers, fathers who hit baseball referees when their son strikes out and over-achiever moms and dads pushing their children to the limit, should we really be surprised when these people step over the edge and are willing to commit murder for their kids?' It is a sad statement.

WANDA WAS OBSESSED BY HER DAUGHTER

Wanda Holloway lived with her third husband, and the children of her first marriage, Shanna and her son Shane, in a modest house in Channelview. Her squat, gated bungalow home is fringed by fir trees, and has a swimming pool in the back garden. A £5,000 air-conditioning system kept the place cool during the long, hot summers.that Texas enjoys

Wanda wanted everything – both for herself and the daughter on whom she doted. The older she got, the more she determined that her daughter Shanna would have the best in life. Psychologists who came to probe Wanda's mind, found that the woman tried to live through her daughter, hoping to intrude in every aspect of the girl's life, from school grades, to her boyfriends, to the clothes she wore, through to Shanna's favourite pastime...

Above: *Wanda Holloway sits impassive in the court as her jealousies and obsessions are laid bare.*

cheerleading. Shanna Holloway longed to be a member of the school cheerleading squad more than anything.

Shanna got the attention and love that her mother never got when she was a child. Wanda Ann Webb was highly strung, hypersensitive to other people's opinions and never got the chance to be on the cheerleading team in her own school. She spent her days in solitary piano playing while she thought about her life as an adult. She hoped that she would have a career as the personal secretary to a corporate executive. She grew up in Channelview and saw her future as part of the town's petro-chemical plants and oil refineries. Tom Curtis, an American author who investigated what came to be known as 'The Cheerleader Murder Plot', said: 'By several accounts, it was her secret yearning as she grew up to become a cheerleader. Cheerleaders were then, and still are, the top of the social heap among teenagers. But her father considered the uniforms they wore too skimpy, the girls in them little better than prostitutes. Wanda never tried out, for this reason as much as any other.'

After a failed marriage to Tony Harper, a former high school football player, father of Shane and Shanna, Wanda did become an executive secretary, working for a small industrial supply company. Former

colleagues there remember her as a glitzy, heavily-made-up woman who was extravagant and careless with money, and who adored her little girl, Shanna.

In 1981 she re-married, this time to divorcé Gordon Inglehart, a salesman in the firm where she worked. She quit her job, moved with the eight-year-old Shane and four-year-old Shanna to a large house on the outskirts of Channelview, and concentrated on ... cheeerleading.

MARRIAGE NUMBER TWO FAILED

Friends recall how that this pastime turned from a deep interest to an obsession. Even when Shanna was still a little girl, Wanda dressed her in little cheerleader outfits to go watch her brother playing in boys' team football. Tony Harper, her first husband, recalled: 'It was the whole thing for Shanna, the entire uniform, pom-poms, the works, even down to Wanda shouting on the sidelines with a megaphone. The boy Shane was embarassed – it was like having your own personal cheerleader when the other kids didn't have one.'

Wanda's second marriage collapsed in 1983, around the same time that the oil industry fell into recession, and this husband's business was affected. When Gordon and Wanda separated, she moved to a smaller home in Channelview. Her new neighbours included Verna and Jack Heath, whose daughter Amber was an enthusiastic and accomplished cheerleader.

However, Wanda met a wealthy local banker Charles Holloway, who became her third husband in 1986. When a former employee of the industrial firm where she worked contacted her for a get-together of old colleagues, Wanda gave a sneer: 'I am married now and my husband has a lot of money, so I don't have time for you lot!' Holloway moved Wanda and her children to a larger home, although the couple did not move neighbourhoods.

Every night after school, Shanna practised with her friends the chants and moves they had learnt from the bigger girls in the high school who were real cheerleaders at the county and state football games. She went everywhere with Amber, her pal and her idol. Good though Shanna was at the intricate moves and the complex baton-twirling, she was no match for Amber. Amber had been practising since she was two. Not only had her mother had been a cheerleading champion, her grandmother had taught dance and tap to two generations of schoolchildren.

GOOD THOUGH SHANNA WAS AT THE INTRICATE MOVES AND THE COMPLEX BATON-TWIRLING, SHE WAS NO MATCH FOR AMBER.

Below: *Moved to emotion when she took the stand, Wanda weeps to convince the jury that she did not plot murder.*

Amber and Shanna were an inseperable duo, although Amber was generally ahead of her friend in athletics and school grades. In a pre-Christmas school election in 1990 both girls sought the presidency of the student council. Amber won. Two months before that they had vied for the title of 'most popular' in a class contest. Amber won. And they both wanted to be in the cheerleading team of Channelview High School when they moved there in September 1991. This honour could only be awarded to one person.

SECOND AGAIN TO AMBER

Before they moved to this school, Amber and Shanna had competed for one place on the team of their former school, the Alice Johnson school. Amber had won this, despite an embarrassing campaign staged on behalf of Shanna by her mother, Mrs Holloway. Wanda paid $50 to a stationery company in Dallas to make up pencils emblazoned with the legend: 'Elect Shanna Harper Cheerleader'. She also distributed pen cases bearing the same message and little sticky badges that she gave to parents when she met them at the school gates.

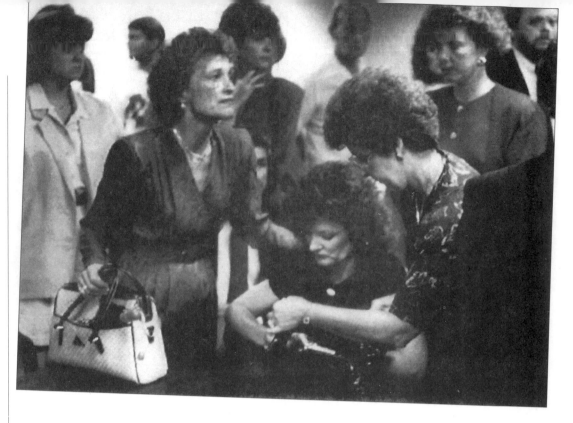

Right: *Wanda's mother, Verna Webb, comforts her daughter after she was found Guilty of solicitation to the murder of her neighbour, Verna Heath.*

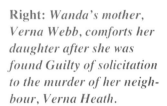

WANDA KNEW THAT TERRY OWNED A .22 HUNTING RIFLE AND DETECTIVES CLAIMED THAT THIS FINALLY DROVE WANDA TO SELECT THIS MAN AS HER HIRED KILLER.

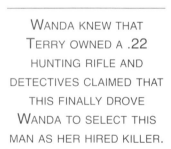

SHE ASKED HIM FOR A 'DOUBLE WHAMMY' – TO KILL BOTH THE MOTHER AND THE DAUGHTER.

But her efforts failed. Her daughter lost to Amber. Police say it was this failure at the earlier school that drove Wanda Holloway into a frenzied obsession, a wild determination to ensure her daughter's success as cheerleader. Assistant district attorney Magliolo gave his views on Wanda's madness: 'I guess you would call her the ultimate stage mom, someone who is living their less-than-fulfilling life through their offspring. We contend that when her daughter's plans were thwarted in a friendly competition she turned to thoughts of murder.'

WANDA HIRED A KILLER

Wanda simply refused to believe that Shanna had been given a fair chance for this team place. She asked the school for a re-count of the judge's votes and was staggered when she saw that in a competition of thirty girls, her daughter was placed a mere third. Wanda did not know the mother of the second girl – but she knew the mother of Amber, the winner. Ann Goodson, whose daughter dated Wanda's son Shane, said: 'Wanda felt she had been cheated. It was really tough on her. She felt that Amber and Verna had conspired together. That's all she ever talked about, all that cheerleading stuff.'

In her home in Mincing Boulevard, Wanda Holloway appeared to live the life of any housewife, watching daytime soaps,

preparing meals for her husband and family, giving dinner parties and running her home. But as she went about her chores, Wanda brooded and fumed over the fate of her daughter, and tried to think of ways to ensure that Shanna would be a cheerleader at her new school. On 4 January, 1991, Wanda arranged the first of three meetings with Terry Lynn Harper, her former brother-in-law.

Terry Lynn Harper must have seemed, to Wanda Holloway, who was looking for a partner in crime, the ideal acquaintance. He has a string of convictions, among them drug peddling. He was given a suspended sentence for drunk driving in 1985, and was also charged with illegal possession of a gun. Wanda knew that Terry owned a .22 hunting rifle and detectives claimed that this finally drove Wanda to select this man as her hired killer. Magliolo explained: 'It was her view that Terry Harper – or someone that Terry Harper knew – would be willing to execute Mrs Heath for money. Initially she asked him for a ''double whammy'' – to kill both the mother and the daughter. Mr Harper informed her that would probably be expensive but that one death would cost about $2,500. She said that was fine – that she could get that much money together.'

Terry Lynn Harper wanted nothing to do with something as dreadful as murder. He went straight to a law officer that he knew, George Helton, a senior narcotics officer with the Harris County Organised Crime and Narcotics Task Force. Helton said: 'The guy has some petty convictions, not much in the way of heavy duty stuff. I couldn't believe him when he said that his brother's ex-wife had turned up after five years and asked him to commit murder – or get someone he knew to do it. It frightened the guy. He did the right thing.' Helton 'wired' Harper with tape recording equipment that would record every word.

DIAMOND EARRINGS AS DOWN PAYMENT

The tapes, played at her trial, make for chilling listening. Phone conversations and meetings between Harper and Holloway were recorded, and include such snippets as: 'This is a critical year. She don't make it this year, she ain't never gonna make it.' When Harper pointed out that it might be difficult to find someone to kill a child Wanda gave an icy reply: 'But Terry, you don't know this little girl. If you knew her – ooh! I can't stand her. I mean, she's a bitch.

Makes me sick. I mean, I could knock her in the face, you know. I want something done – I want them taken care of.'

During one meeting, held in a car park on 14 January, Wanda gave Harper details of the routines followed by the Heath females, both mother and daughter. (Actually, the family were now constantly guarded and watched by the sheriff's deputies, thanks to Harper's report.) Wanda said to Harper: 'The mother's done more damage than the daughter. The mother is the one that screwed me around. I don't care if they ship her out to Cuba and keep her there for fifteen years, okay? I want her gone, I want her gone.' As a down payment for the contract killing, she handed Terry a pair of diamond earrings valued at £1,100.

Then her voice can be heard saying: 'Make it quick. I want the bitch out of the way before the weekend... Burn the car, wreck the house, have a robbery take place in the house – just do whatever it takes. You know, Terry, I just don't think I could pull the trigger on somebody. But I can certainly do it this way.'

> 'MAKE IT QUICK. I WANT THE BITCH OUT OF THE WAY BEFORE THE WEEKEND... BURN THE CAR, WRECK THE HOUSE, DO HATEVER IT TAKES.'

Below: *Wanda, flanked by attorneys, Troy McKinney, left, and Steve Schneider, and her mother Verna Webb leave court during the trial.*

That is the venomous hiss of Wicked Wanda who wanted the woman murdered before a weekend cheerleading practice. She figured that if Mrs Heath was killed before that, Amber would have to drop out of the practise and Shanna would have the chance to shine.

> THEY WERE BEING TAUNTED BY NEIGHBOUR-HOOD KIDS WHO SAID THEIR MOM WAS A MAFIA HITMAN.

There was one more meeting with Harper, and this supplied forty-five minutes of recorded conversation. 'There's nothing in the tapes to indicate that her husband had any knowledge of her diabolical scheme,' said Magliolo. 'This was entirely-her show.' Wanda was obsessed.

Another veteran lawman said: 'Usually there's a monetary gain in these things. Husband wants wife killed for insurance or vice versa. This is a first for me as far as motives in these cases.'

Neighbours watched as the wrought iron gates of the Holloway home opened and Wanda Hollowaywas led out in handcuffs. At a downstairs window of the house Shanna's face could be seen, watching as her murderous mother was led away. Wanda Holloway was allowed bail of $10,000 after a preliminary court hearing in which she pleaded Not Guilty.

Above: Wanda told the court that she was 'sorry' she said 'all that stuff' but claimed that, despite her words, she did not intend to kill. The jury did not accept her apology and found her guilty.

Mrs Holloway was not without friends in Channelview. They claimed that Wanda had been framed by her ex-husband. To support this idea, the friends pointed out that immediately after Wanda's arrest, the man had sought custody of his two young children, Shanna and Shane.

Tony Harper said: 'I was worried about the children's safety and emtional stability after this. Under the circumstances, I think they would be more secure in my home. The children were living in a stressful environment. They were being taunted by neighbourhood kids who said their mom was a Mafia hitman. This was my son's senior year and all this crap took all the good times away from him. It's rubbish to suggest that I was somehow behind all this. Wanda is a very strong-willed woman. This was all her idea.'

The case was a puzzle to many. One neighbour was prepared to give Wanda the benfit of the doubt: 'Maybe she was the victim of a complicated plot. Cheerleading seems a crazy thing to die for. People are big hearted folks down here and we don't hang someone until the full facts are out.' Assistent DA Magliolo said: 'Yeah, I've heard talk about the conspiracy theory and the frame-up. It could even become part of the defence at her re-trial. But you know what? I've heard those tapes – and I can tell you you wouldn't believe your ears! I ain't never heard anything like it. I'm sure she was planning the kill.'

'SHANNA WOULD HAVE MADE THE SQUAD ONE DAY'

There were many citizens in Channelveiw who did not take Wanda's plea of innocence too seriously. One man said: 'It just makes you sick all over. If only she had left it to her daughter. Shanna is a far better loser than she is. The plot was so shocking because the girls were such good friends. If Shanna had been left to her own devices, she would have made the squad one day. It hasn't hit home to Amber that there was very nearly a contract out on her life – that there was indeed one being taken out on her mother.'

Verna, who has been under doctor's sedation since the day the murderous plot on her life was unearthed, said: 'I can't believe the life of a human being, my life,

was to be snuffed out because of something as trivial as cheerleading.'

Wanda Holloway's trial took place in the summer of 1991 and it made front-page news across America, and made the prime-time television news bulletins. Wanda's defence strategy was that although she had said she wanted the Heath women murdered, she had not intended her words to be taken literally. She said that she felt that Terry was trying to pressure her into fulfilling the contract. But when asked by the prosecution in court why she did not back out, she had no convincing explana-tion. Fighting back tears, she turned weakly to the jury and said: 'You don't under-stand... you just don't understand. I am sorry I said all that stuff – I know it sounds awful. Truly I never wanted Amber or Verna killed.' But the tape damned her.

The jury of four women and eight men took just six hours to find her Guilty and under Texas law were allowed to set her sentence, which they agreed should be fifteen years. She was bailed on appeal and, just a month after the sentencing, received the news that her trial had been declared a mistrial because one of her jurors did not reveal to the court that he was a felon who had been found Guilty of cocaine posses-sion. He should never have been sitting in judgement on her in the first place.

Her re-trial is scheduled for 1993 but legal experts say it is highly unlikely that the verdict will be any different. The tapes are damning testimony, and Wanda has never denied that it was a her voice on the recordings. But the delay in re-trial has given Wicked Wanda a chance to get rich selling her story to TV and production companies. Her lawyers refuse to comment about any such deals, although the Heaths have admitted to signing up their story with agents in Hollywood.

IN THE WAKE OF WICKED WANDA

Shanna is not attending Channelveiw High School. Friends say that Amber has gone off cheerleading. Verna, her mother, is bitter and confused by Wanda Holloway's jealousy of Amber. 'Why would a cheer-leading position be so important? To leave my kids without a mother? Who would raise them? You know, over cheerleading, not to have a mother? I want to meet her one more time, to ask...to ask: "Why would you do this?" '

Parents and teachers in Channelview have been forced by these sad and silly circumstances to reduce the status of cheer-leading. The entire community was thoroughly frightened by the excesses that, unwittingly, it had allowed to develop around this innocent pastime. The weight chart has been taken down from the school walls; girls on diets to lose weight are carefully monitored, and the new aware-ness of drug abuse keeps parents alert to the health and safety of their children.

Above: *As she waits for a re-trial, Wanda woos the media with a big smile. No wonder – she has reputedly struck a financially reward-ing Hollywood contract for her 'story'.*

THE DELAY IN RE-TRIAL HAS GIVEN WICKED WANDA A CHANCE TO GET RICH SELLING HER STORY TO TV AND PRODUCTION COMPANIES.

CHARLOTTE BRYANT
Killing Killarney Katey

Kate was an Irish beauty who was generous with her charms and beauty. The soldiers loved her. But her obsession with sex drove her into a bizarre marriage and the dreadful role of poisoner.

Her real name was Charlotte McHugh but to scores of British troops garrisoned in her native Ireland she was Killarney Kate. A native of Londonderry, Charlotte was a woman of ill-repute who dispensed her favours to the hated troops then stationed in her homeland. The time was the early Twenties, and sections of Dublin were still in ruins after the abortive Easter Rising by the Irish Republican Army.

Kate's was a dangerous profession made doubly risky by the clientele she sought out. The nationalist militants seeking to overturn Westminster rule to establish an Irish free state did not take kindly to one of their own indulging men whom they regarded as the enemy. But Kate was a free-spirited, determined young woman who brooked no advice and slept with whomsover she chose – and she chose British troops, for the simple reason that they had money to spare.

A SPECIAL QUALITY

She had hair as black as coal, a milky white complexion, full breasts and bright green flashing eyes, and she provoked, not exactly love, but certainly lust in the occupying army. Killarney Kate captured the imagination of many a man and long, long after she swung from a gibbet for her crime, the memory of her lived on in many a soldier's head and heart. She braved the

SHE PROVOKED, NOT EXACTLY LOVE, BUT CERTAINLY LUST IN THE OCCUPYING ARMY.

Opposite: *Killarney Kate as she appeared at the trial for her life.*

Below: *The last home that Kate shared with her husband, Frederick Bryant. The cottage was near the Dorset village of Dover Compton.*

Above: The kitchen of the cottage where Kate, her husband, her gypsy lover, Bill Moss and Kate's five children lived.

'BILL WAS MORE OF A MAN THAN ALL THE REST OF THEM PUT TOGETHER. THERE WAS A MAGIC BETWEEN US.'

threats of tar and featherings from her countrymen, as she boldly flaunted her profession. It could, murmured the Irish sages and righteous gossips who watched her grow up, only end in tragedy.

Regiment after regiment, platoon after platoon, soldier after soldier visited Killarney Kate for her services. But Kate was bored and restless in her native land, fearful that her future offered only more of the same for the rest of her life, and she was searching for that one special soldier who would one day take her to England, where she would bury her past and live happily ever after.

OVER THE WATER

She thought she had realised her dream when she met Frederick Bryant, an easy-going military policeman in the Dorset Regiment. Bryant had served in the last great battle of the First World War when he was shot in the legs during the closing days

of the campaign. His wounds were to cause him pain throughout his life. But all physical and mental pain were forgotten when he met the beautiful Kate, who stole his heart. In him, she saw the passport across the water to the land she dreamed about, the cities like London and Manchester.

In 1925 he was discharged from the army and married Kate in Wells, Somerset. They started their life together on a local farm where he was employed as the head cowman. All went well for the first few months, but rural life in England turned out to be every bit as hard as country living back in Ireland. They lived in a rented cottage with neither electricity nor running water, ate poor food and barely had enough money for the necessities, let alone any of the luxuries that Kate had dreamed about.

Kate turned once again to prostitution while her husband toiled twelve hours a day, often in remote areas of the farm. Her 'gentleman callers' brought her luxury gifts like sides of beef and bottles of champagne

declared her love for the gypsy wanderer and Fred was consigned to the couch. They were evicted from their cottage when Fred's employer heard the village tittle-tattle about the strange arrangement. The three-some were to be evicted from other homes. Once, Fred walked out on Kate, but he soon returned, to live with Kate and Moss in the bizarre three-way relationship.

However, in May 1935, Fred began to suffer from a mysterious illness. He thought, at first, that the shrapnel inside his body was affecting him. Several times that month, and in subsequent months, he was doubled up in agony, unable to move, and was seized by the most excruciating cramps. Doctors diagnosed an acute case of gastro-enteritis, brought on by his rugged

while, with the money she earned, she became one of the best customers at the little village shop in the hamlet of Over Compton. Even though she bore five children for poor cuckolded Fred, she never let her motherly duties interfere with her profession. Local legend has it that she enjoyed sex every bit as much as the men who pleased themselves with her. Her neighbours, of course, painted a black picture of her, but she was never troubled by their wagging tongues. Indeed her motto was: 'To hell with fishwives – and their simpering menfolk too!' Fred, who knew about his wife's activities, appreciated the money she brought to the domestic budget.

But this sweet, if strange, life came to an end when Kate fell madly in love with one of her callers. On 11 December, 1933, she entertained a gypsy called Bill Moss. She believed that she had met a man as darkly mysterious, as sensual as herself. Moss was classically handsome and very charming. She said of him: 'Bill was more of a man than all the rest of them put together. There was a magic between us. It was like trying to hold back the sea at high tide; I couldn't deny what was passing between us even if I had wanted to.' The high-tide washed over them – and caught in its backwash was Fred, who, perhaps wanting to please his wanton wife, invited the swarthy ne'er-do-well to stay in their home.

When Fred went to work in the mornings Moss jumped from his place on the settee into the marital bed. Pretty soon this arrangement came to an end; Kate

Top: *The back of the house with a view of the wash-house where Kate tried to destroy a tin of poison.*

Below: *The bedroom that Kate shared first with her husband, then with her lover, Moss.*

outdoor life and poor diet. Fred began to suspect that Bill Moss was the cause of the illness but then gypsy Moss suddenly moved out, apparently no longer in love with Kate. However, Fred's home was soon occupied by another intruder.

A LADY FRIEND

Kate had struck up an intense friendship with a woman called Lucy Ostler, a widow with six children. Fred suspected that his wife's sexual urges had taken a lesbian turn. He was determined that this new 'friend' would not take over where the gypsy left off. But on 21 December, 1935, Mrs Ostler spent the night in his cottage.

Kate and her children were placed in the care of the local authorities, while the police searched the cottage and questioned neighbours about Fred and Kate's marriage. The investigation went on for many weeks, but there was no evidence to reveal the poisoner. However, after both Kate and her new friend, Mrs. Ostler, were hauled off to an identity parade to be scrutinised by a pharmacist, who had reported selling arsenic to a woman several weeks before Fred's death, Mrs Ostler broke.

THE GREEN TIN

Although neither she nor Kate were picked out in the line-up, Ostler went to police and blurted out her story: 'There was a green tin in her [Kate's] cupboards. She pointed at it and said: "Don't touch that. I must get rid of it." I asked her what was inside it but she refused to tell me. A few days later I was cleaning under the boiler, raking out the old ashes, and I saw the tin, all burned and charred. I threw it into the yard because the ashes were to go on to the compost heap. It's probably still there now.'

Luckily for the police it was – and, even in its charred state, clearly recognisable as the container which the pharmacist claimed he had sold to a woman. The tin was sent for scientific analysis to University College, London where it was confirmed that the tin contained traces of arsenic.

Kate was arrested, charged with wilful murder and told that, if found guilty, she could expect the maximum penalty as prescribed under the legal system – death by hanging. The prosecution built its case

Fred, however, was too ill to argue. That night the excruciating cramps returned and he was rushed to hospital but died the next morning. The surgeon at the hospital could not diagnose the cause of the abdominal pain that brought death. Fred had been a healthy, well–built man, burdened by hard work but nevertheless fit. The surgeon ordered an autopsy; the results revealed that the old soldier, who had survived the bombs and bullets of the Western Front, had been poisoned with arsenic.

Above: *Frederick Bryant in his Dorset Regiment uniform. He was to suffer all his life from wounds sustained in the First World War.*

Below: *The burnt tin of poison that proved to be damning evidence at Kate's trial. It is flanked by undamaged tins of the same brand.*

on the bizarre lifestyle that Kate enjoyed with her husband, Fred Bryant, and Bill Moss, and then with Mrs Ostler. Both these lovers appeared as chief prosecution witnesses, perhaps for fear that otherwise they would be linked with the crime. Moss, whose real name was Leonard Edward Parsons, had tangled with the police previously on account of some petty crimes he had committed, and perhaps he did not wish to incur their displeasure once more. When the trial began on 27 May, 1936, Kate found Ostler and Moss arraigned against her, as were her two eldest children, Lily aged ten and Ernest, twelve. Both had been deeply fond of their father and were extremely aggrieved by their mother.

It seemed that no one would support poor Killarney Kate. Sir Terence O'Connor, the Attorney General, led the prosecution and set the trial's tone when he announced: 'The prosecution contends that the prisoner destroyed her husband in order that her marriage might be at an end... crime for which there can only be one penalty and one we heartily endorse: death.'

THE POISON STORY

Ostler's testimony came first. She said on the night that Fred died, she heard him coughing in the main bedroom. Kate was sleeping on a chair in the sitting room, the same room that Ostler was occupying. Later, she claimed, she heard Kate trying to get Fred to drink some beef extract. 'A few minutes later I heard him vomiting,' she said. 'Later he was taken so queer he had to go to hospital.' She said that Kate wept when she learned her husband had died. But Ostler told the court that she found this strange, claiming that Kate once confided that she hated Fred. Ostler said: 'In that case, I said to her, why didn't she go away and she said she couldn't provide for the children and didn't want to leave them behind.' Perhaps Ostler's most damning evidence was her testimony that she used to read aloud murder accounts from 'penny dreadful' magazines to Kate, who was illiterate. She told the court that she read the story of how a woman in America had poisoned her husband. According to Ostler, Kate's ears had pricked up at this story and she had turned to her friend to ask: 'How do you think I would get rid of someone?'

However, outrage was expressed in court and in the press about the prosecution's use of Kate's children to testify against her. But called they were, although their evidence was of limited use; it centred on a small blue bottle with which they alleged Moss used to threaten their mother.

Kate's passionate eyes burned into her former lover as he was led into the witness box, yet Moss' testimony centred on his affections for her, though he repeated a conversation he had with her concerning a tin of weedkiller. 'It was one day in 1935,' he said. 'I was standing outside the kitchen door when I heard Mr. Bryant say to his

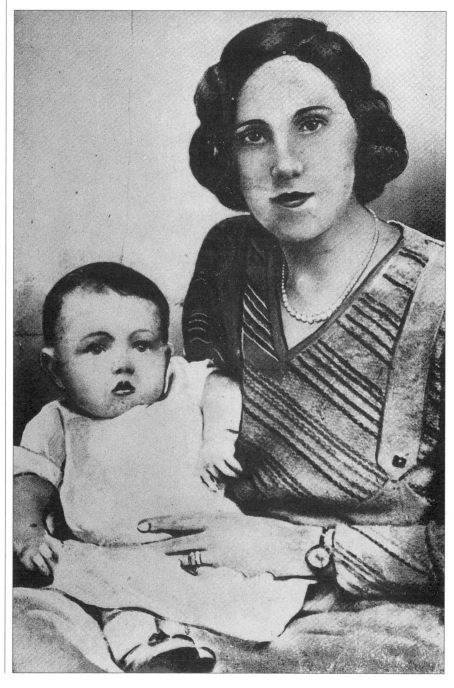

Below: *Kate pictured with Ernest, one of the five children she bore Frederick Bryant. She was, by all accounts, a loving if carefree, mother.*

harm to his wife and, indeed, had gone out of his way to accommodate her special needs and desires, slowly dying in agony from a malady that he could not fight and that he could not understand.

A QUICK JUDGEMENT

In all, there were thirty witnesses against Kate and not one in her defence. She presented a pathetic figure in the dock, a lost case who, unable to read and write, seemed baffled by the weighty and majestic court proceedings unfolding before her. She denied, as best she could in her simple terms, that she had murdered her husband in order to win back Moss. Under further questioning, she said that her relationship with Mrs Ostler was merely a friendship, and did not elaborate upon it.

All Kate could do was refute the suggestion that she had murdered her husband. But the others had no motive to kill him. Moss had returned to his wife, Mrs Ostler had been in Fred's cottage for only one night and was not around him to administer poison over a prolonged period. The trial at

Above: *The majesty of the law, as represented by Mr Justice MacKinnon, frightened the accused, an illiterate country woman.*

Right: *Dr Roche Lynch gave damning testimony on the poison.*

wife. "What's this?." "It's weedkiller." she replied.' With these words, Moss managed to suggest to the court that Killarney Kate had contemplated weedkiller as a means of killing her husband before she switched to the more lethal poison, arsenic.

Expert Home Office testimony seemed to confirm Kate's long, premeditated campaign against her husband. Dr Gerald Lynch, the department's senior analyst, said samples taken from Bryant's corpse showed that he had been slowly and systematically fed the poison over many months. He painted a picture of a man, who had done no

Dorchester Assizes took two weeks, and the jury were out for an hour. When the jury foreman appeared, he pronounced the word 'Guilty'. Kate took this calmly but became hysterical when, moments later, Mr Justice MacKinnon donned the black cap and solemnly announced that she would die upon the scaffold at Exeter jail. In a state of collapse, the frightened prisoner was led by prison warders into the condemned cells beneath the court.

An appeal was lodged and the defence introduced testimony from a professor in London who was an expert on the effects of arsenic. Unfortunately, it was evidence that fell on deaf ears. Lord Chief Justice, Lord Hewart, said: 'This court sets its face like flint against attempts to call evidence which could have been made available at the trial. Moreover, in this case, it is clear that there has been no mistake. The court will not listen to the opinion of scientific

Above: *The local papers gave full coverage to the trial of a murderess. It was unusual to have a woman accused of this crime, and the fact that a mother of five children was sentenced to death caused a horrified reaction throughout the country.*

gentlemen bringing their minds on evidence that they have not heard.' But even though the appeal was dismissed, the public conscience had been aroused by the proceedings. Questions were raised in parliament, and there was a public call for a re–trial. There were press articles about the fate of her children, and of how Kate, in her condemned cell at Exeter jail, had turned to God. Her repeated assertions of her innocence were also widely reported. So vociferous was she in protesting against the wrongful judgement that a leading member of the campaign against the death penalty pledged £50,000 in the poor woman's defence.

DON'T LET THEM KILL ME

Kate was learning to read and write and composed a moving, if simple letter to King Edward VIII in which she stated: 'Mighty King. Have pity on your lowly afflicted subject. Don't let them kill me on Wednesday. From the brink of the cold, dark grave, I, a poor helpless woman, ask you not to let them kill me. I am innocent.' This sad appeal brought no personal response from the king. Did His Majesty even see the letter?

At 8am on 15 July, 1936, Killarney Kate saw dawn come up for the last time. She was led to the scaffold by two warders and the condemned woman listened as a chaplain read the service for the dead. Five minutes later she was pronounced dead.

Was she guilty? The question has echoed down the years. There was no motive to drive the lover, Moss alias Parsons, to murder Fred and as the poison was apparently administered over a long period, no time for the new acquaintance Mrs Ostler to have been the culprit. Criminal historians have looked back time and again on the case of Charlotte McHugh, the girl known to soldiers as 'Killarney Kate'. Charles Skipple, a criminologist in the United States, who specialises in studying doubtful verdicts, said: 'I think she did it. Her's was the classic defence that echoes in jails around the world. "I'm innocent." And yet she couldn't prove that innocence while the jury obviously believed the proof of the guilt. It's the way of the world, the system we live by. Imperfect, of course, but all we have and all we shall probably ever have.'

Above: *The grim and unpitying features of Lord Chief Justice Lord Hewart who turned down Kate's appeal. He announced that the court 'set its face like flint' against new evidence.*

Right: *J.D.Casswell, the defence barrister who fought for Kate's innocence and her life.*

MAD
MURDERERS

JOHN DUFFY
The Railway Rapist

John Duffy used railway timetables to plot his escapes from the scenes of his beastly crimes. Finally it was his frightened wife who lead the police to the elusive rapist-killer, the man whose laser beam eyes mesmerised his terrified victims.

Number One Court, Old Bailey, London. Within these walls have stood some of the most wicked men and women in history. The courtroom, its atmosphere heavy with the full majesty of British law, has been silent witness to the infamous, the gruesome, the chilling, the unbelievable and the shameful. In 1988, yet another villainous soul was brought to justice. He stood before Mr Anthony Hooper, prosecuting Queen's Counsel. The accused was a rapist and a murderer called John Duffy. Thanks to Mr Hooper's eloquence and mastery of courtroom drama, Duffy earned the sobriquet 'the Killer with Laser Beam Eyes'.

That was how Mr Hooper, in his opening arguements at the trial of John Duffy, described the former altar boy. Duffy, who was thirty years old at the time of the trial, had been in custody since November 1986, trapped by his own insatiable thirst for rape and murder. He was suspected of at least three gruesome slayings, and the police attributed two more to him. He was the very worst type of sex criminal – insatiable, ruthless, and absolutely without remorse. After he received a sentence of life imprisonment with the recommendation from judge Mr Justice Farquaharson that the prisoner serve a minimum of forty years, the policeman who trapped him, Deputy Superintendent John Hurst of Surrey CID, said: 'He is a cold-blooded, calculating killer with a razor-sharp mind. In my twenty-two years experience battling crime, I have never come across a man so calculating and cunning. He is very intelligent and alert. He gave me the impression of being able to react to any type of situation in which he found himself. He is purely evil.'

But there will never be total satisfaction for Mr Hurst who believes that, on several of the rapes Duffy committed he was with a partner. That partner has never been found and, while police have a strong suspicion as to his identity, he is still out on the streets.

John Duffy used London's railway network to travel in search of his rape victims. One of six children born to Irish Catholic parents in Eire, he came to Britain as a child and worked at various jobs after leaving school. He married, in 1980, a plump, stocky woman called Margaret Mitchell but the marriage was not a happy one. In fact, his violence towards her helped give the police a clue to his identity as a rapist. He lived in a flat with Margaret in Barlow Road, Kilburn, where the wife who had thought he was a kind-natured, quiet fellow, watched him change into a brooding, silent monster. He would look at her with those eyes... the eyes that burned

Opposite: *John Duffy whose dislike of women drove him to rape, then murder.*

Above: *Maartje Tamboezer who was only fifteen when Duffy killed her.*

into people, instilling fear. The disillusioned Margaret testified at his trial: 'The nice man I married turned into a raving monster with scary, scary eyes. He taunted me that he liked rape. He said it was the natural thing for a man to do.'

Duffy, sensitive about his small stature (he was only five foot four inches), bolstered his confidence with lessons in karate and the martial arts. At a centre near his home, he spent three nights a week building up his muscles and perfecting his skill at strangle holds. He would spend hours of his spare time poring over books that idealized the Nazis and he paid partic-

'HE STARTED TO HAVE KINKY NEEDS IN SEX. HE WANTED TO TIE ME UP BEFORE WE MADE LOVE. HE WANTED SEX EVERY NIGHT AND WE USED TO FIGHT.'

Below: *Police interview commuters at train stations during the search for the 'Railway Rapist'.*

Rail. He was fascinated by the rail network both in and around London, and plotted rail routes he could use to travel to and escape from the locations of his crimes. His wife said: 'The first couple of years were not too bad but, when we tried to have a child and he found out he had a low sperm count, things changed. He started to have kinky needs in sex. He wanted to tie me up before we made love. He wanted sex every night and we used to fight. I used to lie there and let him get on with it. He used the cord from my dressing gown and only enjoyed it if I kept struggling. If I didn't move or protest, the interest was gone. The more I

ular attention when he studied 'The Anarchist's Cookbook', a terrorists' reference book published in the Sixties that taught how to maim and kill. Duffy learnt from this book the importance of planning an escape route from the scene of any crime and because of this lesson, Duffy managed to evade the police, despite his numerous crimes committed over a long period of time.

For the first two years of his marriage Duffy worked as a carpenter for British

Opposite, above: *Squads of policemen looked for clues in wasteland around rail tracks after Maartje's death.*

Opposite, below: *An artist's impression of the criminal based on rape victims' descriptions.*

protested the more he got aroused.' Margaret, who divorced him in 1986, went on: 'Sometimes he got videos out that had blood all over them, all over the cover. He liked those horrific ones, you know, the real nasties.'

Psychiatrists said that Duffy began to hate women, forming in his mind the distorted impression that, somehow, they were to blame for his infertility. It was this hatred that drove him to make violent attacks on women.

THE RISK OF MEETING
HIS VICTIMS WAS TOO GREAT

Police say his first rape was committed in June, 1982, near Hampstead Heath and that Duffy was with his accomplice. A twenty-three-year-old woman was dragged into a derelict building, then she was bound and gagged. She was the first victim of twenty-seven attacks against women and police have linked these to Duffy, claiming that some of the crimes were carried out with his accomplice, some alone. When police investigated that first rape, they made the observation that her attacker probably escaped using the North London Line rail network. Thereafter, getaways by rail proved to be the attacker's hallmark.

In 1985, Duffy, perhaps no longer stimulated by rape, began to kill his victims. He was at Hendon Magistrates Court awaiting arraignment on a charge of assaulting his wife. While he was there he recognised, although she did not recognise him, a woman whom he had raped a few

HE HAD LEFT AN
UNUSUALLY SMALL-SIZE
FOOTPRINT NEXT TO THE
BODY... AND A LENGTH
OF SWEDISH-MADE
STRING AT THE SCENE.

months before. He realised then that he could not risk a possible meeting with his victims after his crimes, and understood, in his twisted mind, that all future victims would have to be silenced for ever.

Duffy often posed as a jogger while out looking for a victim. He donned a loose tracksuit and kept in his pocket a butterfly knife with a razor-sharp blade. To this he added his special 'rapist's kit' that would eventually be used as evidence against him. He carried a box of matches, a length of

Heath, the man whom police had dubbed the 'Railway Rapist'.

Twenty-seven days after his court appearance in Hendon, where he saw one of the girls he had raped, Duffy took a life. On 29 December 29, 1985, he accosted fair-haired Alison Day, nineteen, a girl described at his trial 'as a teenager with a heart of gold'. Alison was travelling on a train between Upminster and Hackney Wick but Duffy forced her off the train at Hackney. Holding a knife against her

Above: *The railway path where Maartje was killed.*

Opposite, above: *Maartje was riding this bicycle when Duffy molested her.*

Opposite, below: *A detective helps cordon off the area where Maartje met her death.*

twine or rag and a piece of wood. These were the tools he used in his role as killer.

He constructed a device known as a 'Spanish Windlass' employed by carpenters to hold glued joints together while they set. Duffy planned to use it as a means of murder, as a garrotte around the necks of the women he chose as victims.

When John Duffy committed the first murder, he was already in the police files. The police, during an exercise called Operation Hart, devised a computer list of all the known sex offenders in Britain and Duffy's name appeared here. And indeed, Operation Hart had been set in motion by Duffy when police set out to find the man responsible for the rape on Hampstead

Duffy, who revelled in using the most foul language on his victims while uttering terrible threats if the girl did comply with his wishes, pushed Alison into a rat-infested garage block, backing on to the filthy waters of the River Lea. There she was raped then garrotted with the Spanish Windlass made from a piece of alderberry wood. Then he attached a weight to her body and dumped it, like garbage into the Lea. She was not found for seventeen days, by which time any evidence of the criminal had decomposed. All police found that could be handed to the forensic laboratories were some clothing fibres from a tracksuit.

Scotland Yard were hesitant to link the crime into Operation Harts being run by

Supt. Hurst's team. The body had been found near a railway line but, the men from the Yard pointed out, the Railway Rapist had never killed before. However, both teams began to feel that the Railway Rapist and the killer were the same man when Dutch-born schoolgirl Maartje Tamboezer, fifteen, was killed.

Maartje was the daughter of a wealthy industrialist whose company had posted him to Britain for several years. She enjoyed the English, often remarking to her friends that she found them so friendly. Maartje was cycling down a footpath near the railway line by her home in West Horsley, Surrey, when Duffy pounced. She was dragged into a nearby copse, her hands were bound around her back and she was raped before Duffy used his Spanish windlass to kill her. Then, he set fire to the lower part of her body, hoping to destroy traces of his semen. But, unwittingly, he

left clues; he had broken a bone in her neck with a blow commonly used by martial arts students; he had left an unusually small-size footprint in the soft earth next to the body; and he left a length of Swedish-made string at the scene.

Next came another rape, this time of a fourteen-year-old girl whose life was spared by Duffy. She gave evidence at his trial, and sobbed uncontrollably, as she described the emotions of a girl who is confronted by a monster like Duffy. She said: 'I was at the train station and he had on a tracksuit with the hood pulled up. He put a knife at my throat and dragged me into woods. He said if I struggled or screamed he would slash my throat. He held me with his other arm so I could not move. He put his arm around me to make it look as if we were a couple from behind, but he still held the knife at my neck. I thought I was about to be killed.

'Before raping me he said: "You had better make it good." Afterwards he seemed pleased. But he did not give a damn about me. I was so frightened and in such a state of shock I did not know what

---

'BEFORE RAPING ME, HE SAID: "YOU HAD BETTER MAKE IT GOOD".'

Below: *Detective Chief Superintendent Vincent McFadden led the hunt for the vicious rapist-killer.*

---

was happening. I thought he was going to slash my throat, or something.'

In May, there was a murder with which Duffy was charged during his trial at the Old Bailey, but on the direction of Justice Farquaharson, he was acquitted of this crime for lack of evidence.

The killing for which he was acquitted was one which attracted a great deal of publicity in Britain. Anne Lock was a vivacious, happy twenty-nine-year-old newly-wed, who worked as a secretary with London Weekend Television. She was murdered just weeks after returning from her honeymoon in the Seychelles in May, 1986. Led down a dark path beside the railway line at Brookmans Park, Hertfordshire, she was bound up, with a stocking pushed into her mouth, the other one wrapped around her throat. Her body was not found until three months after her death, by which time it was badly decomposed.

Six days before the body of Mrs Lock was discovered police interviewed John Duffy. He was one of a group code-named 'Z Men' by police because his blood

matched that found on the body of Maartje Tamboezer. In a large scale search detectives from London, Surrey and Hertfordshire had combined to draw up a list of five thousand suspects taken from the Operation Hart master list of sex and assault criminals. The five thousand men were then investigated by a special team, using computers, that cross-referenced names with indexes detailing descriptions, ages and the methods of attack. Professor David Canter, a leading psychologist from the University of Surrey, helped the police build up a psychological profile of their suspect and Canter predicted correctly the area of London where the killer-rapist lived. There was a special emphasis on any links to railway lines. After all the data was fed into the computers, 1,999 men whose profiles fitted all the categories were given a number and were asked to be interviewed by police officers. Duffy's number came out at 1505 and he was duly seen by officers. If he had never beaten his wife, John Duffy would never have been in the computer system.

This is when the supreme skill at deception employed by Duffy came to the fore. He made up a plausible alibi for the night of the Alison Day attack and managed to convince the officers that he was not a permanent acne sufferer. Several of the rape victims had pointed out that their attacker was badly afflicted with the ailment but Duffy explained that he broke out in spots during moments of high stress only. Police were not entirely happy with his answers, but there was no hard evidence to link him with the attacks. And he refused to give a blood sample, saying he wanted to see a lawyer first. As police marked him down as a 'possible' for re-interviewing, Duffy went to a friend with whom he practised karate and paid him to slash him across the chest with a knife. Then Duffy checked himself into a Middlesex mental hospital, claiming he had been mugged and had lost his memory as a result. This was his last desperate ploy as the police net slowly but surely closed in on him.

In October 1986, while the police worked their way through the rest of the suspects on the list, Duffy checked himself out of the mental hospital to follow his dreadful urge for sexual violence. He picked on another fourteen-year-old

Above: *A murder investigation demands laborious care in the search for clues. Here, officers check thousands of rail tickets looking for a fingerprint to lead them to the 'Railway Rapist'.*

DUFFY CHECKED OUT OF THE MENTAL HOSPITAL TO FOLLOW HIS DREADFUL URGE FOR SEXUAL VIOLENCE.

Above: *Professor David Cantor, of the University of Surrey, was called in by the police to build up a computor-enhanced, psychological profile of the killer.*

HE DEBATED WHETHER TO KILL HER BUT RELENTED AND DECIDED SHE COULD LIVE.

schoolgirl. He blindfolded her, tied her against a tree and raped her. The blindfold slipped as Duffy was attacking the girl and he debated whether to kill her but relented and decided she could live.

THE COMPUTER CAME UP WITH A SINGLE NAME

By this time the police computers were taking over from human guesswork. A rape at Copthall Park, North London, the previous year, was found to have striking similarities to the rape-murder of the Dutch teenager Maartje Tamboezer. Details of that attack and everything else about the offenders – blood type, age, height, weight and methods of attack – were fed into the computer and the machine came up with a single name: Duffy. Professor Canter, who pioneered the system known as Pyschological Offender Profiling, or POP, explained: 'I used a computer programme which I had once used to help a biscuit manufacturer research the popularity of new recipes. A criminal leaves evidence of

his personality through his actions in relation to a crime. Any person's behaviour exhibits characteristics unique to that person, as well as patterns and consistencies which are typical of the sub-group to which he or she belongs.

'To take a simple example, crimes typical of people out of work are more likely to be committed during normal working hours than those typical of people who have jobs. We do not infer a meaning from any one particular clue, however, and that is the way we would differ from Sherlock Holmes. We look for a whole system of patterns. For instance, it is remarkably difficult for people to hide and mask certain aspects of their sexual behaviour, which are indicative of the sort of person they are. There are a great variety of rapes. We look at how the attacker approaches the victim, what goes on in the attack and what happens afterwards. From all the factors taken together we build up the whole picture.'

For two weeks, detectives, under the orders of John Hurst, mounted a massive surveillance operation on Duffy. He was followed literally everywhere and was arrested as he went out one night dressed in his jogging suit, complete with his dreadful 'rape kit' in his pocket.

HIS PERVERTED AMBITION WAS TO BE FAMOUS

Under interrogation he was as cold as ice. One lawmen in on the interviews said: 'He would admit to nothing, just stare at you with those eyes that never blinked. They were like big, black whirlpools in which you could see nothing – no soul, no emotions, no feelings. I imagined my own wife and cringed with pity that those poor women saw those evil eyes as their last image on this earth. He would say nothing, but occasionally, when he knew it looked bad for him, he would murmur: "What can they give me then, eh? Thirty years? No problem. I can do thirty. No trouble?"'

A police search of his flat uncovered clothes that he wore in the attack on Maartje. Forensic experts matched fibres on it with the clothes that she wore on the day she died. And they also found a ball of the Swedish string that he had left alongside the girl's body, together with the four–and-a-half size shoes that he had worn for the attack. They, too, matched the undersized footprint at the scene. Other items taken away included gory videos, 'The Anarchist's Cookbook' terror manual, pornographic magazines, knives and an exercise machine that Duffy used to build up his biceps for the terror locks he used on his victims.

Duffy said nothing during his trial, his eyes remaining unblinking at the judge as the appalling litany of crime was read out. In the end he was found Guilty on two rape charges and two murders.

As he stood to be sentenced, on 26 February, 1988, with the recommendation that he serve forty years in jail, he turned and glared at policeman John Hurst. It was the stare that seemed to say: 'Don't worry – forty years? No trouble.'

But Duffy was hurting inside, not for the people he killed, not for the lives he shattered and the families he tore apart with grief; his own ego was shattered because he had not received more sensational press coverage. While on remand in prison, he

> I CRINGED WITH PITY THAT THOSE POOR WOMEN SAW THOSE EVIL EYES AS THEIR LAST IMAGE ON EARTH.

Below: *John Duffy at the time of his arrest. In court, he was nicknamed 'the killer with laser beam eyes'.*

had boasted to fellow inmates of joining the ranks of the truly notorious such as the Yorkshire Ripper, the Black Panther and Moors Murderer Ian Brady. He was resentful because the trial of Kenneth Erskine, the demented Stockwell Strangler who killed seven elderly people as they slept, started the same day as his, so deflecting some of the spotlight from John Duffy. A detective said after Duffy was sentenced: 'Perhaps that illusion that he is not truly evil – which he is – is the best punishment for him. In Duffy's perverted mind this was when he would join the ranks of the most notorious criminals in Britain. He wanted star status in the gallery of rogues. He was very, very bitter about the Erskine case.'

The hunt had cost £3 million and involved thousands of man hours. But now, at least for the next forty years, women are safe from one of the most infamous rapist-killers of modern times – the Killer with Laser Beam Eyes.

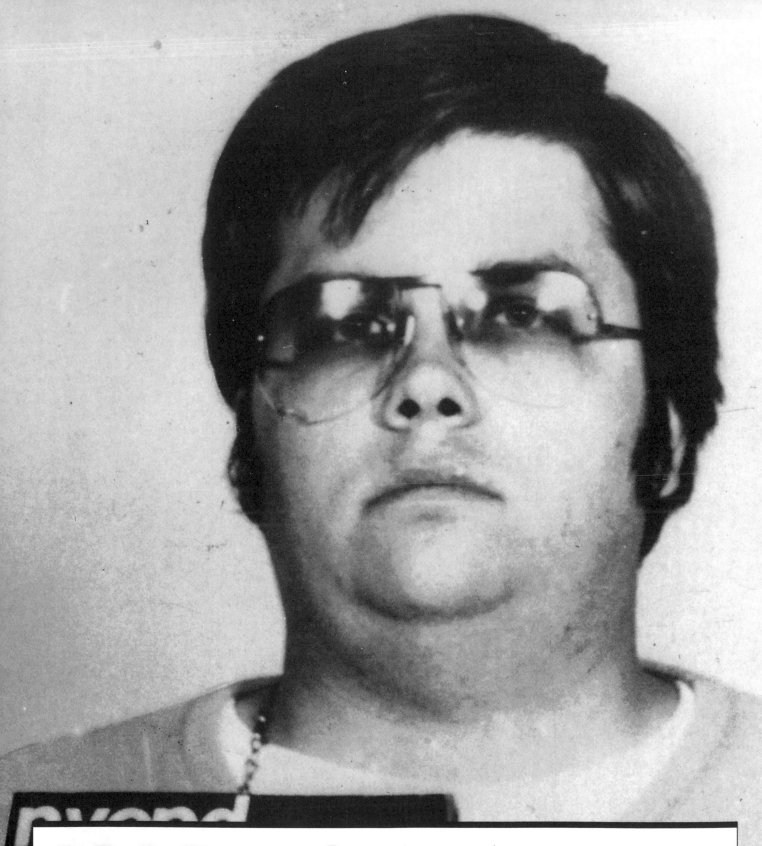

MARK CHAPMAN
D ath of a Dreamer

Mark Chapman was obsessive. His life was dominated by religious fantasies and a wierd idealism. He stalked and shot John Lennon simply because the musician no longer fulfilled his idea of goodness.

During the Seventies, the famous and adored John Lennon, Beatle, was living almost as a hermit in New York's gracious Dakota apartment building, facing the city's Central Park. Although he liked the freewheeling, exciting, easy-going nature of New York, he was increasingly paranoid about his own privacy and his own security. He had received his first death threat in 1964 when, as one of the four lads in the world's first supergroup, a note had been handed to him at a concert in France informing him that he was to die at 9 o'clock that night. That threatened execution, like several others which followed, failed to materialise. However, he was aware of his vulnerability and preferred to spend his days safe in his queen-sized bed with Yoko Ono and cocooned against the dangerous world and a greedy public outside.

Yet 6,000 miles and four time zones away lived a man whose desire to kill John Lennon had become a consuming, overwhelming passion. Mark Chapman had been an intense fan of Lennon's since the star's days with the Fab Four. Chapman loved the philosophy of the songs, loved the way Lennon became an emissary for peace and love. But somewhere within Chapman the spark of love was extinguished and instead there flickered the flames of jealousy and hatred. In order to understand what turned Mark David Chapman into the future killer of John Lennon, it is crucial to know something of his childhood and his interests.

He was born to David and Diane Chapman in Atlanta, capital of America's Deep South, in October 1955. His father was a middle-management bank employee, a former air-force sergeant, his mother a housewife who assisted in local charity groups. There was nothing in his early life that was not shared by millions of teenagers the world over – the usual highs and lows over love affairs, a little dabbling in pot, a few beers when he was under age. At fourteen, he ran away for a week and at fifteen he was a 'Jesus freak' with long hair, tie-dyed shirts, a large cross hanging around his neck, and a Bible always tucked under one arm. Always highly-strung, impressionable and always intensely eager to prove his worth, he switched from one fad to another – including drugs. He 'tripped' on LSD and liked to drift off to sleep in a bedroom cloudy with the fumes of marijuana smoke.

'THE LORD SPOKE TO ME'

When he was sixteen, he finished with marijuana and claims he had an 'intense religious experience, far greater than anything that I had ever experienced, before, whereby the Lord spoke to me and made me realise that I had to show the good person within.' Chapman became

Above: *The respect and admiration that John Lennon inspired is revealed in the mountain of tributes that rose on the pavement outside his home after he was shot.*

Opposite: *Mark Chapman, the man who killed John Lennon.*

'THE LORD SPOKE TO ME AND MADE ME REALISE THAT I HAD TO SHOW THE GOOD PERSON WITHIN.'

assistant director of a summer camp for the local YMCA. Tony Adams, his boss at the local branch, recalled: 'He had real leadership qualities. Mark was a very caring person. Hate was not even in his vocabulary. He said he had experimented with drugs when he was younger but he felt that the Lord had touched him and that his life had been turned around. I think his years working summers here really were magical for him.' Perhaps it was his last happy time.

*Below: **With his head hidden, and wearing a bulletproof vest, Mark Chapman was flanked by lawmen when he appeared in a New York court to answer a charge of murder.***

He was remembered as a 'Pied Piper' among the children, telling them numerous stories and always keeping and holding their attention. But in 1974 he read the book that was to change his life. Someone, it is not known who, gave him 'The Catcher in the Rye' by J.D. Salinger. This novel of disaffected youth, with its central character of Holden Caulfield alone against a cruel and hostile world, touched a deep, raw nerve within Chapman. He identified with Caulfield. His favourite passage from the book, which he kept quoting to anybody who would listen to him, went: 'I keep picturing all these little kids playing some game in this big field of rye. Thousands of little kids, and nobody's around, nobody big, I mean, except me.' The book had become an anthem, a symbol for disillusioned teenagers the world over, but none took it more to heart, or distorted its meaning more, than Mark Chapman.

Around this time there was a second influence in his mixed-up life – rock music. Tod Rundgren, Jimi Hendrix and Bob Dylan were among his favourites. But the Beatles were his all-time top group and his favourite solo singer was John Lennon. It was not just Lennon's music that he adored; he loved his philosophy, his outspokenness on issues like peace and love and fairness. He even played a guitar and tried to imitate him, but he knew he could never attain his 'genius'. Instead, Chapman concentrated on taking a college degree, hopeful that he could get a full-time paid position with the YMCA at the end of the course. In 1975, after taking a college course, he left for Beirut for a short assignment with the youth organization. It was short lived, due to the civil war which started in the Lebanon,

Afterwards he went to Fort Chaffee, Arkansas, a YMCA resettlement camp for Vietnamese refugees. Here he was a resounding success with the Asian immigrants and earned the undying gratitude and praise of the people he worked for. He had also found personal fulfillment with a girl called Jessica Blankenship whom he adored. But she was to claim that soon after he left Fort Chaffee in December 1975, his mood changed. He began to talk with her about death, about how he believed all life was about dying, that the history of man was the history of war. Now in the grip of continual depressions, he began to talk repeatedly about committing suicide.

THE ANGRY AND OVERWEIGHT GUARD

Jessica had persuaded him to enroll in a strict community college to study for a diploma in the humanities. He needed a degree if he was ever to realise his dream of becoming a YMCA director, but he dropped out after just one term. Jessica left him shortly afterwards. He spent the summer of 1976 at a YMCA camp again but quit in the autumn and became a security guard and, a result, an excellent shot with a gun. The security staff for the Atlanta Area Technical School, where he was hoping to be employed, were expected to score at least sixty on a pistol firing test. Chapman scored an amazing eighty-eight. But he was overweight, embarassed by his appearance and, so, growing angrier with the world day by day.

> THE BEATLES WERE HIS ALL-TIME TOP GROUP AND HIS FAVOURITE SOLO SINGER WAS JOHN LENNON.

In 1977, after his parent's marriage split up, he flew to Honolulu, Hawaii.. Hiring a car, he drove to a beauty spot overlooking the Pacific, attached a piece of hosepipe to the exhaust and fed it into the car interior. He was rescued by a passer-by who knocked on the window. Chapman had been in the car for fifteen minutes and wondered why he was not dead. A check on the hosepipe outside showed that the heat of the pipe had burned a hole in it. He was angry that his attempt had been thwarted. He went into hospital for a lengthy period of psychiatric counselling. His mother flew to Hawaii to be near him, but even her presence was unable to lift his spirits; he was aggrieved that with a suicide attempt on his record, he would never attain a decent job with the YMCA.

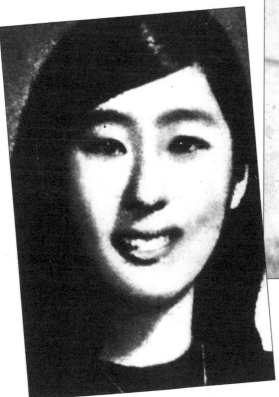

In 1978, with money he had saved, combined with a loan from his mother, he took off on a world tour, taking in Tokyo, Seoul, Singapore, Katmandu, Delhi, Israel, Paris and London. On his return to Honolulu, he worked as a hospital housekeeper before striking up a serious relationship with travel agent Gloria Abe, the Japanese-American woman who had sold him his world ticket. His need for companionship and understanding was crucial, even though Gloria's friends found

Above, left: *Gloria Abe Chapman, wife of the deranged killer.*

Above, right: *The boyish Chapman in a photo taken a few months before he committed his horrible crime.*

him 'weird and possessive'. He married her in June 1979 – just eighteen months before he would turn to murder.

As the marriage came under increasing strain with ever-more erratic behaviour from Chapman – he spent thousands of dollars he could ill afford on fine works of art – he began to talk darkly of John Lennon's 'sellout'. Gloria heard him fixate on the singer in turgid monologues which blamed his wealth and position for making him 'abandon' his ideals. On 10 September, 1980, Chapman wrote a letter to Lynda Irish, a Honolulu schoolteacher he had befriended. On it he had drawn a picture of the sun, moon and stars above a sketch of an Hawaiian beauty spot. He wrote: 'I'm going nuts.' He signed the letter 'The Catcher in the Rye'. On 23

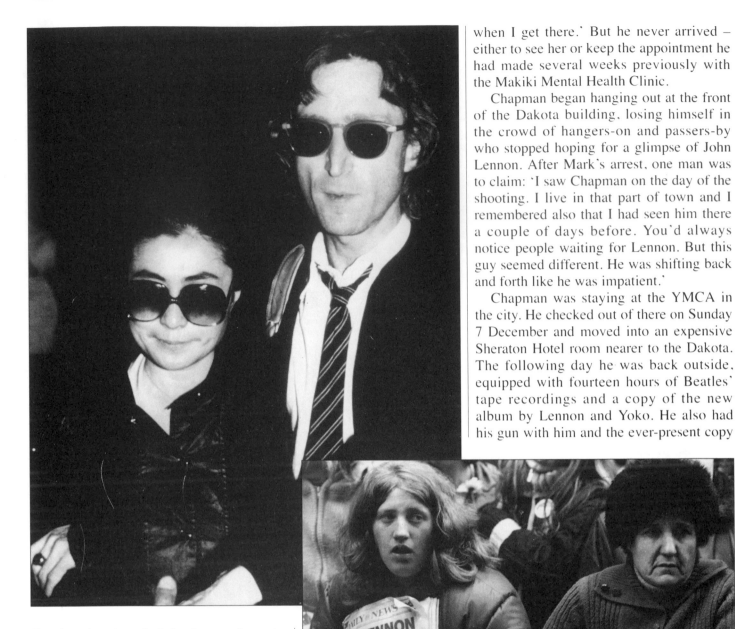

when I get there.' But he never arrived – either to see her or keep the appointment he had made several weeks previously with the Makiki Mental Health Clinic.

Chapman began hanging out at the front of the Dakota building, losing himself in the crowd of hangers-on and passers-by who stopped hoping for a glimpse of John Lennon. After Mark's arrest, one man was to claim: 'I saw Chapman on the day of the shooting. I live in that part of town and I remembered also that I had seen him there a couple of days before. You'd always notice people waiting for Lennon. But this guy seemed different. He was shifting back and forth like he was impatient.'

Chapman was staying at the YMCA in the city. He checked out of there on Sunday 7 December and moved into an expensive Sheraton Hotel room nearer to the Dakota. The following day he was back outside, equipped with fourteen hours of Beatles' tape recordings and a copy of the new album by Lennon and Yoko. He also had his gun with him and the ever-present copy

October, he signed 'John Lennon' on the worksheet at his workplace and four days later purchased a .38 snub nosed revolver.

A few days later, Mark Chapman was in New York, driven by demons whose strength only he fully comprehended. He returned to his birthplace of Atlanta shortly afterwards, telling a local minister that he had been wrestling with the 'good and evil within' but refusing to elaborate. He looked up his old girlfriend Jessica – she would later say that he looked 'disturbed'.

Chapman returned to New York, further depressed when a visit to the YMCA where he had spent happy summers proved to him that he had been virtually forgotten. But his spirits lifted and he telephoned Gloria with news of another religious revelation. 'I've won a great victory,' he said breathlessly. 'I'm coming home. I'll tell you about it

Above, left: *John Lennon with his wife, Yoko Ono, in New York two months before his murder.*

Above, right: *A mother and daughter were among mourners gathered at the death site.*

of 'The Catcher in the Rye'. In a huddle with other fans, he struck up a conversation with a young blonde fan who was always there. They had lunch together in a restaurant opposite the entrance and returned in the late afternoon, to be joined by another fan called Paul Goresh, an amateur photographer. A few minutes later, at 4.30pm, Lennon stepped outside, accompanied by Yoko. As he walked towards a waiting limousine Chapman stepped forward with a copy of his Double Fantasy LP in his hand. 'Could I have your autograph, please,' he said almost breathlessly. John paused briefly as Goresh snapped a picture. 'Did I have my hat on or off in the picture?' enquired Chapman. 'I wanted my hat off – they'll never believe this in Hawaii!'

'I JUST SHOT JOHN LENNON'

John Lennon returned again at 11.30pm and Mark Chapman was waiting for him in the shadows. 'Mr Lennon,' he cried out. Then as John turned to see who had spoken, the tormented Chapman assumed the combat stance and killed the musician with five shots. Yoko Ono cradled her husband's head in her arms as the doorman shouted to Chapman: 'Do you know what you just did?' 'I just shot John Lennon,' he calmly replied. Chapman was arrested sitting outside the Dakota building as Lennon was rushed to the Rossevelt Hospital. He was semi-conscious and still-alive, but he had already lost massive amounts of blood. 'It wasn't possible to resuscitate him by any means,' said Dr Stephen Lynn, the hospital's director of emergency services. 'He had lost three to four quarts of blood from the gun wounds, about eighty per cent of his blood volume. The word of his death was broken to Yoko as gently as possible.'

Word spread through the New York night like wildfire. Within one hour one thousand people were outside the Dakota and they stood with candles in a vigil to his memory. The crowd sang Lennon's songs as the tickertapes in countless newspaper offices all over the world clattered out the details of his appalling murder. President Jimmy Carter spoke of the irony that 'Lennon died by violence though he had long campaigned for peace' and President-elect Ronald Reagan called it 'a great tragedy'. The world was saddened.

Chapman was charged with murder and ordered, initially, to undergo thirty days of psychiatric testing. He was first sent, under heavy guard, to a cell at the city's famous Bellvue Hospital where he was placed under a twenty-four-hour suicide watch. But as fears of a revenge killing grew, he was moved to Rikers Island, the city's maximum security jail where his safety could be better guarded. His second

attorney – his first quit as the groundswell of public opinion grew more menacing towards Chapman by the day – announced that at his trial the accused would plead Not Guilty by reason of insanity.

When it came to his court hearing in August 1981 Jonathan Marks, his attorney, argued against the prosecution case that Chapman had stalked Lennon before murdering him and had shown no regret. He painted him as a deeply disturbed young man, saying:'All the reports came to the conclusion that he is not a sane man. It was not a sane crime. It was a monstrously irrational killing.' But Chapman himself pleaded Guilty to murder. However, his sanity was definitely in question; whenhe was given time in court to say a few words, he merely quoted a passage from 'The Catcher in the Rye', the book that had become his own gospel.

After he was sentenced to twenty years to life in prison, psychiatrists flocked to America's daytime talk shows to try to explain exactly why Lennon died. Perhaps

'HE STARTED SIGNING HIS NAME AS LENNON. I THINK IT IS SAFE TO ASSUME THAT HE BELIEVED HE WAS JOHN LENNON.'

Below: *Mark Chapman at Fort Chaffee, Arkansas where he worked in a resettlement camp for Vietnamese refugees. He was well liked by the people in the camp.*

one of the most convincing theories about the motives of Mark Chapman came from Robert Marvit, an Hawaiian psychiatrist. He said: 'He started signing his name as Lennon. I think it is safe to assume that he believed he was John Lennon, or was turning into him. Chapman could have said to himself at the critical point: "My God, Lennon knows there are two of us. I have to reduce it to one." But in the complex package of emotions and hostility which was Mark David Chapman, I am not sure that we shall ever really know what drove him, just what made the ghost in the machine.' But there was no excuse.

'DEMONS' DROVE HIM TO MURDER

It was many years later that the deranged assassin of Lennon spoke for the first time of the 'demons' which drove him to murder – and of how he prays for forgiveness for the awful murder. In 1991 he granted an interview about the events that led up to the shooting, and the killing itself, and he recalled hearing evil whisperings in his head – 'Do it! Do it! Do it!' He claims that he practiced in his hotel room for three days before waiting for Lennon outside his New York apartment building.

'I prayed for demons to enter my body to give me the power to kill,' says Chapman from his cell at Attica Prison in New York State.

Since he was imprisoned, Chapman has received more death threats than any other prisoner in America. Raging Beatle fans

Above: *The murderer as a normal person, playing with a child, before his crazy shooting of John Lennon pushed him to the edge of society and turned him into an outsider.*

Above, top: *Japanese fans in Tokyo mourn the death of John Lennon.*

have never forgiven him for killing peace-loving Lennon, even his own father cannot forgive him and has never visited him in jail. However, Chapman says he begs forgiveness from God and the world.

He says: 'I became hurt. Enraged at what I perceived to be Lennon's phoniness. I read a photo essay. Put yourself where I was. I saw him on the roof of the luxurious, gabled Dakota building and I showed it to my wife, explaining all about my rage. He told us to imagine. He told us not to be greedy. And I had believed in him! I mean, I had the Beatles pictures on my walls! I believed in those things. They weren't doing them for money. From the time I was ten years old I was listening to all the idealism and truth of John Lennon and I was taking it to heart.

'When it came to the point when my own life was failing I tried to strike it down.' The demented Chapman said he invented 'little people' in his head that he talked with every day, asking them what he should do. It was those 'little people' that who had convinced him he had to murder the famous musician, John Lennon.

'They were appalled,' he said. 'They were shocked. They were still part of my conscience and when I didn't follow my conscience there was no longer any government inside of me. I was on my own. Alone in my apartment, I would strip naked and put on Beatles records and pray to Satan. I prayed for the demons to enter my body to give me the power to kill. I would scream and screech into a tape recorder: "John Lennon must die! John Lennon is a phony!"' The delerious chanting was accompanied by lurid black magic lyrics he taped over John's poignant song 'Strawberry Fields'.

Chapman says he wavered between God and the Devil for two months in 1980 before slipping out to a hardware store where he bought the .38 calibre pistol for £150 and this was the pistol he was to use to shoot John Lennon.

He says he wandered for days 'in a homicidal and suicidal cloud.'

'I prayed, and after struggling back and forth, I won a victory with God's help. I called my wife Gloria and said "your love has saved me. I have won a great victory. I'm coming home." But the demons returned. I went back in December.'

Chapman waited for three days and went to the Dakota building on 8 December with a copy of Lennon's new album 'Double Fantasy'. Chapman said: 'Lennon was very cordial to me. That's something I regret to this day. I handed him the album and he took the black retractable Bic pen and scratched on the album cover to get it going. He stood there trying to get the J going in John and he scratched it a couple of times and laughed. Then he signed 'John Lennon' and wrote 1980 underneath that. Then he handed the album to me and said: "Is this all you want?" His wife was in the car waiting. The door was open. And...I said: "No." I said: "Thanks John." I think of him saying that now: "Is that all you want?" And it seems like, maybe, he had a premonition of his death.

THE DEMONS' ORDERS

'And I was full of wonder that I had a signed album by John Lennon. So much so that I wanted to call the nearest cab and go home to my wife. I wanted to get out of there. But I didn't. I couldn't have gotten out of there. I was totally compelled.'

He returned later that night to complete his berserk quest.

'"Do it! Do it! Do it!" said my demons. And I did it. I took the combat stance, just as I had practiced in my hotel room. As he walked past I aimed right at his back and pulled the trigger five times. I remember him sprinting up the stairs, his body turning slowly, jerking forward. The doorman, Jose, I remember him shaking the gun out of my hand. He was crying. He was yelling at me: "Look what you've done! Get out of here. Get out of here." And I said: "Where would I go?"' When police arrived they found Chapman sitting on the pavement reading his beloved - and misinterpreted - 'The Catcher in the Rye'.

He will not be eligible for parole until the year 2000. Chapman says he is talking now because he feels remorse. He claims to have suffered nightmares that he is a visitor in Lennon's home. He said: 'I was talking to Yoko and his sons like a friend of the family. We were all very sad but they understood that I was very sorry for the killing. They understood because they knew that I really didn't mean to kill him. John Lennon was a seeker in the spiritual sense. He knew that a perfect world would never be but he said to just think about it. To have the power to imagine it in the first place is the power to bring us closer to it. The idea is not to hurt everything. The idea is to help everything. I regret that I was the author of this kind of hurt. Perhaps now I can be the author of something helpful.

'It is still very, very difficult to know who I am. There are many times when I just feel utter confusion and pain at being Mark David Chapman.'

'AS HE WALLKED PAST I AIMED RIGHT AT HIS BACK AND PULLED THE TRIGGER FIVE TIMES.'

Above: *John Lennon and Yoko Ono demonstrate their interpretation of love and peace. Their bizarre public appearance in bed was seen by the youth of the Sixties as a radical and significant statement of pacifism. It was this generation that mourned John's death most strongly.*

Left: *Police guard the floral tributes left by fans outside the Dakota building where John and Yoko lived.*

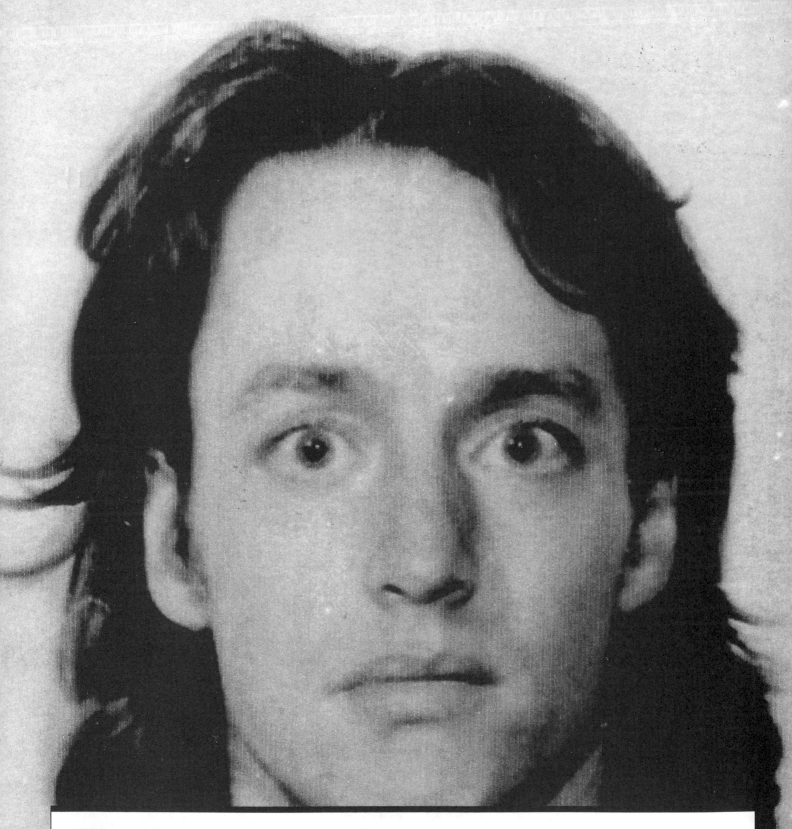

RALPH NAU
Love Among the Stars

After Lennon's death, stars began to pay thousands of dollars to protect themselves from 'celebrity stalkers'. Some fans may want only an autograph but madmen like Ralph Nau have robbed the stars of a most precious asset – peace of mind.

America's most deranged celebrity stalker will make his next bid for freedom soon – the same bid he has made every two months since 1989 – but it is a move that sends shivers through Hollywood. Some of America's biggest names fear Ralph Nau, a chilling, deranged killer who has made his life's work an obsessive quest for love among the stars.

He is one of a new brand of fiend bred by America in the latter half of the twentieth century: the tribe of loners and losers who fixate on rich and famous strangers... often loving their heroes to death.

Nau would have stayed a nameless face within America's penal and mental institutions if he had not chosen to prey on famous film stars. He leapt to notoriety in December 1989, when a bevy of celebrities – including Cher and Farrah Fawcett, both of whom had been his victims – blocked his release from a mental institution by revealing that he had bombarded them with letters from behind bars while making bizarre claims that singer Sheena Easton had bought his family farm, that Olivia Newton-John is a murderer, that Madonna is waiting to marry him.

The killing of starlet Rebecca Schaeffer in Hollywood occurred the same year that Cher and Farrah Fawcett stepped forward to complain about Nau and her murder proved their fears regarding Nau's potential release were not unfounded. Schaeffer, just twenty, was a bright, vivacious young girl who had become the obsession of warped loner Robert Bardo, a predator who wasted his life watching daytime soap operas and worthless late-night melodramas . He would later say 'She became my goddess... I worshipped her.' Bardo is serving a life sentence for her murder.

THE BEGINNINGS OF OBSESSION

Ralf Nau is another one of those lonely, lonely people – a man, a psychiatrist once said, who 'wants to assassinate the world'.

At school he was a loner, never able to find a girl to date, or to strike up close friendships with boys his own age. After he left at the age of sixteen, his brother Kerry claimed Ralph joined a club which advertised its services as 'a club to help mature single men find happiness with women.' 'Actually it was a club where one paid a subscription and, in return, received dirty letters through the post.

Ralph paid his money and got letters from 'Candy' that he treasured. He showed these to several people in his hometown of Antioch in Illinois. He was laying the groundwork for his obsession... that it was perfectly possible for people, who had never met, to love each other.

He started writing letters to showbiz stars when he moved to Hollywood in 1980. He began with Cher because he had had a schoolboy crush on her and to another woman named Maria. Ralph said that Maria was 'a sorceress – the magic lady who led me to things with Olivia Newton-John.' It was then that he knew he had to live in California.

OBSESSIVE LOVE, WEAPONS, DEATH, SUICIDE, RELIGION

He signed the first missives to Cher as 'Shawn Newson-John' and put the return address on the back as Xanadu. Initially, the letters were outpourings of love, but then veiled threats began to appear, hinting at what violence he would commit if his love was unrequited.

At home, in his solitary room, he penned more of the sick love letters, adding Sheena Easton, Farrah Fawcett and Madonna to his list. He turned his room into a shrine to Olivia Newton-John and named a dog Sam, after the love song of the same name that was one of her hits.

THESE POOR WRETCHES, BRANDED 'STALKERS' BY THE LEGAL AND MEDICAL WORLD, CAN FORM NO REAL OR WORTHWHILE RELATIONSHIPS.

IT WAS A CLUB WHERE ONE PAID A SUBSCRIPTION AND, IN RETURN, RECEIVED DIRTY LETTERS THROUGH THE POST.

HE WAS A MODEL EMPLOYEE. BUT AT NIGHT, AT HOME, HE CHANGED. IN HIS SOLITARY ROOM, HE PENNED MORE OF THE SICK LOVE LETTERS.

Opposite: *Ralph Nau revealed his incipient insanity in letters to celebrity women but proved his madness in the murder of his little step-brother.*

But then he had to kill the dog with an overdose of sleeping tablets because, in Ralph's twisted mind, Sam was keeping Olivia away from him.

Diana Ross became a victim. So did Connie Chung, one of America's top newscasters. But Olivia was the main target and he began signing his letters with his real name. Olivia hired a top security firm in Hollywood run by Gavin DeBecker, who though he followed Nau, did not report to the police. DeBecker said 'The criminal justice system is looking for something very clear to commit a man to prison or hospital, like the fact that he struck his mother or bought a gun and pointed it at someone. But here was a guy who went to work every day, who was doing no harm. A court would have laughed us out of the room. Hell, they'd say, who cares if he has a few obsessions about Olivia Newton-John? Who doesn't?'

For the next three years, at Olivia's request, DeBecker and his men monitored virtually every move that Ralph Nau made.

Nau saved his money up to see Sheena Easton and Olivia at concerts in Los Angeles. He travelled to the set of 'Mask' to catch a glimpse of Cher making the movie. And all around him were DeBecker's men, who were now on a twenty-four-hour-surveillance of their most dangerous suspect.

At one Newton-John concert Nau scrambled on to the stage but was hauled off by DeBecker's toughs. 'I knew the concert stopped after I ran away,' he wrote to her later, 'because I know you were only playing for me.' He hung around Cher's movie studio. He stalked Sheena Easton and Farrah Fawcett to their homes. He travelled across America in pursuit of the women who, he was convinced, loved him.

In 1983 the vet's business where he worked was sold and Nau, who neither smoked, drank nor dated, used his saving to fly to Australia to track down Olivia.

He spent a week sleeping in a hired car as he tried to get close to her ranch. Police believe that while he was there, he may have murdered a vagrant, although it was never proved and he was never charged.

Nau returned, dejected to America, and used the last of his savings on a jaunt to Scotland to see Sheena Easton who, he had read somewhere, had returned to her

Above: *Cher was Ralph's 'first love'. He never met her yet was convinced that he enjoyed a relationship with the beautiful and famous stranger.*

HE HAD TO KILL THE DOG WITH AN OVERDOSE OF SLEEPING TABLETS BECAUSE SAM WAS KEEPING OLIVIA AWAY FROM HIM.

homeland. He was turned back by customs officers who had been informed by DeBecker of the real reason for his visit.

Ralph Nau returned home to his father's farm where his family noted, with rising alarm, his ever-more crazy behaviour. He began taking three-hour-long showers with the family dog.

DeBecker rang Ralph's father, and warned him of his son's obsession with celebrities, for Ralph's letters were still pouring in. Delmar Nau contacted a lawyer who said there was little that could be done until Ralph actually harmed someone.

In January, 1984, he sold his beat-up car and with the last of his savings made a second pilgrimage to Australia, in a bid to 'reconcile once and for all' with Olivia. This time DeBecker knew Nau's plans and arranged for the superstar to be away from her ranch. His security people followed Nau every inch of the journey. Ralph wandered around the outback for a week on his own. He never saw Olivia.

Within months he was sitting in a jail on a murder charge. He had axed to death eight-year-old Denis Gerken, his mentally retarded stepbrother. Denis could neither read nor write, could not talk or even dress himself. He was a totally vulnerable child.

When Nau returned from Australia, his parent's marriage was over and his mother, Shirley, had married egg farmer Ken Gerken. Ralph was given a job on Ken's farm and, on a steamy August night, his madness finally overwhelmed him.

When he was being interrogated for the murder, Ralph Nau told the police: 'Olivia sends me messages all the time. She tells me how much she loves me and how much she wants me to be with her. She paid my way back to the United States.

'I think you might find Denny with a dog I buried. Yes, you might find him there...' Police found the little boy's body in a cornfield. There was no dog's corpse.

Psychiatrists at his trial said the boy was killed because he tried to change channels on the TV set as Ralph was watching one of his heroines, Nadia Comaneci, performing. At concerts and film sets and airports,

---

'I KNEW HE HAD DONE THE BOY. HE COULDN'T ADMIT TO IT DIRECTLY — TOLD US A STORY ABOUT FINDING HIM WITH A DOG. I GUESS THE POOR BOY WOKE UP AND WANTED TO SWITCH CHANNELS... RALPH JUST FLIPPED.'

Below: *Olivia Newton-John, the Australian singer whose life was made a misery by the unwanted attentions of Ralph Nau, a man she had never met. She hired a major security firm to protect herself from the man.*

burly security men had stopped Ralph getting close to his ladies and now, here was Denis, stopping him in his own home. The boy had to pay for it with his life.

Police said that on the night of 8 August, 1984, Ralph's mother put Denis to bed. She and her husband were watching TV in a family room at one end of the house while Denis was asleep in his room. Ralph was watching TV in the living room. Nadia Comaneci was on and he was spellbound.

THE STARING EYES OF A MADMAN

Around 10pm Ralph told the family that he had heard Denis crying, went to check on him, but then found that he was not there. While the family searched the house and nearby land Ralph hurriedly washed his clothes and cleaned his boots. Sherrifs arrived half-an-hour later and their only suspect was Ralph. 'He has strange, staring eyes,' said Lt Chester Iwan, of the Lake County Sherrif's Department. 'I had to interrogate him. I knew he had done the boy. He couldn't admit to it directly – told us a story about finding him with a dog. I guess the poor boy woke up and wanted to switch channels. Ralph's 'beloved' was on and he just flipped.'

At the Chester Mental Health Facility where he was sent initially, psychiatrists began to realize that Ralph Nau was seriously disturbed. He was confined for just six months before a court ruled that his confession was inadmissible, because he could not be regarded as sane or responsible for his actions. There followed five years of legal wrangling until he was confined, in 1989, to the Elgin Mental Health Centre in Illinois. But the legal system in the United States allows a mental patient the right to apply every sixty days for release from an institution. At every opportunity Ralph Nau applies for his freedom, but his requests are counteracted by the star victims of his letters.

'However, he will be out one day and there are people who may not have the money it takes to hire a DeBecker,' said one disillusioned lawman, who fought to get Ralph Nau sentenced to life imprisonment for the murder of the little boy.

JOE DOHERTY
IRA Hitman

He grew up in bitterness and with a strong sense that he was a victim. Joe Doherty took his revenge with evil acts of killing and maiming the innocent – all in the name of patriotism.

The murder of a Special Air Services officer in a grubby Belfast street in 1980 would, on the surface, have little connection with the 1986 bombing of Libya's deranged dictator Colonel Gaddafi in Tripoli. One was carried out by a psychopathic Irish Republican Army terrorist called Joe Doherty who dressed up his murderous outrage in the guise of freedom fighter. The other was carried out by trained pilots on the orders of Ronald Reagan, US president, as a warning to Ghaddafi to desist from his global sponsorship of terrorist causes.

Not until 1992, when the fugitive gunman Doherty was finally brought back in chains from America to serve a life sentence for his killing of Captain Herbert Richard Westmacott did the correlation between his murder and the Tripoli bombing raid become clear. For it was Mrs Thatcher, as much as any police officer, intelligence operative and FBI agent whose long arm stretched across the Atlantic to bring Doherty home from America – where he sought political sanctuary – to face justice. Doherty was 'payback' for Tripoli because Mrs Thatcher had allowed US warplanes to take off from British bases on their mission. She weathered a great deal of criticism at the time over the decision and made it plain to her American opposite numbers that, one day, a favour might have to be returned. That favour came in the form of thirty-seven-year-old Joseph Patrick Doherty, the killer that Mrs Thatcher would not let get away.

The story of Joseph Doherty – street-thug, rioter, ambusher, political assassin and propaganda pawn – is an odyssey from the breeding ground of hatred through to the highest levels of international intrigue and diplomacy. If he had chosen another path as a youngster, one away from the gun and the hard men who rule his ghetto area of West Belfast, he might now be a father with a secure job and a bright future. Instead, he will be almost a pensioner when he is finally released. The only value he has to the IRA now is to embellish the memories of 'the cause' when the stories are told around pub fires and in meeting halls where the Republican ethos is worshipped like a religion.

Before he became infamous, Joe Doherty was born into a system that preached and practised unfairness towards the Catholic minority in Northern Ireland. Artificial electoral boundaries, discrimination towards Catholics in schools, housing, jobs and civil rights and terror in the form of the police 'B Specials' combined to fuel the resurgence of the Republican movement that was dormant, if not dying, by the time Doherty was born in 1955. to a family that celebrated Irish rebel heroes in the uprising with Britain in the early part of the century that won the south its independence. Doherty says when he was five he felt the first stirrings of a grave injustice being committed in his country. He said: 'I remember going to school and being taught English instead of our national language. You take the history classes we went to. It

Below: *A priest kneels by the body of David Howe, killed when he inadvertently blundered into an IRA funeral procession.*

Opposite: *Joe Doherty, the IRA man who murdered in cold blood, then sought sanctuary in the United States by claiming he was a political refugee.*

The glamour of the gun soon lured Doherty into the clutches of the IRA, the illegal but best guerilla operation in the world. Involved with petty crime from the age of fourteen – offences like housebreaking and thieving – he joined the organization Na Fianna Eireann, the junior wing of the Provisional IRA. In these early days, with the burning resentment against British troops in his land growing inside him, he was a willing recruit. In the far-flung, remote regions of County Donegal and on the west coast of Ireland, he attended the indoctrination and training sessions that would give him both the spirit and the practical tools to become an effective IRA operative. In this role he became an intelligence scout for the IRA killers on the streets of Belfast; warning of the approach of a police or army patrol,

Above: *On the right, the then-Mayor of New York, David Dinkins, his political antennae keenly aware of the massive Irish-American vote in his city, woos the Irish murderer, Joe Doherty. Dinkins was not heard to give sympathy to Irish – or other – victims of Doherty's killing habits.*

Right: *The reality of the IRA's actions was seen yet again in London when nine soldiers and seven cavalry horses were blown apart by terrorist bombs in Hyde Park in 1982.*

THE GLAMOUR OF THE GUN SOON LURED DOHERTY INTO THE CLUTCHES OF THE IRA.

was mostly on the Tudors and royal heads, kings and queens of England. We were told nothing about our own country. When we took geography we were given the map of England, Scotland and Wales, Europe, the United States, but we were never given a map of our own country. So it was resented by a young person at my age that I couldn't learn where the hell I am living. I knew more about Birmingham and Manchester than I knew about my own city and the beautiful countryside that was around it.' Bitter words from one of the oppressed.

luring soldiers into ambushes and assisting in diversions when terrorists or arms had to be removed from an area rapidly.

He also became a member of the notorious knee-capping squads. These vigilantes were an important factor in IRA rule in the early days of the troubles – patrolling dances and drinking halls, dispensing rough and ready justice to those who they deemed were either drunkards, drug pushers or potential enemies of the IRA. Doherty would later claim that he was little more than a concerned citizen when he carried out these vigilante duties – but he had shown himself, to his IRA superiors, ruthless and efficient – two qualities which they prized very highly indeed.

PRISON LESSONS IN TERRORISM

Doherty's pathological loathing of the British continued to rise as army attempts to root out and contain terrorism spilled over into his own neighbourhood. He witnessed his family being pulled from their beds at midnight by soldiers and was continually quizzed by intelligence officers about his membership of the junior IRA. On 22 January 1972, a day after his seventeenth birthday, he found himself interned without trial at one of the several British camps. He claimed he was tortured in Girdwood camp. While human rights investigators have determined that some terrorists were subjected to cruel and inhuman treatement while in internment camps, not a shred of evidence exists to say that Doherty was mistreated, and certainly he never suffered the use of electric shock apparatus which he claimed was in common use in the camp.

Later he was interned on the prison ship Maidstone and in Long Kesh where IRA cell leaders marked him down as a zealot who would soon be ready for active service in the field – namely, killing people. Inside the camps was a well-organized IRA network that kept prisoners indoctrinated with the lectures on the Republican movement and weapons they would be using on their release. Doherty joined the adult arm of the IRA upon his release, swearing his allegiance to the terrorists in the traditional way; placing his hand upon a Bible, a .45 revolver and the Irish tricolour, he thus became a volunteer in C Company, 3rd Battalion of the Irish Republican Army. During the early Seventies, outfits like Doherty's caused tremendous civilian loss of life with indiscriminate bombings, sectarian murders and numerous shootings of security and police personnel, but he was never charged with any specific murders, although security personnel had plenty of suspicion. The only charge they nailed him on came in 1973 when he served three months for being caught in possession of a starting pistol; a tool he used to intimidate neighbourhood youths.

NOT A SHRED OF EVIDENCE EXISTS TO SAY THAT DOHERTY WAS MISTREATED, AND CERTAINLY NEVER SUFFERED THE USE OF ELECTRIC SHOCK APPARATUS.

Below: *Another view of the bombing in Hyde Park, where men died like animals and animals died like men.*

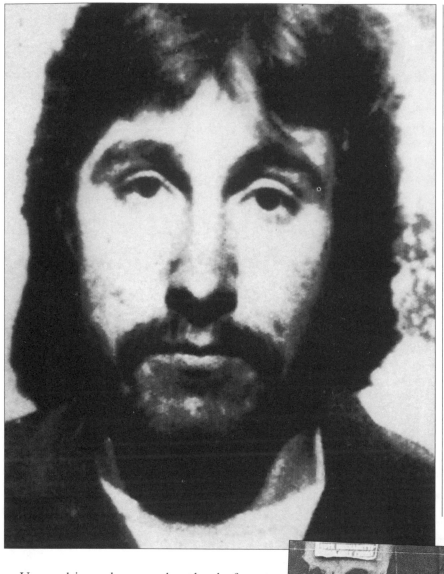

He was released shortly before Christmas 1979 – the last Christmas he would know as a free man. When he was neither a fugitive on the run, or a man held behind bars.

MASTERING A LETHAL WEAPON

After he walked free again Joe Doherty was singled out for special training with the M60 heavy machine gun, a fearsome weapon capable of cutting a man in two with a split-second burst. He later denied ever being trained in the handling of these, but an IRA informer told his Special Branch handlers in Ulster that Doherty was so familiar with every nut and rivet of the weapon, that he could break it down and then re-assemble it wearing a blindfold. This gun, one of a batch stolen from an armoury in America, was to play a major part in his designated IRA 'mission' the following year.

His unit was assigned to kill policemen and soldiers by using the high-powered weaponry acquired from America. Again, Doherty and his cohorts were not charged in this period with any offences and, naturally, he has been at pains to play down any of his activities. The incident which would land him with a life sentence for

Upon his release, shortly before Christmas of that year, he was told to report for active duty to the 3rd Battalion. He was ordered to stay 'on the run', avoiding the homes of friends and family in favour of unknown IRA sympathisers, because the IRA had plans for him. In February 1974 he removed eighty pounds of gelignite from one of the organization's dumps and moved it by car to another unit across town. Unfortunately for him an army spot check found him and his portable, unprimed bomb and both were taken into custody. He was given a three-year sentence, compounded shortly afterwards with another eighteen months after a futile prison escape attempt ended in abject failure. In jail he rose in the IRA ranks and was an officer in charge of other men. His masters on the other side of the wire bided their time for Joe Doherty, because they were nurturing big plans.

murder came towards the middle of 1980. His IRA masters chose to mount an attack on a British army patrol – any patrol, it did not matter which – that passed by a house that his unit would take over on the Antrim Road .Doherty knew that military vehicles from the Girdwood base passed by all the time; there was bound to be a rich target. Almost certainly 'blooded' in IRA actions by this time, Doherty and his gang were chosen for the operation on the direct instructions of the leader of the Belfast Brigade of the terror organisation.

Doherty personally planned the operation, ordering that the M60 heavy machine gun was to be fired from one window while the rifles and revolvers used

by the gang were positioned at another. He ordered his gang to hijack a vehicle the evening before the ambush in order to transport themselves and their weapons to the scene. He gave orders for the family in a house overlooking the spot where they intended to spring the trap to be held hostage. Both were standard IRA procedures for this kind of assassination. But unknown to Doherty and his allies the eyes of army intelligence were already upon them. Members of the 14th Intelligence Company had, through an IRA informer, learned of the operation planned for 2 May, 1980. A unit of the Special Air Services was given careful instruction to tackle them on the day.

Above, right: *Police check vehicles for IRA car bombs after the terrorist attack on military bandsmen in Deal in Kent, 1989.*

Above, left: *The army on full alert during an IRA funeral in Belfast.*

Opposite, above: *Joe Doherty hid behind a beard and long hair when he fled to the USA.*

Opposite, below: *Hooded IRA men patrol in Belfast.*

The night before the ambush, a blue Ford Transit van was hi-jacked by volunteers and handed over to Doherty's team and driven to the rear of house number 371 in the Antrim Road – designated for the take-over the next day and the base for the ambush. The following morning nineteen-year-old Rosemary Comerford and her two-year-old son Gerard were alone in the house.

She recalled: 'At 10.30am a knock came on the door and I opened it. Two men were standing there and one of them said they were Irish Republican Army. The man who spoke had a handgun pointing at me. This man said they were going to take over the house and they were going to hold me and my son as hostages. He then took us into the bedroom at the rear of the house. The other man who did not speak remained in the bedroom with us. I could hear the other man moving about. I think the man who stayed in the bedroom with us brought the handgun with him. At about 12.30pm my sister Theresa called and the man who was in the bedroom with me told me to go and see who it was. He told me to let her in and said she'd have to stay in the bedroom with us. My husband Gerard came home and the same thing happened.'

At 2pm that day, as Doherty and his 'freedom fighters' took up positions in the occupied house that gave them the best view on to the anticipated killing zone, Captain Herbert Westmacott, thirty-four, and his men were on their way to the scene. The SAS career veteran and his men were trained precisely for this kind of urban assault. SAS headquarters in England were equipped with houses such as these which Westmacott and his men had neutralized time and time again in their training missions. But a terrible blunder in trying to determine what was the exact entrance to the house gave the gunmen inside vital seconds. The entrance to the house was actually through 369 and not through the door marked 371. Captain Westmacott fell

would leave no prisoners. But, as if to disappoint the IRA propaganda machine about such atrocities, they gave the killers inside the kind of chance never afforded to Captain Westmacott. A priest was brought in at Doherty's request to oversee their surrender after the SAS had surrounded them for several hours. Forensic tests taken later on his clothing showed that, of the four-man gang, he had the most ballistic

CAPTAIN WESTMACOTT FELL IN A POOL OF BLOOD OUTSIDE THE ENTRANCE TO 371 AFTER THE HITMEN IINSIDE OPENED UP FIRST.

Right: *Airey Neave, on the left, survived the Nazi prisoner-of-war camp at Colditz Castle, only to die in a cowardly IRA killing. They planted a bomb in his car on 30 March, 1979 that killed him the instant he started the vehicle.*

in a pool of blood outside the entrance to 371 after the hitmen inside opened up first. The British government would later charge Doherty, who as he was led away from the scene of the murder said of the M60 that killed Captain Westmacott said: 'that's my baby', with being the triggerman.

Trapped inside like rats Doherty and his men believed they would endure first smoke, then stun grenades before the SAS mounted a charge on their positions that

residue on him, indicating that it was probably him who fired the M60 which killed Captain Westmacott.

British interrogators were intent on breaking down Doherty when he was in custody; they knew he was a valued IRA operative who had probably killed before. But he was well versed in the cat-and-mouse games that his handlers had taught him. Every question that was not answered with a refusal was answered with a

FORENSIC TESTS TAKEN LATER ON HIS CLOTHING SHOWED THAT, OF THE FOUR-MAN GANG, DOHERTY HAD THE MOST BALLISTIC RESIDUE ON HIM.

and the fact that he had killed a member of Her Majesty's most elite force ensured that his name was already high up in the newspapers. His leaders instructed him to work on escape plans for him and seven of his fellow inmates.

Doherty handed his commanders their much-needed propaganda victory on 10 June, 1981, when he and seven others made a successful break out from the jail. Using guns smuggled in by IRA sympathisers they overpowered guards – clubbing one brutally – and dressed in prison uniforms to pass a series of checkpoints leading to the staff entrance to the jail. Finally out in the street, a gun battle ensued in a car park between the security forces and the IRA units sent to pick up the escapers. Doherty fled through the warren of streets in the Shankhill area of town – a fiercely loyalist enclave, but nothing happened to him and he was able to reach his own turf unscathed. Once there he was kept away from his family and friends – the first target of searches by the army – and sheltered at the homes of sympathisers who had no record of IRA membership or of terrorist offences. Within days he was moved south of the border into the Irish Republic where he was hidden in an even more remote region. As he bided his time for several months he heard the news from Belfast that Lord Justice Hutton had found him Guilty of murder *in absentia*, sentenc-

question. Doherty was a misty-eyed Republican who fondly remembered his grandfather's medals from his time spent fighting the British earlier in the century. He wavered between bravado and mute silence to arrogance and foul language during his interrogation sessions, but he finally cracked when his mother's name was mentioned. He admitted he had tried to get out of the movement but had failed and only wanted a better Ireland to live in. He did not admit to killing Westmacott specifically, only that he had fired a gun.

BACK IN THE BOSOM OF THE IRA

Doherty soon found himself back in the cold familiarity of the Crumlin Road jail after his inquisitors had finished with him. Here he was among familiar faces and old IRA comrades and the bravado that led him to kill easily returned. He was back under the discipline of the IRA where top-level decisions were taken by his masters to turn him into a cross between a martyr and Robin Hood. At the time of the beginning of his trial in April 1987 things were going badly for the IRA leadership; the hunger strike at the Maze prison was claiming lives with five volunteers dead and no sign of the Thatcher government backing down. The leadership of the terror gang badly needed a propaganda break and they saw their opportunity in gaining it with Doherty. He had already refused to recognize the court sitting in justice on him

Above: In 1988, a girl walked into an army disco in Mill Hill, North London and laid an IRA bomb. A young man lost his life in the blast.

Below: British soldiers returning to their barracks after home leave in 1988 were blown apart by the IRA. Eight men lost their lives as the bus in which they travelled exploded.

ing him to life imprisonment with a recommendation to the Home Secretary that he should serve a minimum of thirty years inside. It did much to take the edge from his fame as 'The Great Escaper' as he was now known among Republican sympathisers. His masters in Belfast knew that his pursuers would leave no stone unturned in their hunt for him and so took the decision to give him a new identity and send him off to America where a massive Irish community – which gave literally millions of dollars each year to the war chests of their fighting units – would ensure his safety as a fugitive. He left Ireland under the name of Henry J. O'Reilly in February 1982... ready to bury himself in anonymity until his overlords called him to service once again when the heat was off.

Margaret Thatcher was not prepared to let the killer of a British officer escape so easily. In his authoritative book on Doherty entitled 'Killer in Clowntown' author Martin Dillon wrote: 'Doherty was a prestige target and, little did he know then, to the British prime minister at the time, Margaret Thatcher. The killing of Westmacott and the escape of his killers angered her. Doherty was the only one

Above: Eighteen soldiers were killed when the IRA ambushed a convoy in Warrenpoint, County Ulster in 1979.

Right: Funerals for IRA men are given the importance and ritual suited to matyrs. These men are bearing the coffin of IRA hitman, Brian Mullin.

> HIS MASTERS IN BELFAST KNEW THAT HIS PURSUERS WOULD LEAVE NO STONE UNTURNED AND DECIDED TO GIVE HIM A NEW IDENTITY AND SEND HIM TO AMERICA.

unaccounted for and eventually become so important that she would demand to be personally briefed about him. Thatcher believed that his recapture would enhance relations between Britain and Ireland and repair damage to security in Northern Ireland resulting from the 'Great Escape.' Neither the IRA nor Doherty needed to be convinced of her intentions or her determi-

physical trait of the wanted man together with a profile of his habits and psychological breakdown. Soon questions were being asked around town among a network of IRA informers and it came to the notice of FBI agent Frank Schulte that there was a young man working at Clancy's Bar who fitted the bill. On 18 June 1983, he was seized at work. Margaret Thatcher was informed later that same day and she thought that he would be home in a matter of days to begin his thirty-year sentence. But it would be many years of tortured manouvreings and murky intrigue before Doherty heard the slam of a British cell door clang behind him.

Below: *Joe Doherty, healthy, defiant and fighting against an extradition order requested by the British government. Doherty was detained for eight years in custody in the USA during his determined attempts to appeal against the order. He lost his case and was returned to Britain where he resumed a life sentence for murder.*

nation to see them fulfilled. But they were unaware then of her growing personal interest in him.'

DOHERTY'S NEW LIFE IN NEW YORK

In New York, Doherty got a job with a construction company while lodging with a family sympathetic to the Republican cause in Ulster. He also worked as a shoe-shine boy, a bell-hop in a hotel and, with a fake social security number, managed to get a job as a barman at Clancy's Bar in Manhattan. Here he earned upwards of $120 per day with tips and thought the going was good. He had a girlfriend, a comfortable apartment in New Jersey and had adapted to life outside the strict discipline of the IRA with ease. He thought he had it made.

But the heat was on in Ireland to get him back. Thatcher, receiving almost weekly intelligence briefings on his suspected whereabouts, gave her Royal Ulster Constabulary chiefs and army intelligence officers but one brief: find him. The Federal Bureau of Investigation in America was contacted in 1983 and a full file sent over to officers in New York listing every

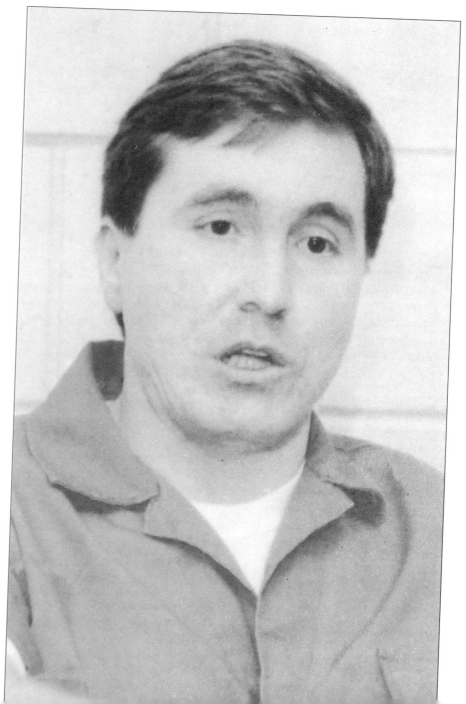

Above: *The scene of horror at Enniskillen, Northern Ireland, when the IRA slaughtered worshippers at a Remembrance Day service in 1987. Eleven people were killed.*

JOE DOHERTY FOUND HIMSELF IN THE ENVIABLE POSITION OF BEING A HERO TO A LARGE PART OF THE IRISH-AMERICAN POPULATION IN NEW YORK.

Joe Doherty found himself in the enviable position of being a hero to a large part of the Irish-American population in New York. To these citizens of the Big Apple he was not the common murderer as depicted by Mrs Thatcher and the British establishment; rather he was a freedom fighter, a hero in the armed struggle to rid Ireland of the English 'oppressor'. He soon found himself with the kind of fame usually reserved for a showbusiness celebrity. Everyone wanted to press Doherty's flesh – the American senator Jesse Jackson was among one hundred politicians who petitioned for him to be granted political asylum in America. Eventually Mayor David Dinkins of New York would come to name the block outside the Manhattan Correctional Centre where he was held 'Joe Doherty Corner.' To Mrs Thatcher and all the victims of IRA terrorism it was the equivalent of re-naming a London street after the Boston strangler for Doherty is also a crude killer.

Initially Doherty was charged with illegal entry into the USA – he had, after all, committed no crimes in America. Time after time after time courts ordered his release on bail and a full immigration hearing, only to have the legal process blocked from on high. Clearly, the hand of something or someone much bigger than the usual legal process was being brought into play repeatedly. Ronald Reagan, who enjoyed an unusually cozy relationship with Mrs Thatcher, was, like her, a man dedicated to the opposition of terrorism. She expected him to deliver Doherty up to her, but he was thwarted at every turn by the procedures of the US judicial system. In 1986 came the Libyan bombing when Reagan took his own stand against world terrorism by attempting to kill Colonel Gaddafi. Mrs Thatcher stood alone among western leaders by allowing the American warplanes to take off from British bases on their mission. When Britain continued to be frustrated by the American courts Mrs

Thatcher's emissaires diplomatically reminded America that they 'owed' Britain a favour. The favour was Doherty for Tripoli and it was said so by Sherard Cowper Coles, a senior British diplomat, to Otto Obermaier, US attorney assigned to prosecuting him. He told Obermaier: 'The prime minister believes you owe us this one. She allowed your government to use our territory for your F1-11s when they were on their way to bomb Tripoli.'

But the legal process ground on and on in Doherty's favour. The American court system, examining the statues of the constitution of the United States and every similar case that had gone before, could not find sufficient arguments to warrant the deportation of Doherty. At one bail hearing in September 1990, after he had won over a dozen court cases that kept being referred to higher and higher authorities, Doherty gave a classic terrorist's 'doublespeak' account for his killing of Westmacott. He said: 'It was to bring pressure on the British government, to force them to negotiations. That was the reason I was involved in the operation, to bring to the British government that their presence in the North of Ireland is unworkable, politically and militarily, and that they cannot suppress the IRA, that the IRA can survive and strike back.' This from a man who lied to the American courts that he had left the organization in 1982.

THE SUPREME COURT REJECTED ANY FURTHER HEARINGS

By 1992 he was the longest held political prisoner, held without a charge other than that he had come into the country illegally, in America. There was still intense pressure on the White House – now under the occupancy of the Bush administration – from No.10 Downing Street, whose keys had passed to John Major. By February 1992 Joe Doherty's case reached the highest court in the land, the Supreme Court. He prayed for an immigration hearing, a separate tribunal that might allow him the political sanctuary he craved. But, almost nine years after he had first been arrested and locked up, it ended for him. The Supreme Court rejected any and all further hearings. On 19 February they came for him – as he rightly predicted they

> TIME AFTER TIME AFTER TIME COURTS ORDERED HIS RELEASE ON BAIL AND A FULL IMMIGRATION HEARING, ONLY TO HAVE THE LEGAL PROCESS BLOCKED FROM ON HIGH.

Below: *Mrs Thatcher was guarded by a young marine as she went to show her respects to the dead bandsmen in Deal, Kent. She called the IRA terrorists 'monsters' and was relentless in her fight against them.*

would – to, in his own words, 'complete my sentence in the hell of a British prison.' Doherty was taken from a new lock-up in Kentucky and flown to Northern Ireland where IRA men in Belfast's Crumlin Road jail, scene of his great escape, welcomed him with cake and tea.

The saga of Joe Doherty ended in complete victory for Mrs Thatcher and the opponents of terrorism everywhere. Doherty's supporters, and particularly his lawyer in America, Mary Pike, argued that the American judicial system had been bent, perverted to the cause of Britain and not the interests of the Stars and Stripes.

However, one senior British diplomat, who wishes to remain anonymous, said: 'He was a top operative before he got caught and he tried to con the people of America that he had seen the senselesness of violence, that he had reformed.

'He cannot complain of dirty tricks because he formerly employed every one in the book. Yes, America did owe Britain one for Tripoli – and now the debt has been repaid in full.'

CARLOS THE JACKAL
The Supreme Terrorist

As a boy he was trained in hatred; as an adult he has terrorised the entire globe with his murderous acts. Yet Carlos the Jackal has never been caught and the whereabouts of one of the world's most wanted men remains a mystery.

H e has written his name in blood across the world. A master of disguise, an expert urban guerilla, a killer without compunction or compassion, he moves at ease within the terror networks who support him or hire him, with a slush fund of ready cash and an inexhaustible supply of passports. At various times in various places, he has gone under the names of Carlos Andres Martinez-Torres, Hector Lugo Dupont, Cenon Marie Clarke, Adolf Jose Muller Bernal, Flick Ramirez, Glenn Gebhard and Ahmed Adil Fawaz. His real name is Illyich Ramirez Sanchez. But to police forces all over the globe he is known simply as Carlos the Jackal.

This master of global terrorism is as elusive as he is infamous. Interpol dragnets, complex deals within deals of the diplomatic and espionage worlds, and operations masterminded by the world's leading anti-terrorist units have failed to flush him out and bring him to justice for his crimes – crimes that include the attempted assassination of Joseph Sieff, head of Marks and Spencer; the murder of two French counter-espionage agents; the mass kidnap of OPEC delegates in Vienna; car bombings in France that claimed five people; the machine-gun massacre at Israel's Lod Airport which claimed twenty-five lives; and rocket attacks on aircraft at a Paris airport.

This bloody killer, who mocks the combined efforts of the civilized world to capture him, comes from simple roots. Born in 1949 in Venezuala, he was the son of a left-wing lawyer who admired Stalin.

Instead of nursery rhymes and picture books, Carlos grew up on a diet of orthodox Marxist-Leninism. His father believed violent, global revolution was the only lesson worth teaching and by the time he was a teenager, Illyich – named after Vladimir Illyich Ulyanov, Lenin's real name – was a willing disciple of his father's beliefs. Clever, dispassionate, Carlos believed in the overthrow of world capitalism, and he identified with the minorities of the world. The IRA in Ulster, the Palestinians in Israel, the ETA terrorists in the Basque region of Spain – these were the heroes of the young Carlos. When he was seventeen, his father packed him off to a terrorist training camp in Cuba.

THIS BLOODY KILLER, WHO MOCKS THE COMBINED EFFORTS OF THE CIVILIZED WORLD TO CAPTURE HIM, COMES FROM SIMPLE ROOTS.

At the camp near Havana, Carlos learned the rudiments of handling explosives, unarmed combat and weaponry. In the latter field he was particularly adept, proving himself a crack shot with any calibre of weapon from a pistol to an automatic rifle. He also developed a thorough disregard for human life which served him well in his chosen profession. One of his instructors gave an interview to a Paris newspaper several years later: 'He was clinically detached from everything he

Above: *Scene after the 1983 terror bombing of the US Marine base in Beirut which many suspect was masterminded by Carlos.*

Opposite: *Carlos the Jackal, master of disguise and ruthless terrorist.*

did, mechanical, a superb pupil to train. You could tell from the way he pulled a trigger or pulled down an opponent on the judo mat that there was no emotion attached to anything. It was all just business for him.'

After his initial training in terrorism in Cuba, he was shipped to London where he lived briefly with his mother – estranged from his father – at addresses in Wimpole Street and the King's Road, Chelsea. His brother Lenin – his real name – was with him during this time, around 1968, and the two of them spent endless hours with

Opposite, top: *Carlos pictured at a cocktail party in London in the Seventies. He is with his mother and a girlfriend.*

Opposite, bellow: *The collection of arms and ammunition that Carlos left behind when he fled a Paris flat.*

Here he learned about the various guerilla groups who needed help and were willing to pay for it. From the Middle East to the killing fields of Asia, from the back alleys of Belfast to the sun drenched plains of Spain's Basque region, there were wars for 'freedom' by minority groups. Also at Patrice Lumumba, he forged contacts that were to be invaluable to him, and he mastered the intricacies of the world banking system. This latter lesson was to serve him well when he began to procure arms and secure payment for his own terrorist operations.

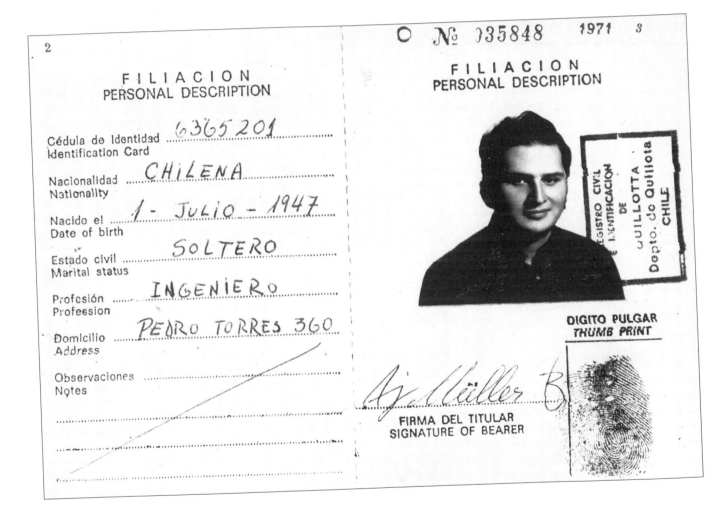

anarchists in bars where they talked about changing the world through violence. In 1969, Carlos moved on again – this time to the 'finishing school' for terrorists, the Patrice Lumumba Friendship University in Moscow. This seat of learning was in reality the world's top terror academy. Within its walls the Soviets trained some of the most diabolical killers in the world, all of them intent on changing society to fit in with the Marxist-Leninist doctrine.

Above: *A false passport found in a Paris flat after French law officers had been shot by Carlos.*

He spent a year here before he was dismissed for 'riotous and dilettante behaviour.' But western intelligence experts regard this cumbersome phrase as a feint dreamed up by the spy lecturers in order to fool the west that Carlos was never going to be part of international terrorism. Equipped with his new, lethal knowledge, he wrote a letter to his father : 'I am ready for what I must do. Thank you for pointing me on the true and correct path.'

Red Army terrorist, Kozo Okamoto, to lead a kamikaze-squad of terrorists in one the most heinous acts of terrorism ever perpetrated against innocent people. Okamoto and two others were flown to Israel on an Air France flight from Rome. In Rome they checked in luggage packed with automatic weapons and grenades – luggage which in those innocent days of air travel was not checked. Upon arrival in Israel, Okamoto and his accomplices, Rakeshi Okudeira and Yoshuyiki Yasuda, opened their luggage and began spraying the crowded terminal with automatic weapons fire, and hurling grenades into the lines of passengers. A defective grenade accounted for one terrorist, a second was shot by a policeman. Okamoto, who had intended to die in the assault, was knocked to the ground by an El Al maintenance worker as he aimed his machine gun at aircraft on the tarmac. On that dark day, 30 May, twenty-four people died, four more died from their wounds in hospital and seventy-six were wounded, many seriously. It was Carlos' grand opening venue on the stage of world terrorism.

He was paid £1 million for organizing the successful killing mission and his name – taken from the title of 'The Day of the Jackal', the Frederick Forsyth novel about

A BLOODTHIRSTY CREW

He spent some time in Paris with a cell of the Popular Front for the Liberation of Palestine, the PFLP, whom he had befriended in Moscow. He would become the leader of this bloodthirsty crew when the Israeli secret service assassinated its head. The first outrage committed by him is believed to be a bomb aboard a Swissair plane bound for Tel Aviv from Zurich on 21 February, 1970. The bomb exploded within minutes of take-off in the baggage hold, causing a massive fire which brought the jetliner down, killing all two hundred people on board. But Carlos revealed his masterly flair for planning when he organized a 'big target' as he referred to the 1972 massacre at Israel's Lod Airport.

Thanks to the contacts he made in Moscow, Carlos employed the Japanese

an assassin stalking Charles de Gaulle – was widely broadcast in terrorist circles as a man who gets things done. Next, Carlos turned his sights on a prominent Jewish figure in Britain: Joseph Sieff, boss of the Marks and Spencer stores and a prominent supporter of Israel. But Carlos botched the assassination and, six years later, he discussed it in a newspaper interview given to a French journalist for the Parisian-based Arabic publication Al Watan Al Arabi. The two men met at a secret hideout in the Middle East and Carlos erroneously referred to Mr Sieff as Lord throughout his interview and said he had been chosen to die 'because he was the most important

> THE ATTEMPTED MURDER OF SIEFF WAS THE ONLY MISSION THAT CARLOS IS EVER KNOWN TO HAVE BOTCHED.

opened the bathroom door I fired my old Beretta. He was wounded at the upper lip below the nose. I usually fire three times around the nose. It's sure death. But in Lord Sieff's case only one bullet went off, though I fired three times. When Lord Sieff survived I decided to try again. But by the time I managed to get the necessary weapons two weeks later he had gone off to Bermuda.' The attempted murder of Sieff was the one and only mission that Carlos is ever known to have botched.

In 1974, he struck at the Hague in Holland. He again used Japanese Red Army fanatics for this mission. The terrorists seized the French ambassador and his

Above: *Captives taken from OPEC's headquarters in Vienna by Carlos' terror gang are forced to board an aircraft to Algeria.*

Zionist in Britain.' Carlos elected to carry out the assasination himself because of his expertise with small arms weapons.

His first operation in England started on 30 December, 1973. Here is how Carlos described it: 'I drove to the Lord's home, parked my car, rang the bell and held the butler at gunpoint. It was 6.45 in the evening. I ordered the butler to call out for his master from the bathroom. The butler did so and fainted. When Lord Sieff

staff and held them hostage, while Carlos demanded the release of another Red Army terrorist held in Paris. To prove he was not bluffing, and to stave off any 'cheating' from the governments he was blackmailing, Carlos bombed the Drugstore Publics in St Germain-des-Pres in the heart of Paris, killing two and injuring thirty. In the same interview with the Arab paper in which he boasted of the attempted killing of Sieff he said: 'The French authorities

Above: *Israelis celebrate their successful raid on terrorists who held an aeroplane and its passengers hostage at Entebbe, Uganda.*

panicked. A Boeing 707 was sent to Holland along with the freed Red Army terrorist to pick up the embassy assailants in the Hague. The operation succeeded completely.' Carlos was boastful.

ELUSIVE AND EFFICIENT

By now the western intelligence agencies were building up a profile of this master terrorist. They knew he was based in Europe, but he never stayed in one place long. He was as elusive as he was efficient. The French authorities came close to capturing him, when on 27 June, 1975, a Lebanese informer of the PFLP led two agents of the French Direction de la Surveilance du Territoire to Carlos' apartment in the centre of the city. Michel Mourkabel, the informer, had been at one time Carlos' liason man with the PFLP leadership in the Middle East. Carlos

described what happened when Mourkabel brought agents Jean Donatini, thirty-four, and Raymond Dous, fifty-five, to his apartment on the third-floor of a block on the Rue Toullier in the Latin quarter of the city. Carlos has always claimed that there were three French agents present, although the authorities have only ever admitted to two agents. Carlos said to the Arabic newspaper journalist: 'It was 8.45 in the evening when they knocked on the door. I was with two Venezualans and a student girlfriend. One of the Venezualans opened the door and shouted "police."'

'We asked the policeman to have a drink with us. They sat for a while and asked for our passports. We produced them and then they started questioning me about Moukarbel. I denied that I had ever met him. But they said he told them that he knew me and that he was waiting outside to identify me. I then challenged them to

HE NEVER STAYED IN ONE PLACE LONG. HE WAS AS ELUSIVE AS HE WAS EFFICIENT.

bring him in. They consulted among themselves and then one of them went out. Fifteen minutes later Moukarbel was brought in. When he started to point his finger at me I realised I had to shoot it out. I realised I had to execute the death sentence. I whipped out my Russian-made pistol and fired first at Donatini who was going for his gun. He was reputed to be a fast marksman. But I was faster and slugged a bullet into his left temple. Then I shot Dous between his eyes. Then I put a bullet under the ear of the third Frenchman.

Only Michel was left. He moved towards me, covering his face with his hands. He must have realised at that moment that he who cracks in this field of action is bound to be executed. These are the rules of the game. When he was almost at point-blank range I fired between his eyes. He slumped. I fired a second bullet into his left temple and then raced out into the darkness through the neighbouring apartment. The whole operation took six seconds.'

Carlos fled to London where he holed up with beautiful revolutionary, Nydia Tobon,

Below: *Marines lay a dead comrade on a stretcher after the massive Beirut bombing, probably organised by Carlos, that took two hundred American lives.*

Above: *Rescuers dig through the rubble, looking for survivors, after the US Marine base was blown up during the troubles in the Lebanon.*

'CARLOS WANTED TO KILLTHE COP. I TOLD HIM TO USE A BIT OF CHARM INSTEAD.'

when police raided the Hereford Road, Bayswater, apartment he had previously shared with twenty-three-year-old Spanish waitress Angela Otaola. They found a cache of arms and in one of the suitcases stashed with weapons, was a shopping list of death. Among the prominent members of British society on the list were Lord and Lady Sainsbury, Sir Keith Joseph, Sir Bernard Delfont and violinist Yehudi Menuhin. Later, Carlos was stopped on the M4 motorway near Reading by Thames Valley police. Tobon, who was expelled from Britain two years after the incident, returned to her native Columbia where she said: 'He had been driving way too fast and we were stopped. The policeman came over and he reached for his pistol. He wanted to kill the cop. I told him to use a bit of charm instead and he let him go with a warning. In the back of the car he had several more weapons and at least eight passports.' Carlos had luck on his side.

In December of the same year Carlos pulled off his most daring exploit.

Working for the PFLP, Carlos masterminded and led a team of daring guerillas in an assault on the OPEC delegates, assembled in Vienna for a conference on world petroleum pricing. Eighty-one delegates of rich Middle Eastern states were present on 21 December when Carlos and his fanatics struck. The PFLP were angry at what they regarded as an Arabic 'sell-out' by states to the 'imperialist' Americans who gave so much support to their arch-enemy Israel. There was an element of that to it, but the main purpose of the mission was to raise funds for future operations – and to line the Swiss bank account of Carlos, Illyich Ramirez Sanchez.

The OPEC meeting was in its second day when Carlos, accompanied by two West German terrorists linked with the Baader-Meinhof gang, two Palestinians and a Lebanese burst into the meeting hall after a shootout with Austrian security guards. They killed three people, including the Libyan delegate to the conference, a bad move, as Libya was one of Carlos' main weapons suppliers, a policeman and an Iraqi employee of that nation's delegation and they wounded seven.

> THE MEN WERE RELEASED INTO THE DESERT AFTER AN ESTIMATED 50 MILLION DOLLARS WAS PAID IN RANSOM.

Below: *One of Carlos' men was wounded in the OPEC seige in Vienna. He was furious that the authorities removed the man to give him medical care.*

A SAFE PASSAGE OUT OF AUSTRIA

The terrorist gang then seized dozens of hostages, among them Sheik Yamini and Jamshid Amouzegar, Iranian Minister of the Interior. Responsibility for this attack was claimed by the Arm of the Arab Revolution, but it was in reality a PFLP operation. Carlos demanded massive amounts of ransom cash for several of the wealthier delegates and a safe passage for his gang out of Austria. One of the gang members who was wounded by return fire in the initial storming of the conference was treated at a city hospital and returned to Carlos. In return for the freedom of forty-one Austrian hostages the government allowed Carlos to fly out with his hostages from Iraq, Saudi Arabia, Gabon, Ecuador, Venezuala, Nigeria and Indonesia. They flew to Algiers and from there to Libya and the men were eventually released into the desert after an estimated $50 million was paid in ransom by the hostages' nations. It was a stunningly

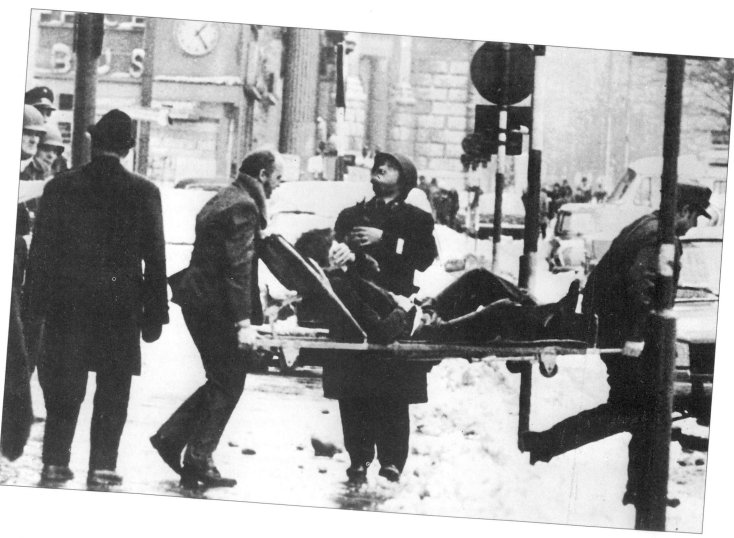

brilliant terrorist operation thanks to the masterful cunning of Carlos.

In the following months he committed a string of assassinations across the world, including the murders of a dissident Syrian exile, a Palestinian rival guerilla leader and several PFLP commanders who needed to be 'purged' from the movement. After resting in a guerilla training camp in Libya, he masterminded, in 1976, the hijacking of an Air France jet en route from Tel Aviv to Paris with two hundred and fifty–eight passengers on board. The plane was diverted and hi-jacked in order to obtain the release of imprisoned terrorists, among them the crazed Okamoto who had caused such carnage at Lod Airport. The hijacked plane landed at Entebbe in Uganda, where Israeli commandos stormed the parked aircraft and released the hostages in a brilliant display of anti-terror tactics. Carlos was said to be angry that the terrorists he sub-contracted for the operation were 'not up to the task'.

After the Entebbe fiasco, Carlos faded into some obscurity. He began training guerillas for Gaddafi in Libya and was said by intelligence agencies to be, at various times, in East Berlin, in Syria, in Czechoslovakia, Iraq, South Yemen and Hungary. He was a man admired for his cool skill but derided by his fellow murderers as a vain, egotistical urban warrior who spent hours on personal grooming. Hans Joachim-Klein, the terrorist badly injured in the OPEC operation, gave an interview to a German newspaper in 1978: 'He was mocked, certainly by his German accomplices, for his vanity. He was always taking showers and powdering himself from head to foot. But no-one could fault him professionally although he did upset

Opposite, left: Carlos as he appeared in a 'wanted' poster after he killed two lawmen in Paris.

Opposite, right: Sheik Yamani, the Saudi Arabian oil minister who was furious that Carlos had sabotaged his meeting in Vienna.

Above: *Terrorist Hans-Joachim Klein, wanted in connection with the OPEC assault, in a car with the French philosopher, Jean-Paul Sartre (front of car) and left wing lawyer, Klaus Croissant. The urban terrorists attracted some unexpected support.*

HIS MURDERS WERE PLANNED TO COINCIDE WITH THE THIRTIETH ANNIVERSARY OF THE FOUNDING OF THE STATE OF ISRAEL.

several with his constant attempts to take over German revolutionay groups that had nothing to do with him. He was very cool during the whole OPEC operation – he even rode the tram to the hall with all his weapons.' And always well-groomed.

In May 1978 Carlos surfaced in London where he was spotted in Notting Hill by a man working for a foreign embassy in London. Scotland Yard's anti-terrorist branch was put on full alert and the Notting Hill area of the city, where he was seen, was combed, but he was not found. There is speculation that he came to fulfill the contracts on several of the people on the death list drawn up years earlier, and his murders were planned to coincide with the thirtieth anniversary of the founding of the state of Israel.

A WORLDWIDE TERROR CAMPAIGN

When Israel launched the 1982 invasion of Beirut for a full and final reckoning with

the Palestine Liberation Organization Carlos hired himself out to Hezbollah fanatics. He is credited with numerous assassinations committed at this time, including the killing of fifty-eight people at the French military headquarters in Beirut.

His last known mission happened just before the outbreak of the Gulf War in 1991. Intelligence sources say Carlos was summoned to Bagdhad by Saddam Hussein and asked to organize a world-wide terror campaign if the West resorted to military action to free Kuwait from the Iraqi invasion. Carlos was alledgedly offered $10 million to organize the terror squads, but pressure was put on him by Syrian and other Arab governments to stay out of this one. Many Arab nations that he had worked for in the past were actually allied with the West against Saddam. Carlos backed out, reputedly with a million-dollar 'consultancy fee' in his back pocket.

Apart from the crimes he is known to have masterminded and committed, he is wanted for questioning on many, many more. His bloody handprints are seen in the murder of Swedish premier Olaf Palme and in the murder of more than two hundred US Marines in Beirut. But with the ruthlessness and cunning he displays, and the number of nations in the world willing to give terrorists refuge, it is highly unlikely that Carlos the Jackal will ever be brought to justice.

His nest is nicely feathered with booty from his bloody games and he may find retirement easier to enjoy than the danger of his terrorist existence. He is reported to have travelled in November 1991, on a Yemeni passport, to Yemen after a falling out with Colonel Gaddafi over the political direction of terrorism. It is believed that Carlos is living with Magdalene Kopp, a Baader-Meinhoff terrorist that he somehow found time to marry at some point during his bizarre international odyssey of death and mayhem.

But perhaps there is a kind of justice waiting for Carlos – the same kind of justice that he himself has dispensed without mercy. According to America's CIA, there is a group of wealthy Arab businessmen which has put out a contract on his head. Aware that fanatics like Carlos pose a threat to everyone in any society, these men are said to have pooled millions of dollars that will go as a reward to the person who assassinates Carlos. But international terror expert, David Funnel, said in Washington: 'It will take a killer of very high calibre indeed to catch Carlos. He has been schooled for too long and is too wily to allow himself to become vulnerable. If his antennae sense danger, he will uproot from one spot and move to another. He is that clever and that cunning.'

'IT WILL TAKE A KILLER OF VERY HIGH CALIBRE INDEED TO CATCH CARLOS.'

Below: *Red Army guerilla, Kozo Okamoto, the killer who opened fire on the crowds at Lod Airport, Israel, in 1980. He was freed for an exchange of Israeli prisoners in a deal between the Palestinians and Israel.*

HAUPTMANN
The Lindbergh Kidnaping

America wept when the darling child of their aviator hero was kid-napped and murdered. The criminal was tracked down and caught by a brilliant piece of detection, yet he denied his horrible guilt right up to the end.

Stormin' Norman Schwarzkopf was the man of the moment with the US people as he led the allied armies on the road to victory in Operation Desert Storm. But over fifty years before this campaign, it was his father in the glare of publicity. Colonel Norman Schwarzkopf was the head of the police force that investigated the snatching of little Charles Augustus Lindbergh, the son of famed Atlantic solo flier Charles Lindbergh. The kidnapping, and subsequent murder of the little boy, arouses passions to this day. From the time the crime was committed until the day that the kidnapper 'fried' in the electric chair, was four years. Even now, the memory of what befell the son of one of America's great heroes, tweaks the conscience of the nation. Crime expert John Rowland wrote: 'In all countries there are a few criminal cases which have stirred the nation. The British case of this kind was probably Jack the Ripper, the French case was probably that of Landru, the German case probably that of Troppmann. If anyone in the USA is asked what case has created the greatest stir it is what the British press called the 'Lindbergh Baby Case'. It is a tragic story.

Charles Lindbergh caught the imagination of the world when he flew solo over the Atlantic for thirty-three hours in 1927 in his little plane 'The Spirit of St. Louis'. He was honoured in fifty countries around the world. At home, he was more celebrated, more revered than the movie stars who were the true demi-gods of

society. Lindbergh could not move anywhere in America without being mobbed, and without his private life being discussed. It was because of this that Charles Lindbergh sought seclusion in the New Jersey town of Hopewell. Situated in Hunterdon County, it was near enough to New York to be convenient for travel and business meetings, and secluded enough to keep sightseers and the ravening hounds of the media away.

But its very location made it the perfect place for a crime – the crime of kidnap. On 1 March, 1932, Charles Lindbergh Jnr was taken from the country mansion and never seen again.

Colonel Lindbergh and his wife Anne retained an apartment in Manhattan and always telephoned the baby's nursemaid, Betty Gow, when they intended returning to their country house. On the night of the kidnapping, the Lindberghs and Gow dined

> 'IF ANYONE IN THE USA IS ASKED WHAT CRIMINAL CASE CAUSED THE GREATEST PUBLIC STIR, IT IS THE LINDBERGH CASE.'

Above: *Charles Lindbergh, the aviator hero who was the first man to fly across the Atlantic. This picture shows him in front of his plane before he took off.*

Opposite: *Bruno Hauptmann in his cell hours before his execution.*

together after the twenty-month-old baby was put to bed at 8pm. The Colonel heard what he decsribed as a 'queer, crackling noise' as he sat in the sitting room after dinner, but dismissed it as something Mrs Gow had dropped in the kitchen, where she was speaking with Mr and Mrs Whateley, an English couple who acted as butler and housekeeper to the family.

At 10pm Betty Gow went up to the nursery to look in on the child. He was gone, but the woman was not unduly worried, believing that her mistress had come in and taken the tot into her room as she often did. When she saw Mrs Lindbergh, however, the panic alarms went off. The mother had not been into see her child and had definitely not removed him to her room. As all five people in the mansion now began a frantic search, it was Colonel Lindbergh who found the heartbreaking note – the note that would feature so prominently in the sensational kidnap and murder trial. Pinned to the radiator and contain some gross spelling mistakes, it read: 'Dear Sir!

Below: These photographs show the glamorous good looks of the aviator, Charles Lindbergh. He was, however, a modest man who disliked publicity. His life was cruelly shattered by his fame which attracted not only applause but also tragedy.

'Have $50,000 ready, $25,000 in $20 bills 15,000 in $10 bills and 10,000 in $5 bills. After 2-4 days we will inform you were to deliver the Mony. We warn you for making anyding public or for notify the Police the chld is in gute care. Indication for all letters are signature and 3 holds.'

Close to the signature was a combination of perforations, leading police to

believe the semi-illiterate fiend meant holes, not holds. Colonel Lindbergh made one more frantic search of the grounds outside, hoping to see some clue as to which direction his son had been taken, then ran back into the house and immediately telephoned the police. Detectives were on the scene within thirty minutes.

SCANT CLUES INDEED

Initial inspections discovered footprints of yellow clay in the nursery and the indentation of a ladder in the flower bed below the nursery window – obviously the kidnapper's means of entry into the house. A carpenter's chisel was found half-buried in the soft mud – it had rained for days prior to the kidnapping – and there were ladder scuff marks on the whitewashed wall of the house. But these were scant clues indeed. Within forty-eight hours, President Hoover himself had become involved. Because of the fame of Colonel Lindbergh, and the dastardly nature of the crime perpetrated against him, Hoover ordered the FBI to provide limitless assistance to the New Jersey police. The investigation was headed by Colonel Norman Schwarzkopf who

cancelled all police leave in a bid to get the case wrapped up quickly. Neither he, nor anyone else, could conceive that it would be four long years before justice was done.

Experts called in to examine the note speculated that the villain was German or Scandinavian – the spelling of 'gute' and 'anyding' pointed in this direction. The ink was analysed, but found to be a commer-

Below: The baby Lindbergh, Charles Jnr., on his first birthday. He was adored by his parents and his father described him as 'the perfect son.'

newspapers, which her husband had once loathed with such venom, to print details of the baby's diet. It was a special diet for the boy, as he had recently been unwell.

Anne Lindbergh thought that the massive police operation to find the kidnappers might make the criminals afraid to surface. Anne wrote to her mother: 'The detectives are very optimistic although they

cial brand easily available right across America, as was the paper it was written on. After questioning the servants, delving into their backgrounds and the ethnic make-up of their families, the police investigation did not move forward one inch. There came a tearful plea from Colonel Lindbergh himself. Ignoring the kidnappers' demands not to tell the police, which in turn meant keeping silent to the public, he published an appeal in big city newspapers across the USA, begging that his son be treated well and safely returned. His wife, in turn, managed to get the

'THE DETECTIVES ARE
VERY OPTIMISTIC
ALTHOUGH THEY THINK IT
WILL TAKE TIME AND
PATIENCE.'

think it will take time and patience. In fact, they think the kidnappers have gotten themselves into a terrible jam – so much pressure, such a close net all over the country.' She did not think about murder.

For two weeks they heard nothing, but then another note was delivered, followed rapidly by several more. The first read: 'We will holt the baby untill everyding is quiet.' The next: 'We are interested to send your Boy back in gud health.' Charles Lindbergh, the aviator with steel nerves, found those same nerves now stretched to breaking point. Concerned about the lack of progress in the police investigation, he went behind the back of the police to negotiate with the kidnappers and one month later paid the ransom through an intermediary called Dr John Condon.

Condon was an eccentric old man who had retired after fifty years teaching, then secured an appointment as a professor at New York's Fordham University. Condon approached Lindbergh and offered himself as the intermediary in negotiations because he had provoked the criminals, and so began to receive the same kind of ransom

NEITHER LINDBERGH NOR CONDON TRIED TO GRAB THE MYSTERIOUS CHARACTER WHO LED THEM TO THE CEMETARY.

Above: *Charles and Anne Lindbergh in carefree days.*

demands marked with the unique cluster of holes at the bottom of the notes next to a signature. The first note to him, delivered after Condon placed an advertisement in a New York newspaper outlining his proposition to be a negotiator, read: 'Dear Sir: If you are willing to act as go-between in the Lindbergh cace pleace follow stricly

instruction.' Lindbergh, at first, was suspicious of Condon, but when he showed him the note with the coded circles at the bottom, he allowed himself to go along with the plan.

Condon was given the code-name 'Jafsie' by Lindbergh, who then authorised the old man to place the coded message: 'Mony is Ready, Jafsie' in a New York newspaper. This was in response to a demand for money in the second note the kidnappers sent to Condon. A month later, Condon received another note informing him to read an advertment in the personal section of the New York Times. That ad told him to go to a New York subway station with the money. At the subway station he found, at the pre-arranged rendezvous spot, a note that read: 'cross the street and follow the fence from the cemetary. direction to 233 street. I will meet you.' In the cemetery, lurking between the gravestones, Condon met a man who told him that the baby was safe. 'Colonel Lindbergh needs some proof,' Condon said, 'before he can hand over the money.' The man said he would send the boy's sleeping suit through the mail within the next day or so. But he said, also, that the ransom demand had been increased to $70,000. Condon replied that it was short notice for such an amount of money. The man seemed to panic then, and asked sharply: 'Have you brought the police?' 'No, you can trust me, I assure you,' replied Condon. Two days later, the baby suit arrived, and was identified by Mrs Lindbergh as the one that little Charles was wearing that fateful night.

MYSTERIOUS MAN CALLED 'JOHN'

Fifty thousand dollars was dropped off by Condon in a subsequent meeting at the cemetery in the Bronx section of New York; and this time, Colonel Lindbergh accompanied Condon, although neither of these two men tried to apprehend or grab the mysterious character who had led them to the cemetery. He called himself 'John' and accepted the box of money handed to him by Condon. He promised to send details of the whereabouts of the child by the next morning's post. This strange encounter was indeed followed by an anonymous letter, marked with the familiar puncture holes,

'The boy is on the Boad Nelly – you will find the Boad between Horseneck Beach and Gay Head near Elizabeth Island.' Lindbergh took 'Boad' to be a misspelling for boat and searched the area near Martha's Vineyard in New England without success. He returned home on 12 May to the dreadful news that the decomposed body of a little boy had been found in a thicket by William Allen, a truck driver, just six miles from his home. The child had died from a severe blow to the skull. The dead baby was identified as Charles Lindbergh, Jnr. The discovery shattered Charles Lindbergh's heart, and the pain of his loss was intensified when he was informed that the baby had died on the night that he was kidnapped.

It was also distressing that the police investigation had not unearthed a single clue as to the identity of the murdering kidnappers. The Lindberghs said that they would have derived some kind of comfort if they knew that the murderer was behind bars, or executed for his crime, but that such wickedness should go unpunished was a hard cross to bear.

As the story gradually disappeared off the front pages, and Charles Lindbergh began to immerse himself in the politics of fascism, at that time gaining popularity in

Above: *Bruno Hauptmann who, for greed, cruelly kidnapped and killed a small child.*

Left: *A scene during the hunt for evidence in the first hours after the baby's disappearance.*

Europe, the police continued their dogged, patient detective work. The money paid over by 'Jafsie' was their chief clue, for Lindbergh had been careful to record the serial numbers of the notes he handed over and some of these were readily-convertible gold certificates whose numbers were quickly distributed throughout the country. All banks had been told to be on alert for anyone cashing in certificates that bore the serial numbers of the ones paid out in the Bronx cemetery.

RANSOM CASH DISCOVERED

On 15 September, 1934, a thirty-five-year-old German-born carpenter was arrested after paying for ten gallons of petrol with a $10 gold certificate that carried one of the 'hot' serial numbers – 4U13-41. The quick-thinking petrol pump attendant noted the customer's car registration number and informed police. A quick check on the

Above: *Charles Lindbergh at Croydon Aerodrome, England, after his courageous flight.*

Right: *Bruno Hauptmann leans across to address his wife before his murder trial gets underway.*

licence plate of the car revealed that the owner was one Bruno Hauptmann, of 1979 East 222nd Street in the Bronx. When he was arrested several of the ransom certificates were found in his possession. A search of Hauptmann's garage unearthed a further $14,000 of the ransom cash. And a search of his apartment revealed, stencilled behind a cupboard door, the telephone number of go-between Condon.

Hauptmann told his captors that he had come to America in 1923 and that he had been speculating in stocks and shares. 'I have been lucky,' he claimed. 'I am not a criminal. Everything I have is my own, not some fruits of a criminal enterprise.' Hauptmann then explained that the bulk of the cash was, in fact, not his, that it was was given to him by a friend called Isidor Fisch, a wealthy fur dealer, to look after until he returned from a trip to Germany. Fisch died in Germany and was never able to corroborate his story.

Interpol did not exist in those days, but a quick cable to Germany proved that Hauptmann was a liar on at least one point: he was a criminal and in his homeland had been convicted of robbery and managed to escape to America, entering the country illegally under a false name. And further proof was arrayed against him when a taxi-driver identified him as a man who had once asked him to deliver a note to Condon. On 11 October, 1934, Bruno Hauptmann was charged with murder and for attempting to extort money out of Colonel Lindbergh.

The trial was a sensation when it opened on 2 January, 1935, almost three years after the crime. David Wilentz, the New York State Attorney General,

Above: *Anne Lindbergh before the dreadful murder of her baby. It was a tragedy from which she never fully recovered.*

HAUPTMANN WAS A CRIMINAL AND IN HIS HOMELAND HAD BEEN CONVICTED OF ROBBERY.

outlined the prosecution's case to a court packed with pressmen, sketch artists and the curious public. Mrs Lindbergh took the stand and courageously told the events of that tragic night. Colonel Lindbergh rejected assertions from the defence team that members of his staff may have committed the crime. And Betty Gow, who had gone back to her native Scotland, returned to give evidence.

Condon held the court's attention when it was his turn to testify. As the go-between, the man who had handled the negotiations between the kidnapper and Lindbergh, his evidence was vital. He said that, after hearing Hauptmann speak, he was convinced that the man he met in the cemetery was, in fact, the accused.

Part of the door jamb of the cupboard, on which Condon's phone number had been scratched, was brought into court. Hauptmann tried to explain it away thus: 'I became interested in the case through reading about it in the newspapers. I jotted it down when Condon's name had been

Above: *During the trial, Charles Lindbergh was obliged to read yet again the ill-educated but cruel ransom letters the kidnapper sent to him and his wife.*

Opposite, above: *The jury who judged John Case. He was charged with obstructing justice in the recovery of the kidnapped baby.*

Opposite, below: *The accused listens to the evidence mounting against him. The investigation had unearthed detailed and damning proof of his crime, yet Bruno Hauptmann continued to plead his innocence.*

featured, but I did not deliver ransom demands to him.' The evidence continued to mount against Hauptmann. As he sat slumped in the dock, he could hear the cries of the newspaper sellers outside as they hawked the sensational story of the trial. The most damning evidence came from a firm of accountants that had been hired by police to investigate Hauptmann's financial affairs. The accountants calculated that, with his wages and those of his wife Annie's, Hauptmann could only have accrued a capital of just over 6,000 dollars; yet, he had $41,000 although not even his 'speculations' on the stock market had made such profits. The accountants, the police, the Lindberghs and the defence counsel itself were forced to admit that it seemed likely that Hauptmann was holding some of the $35,000 that the Colonel had paid in ransom money for the return of his baby son.

Handwriting experts testified that the accused's writing was the same as that on the ransom notes, and that he was a notoriously bad speller when writing English. One witness said in reference to Hauptmann's spelling: 'He was quite atrocious – simply the worst I have ever come across.'

Finally, police offered up a ladder as the final piece of evidence to link Hauptmann with the crime. A ladder, that was not the Lindbergh's property, had been found at their home after the kidnapping. On closer examination, it proved to be a handmade affair and was designed as three pieces, that could be quickly assembled to form the ladder, but, also, they could be taken apart in seconds to fit neatly in the boot of a car. Such a ladder was perfect equipment for a burglar or a kidnapper. Arthur Koechler appeared before the jury. He was an expert

Right: *Bruno Hauptmann with his defence attorney, Edward J. Reilly.*

Below: *Aerial view of the Lindbergh estate in New Jersey from which the baby was taken.*

in wood, and his testimany proved that this ladder had been crafted by the carpenter, Bruno Hauptmann.

LADDER WAS THE KEY TO THE CASE

Koechler's testimony became a classic in courtroom evidence, so thorough was both his knowledge of his subject and his investigation into the provenance of the ladder found at the scene of the crime. The author of fifty published works on timber and its uses, Koechler told the court he had examined timbers in Hauptmann's home and could swear on oath that part of the ladder was made from a board lifted from the floor in Hauptmann's attic. Nail holes in the floor corresponded with nail holes in the wood of the ladder, as did the grain of the wood itself. But Koechler was not satisfied with this evidence. He checked and found the sawmill where the wood had been bought. He discovered, too, that Hauptmann once worked at this very sawmill and that he had purchased timber from his employer on 29 Deecember, 1931, three months before the kidnapping.

But despite the overwhelming mass of evidence that proved his guilty involvement in the crime, Bruno Hauptmann continued to plead his innocence. He insisted that everything was circumstantial,

*Above: **Bruno Richard Hauptmann is strapped into the electric chair. He was found Guilty and sentenced to death for the murder of baby Lindbergh.***

'WHY HE CHOSE TO KILL THAT LITTLE BABY BY BASHING HIS HEAD IN, WE'LL NEVER KNOW.'

that he was spending time with friends at the time that he was supposed to have met Condon and Lindbergh in the cemetery. And he even claimed that the words he misspelled when asked to write them for the police, words that happened to repeat the exact errors of the ransom notes, proved nothing, except that he had been under strain from the long interrogations and abusive treatment meted out by the detectives grilling him. Attorney General Wilentz glared at him during the trial summing up, saying: 'You are a liar and a rather unskillful liar at that.'

THE JURY WERE UNANIMOUS IN THEIR VERDICT

The trial lasted until 11 February, 1935, thirty-two days in all, and the transcript of court proceedings filled four thousand pages of closely-typed law books. And the jury, which was out for over eleven hours, were unanimous in their verdict: Guilty. It was Judge Thomas Trenchard's duty to hand down the maximum penalty prescribed under the law. Bruno Hauptmann was to die in the electric chair for his hienous crime.

The prisoner lodged several appeals through the cumbersome American legal system and this delayed his execution. But in the end Bruno Hauptmann, proclaiming his innocence until the end, died at New Jersey's State Jail on 3 April, 1936. His widow Annie is now ninety-three, frail and weak, but she remains convinced that a great miscarriage of justice was done. She still calls repeatedly for a pardon for her husband. She is repeatedly ignored.

Norman Schwarzkopf Senior, whose career took him to police posts in the Middle East and other parts of the world, remained confident that justice had been served. He said: 'Hauptmann was a greedy man who concocted a scheme to get rich quick. Only the scheme he chose is probably one of the most heinous known to man. Why he chose to kill that little baby by bashing his head in, we'll probably never know. It's almost certain that he panicked; men have a peculiar habit of being over-awed by little children. Whatever happened, I for one never doubted his guilt.' And the evidence against Hauptmann was very convincing.

JEFFREY DAHMER
The Cannibal Killer

He seemed to be just another quiet worker at the chocolate factory but there have been few monsters to equal Jeffrey Dahmer – sadist, sodomite, killer and cannibal.

It was a balmy Milwaukee night in July 1991 when horrified police uncovered the secret life of America's most twisted serial killer, Jeffrey Dahmer. His one-bedroomed flat had been turned into a slaughterhouse for his hapless victims and, as the case unfolded, revelations of cannibalism, perverted sex, brutal murder and other unspeakable horrors shocked the whole world.

Photos of police forensic experts carting out vats of acid filled with bones and decomposing body parts, filled television screens around the world and ensured that Milwaukee would forever be known for something other than its beer.

Even though thirty-one year-old Dahmer pleaded Guilty to the murders of fifteen young men he still had to go to trial because he claimed that he was insane – and only a jury could decide whether his acts were the work of a twisted madman or of a cold, calculating, killing machine. The trial itself was one of the most disturbing America had ever witnessed and a national audience of millions of television viewers were to hear tales of human carnage, bizarre sex, sick killings and grisly fantasies that would have ensured a XXX rating had it been a movie.

The strange case of Jeffrey Dahmer ended with a verdict of Guilty and sane. The judge was forced to sentence Dahmer to mandatory, consecutive life terms in prison with no chance of parole for 930 years. The jury disregarded the testimony of psychiatric experts who said that Dahmer was 'psychotic' and suffered from unstoppable sexual urges caused by the mental disease of necrophilia. Dahmer himself appeared to undergo a physical change when he was in prison for the six months before the trial. Expressing remorse and asking to be put to death, the Milwaukee Monster had lost the mad, staring eyes that he had when he was first arrested. But experts still could not agree about his thought processes.

Like the capture of many serial killers, the arrest of Jeffrey Dahmer happened

almost by accident. It had been a routine night for Milwaukee police patrolmen Robert Rauth and Rolf Mueller on 22 July 1991 when they spotted a black man running towards their car with a pair of handcuffs dangling from his wrist.

HE HAD FLED FOR HIS LIFE

The man with the handcuffs was Tracy Edwards and he told them a wild story about a man in the Oxford Apartments who had threatened to cut out Tracy's heart and eat it. He had fled for his life. It would turn out that Edwards had narrowly avoided becoming victim number eighteen for America's most bizarre and warped serial killer, Jeffrey Dahmer.

The two veteran policemen, used to responding to trouble in the rundown section of Milwaukee that had become their beat, took Edwards back to the ordinary looking block of flats and rang the buzzer of one of Dahmer's neighbours. 'Open up, this is the police,' they told John Batchelor through the intercom. He let them in and looked at his watch – it was 11:25pm.

Opposite: *Jeffrey Dahmer, the man who shocked the world when his depravity was revealed in a criminal court.*

Above: *Carolyn Smith weeps as court testimony describes the horrible death that her son, Eddie, suffered in the hands of Dahmer.*

THEY SPOTTED A BLACK MAN RUNNING TOWARDS THEIR CAR WITH A PAIR OF HANDCUFFS DANGLING FROM HIS WRISTS.

Nothing had prepared the two cops for what they would find after they rapped on the door of apartment number 213 as Tracy Edwards stayed a safe distance away down the corridor. A slight man with dirty-blonde hair and wearing a blue T-shirt and jeans opened the door. As they entered the dingy flat the policemen smelled a foul stench. A hi-tech electronic lock on Dahmer's front door further heightened their suspicions and they started to ask what had been going on. Mueller spotted some pots on top of the stove, some of them filled with a gooey substance and lots of dirty dishes.

Edwards had told the policemen that he had met Dahmer at a downtown shopping mall and agreed to come back to his flat to drink some beer. When he said he wanted to leave Dahmer threatened him with a knife and put the handcuffs on one of his wrists, holding the other end in his hand. When Edwards later recounted his incredibly lucky escape from the Milwaukee Monster to a packed courtroom, he was too frightened to even look across at the

Above: *In 1978, Jeffrey Dahmer was normal enough to go to the high school prom with a girl, Bridget Geiger. In 1982, he was photographed by the police when he was arrested for disorderly conduct.(Below)*

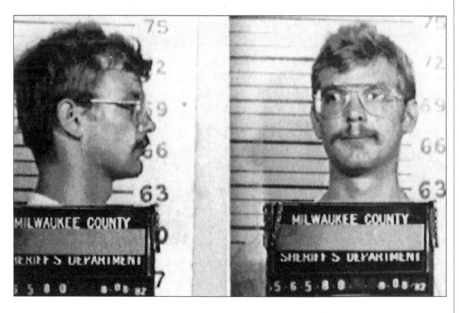

defendant. We must assume that Jeffrey Dahmer had wielded a similar dread power over most of his victims.

After several hours inside the Dahmer lair, during which time Dahmer lay on top of Edwards' chest and listened to his heart, the killer began to get restless. Edwards testified that Dahmer began going in and out of a trance, chanting and swaying back and forth. This gave Edwards the opportunity to escape. Officer Mueller radioed back to police headquarters to 'run a make'

'OH MY GOD! THERE'S A GODDAMN HEAD IN THERE. HE'S ONE SICK SON OF A BITCH.'

---

on Dahmer. When they replied that the man was still on probation for a second degree sexual assault charge against a thirteen-year-old boy, the officers instructed Dahmer to lie face down on the floor so they could handcuff him and take him in. It was then that Officer Mueller wandered over to the refigerator and opened it. 'Oh my God! There's a goddamn head in there. He's one sick son of a bitch.'

Jeffrey Dahmer had been found out and his killing spree had been brought to an abrupt end, but as the gory details of his murderous orgy began to emerge it became clear that for more than a year, he had been killing people and chopping them up.

A COLLECTION OF POLAROIDS SHOWING DAHMER'S VICTIMS

As forensic specialists began to pour into the apartment building to catalogue the series of horrors, neighbours, awakened by all the commotion, started filing out into the streets. Police found a barrel drum filled with acid and the remains of three human torsos. Decomposed hands and genitals were kept in a lobster pot in one of his cupboards along with human skulls, hands and fingers. A collection of Polaroids was found showing each of Dahmer's fifteen victims in various states of undress and then, according to the forensic report 'in different degrees of surgical excision'. They had been slaughtered, butchered and then dissolved.

Photographs from gay magazines hung on Dahmer's bedroom walls and a collection of pornographic videos, heavy metal records and a tape of 'The Exorcist II' littered the living room. The only normal foodstuffs police found in Dahmer's flat were packets of crisps, a jar of mustard, and some beer. Not only had he been murdering and butchering his prey, he had been eating their flesh as well. He would later tell police how he fried one of his victim's biceps in oil and had it for dinner. In his freezer, police found human hamburgers made up of strips of muscle and flesh. Horrified neighbours watched as police in protective anti-toxic suits carried the evidence out of the building.

Dahmer grew up in a normal American family. His father Lionel worked as a research chemist in Bath, Ohio where he married Joyce Flint in 1959. Jeffrey was born exactly nine months after his parents got married, and doesn't seem to have had a terribly traumatic childhood. His parents divorced when he was eighteen and he was left to fend for himself. He was just about to graduate from the Revere High School and he moved into a motel to be by himself while his mother and father sorted out custody of his eleven-year-old brother. By this time, however, Dahmer was beginning to show signs of being 'a little odd'. He had trouble having relationships with girls, he was considered 'weird' by many of his classmates, and his favourite pastime was imitating mentally retarded people. 'He was a class clown but not in a wholesome sense,' recalled Dave Borsvold. 'He was only amused by the bizarre. He used to trace outlines of bodies out on the floor with chalk. He was definitely a little bit different.' But he did not seem dangerous.

His high school guidance counsellor George Kungle said: 'Jeff was never a discipline problem – he was a quiet but not necessarily introverted guy. He never let anyone get to know him well. I would try and talk to him, like you would any kid, hoping to get some insights. He just never said a whole lot about himself.'

A FATHER'S SENSE OF SHAME

During a bitter divorce Jeffrey's father accused his wife of 'extreme cruelty and gross neglect' and he made references to her 'mental illness' and the medical treatment she was receiving. Even the experts do not know what causes a serial killer to develop, but in Dahmer's case an hereditary mental illness might not be too far from the mark. 'In retrospect I wish I had done more in terms of keeping in touch of what he was doing and visiting him more often,' said Dahmer's father when he discovered what his son had been doing. 'I don't know about feeling guilty for what he did, but I feel guilty that I didn't do more. I feel a deep sense of shame. I think any father who has some sense of responsiblity feels the transfer of shame or the responsi-bility somehow for this. When I first heard about it I could not associate him with what I was hearing was done. Absolutely not. I didn't think in my wildest dreams he was capable of something like that,' added

> 'JEFF WAS NEVER A DISCIPLINE PROBLEM – HE WAS A QUIET BUT NOT NECESSARILY INTROVERTED GUY.'

Dahmer Sr. who paid for an expensive criminal defence lawyer, Gerald Boyle, to act for his son.

'I didn't look at him and see a monster. He acts – under most conditions – polite, kind, courteous. I can only imagine in my mind those occasions when he attacked the victims that was the monster who was out of control.' In Revere High School's yearbook Dahmer is described as a 'very valuable' member of the tennis team. He also played in the school band. In the space reserved for what he would like to do with his life, he said he wanted to attend Ohio State University and then pursue a career in business. It would later emerge that

Above: *Jeffrey Dahmer, was at last, in 1991, unmasked for the monster he is. Here he is led into court to face charges of murder and cannibalism .*

Dahmer had already committed his first murder the year he left school. He often killed and mutilated animals in the woods behind his home, before he killed a young male hitch hiker, Stephen Hicks, who was on his way to a rock concert. Dahmer did indeed go to Ohio State in September of 1978 but he dropped out in January the next year to join the army. Friends who remember him say he was set on the idea of becoming a military policeman.

Instead, Dahmer ended up becoming a medical orderly and was sent to Germany to the Baumholder base in Rhineland-Palatinate state. The army has not revealed why he was discharged before his commis-

THE YEAR WAS 1988 AND, UNKNOWN TO THE LAW, HE HAD ALREADY KILLED FOUR TIMES...

Right: *His defence team pleaded insanity on Dahmer's behalf, but the jury were to hear that he had planned his crimes with cunning forethought and in full awareness of his dreadful acts.*

FOR ALMOST TWO YEARS THE PROBABTION OFFICER SAT ACROSS A TABLE FROM DAHMER EVERY FIRST TUESDAY OF EACH MONTH. NEVER IN A MILLION YEARS DID SHE DREAM THAT HE COULD BE CAPABLE OF THE BRUTAL BUTCHERY OF THE ELEVEN YOUNG MEN.

sion was up, but members of Dahmer's family say it was because of alcoholism. His time in the forces equipped him with a rudimentary knowledge of anatomy. When Dahmer returned to America he started drifting into casual, blue collar jobs that paid little and afforded little respect from anyone. After six months in Miami he moved to Bath, Ohio, where he received a disorderly conduct charge for having an open container of alcohol on the street. In January 1982 he moved to Milwaukee to live with his grandmother, where he dispalyed a pattern of bizarre sexual activity by exposing himself to young

and was told to report regularly to a probation officer.

For almost two years probation officer Donna Chester sat across a table from Dahmer every first Tuesday of each month for fifteen minutes. Never in a million years did she dream that he could be capable of the brutal butchery of the eleven young men. Thirty-five-year-old Chester, who still works for the Wisconsin State Probation Service, was assigned to Dahmer's case in March 1990 after he was released from prison. To Chester, Jeffrey Dahmer was no different from most of the one hundred and twenty-one criminals that

children until he was charged with sexual abuse of a thirteen-year-old boy. The young boy's brother was to be a murder victim.

Shortly before he was due to be sentenced for the abuse of the boy, Dahmer wrote a lucid letter to the judge in the case asking for leniency and promising never to do it again. 'The world has enough misery in it without my adding more to it,' he wrote. 'That is why I am requesting a sentence modification. So that I may be allowed to continue my life as a productive member of our society.'

The year was 1988 and, unknown to the law, he had already killed four times. Regardless of his letter Dahmer was sentenced to eight years in jail, though he was released after serving just ten months because he proved to be a model prisoner

were part of her caseload. He was trying to make his way back into society with the help of counselling and supervision after a bout in jail time that he said he regretted.

As he sat in her room in the district office he would tell Donna how his counselling sessions were going, he would talk about his hobbies, his personal life and the things he did in his spare time. What she did not realise was that this was no ordinary sex offender working his way diligently through rehabilitation. Jeffrey Dahmer held a dark secret close to him. And he was so good at it that Donna even cancelled a home visit to his apartment. A spokesman for the Department of Corrections, Joe Scislowicz, said it was unfair to blame Donna Chester for what happened. He remembered Dahmer as polite, punctual and reliable. 'He was only unable to report on two occasions in two years, otherwise he was here at the same time every month,' said Scislowicz. 'Both times he called ahead and said he wouldn't be able to make it and gave a good reason. He was excused from appearing both times. He was very meticulous about reporting to his probation officer once a month. I'm told he was like that in his work, too.'

NAKED AND BLEEDING, HE RAN FROM DAHMER

Scislowicz would not elaborate on the kind of rehabilitation treatment Dahmer was going through – saying it was a breach of privacy – he said his case file shows that Dahmer felt he was making some progress at working towards his goal of becoming a 'useful contributor to society'. Chester's inability to see through Dahmer's tissue of lies brought criticism from Milwaukee police chief Philip Arreola who spoke out about how the system failed its people and its policemen. 'We try to put these people away for a long time and they get let back out on to the streets,' he said. 'Now we can see the tragic results of a system that has simply ceased to function.'

It was a hard pill for the probation department, and Chester to swallow. They felt they had done all they needed to keep tabs on Dahmer. As Scislowicz said: 'There was a lot of evidence he was doing alright. Most people who have a residence and a good paying job tend to stay out of trouble. This is such an exception, it's not fair to blame it on any individual.'

Arreola got a taste of his own medicine just a few days later when it emerged that a tragic, careless act by three bigoted policemen allowed Dahmer to continue with his killing spree unabated. Choking back tears of embarassment the police chief had to admit that he was bringing in the Internal Affairs Division to investigate reports that three officers actually came face to face with Dahmer on the night of 27 May. One even went inside his flat – and not one of them thought anything was wrong.

The incident involved Konerak Sinthasomphone, a fourteen-year-old Laotian refugee who was seen running out of Dahmer's apartment apparently bleeding. Neighbours, mostly black people, called in the police but were more or less told to 'stop bothering the white guy' according to witnesses. Not only was Sinthasomphone naked and bleeding, but he had been drugged with a heavy dose of sleeping pills – Dahmer's favourite form of rendering his victims unconscious before strangling them – and there were tiny drill marks in his head. Dahmer had fantasised about creating zombie-like lovers that could be his sex slaves and he began to experiment on some of them by doing crude lobotomies with an electric drill and some acid. One poor victim stayed awake for an entire day before finally dying. As soon as the police left the building Dahmer, who told them the boy was his lover, strangled Sinthasomphone, and dismembered his body – all the while taking polaroid pictures. The three policemen responsible have been fired.

Within hours of his arrest Dahmer admitted to killing seventeen people, twelve of them inside his Milwaukee flat and two in a different state. He identified photographs of missing persons for detectives. Forensic psychologists and other experts all testified at his trial, which drew large crowds for three weeks at the Milwaukee County Safety Building. But they could not agree on whether he was able to stop his urge to kill, a crucial aspect of his insanity defence. Dahmer sat emotionless, occasionally stifling yawns, as he listened to detectives and psychiatrists recount hundreds of hours of interviews they conducted with him to trying to understand his vile and terrible acts.

DAHMER HAD FANTASISED ABOUT CREATING ZOMBIE-LIKE LOVERS WHO WOULD BE HIS SEX SLAVES.

Below: *This young boy, Konarak Sinthaomphona, ran screaming from Dahmer's flat but passing policemen were convinced by Dahmer that he and the boy were playing a 'homosexual game'. They let the boy go. Dahmer killed him*

Below, left: *Konarak's brother and sister are haunted by their brother's desperate death.*

Relatives of his victims, who were almost all black, listened intently to the gruesome testimony. They hugged each other and cried as they heard for the first time what really happened to their loved ones. At the end of the trial, after a jury found that Dahmer was sane, the relatives gave voice to their horror and grief.

For one young woman, seeing Dahmer face to face was too much. Rita Isbell stared into the eyes of the Milwaukee Monster as Judge Laurence Gram invited her to make a statement before sentence was to be imposed. Rita became hysterical

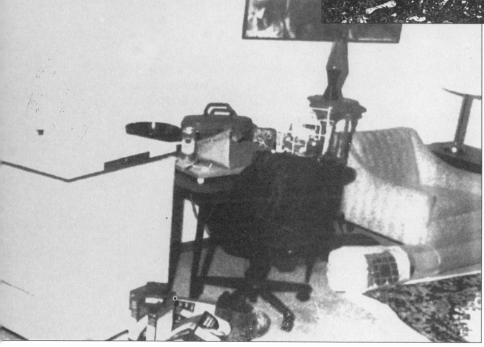

when she started talking about her dead brother, Errol Lindsey, who was just nineteen when he was butchered and dismembered by Dahmer in his Milwaukee apartment in 1991. Dahmer had satisfied his twisted fantasies by having sex with the corpse.'I never want to see my mother go through what she went through because of you,' said Isbell. 'Do you understand Jeffrey? Jeffrey, I hate you,' she shouted. Isbell, wearing a sweatshirt that read '100 per cent black', then ran around the outside of the witness box and towards the table where Dahmer was sitting with his lawyers. 'You Mother ****er, I'll kill you Jeffrey,' she screamed hysterically as five court officers held her back.

After other families called him 'a devil' and asked the judge to ensure that he never

Top: *A Milwaukee policeman is obliged to photograph human bones found in the alley behind Dahmer's apartment.*

Above: *The freezer where Dahmer kept his nasty store of human flesh.*

saw daylight again, Dahmer surprised and stunned everyone by asking to make his own statement – an articulate and far reaching apology he had composed himself in his prison cell. Asking for 'no consideration' in his sentencing and declaring that he would have rather had the death penalty – something the state of Wisconsin does not have – Dahmer said: 'It is over now. This has never been a case of trying to get free. I really wanted death for myself. I hope God can forgive me. I know society and the families can never forgive me. I promise to pray every day for their forgiveness. I have seen their tears. If I could give my life right now to bring their loved ones back I would. This was not about hate. I never hated anyone. I knew I was sick or evil or both. Now I have some peace. I know the harm I have caused. I can't undo the terrible harm I have caused but I cooperated as best I could. I am very sorry.

'I understand their rightful hate,' he said of the victims' families, some of whom said they wished he would go to hell. 'I know I will be in prison for the rest of my life. I will turn back to God. I should have stayed with God. I tried and failed and created a holocaust. Only the Lord Jesus Christ can save me from my sins.' Dahmer promised to devote his time behind bars as a study for doctors and psychologists. He said he would to turn himself into a human guinea pig so that they can further examine his bizarre mind to try and find out what would make a human being turn into such a monster. The killer vowed to help psychiatrists to understand what made him do the ghastly things that he did on his killing, mutilation and cannibalistic spree.

'I pledge to talk to the doctors to help find some answers,' Dahmer said in a prepared statement. 'I know my time in jail will be terrible but I deserve whatever I get because of what I did.' Dahmer – who admitted to detectives that he studied the Satanic scripts – read a passage from the Bible and declared: 'Jesus Christ came to the world to save the sinners, of whom I am the worst.' Dahmer apologised to the victims' families, his probation officer, and even the policemen who were fired. Dahmer also apologised to his father Lionel and step-mother Shari, who both sat quietly and listened intently every day of the court proceedings.

'I regret that the policemen lost their jobs,' said Dahmer. 'I know they did their best. I have hurt my mother, father, step-mother and family. I love them all so much. I only hope they find the same peace I have. I take all the blame for what I did. I hurt many people. I decided to go through with this trial for a number of reasons. I wanted to show these were not hate crimes. I wanted the world to know the truth. I didn't want any unanswered questions. I wanted to find out what it was that caused me to be bad or evil. Perhaps if there are others out there, this all might have helped them.'

ROUND-THE-CLOCK SURVEILLANCE IN ISOLATION

Dahmer was sentenced to a total of one thousand and seventy years in prison on fifteen consecutive counts of murder plus extra sentences for habitual criminality with no possibility of parole for nine hundred and thirty years. Just one day after the sentence he was taken to Wisconsin's toughest jail – the maximum security Columbia Correctional Institution where he is held in a segregated cell. The Portage prison houses five hundred and seventy-five of the worst criminals in the state – sex offenders, murderers, drug dealers and now Jeffrey Dahmer. There is a chance that he could be absorbed into the main prison population but for now he will be under round-the-clock surveillance in isolation. 'At the beginning we will be observing him twenty-four hours a day to ensure that he is not a danger to himself,' said Columbia's

warden Jeffrey Endicott. 'The best way for us to do that is to have him in that section of the prison. It is safest for all concerned.'

Endicott added that many inmates are moved out of the isolation block after a few days, but that Dahmer may be kept there longer than others. Many of the one hundred and fifty sex offenders in the prison never leave their single cells or mingle with other prisoners. Fellow serial killer Henry Lee Lucas, who is on death row in a Texas prison said that life in jail for him was 'pure hell'. Lucas, who was convicted of eleven murders and suspected of committing one hundred and forty more, says Dahmer will have a rough time of it. 'He'll be lucky to stay alive in prison. There's a thing in prison about kids, you know,' he said.'If somebody kills a kid like that he'll have a hard way to go.'

Dahmer will have no contact with other prisoners at first and even though he says he no longer wants to kill, guards have been told to take every precaution when dealing with him. All of his food is passed to him through a drawer in a wall to avoid contact

and he will be kept under constant surveillance twenty-four hours a day by guards who sit inside a protected 'control bubble'. Columbia Correctional Institution is a large complex, with five watchtowers, razor wire topped high security fences and electronic surveillance of its nineteen-acre perimeter. There is no chance that Dahmer could escape. He is allowed to exercise once a day but is always accompanied by several guards. And he must wear the bright orange jumpsuit uniform he was given when he walked in the front door of the prison.

DAHMER WAS SENTENCED TO A TOTAL OF ONE THOUSAND AND SEVENTY YEARS IN PRISON ON FIFTEEN CONSECUTIVE COUNTS OF MURDER.

Above: *The freezer, vital evidence to support the charge that Dahmer was a cannibal, is loaded on a police van.*

Right: *Another mother grieves for her son during a candlelit vigil held in Milwaukee for the murdered boys. Her son was Tony Hughes, and he was dismembered by the monster.*

Below: *Oliver Lacy, one of the many victims. Dahmer decapitated the corpse and kept the head.*

HE IS SIMILAR TO MANY OF AMERICA'S WORST MASS MURDERERS IN THAT HE CAN BE PERFECTLY NORMAL WHILE HE IS NOT IN HIS 'KILLING MODE'.

Dahmer will not be allowed any more than six books, four magazines, ten pictures and fifteen letters. Each week he receives more than two dozen letters – some from women who want to meet him and fall in love. Dahmer came from a middle-class family, but was affected in early life by a trauma or rejection which sent him over the edge.

He is similar to many of America's worst mass murderers, in that he can be perfectly normal while he is not in his 'killing mode', and that may work to his advantage in jail. Ed Gein was working as a babysitter while he was spending his nights digging up graves; Ted Bundy worked at a Samaritans' hotline in Seattle in between killings; John Wayne Gacy performed as a clown at childrens' parties; amd David Berkowitz now spends much of his time counselling other inmates at a New York state high security prison.

He helps them with their problems, reads their mail to them and cleans floors. He is considered a model prisoner and will be elligible for parole in ten years. 'Many of these killers are frequently glib and superficially charming, helpful, sweet and kind,' said Helen Morrison, a Chicago psychiatrist and serial killer expert. 'I'm sure Dahmer falls into that same category.' Judith Becker, who testified at the Dahmer trial for the defence, says it is too soon to tell how the prison term will affect Dahmer's personality or his mind. 'He did indicate to me that he hated what he had been doing and he talked about a 'nuclear explosion' that had happened within him since he had been caught,' she said. 'He's talked about killing himself, but obviously he won't be able to do that in prison. He says he is sorry for what he did and that he feels pain for the relatives of the victims. He has already had a lot of time on his own to think about that, and he seems to be coping with it now. The fantasies have stopped, he says. But there is no way of really knowing if they will start up again.'

THE CHANCES ARE THAT HE COULD BECOME A MODEL PRISONER

'The prosecution made a strong case by identifying that Dahmer was able to make definite decisions not to do things at certain times,' said David Barlow, an assistant professor of criminal justice at the University of Wisconsin. Richard Kling, who defended serial killer John Wayne Gacy, added: 'I don't think there is a person in the world who would come in and say Dahmer isn't abnormal. The problem is that abnormal doesn't add up to insanity.' How he deals with being in prison is something that will fascinate psychiatric experts for years to come. The chances are that he could become a model prisoner, with the ability to be outwardly friendly to both fellow inmates and guards.

During the trial McCann pointed out Dahmer's ability to manipulate doctors and psychiatrists for his own ends. His supply of prescription sleeping pills – which he used for drugging his victims before he strangled them – came from doctors who thought he was having trouble sleeping.

Dahmer also deliberately misled court appointed therapists who were trying to help him after he was convicted of sexual assault. He rejected the hand that could have helped him,' said McCann. 'He knew what he was doing.' No matter what happens the files of Jeffrey Dahmer will provide endless hours of research material for the FBI's academy in Quantico, Virginia – where special agents are trained to produce profiles of serial killers. Although the project is temporarily dormant after the departure of its director, Robert Ressler, Dahmer's court files will be entered into the FBI's extensive databanks on serial killers.

'SILENCE OF THE LAMBS'

Ressler, who has interviewed such killers as Charles Manson, Sirhan Sirhan, Ted Bundy, John Wayne Gacy, and 'Son of Sam' killer David Berkowitz will attempt to see Dahmer so that he can include his files in his rogue's gallery.'How can a person be sane and do these horrendous acts ?'. He would be a fascinating study for me,' said Ressler, who now runs his own investigating company. 'Any information we can collect on individuals like Dahmer is like gold dust in tracking down others out there who might be doing the same thing.'

In the film 'Silence of the Lambs' Jodie Foster played a young FBI agent who had to befriend the demented Hopkins character – Hannibal the Cannibal – so that she could help catch another serial killer, a murderer based on Wisconsin's other famous maniac, Ed Gein. Gein killed women and then skinned them to satisfy his twisted transvestite fantasies. He also dug up freshly buried bodies so that he could use their skin to build himself a body. He was found mentally incompetent to stand trial in 1957 and so never had the opportunity to

> DAHMER DELIBERATELY MISLED COURT-APPOINTED THERAPISTS WHO WERE TRYING TO HELP HIM AFTER HE WAS CONVICTED OF SEXUAL ASSAULT.

plead guilty. He died at the Mendota Mental Health Institute in Madison in 1984. Other psychiatric experts have pointed out that a thorough investigation of Dahmer would be invaluable as research material into sexual perversion.

Judith Becker said: 'We could learn a tremendous amount from studying Dahmer because necrophiliacs are extremely rare. I have not seen anywhere in the literature the sucessful treatment of this disorder.' Even the most highly qualified experts cannot agree on what kind of demons live inside the mind of Jeffrey Dahmer. He showed early on in his life a twisted fascination with the macabre and the bizarre. Some psychiatrists claim that the emotional distance between him and his parents might have contributed to his feelings of abandonment. Those feelings fuelled his

Above: *Jeffrey Dahmer claimed to feel 'remorse' for his acts. But it needed a police investigation to provoke these feelings in him.*

ghastly killing spree – he told doctors that he killed his victims because he didn't want them to leave him. Some experts say being locked up for life with other criminals who won't be leaving might actually appeal to the perverse needs of Jeffrey Dahmer.

'One great myth about serial killers is that they secretly want to get caught,' said James Fox, a professor of criminal justice

SOUVENIRS ARE VERY IMPORTANT TO THE DISORGANISED SERIAL KILLERS BECAUSE THEY REMIND THEM OF THE BEST TIMES THEY HAD. DAHMER'S MURDERS WERE DRIVEN BY HIS FANTASIES OF DESTRUCTION, TIED UP WITH A SEXUAL DESIRE.'

at Boston's Northeastern University and author of 'Mass Murder: The Growing Menace'. 'That's just not true, these guys enjoy what they do. They might get a little guilty afterwards for a while, but the fantasies that drive them are so powerful that they have to do it again soon. Dahmer will not be able to do it again now that he's in jail and I'm sure he won't be happy about that. He doesn't even have any of his souvenirs – the photos or even the body parts – to look at anymore. That may be why he has asked for the death penalty, he has nothing else to live for. Souvenirs are

very important to the disorganised serial killers because they remind them of the best times they had. Dahmer's murders were driven by his fantasies of destruction, tied up with a sexual desire.'

Prosecutor E. Michael McCann said that Dahmer has always managed to control his violent tendencies when he has been in closely controlled situations and some feel that prison life will do him a lot of good.

DAHMER LONGS FOR DEATH

Worst of all for Dahmer will be the long hours of contemplation he will have to spend alone. He told detectives after his arrest that he wished Wisconsin or Ohio had the death penalty. Now he will have to spend the next forty years thinking about what he did. 'It will probably tear him apart,' said one expert. 'If the court didn't think he was insane when he killed, just wait a few years and see what the torture of his acts does to his mind.'

Dahmer may have to go through the trial process all over again in Ohio where he killed his first victim in 1978. But Ohio, like Wisconsin, has no death penalty – the one thing that Dahmer has wished for.

The world will be a safer place without Jeffrey Dahmer. But the world might never know what it was that drove him to commit some of the worst crimes in American history. One thing is certain, inmates at Columbia will not be jumping over each other for a chance to share a cell with him.

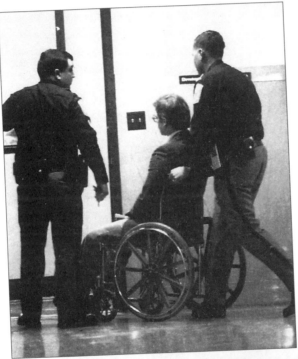

Above: *The Milwaukee Monster is wheeled into court. His hands and legs were shackled in irons as befits a dangerous beast.*

Right: *Lionel and Shane Dahmer, Jeffrey's father and stepmother, sat in court throughout his trial.*

VICTIMS AS NAMED BY PROSECUTOR'S OFFICE:

1 January 1988 – James Doxtator
Killed at age fifteen at Dahmer's grandmother's house. Strangled after drinking sleeping potion. Dismembered, bones smashed with a sledgehammer.

2 March 1988 – Richard Guerrero
Killed at age twenty-three at grandmother's house. Drugged him and then dismembered the body.

3 March 1989 – Anthony Sears
Killed at age twenty-four at grandmother's house. Strangled and dismembered. Dahmer kept his skull, boiled off the skin and then painted the skull as a souvenir.

**4 May 1990 – Raymond Smith,
aka Ricky Beeks**
Killed at age thirty in Apartment 213. Strangled after being drugged. Dahmer had sex with the dead body. Dismembered him but kept the skull and painted it.

5 July 1990 – Edward Smith
Killed at age twenty-eight. Dismembered and disposed of in rubbish bags.

6 September 1990 – Ernest Miller
Killed at age twenty-three. Dahmer slit his throat, dismembered him and kept his biceps in the freezer to eat later. Also kept the skull and skeleton which he bleached.

7 October 1990 – David Thomas
Killed at age twenty-three. Killed even though he was not Dahmer's 'type' for fear that he would tell police he had been drugged. Body disposed of.

8 February 1991 – Curtis Straughter
Killed at age seventeen. Strangled with a strap after being drugged. Dismembered him but kept the skull.

9 April 1991 – Errol Lindsey
Killed at age nineteen. Strangled him and then had sex. Dismembered the body and kept the skull.

10 May 1991 – Anthony Hughes
Killed at age thirty-two. Strangled and dismembered him but kept the skull.

**11 May 1991 – Konerak
Sinthasomphone**
Killed at age fifteen. Murdered after police left Dahmer's apartment following telephone call from neighbours. Strangled, dismembered but kept the skull.

**12 June 1991 – Matt Turner aka Donald
Montrell**
Killed at age twenty-one. Strangled with a strap. Kept his head in the freezer and put his body in the acid-filled barrel.

13 July 1991 – Jeremiah Weinberger
Killed at age twenty-four. Strangled with his hands. Put his head in the freezer and his body in the barrel.

14 July 1991 – Oliver Lacy
Killed at age twenty-five. Strangled him and then had sex. Placed head in the bottom of the fridge and kept his heart in the freezer to eat later. Also kept his body in the freezer.

15 July 1991 – Joseph Bradehoft
Killed at age twenty-five. Strangled with a strap while he slept. Dismembered, head put in the freezer and body in the barrel.

Two additional victims Dahmer has admitted killing were not in the Milwaukee charges. They were:

Stephen Hicks was killed in Dahmer's parents' home in Bath, Ohio. Dahmer killed him with a barbell, then disposed of the body in the woods.

Stephen Tuomi killed in Milwaukee hotel room in September 1987. Dahmer says he doesn't remember how he killed the man, but he took his body back to his grandmother's house in a trunk and dismembered him.

Above: *Investigators were sent to Dahmer's boyhood home to look for the remains of the Monster's first victim, killed in 1978.*

HE DOESN'T REMEMBER HOW HE KILLED, BUT HE TOOK THE BODY BACK TO HIS GRANDMOTHER'S HOUSE AND DISMEMBERED IT.

GRAHAM YOUNG
The Broadmoor Poisoner

Is it possible for a child to be born evil? Graham Young was a prodigy in poison, experimenting with deadly potions even before he was sixteen. And he killed his family and friends as if they were laboratory rats.

Even as a small child, Graham Young was entranced by poisons. Other people may regard such substances with alarm and caution but Graham played with them, learnt their various deadly properties and longed to use them.

Like Ian Brady, the infamous Moors Murderer, Graham Young had a lonely childhood, and in his sullen resentment of the world, turned to other outsiders in his search for role models. Dr Crippen, the wife murderer, was an idol, as was the Victorian poisoner, William Palmer. In contemplating their lives and dreadful acts, Graham Young found a kind of solace which he never got from his family.

He was born in September 1947, and his mother died when he was just three months old. He was cared for by his father's sister, Auntie Winifred, and her husband, Uncle Jack and their's was an affectionate household. But at the age of two his life changed when he was sent to live with his father, who had married a twenty-six-year-old woman called Molly. Psychologists would later say that 'the terrible coldness' that characterised Young was formed by the truama of separation from his first home. He never trusted any affection after that, believing only that it would end in pain and rejection.

Relations with his stepmother were cordial but she never lavished on him the brand of intense loving he craved. Perhaps she found it difficult, for Graham was rummaging through the chemist's rubbish bins in his search for poisons, and was reading books on Satanism by the time he was nine years old. He began wearing a swastika badge that he found at a jumble sale and refused to take it off, even for his teachers at school. Yet Graham was an exceptionally intelligent child, with a strong scientific ability. To celebrate his achievement in passing the eleven-plus examination, his father gave the boy his first chemistry set.

Opposite: **The child prodigy in poison, Graham Young, is led into custody.**

Below: **David Tilson, a victim who survived the poisons.**

This gift was the key to the wonderful world of poisons that Graham longed to master. The phials and bunsen burners, the laboratory pipettes and crucibles became his toys at an age when most boys have their pockets stuffed with conkers and fudge. His private games were also more sinister than those of the normal child. Graham liked to witness the death throes of the mice that he fed with the poisons he brewed from his chemistry set. When his stepmother angrily removed a live mouse, and demanded that he stop bringing them into the house, he drew a picture of a craggy tombstone toppling over a mound, inscribed with the words: 'In Hateful Memory of Molly Young, R.I.P.' Graham made sure that the poor woman saw this nasty little drawing.

HE NEVER TRUSTED ANY AFFECTION, BELIEVING ONLY THAT IT WOULD END IN PAIN AND REJECTION.

The youngster took to stealing chemicals from his school and he took to carrying a bottle of ether from which he would frequently take sniffs; he raided his stepmother's cosmetics cabinet to get at nail polish remover, which he used to kill a frog in one of his experiments in the effects of poison. By the time he was twelve, his teachers at the John Kelly Secondary School in Willesden knew that Graham had an unusual expertise, not only in poisons, but in his general pharmaceutical knowledge. The child knew the ingredients

of most household medicines, and was able to diagnose minor illnesses.

But medicine and its life-saving properties were not of real interest to the child boffin. He preferred poisons and their deadly effects. When he was thirteen, Graham found a book that would forever change his life. It was the story of the nineteenth-century poisoner Dr Edward Pritchard, who killed his wife and his mother with the poison antimony. Antimony, a slow working toxin, causes cramps, nausea and swellings in the victim. These symptoms have often led to an incorrect diagnoses from doctors, and this fact has, naturally, made the poison a favourite among murderers.

> CHRIS HAD TO BE PUNISHED. GRAHAM BEGAN TO LACE HIS FRIEND'S SANDWICHES WITH ANTIMONY AND WATCHED THE RESULTS WITH SATISFACTION.

Left: *Graham Young was incarcerated in hospitals and prisons, but he still managed to experiment with his poisons.*

Opposite, above: *The poisoner, whose youth and ruthlessness horrified the nation, was obscured by a blanket as he was bundled into a police van.*

Opposite, below: *The sweet face of a boy but the Young family were not entirley fooled. They knew something was wrong with the child, Graham.*

> MRS YOUNG SUFFERED SEVERE VOMITING ATTACKS. THEN GRAHAM'S FATHER EXPERIENCED SIMILAR SYMPTOMS, AS DID HIS AUNTIE WINIFRED.

Chemist Geoffrey Reis in High Street, Neasden, sold Graham Young the poison antimony. The boy lied about his age and claimed he was seventeen. Reis explained to the police that the boy's knowledge of poisons was so vast, and he outlined in such detail the chemical experiments in which he intended to use the restricted merchandise, that the chemist naturally assumed him to be older than a mere thirteen-year-old. And neither was Graham Young strictly truthful in describing his experiments to the chemist.

Chris Williams was one of Graham's few schoolboy friends who shared his love of chemistry. He had even invited Chris to his bedroom laboratory to share the pleasure of watching mice die in agony. But Chris Williams began hanging around with another boy, and Graham interpreted this as a persoanl rejection. Chris had to be punished. Graham began to lace his friend's sandwiches with antimony and watched the results with satisfaction. After Chris had suffered two violent vomiting attacks, his family sent him to a specialist who was unable to diagnose the problem. Throughout the early part of 1961, Graham continued to administer doses of poison to his school chum.

EPIDEMIC OF POISONING

Young took to carrying a phial of antimony around with him all the time, calling it 'my little friend'. But his stepmother found the bottle, marked with a skull and crossbones, and put a stop to her stepson's shopping trips when she herself informed the chemist, Mr Reis, of Graham's age. Thwarted but by no means defeated, Graham switched to a new supplier, and a new target. Molly Young would be punished for this.

In October and November, 1961, Mrs Young suffered severe vomiting attacks. Then Graham's father experienced similar symptoms, as did his Auntie Winifred. On one occasion, Graham spiked his own food in error, and he, too, was violently ill, but this did not deter the young poisoner. Using antimony tartrate which he bought from Edgar Davies – another chemist similarly fooled by his advanced knowledge of poisons – he moved on to his step-sister. The girl tasted something odd, and spat out her tea, accusing her mother of leaving some washing-up liquid in the cup.

Winifred was the first to be diagnosed as a poison victim when she had to be helped from a London Underground train on her way to work one morning, in the summer of 1962. Dizzy, her eyes blinded with pain and feeling very ill, she was rushed by ambulance to the Middlesex Hospital where a doctor said she was suffering from belladonna poisoning, the toxin released from the berries of the deadly nightshade

> HIS FATHER WAS INFORMED THAT HE WAS LUCKY TO BE ALIVE, BUT THAT HIS LIVER WAS PERMANENTLY DAMAGED.

weed. Winifred believed that her nephew was to blame, but a search of his room failed to give evidence to her fears. Molly Young's health continued to decline as Graham fed her increasing doses of the antimony tartrate. Early in 1962 she died. At the age of fourteen, Graham Young had committed the perfect murder. He was arrested on suspicion of causing his stepmother's death, but he was released without charge. Molly was cremated and the evidence, the poison in her bloodstream, went with her.

Graham Young was now assured of his powers to punish those who annoyed or rejected him. Besides, he still had some unfinished business. Dad was to be fed further doses of antimony, as was his unfortunate schoolfriend who continued to suffer violent attacks of nausea, but was still alive. Fred Young collapsed and was rushed to Willesden Hospital where doctors diagnosed arsenic poisoning. 'How ridiculous!' sneered Graham when he visited his father in hospital. 'Fancy not knowing how to tell the difference between antimony and arsenic poisoning!' He explained to the doctors that his father showed all the symptoms of antimony poisoning, but offered no explanation as to how the poison entered his father's system. His father was informed that he was lucky to be alive, but that his liver was permanently damaged. He was allowed home, but was back in hospital within a couple of days because Graham could not resist giving his father another dose in his morning tea.

The Young family were, by now, thoroughly alarmed by their suspicions that their own Graham might be causing their various illnesses. They did not like the way Graham seemed to brighten up and become keenly interested whenever he was discussing the finer points of poison with hospital staff. His father told Aunt Winifred to keep an eye on him, but it was to be his chemistry master at school who spotted the boy's toxic ways. The teacher went through Graham's desk at school, discovering notebooks with lurid pictures of men in their death throes, empty bottles of poison by their sides. He discovered phials of antimony tartrate alongside the drawings, plus detailed notes of what doseages of particular poisons are needed to kill an adult human being. After voicing his concerns to the school headmaster, the two teachers decided to inform the police. The police, in turn, decided to get a psychiatrist to help them trap Graham.

Posing as a careers guidance officer, the psychiatrist interviewed the boy, asking him what he would like to do when he left

school. The doctor was both astounded and horrified at the detailed knowledge the boy had about poisons and their effects. One by one Graham reeled them off, leaving no doubt whatsoever in the psychiatrist's mind that this boy was a psycopath. His report prompted the police to search Young's room. This revealed seven different types of poison stashed in various hiding places, and included a copious amount of antimony tartrate.

Graham Young encountered the police when he came home from school. He reeked of the ether he habitually sniffed, and vehemently denied any involvement in the poisoning of his family. But Young's vanity overcame him. As he liked to brag to the doctors and the psychiatrist, showing off his knowledge of poison, so he could not resist telling the police that he was a successful poisoner. He confessed all, listing the doseages, the times and the methods he used to dispense the poison.

Left: *Jethro Batt whose evidence helped convict the mad poisoner.*

Below: *John Williams who told the court of Young's repeated attempts to kill him with poison.*

At Ashford Remand Centre he was subjected to a battery of psychiatric and psychological testing. The doctors who examined him recognised that his was a rare problem, for Young was incapable of comprehending his guilt. 'He has a distinct lack of moral sense, an idea that he is neither bound to nor governed by the rules which apply to other members in society,' was the official verdict. Indeed, Young relished telling the doctors, who were probing his warped emotional state, about his potions and how he loved his father, but that he came to view his parent as a guinea pig for experiments in poison. He told them: 'I chose my family because they were close at hand, where I could observe and note the results of my experiments.' There was no remorse, however. 'I love my antimony,' he explained. 'I love the power it gives me.'

The case of the schoolboy poisoner captured the public imagination when he came before the stern judge Mr Justice

Melford Stevenson on 6 July, 1962, at the Old Bailey. This is Britain's highest court, where half-a-century before, Graham's hero Dr Crippen, had been condemned to death.

Graham Young was charged with poisoning his father, his aunt and his school chum. He spoke only once at his trial, to plead guilty to the charges, but a statement that he made while in custody was read out. Graham told the police: 'I knew that the doses I was giving were not fatal, but I knew I was doing wrong. It grew on me like a drug habit, except it was not me who was taking the drugs. I realised how stupid I have been with these poisons. I knew this all along but I could not stop it.'

A psychiatrist, after testifying that Young was suffering from a psychopathic disorder, recommended the accused be incarcerated in Broadmoor, Britain's top security mental hospital. The judge asked whether a grim, forbidding place such as Broadmoor was the right institution for such a young boy, but after further testimony from Dr Donald Blair, a psychiatrist who had also examined Young, he – the judge – was left with little choice. Blair told the court: 'There is no doubt in my mind that this youth is, at present, a very serious danger to other people. His intense obsession and almost exclusive interest in drugs and their poisoning effect is not likely to change, and he could well repeat his cool, calm, calculating administration of these poisons at any time.'

Young was sent to Broadmoor with an instruction that he should not be released without the permission of the Home Secretary. It was not, however, the last that the world would hear of Graham Young and his potions.

POISONER BEHIND BARS

Far from being an unsuitable place for Graham, Broadmoor was actually a home-from-home for him. The institute is a hospital, after all, and the young poisoner was surrounded by all the medicines and drugs and poisons that he could wish for. He enjoyed lecturing the staff on toxins, and often gave advice to nurses on drugs when no doctors were on hand. Suspicion, however, fell upon him when a fellow inmate, twenty-three-year-old double-murderer John Berridge, died of cyanide

poisoning. But Graham was never charged with his murder, although he spent many hours explaining to other inmates how the poison could be extracted from the leaves of the laurel bushes which grew in the hospital grounds.

Young's room in Broadmoor became a shrine to Nazism, heavily decorated with swastikas. He even grew a toothbrush moustache and combed his hair in a fashion that imitated that of Adolf Hitler. He managed to secure a 'green card' – the special pass allowing him to freely roam the hospital wards and gardens. The pass was issued by the psychiatric staff in contradiction to the wishes and advice of the day-to-day nursing staff. The card gave Young the opportunity to collect leaves and plants that contained poisonous materials, and to steal chemicals. The nursing staff often found jars of poison, not on the shelves where they were supposed to be, but in odd places. Young owned up to hiding some of these, but not all. Inexplicable outbreaks of stomach aches and cramps were endured by both staff and

Above: *Winifred Young, Graham's sister, and his aunt who listened intently to the court evidence against him.*

'THERE IS NO DOUBT IN MY MIND THAT THIS YOUTH IS, AT PRESENT, A VERY SERIOUS DANGER TO OTHER PEOPLE.'

Above: Broadmoor, the mental hospital where Young was confined.
Below: Frederick Young, the father who nearly died.

patients; hindsight dictates that Young had been busy dispensing his potions freely-round the large prison hospital.

With the support of two senior doctors who did not want to see him institution-alised for the rest of his life, Graham was able to convince the parole board to free him for Christmas in 1970. He spent it with his Auntie Win, but his return to Broadmoor after the holidays made him more resentful than ever. He wrote a note that nursing staff found, saying: 'When I get out of here I intend to kill one person for every year I have spent inside.'

Nursing staff say they heard him boasting, when he thought no staff were listening, how he wanted to be the most infamous poisoner since Crippen. And the note he wrote remained on their files. Yet Graham Young was released after nine years. At the age of twenty-three he returned to his forgiving Auntie Winifred at her home in Hemel Hempstead, Hertfordshire, before moving on to a hostel in Chippenham where he began his new life.

ANOTHER FRIEND POISONED

Within weeks he was up to his old tricks again. A keen amateur footballer called Trevor Sparkes, who was with Young at a training centre, suffered cramps and pain over a six-month period, and was so debili-tated by the mysterious 'illness' that he would never play football again. Sparkes would testify that he and Young enjoyed a friendship, and it never occurred to the footballer that he was being systematically poisoned by his friend.

In April, 1971, Graham saw an advertisement, offering employment for a storeman with the John Hadland Company of Bovingdon, in Hertfordshire. Hadland's was a well-established family firm that manufactured high grade optical and photographic equipment. Graham impressed Managing Director, Godfrey Foster, at the interview, and explained that his long break from regular employment was due to a nervous breakdown. Foster checked up with the training centre and also Broadmoor, and he received such glowing references as to the young man's abilities and recovery that he offered him the job without hesitation..

On Monday 10 May, 1971, Graham Young arrived at Hadlands. The company thought they were getting a storeman. In reality, they had hired an angel of death. Young rented a bedsitter, and the cupboards and shelves were soon filled with a collection of poisons. At work he was regarded as a quiet, remote young man unless the conversation turned to politics or chemistry when he became belligerent and articulate. His best friend at work was forty-one-year-

inquest on his body because doctors diagnosed his illness as bronchial-pneumonia linked to polyneuritis.

In September, after a relatively pain-free summer for the staff at Hadlands, because

Below: *Frederick Young, Graham's father and the long-suffering Aunt Winnie. Graham tried to poison both of them.*

old Ron Hewitt whose job he was taking. Ron stayed on to show the new man the ropes and introduced him to the other hands in the plant. Many showed great kindness to Young, lending him money and giving him cigarettes when he had none. Young repaid their warmth by rushing to serve them from the morning tea trolley.

On Thursday 3 June, less than a month after Graham started work, Bob Egle, fifty-nine, who worked as storeroom boss, was taken ill with diarrhoea, cramps and nausea. Next, Ron Hewitt fell violently ill, suffering the same symptoms but with burning sensations at the back of his throat. Workers at Hadlands called the mystery pains 'the bug'. In fact, the symptoms were caused by doses of Thallium, an extremely toxic poison. Young bought the poison from chemists in London, and then laced his workmates' tea with the deadly, but tasteless and odourless chemical. On Wednesday, 7 July, Bob Egle died. His was a horrible, painful death, yet there was no

Young was often absent from work, Fred Biggs, a part-time worker, died after suffering agonising cramps and pains over a twenty-day period. Young feigned sympathy for him, as he had for his other victims. 'Poor old Fred,' he said to colleague, Diana Smart. 'It's terrible. I wonder what went wrong with him. I was very fond of Fred.' Four other workers fell victim to awful illnesses, two of them losing all their hair, followed by severe cases of depression.

The company became so concerned by the poor health of their workforce, that they called in a local doctor, Iain Anderson, to check the employees, but he was unable to determine the source of the 'bug'. But then Anderson talked to Graham Young, who unable to suppress his vanity, reeled off mind-numbing statistics about poisons and their effects and Anderson's amazement turned to suspicion. He consulted the company management, who called Scotland Yard. The police ran a background check on

IT WAS A RELATIVELY PAIN-FREE SUMMER FOR THE STAFF AT HADLANDS BECAUSE YOUNG WAS OFTEN ABSENT FROM WORK.

FOUR OTHER WORKERS FELL VICTIM TO AWFUL ILLNESSES, TWO OF THEM LOSING ALL THEIR HAIR, FOLLOWED BY SEVERE CASES OF DEPRESSION.

Above: Graham Young taken into court by law officers. He was given a long sentence, but died in prison – not of self-administered poison, but a heart attack.

this confession could put him in jail for life. But the prisoner said: 'You have to prove that I did it.' He intended to withdraw his statement in court, which in due course he did.

On 3 December, Graham Young was charged with murdering Egle after the analysis of the ashes of his cremated corpse showed traces of Thallium in them. He pleaded Not Guilty. He was also charged with the murder of Fred Biggs and the attempted murders of two others and of further administering poison to two others.

In prison , Young enquired of his guards whether Madame Tussaud's waxworks in London were planning to put his effigy next to those of his heroes, Hitler and the poisoner, Palmer. He threatened to kill himself in the dock of the court if he were found Guilty. But there were no theatricals from the prisoner when he was convicted on all charges by a jury that took less than an hour to deliberate on the evidence.After a brief chat with his family, he was taken away to begin a life sentence in July 1972.

A DEADLY FUNGUS

all company employees, while forensic scientists from the government research station at Aldermaston were asked to analyse samples taken from the poorly members of staff. The scientists proved that Thallium had caused the deaths and the illnesses among the staff at Hadlands. Graham Young was arrested at his father's house, and as he was led away, asked the police: 'Which ones are they doing me for, then?'

However, in custody Young claimed that he was innocent, despite the fact that a phial of Thallium was found in his jacket pocket, and a list of six names of Hadland's employees was found in his bedsitter. The list was significant: it included the two men who had died, and the four stricken with horrible illnesses. But Young could not resist for long his need to boast.

He detailed his first murder, that of his stepmother, and explained why he decided to poison his workmates. Graham Young said: 'I suppose I had ceased to see them as people – or, more correctly, a part of me had. They became guinea pigs.' Detective Chief Superintendent Harvey Young, in charge of the case, warned Graham that

Young was not sent back to Broadmoor but, initially, was sent to Wormwood Scrubs, then, to the top security Park Lane Mental Hospital near Liverpool. He was in this institution for two years before officials realised he had lost none of his madness. In 1990, they discovered that Graham had grown, in the prison grounds, a deadly fungus that he mixed with his own excrement to concoct a deadly toxin.

He was transferred to the top security prison of Parkhurst on the Isle of Wight where he was found dead in his cell on 2 August 1990. At first, officials thought that he had killed himself with one of his own poisons, but a post mortem revealed that a heart attack had been cause of death.

There were few people to weep for him, his sister, also called Winifred, felt sad for him. She said that he craved publicity and infamy, and he certainly achieved these ambitions. But she said that he was depressive and lonely. When she suggested he ease his loneliness by going to social clubs or dances, he replied; 'Nothing like that can help me, I'm afraid. You see, there is this terrible coldness inside of me...'

WAR CRIMES

POL POT
The Murder Machine

A gentle nation, ancient in its culture, pious in its faith, was cruelly dismembered by a Marxist fanatic. Pol Pot turned Cambodia into a killing field while the world turned its back on this lost nation.

I magine a government that comes to power, then declares that money is banned. Not only money, but the forces which provide money – commerce, industry, banking – are also proscribed. The new government decrees that society will become agrarian again, just like it had been in the Middle Ages. Great cities and towns will be de-populated and the people will be moved to the countryside, where they will live and work raising crops and cattle. But families will not be allowed to stay together. The government, in its infinite wisdom, realises that children must not be influenced by outdated and archaic bourgois thoughts passed down by their parents. So they are taken away and brought up as the vanguard of the regime, imbued with and steeped in the philosophy of the new order. No messing about with books until they are in the late teens – there is no need for books anymore, so they are burned – and children from the age of seven will begin working for the state.

For the new agrarian class, there are eighteen-hour days, back-breaking work, followed by 're-education' in Marxist-Leninist thought from their new masters. Anyone who dissents, or who shows signs of 'regression' to the old ways is not allowed to live – nor are intellectuals, teachers and college professors; nor those people who are literate because they might read thoughts which are not Marxist-Leninist, and spread a poisonous philosophy among the re-educated workers in the fields. Priests, with their outmoded theology, politicians of any hue other than that of the ruling party and those who made

fortunes under previous governments are no longer needed: they too are eliminated. There is no trade, there are no telephones, there are no churches or temples, here are no bicycles, birthday parties, marriages, anniversaries, love or kindness. At best, there is work for the state – torture, degradation and at worst, death.

This nightmare scenario was not a figment of some science fiction writer's imagination. It became a terrible reality in Cambodia, where leader Pol Pot turned the clock back and pushed civilisation out, hoping to find his own warped vision of a classless society. His 'killing fields' were littered with the corpses of those who did not fit into the new world that his brutal

Above: *The grinning face of evil – Pol Pot is a study in tyranny and murder. He turned his gentle land into a vast 'killing field'.*

AS MANY AS THREE MILLION PEOPLE MAY HAVE PERISHED DURING POL POT'S REGIME IN CAMBODIA.

subordinates were shaping. As many as three million people may have perished during Pol Pot's regime in Cambodia – the same number of unfortunates killed in the gas chambers of the Auschwitz death factory run by the Nazis in the Second World War. Life under Pol Pot was intolerable and Cambodians were forced to tragically re-christen their South-East Asian country. They gave it the macabre name of the Land of the Walking Dead.

The Cambodian tragedy was a legacy of the Vietnam War that first marked the end of French colonialism before escalating into the conflict against the Americans. Fifty-three thousand Cambodians were slain on the fields of battle. Between 1969 and 1973 American B-52 aircraft carpet-bombed huge tracts of Cambodia, dropping as many tons of high-explosive on the tiny land as had fallen on Germany in the last two years of the Second World War. The Viet Cong fighters in Vietnam used its neighbour's lush jungles as encampments

Above: *Leading a column of his faithful followers, Pol Pot treks through the Cambodian jungle.*

HE ORDERED THE ABOLI-TION OF ALL MARKETS, THE DESTRUCTION OF CHURCHES AND THE PERSECUTION OF ALL RELIGIOUS ORDERS.

and staging posts for operations against the Americans, and these hideouts were the targets of the war planes.

Prince Norodom Sihanouk, ruler of Cambodia and heir to its great religious and cultural traditions, renounced his royal title ten years before the onset of the Vietnam War, but remained the head of his country. He tried to guide his country along a path of neutrality, a delicate balancing act for a country surrounded by warring states and conflicting ideologies. He had been crowned King of Cambodia, a French protectorate, in 1941, but abdicated in 1955. However, he returned, after free and fair elections, as head of state.

Between 1966 and 1969, as the Vietnam War escalated in intensity, he upset policy-makers in Washington by ignoring the arms smuggling and the Vietnamese guerilla camps in the jungles of Cambodia. At the same time, he was only mildly critical of the punishing air raids being launched by America. On 18 March, 1970, while he was in Moscow, his prime minister, General Lon Nol, with the backing of the White House, staged a coup, after which he changed the name of Cambodia back to its ancient title, Khmer. The Khmer Republic was recognised by the United States, which, however, one month later, chose to launch an invasion against the newly-named land. Sihanouk went into exile in Peking... and here the ex-king chose to form an alliance with the devil himself.

Not much is known about Pol Pot, the man with the fat face and sparkling eyes, the man with the face of an avuncular old grandfather and the heart of a murderous tyrant. He was the monster with whom

Sihanouk threw in his lot, swearing with this Communist guerilla chief that they would mould their forces into a single entity with the aim of destroying American forces. Pot, brought up by a peasant family in the Kampong Thom province of the country, had been educated at a Buddhist monastery where, for two years, he lived as a monk. In the 1950s he won a scholarship to study electronics in Paris where, like so many other students of the time, he became involved in left-wing causes. Here he heard about – although it is unclear whether they actually met – another Cambodian student, Khieu Samphan, a political science student whose controversial but exhilarating plans for an 'agrarian revolution' were to inspire the ambitions of the peasant, Pol Pot.

Above: *Government troops surround refugees during the Khmer Rouge fighting.*

Top: *Refugees flee from the city of Phnom Penh.*

POL POT, THE MAN WITH THE FACE OF AN AVUNCULAR OLD GRANDFATHER AND THE HEART OF A MURDEROUS TYRANT.

A TERRIBLE REALITY

Samphan's theory was that, in order to progress, Cambodia must regress; it must turn its back on capitalist exploitation, fat-cat bosses created by the former French colonial overlords, reject corrupted bourgeois values and ideals. Samphan's twisted theory decreed that people must live in the fields and that all the trappings of modern life must be annihilated. If Pol Pot himself had remained an obscure figure, this theory may have remained a coffee bar philosopy rattling around the boulevards and parks of Paris. Instead, it became a terrible reality.

Between 1970 and 1975 the Khmer Rouge – the Red Army led by Pol Pot – became a formidable force in Cambodia, controlling huge tracts of the countryside. On 17 April, 1975, Pol Pot's dream of power became a reality when his armies, marching under the red flag, entered the capital, Phnom Penh. Within hours of the coup, Pol Pot called a special meeting of his new cabinet members and told them the country was now called Kampuchea. He outlined the plans for his brave new world which would begin taking shape within days.

He ordered the evacuation of all cities and towns, a process to be overseen by newly-created regional and zonal chiefs. He ordered the abolition of all markets, the destruction of churches and the persecution of all religious orders. Although privileged himself, in having been educated abroad, he harboured a loathing for the educated classes, and so all teachers, professors and even kindergarten teachers were ordered to be executed. The educated peasant, Pol Pot, feared the educated classes.

The first to die were the senior cabinet members and functionaries of Lon Nol's regime, followed by the officer corps of the old army. All were buried in mass graves. Then came the evacuation of the city, towns and villages. Pol Pot's twisted dream was to put the clock back and make his people the dwellers of an agrarian, Marxist society. Pol Pot was aided by his evil deputy, Ieng Sary. Doctors were murdered because they, too, were 'educated'. All religious groups were exterminated because they were 'reactionary'. The term Pol Pot used for his extermination policy was '*Khchat-khchay os roling*' – it translates as 'scatter them out of sight'. The sinister reality meant the death of thousands.

Buddhist temples were desecrated or turned into whorehouses for the troops or even became abbatoirs. Before the terror, there were some sixty thousand monks in Cambodia; after it was over, just three thousand returned to their shattered shrines and their holy places of worship.

Pol Pot also decreed that ethnic minorities did not, in fact, exist. Vietnamese, Thai and Chinese festivals, languages and cultures were ruled illegal, to be practised under punishment of death. His was to be a pure Khmer society. The deliberate and forceful eradication of ethnic groups fell most heavily on the 'Cham' people. Their ancestors had formed the Kingdom of Champa, once a country in what is now Vietnam. The Cham migrated to Cambodia during the eighteenth century to live as fishermen along Cambodia's rivers and the Tonle Sap lake. They were an Islamic people and were, perhaps, the most distinctive ethnic group in modern Cambodia, for they never adandoned or diluted their language, cuisine, costume, hairstyles, burial customs or religion.

The Cham were obvious targets for the young fanatics of the Khmer Rouge who fell upon them like a plague of locusts. The villages were torched, the people marched into the swampy, mosquito-plagued hinterland, fed pork – strictly against their religion – and the religious leaders executed. When villagers resisted whole communities were murdered, their bodies flung into huge pits and covered over with lime. Of two hundred thousand Cham people alive before the new order, barely one hundred thousand survive today. Those who survived the initial terror found that life

Below: *Cambodian defence minister, Keieu Sampen receives a warm hug from Prince Sihanouk (right).*

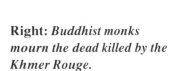

Right: *Buddhist monks mourn the dead killed by the Khmer Rouge.*

BUDDHIST TEMPLES WERE DESECRATED OR TURNED INTO WHOREHOUSES FOR THE TROOPS.

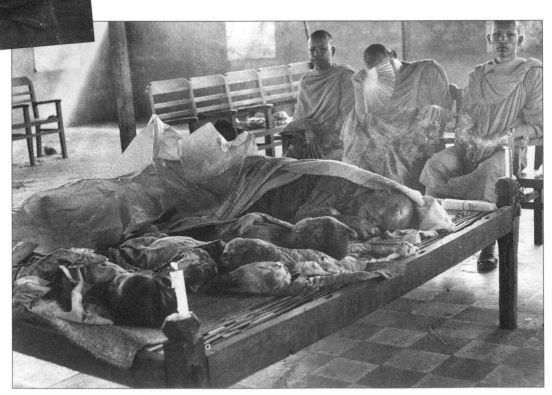

under the new regime was infinitely harder than a quick death – hence the phrase 'Land of the Living Dead', coined by those forced to live under these conditions.

BOURGEOIS CRIMINALS

Pol Pot believed that all adults were tainted by feudal, bourgeois attitudes, with 'sympathies' for foreign regimes which Pol Pot had decreed were alien to the national way of life. Urbanites, in particular, were rooted out and placed in work camps where hundreds of thousands were literally worked to death or murdered if they spoke French – a major crime in Khmer Rouge eyes because it showed a bourgeois attitude, with a link to, and sympathy with, the colonial reign of the past.

In vast encampments, devoid of any comforts save a straw mat to sleep on and a bowl of rice at the end of every day, the tradesmen, dockers, clerks, bankers – many alive only because they managed to hide their professions – and numerous other citizens, toiled in conditions that would have shamed Japanese prison-of-war camps in the Second World War. The camps were organized, much like the concentration camps of the Nazis, to ensure that 'natural selection' took its toll of the aged and the ill, the very young, and pregnant women. Given a poor diet, deprived of strength, hundreds and thousands succumbed to disease, starvation and the clubbings of their brutal overseers. With no medical men to treat them, save for the attention of a few 'traditional' herbalists whom the new government tolerated, the life span of a prisoner in the camps was pathetically low. They were frog-marched out at dawn into malaria-ridden swamps where they worked twelve hours a day, planting rice and clearing jungles in futile attempts to reclaim more farmland. Then they were frog-marched back at night, under gunpoint and often under the blows and bayonet-thrusts of their guards, to a bowl of rice, gruel and a morsel of dried fish. Then, exhausted though they were, they had to endure Marxist indoctrination sessions, when irredeemable bourgeois elements were rooted out to be taken away for punishment while the others chanted, parrot-fashion, the benefits and joys of the new state. There was one day off in every ten, when people could look forward to twelve hours of indoctrination. Wives were separated from

Above: *A weary soldier is welcomed by hysterical refugees fleeing the guerilla onslaught.*

THEY WERE FROG-MARCHED OUT AT DAWN INTO MALARIA-RIDDEN SWAMPS WHERE THEY WORKED TWELVE HOURS A DAY

To re-inforce his battle against enemies real and imagined, Pol Pot set up a system of interrogations, tortures and executions in his prison camps. Much like the Spanish Inquisition of old, Pol Pot and his henchmen knew that all who came through the portals of these grim places were guilty – all they had to do was to confess that guilt. To convince its followers that cruelty was necessary and good for the nation, the regime taught its young bureacrats that torture had a special, political significance.

Taught by the Chinese, the Khmer security officers were enmeshed in a hard and cruel ideology, revealed in documents captured after the overthrow of Pol Pot. These dossiers show that torture attained a high level in his nation. One document, the 'S-21 Interrogator's Manual', later handed over to United Nations' investigators, reads: 'The purpose of doing torture is to get their responses. It's not something we do for the fun of it. Thus, we must make them hurt so they will respond quickly. Another purpose is to break them psychologically and make them lose their will. It's not something that is done out of individual anger or for self-satisfaction. Thus we beat them to make them afraid but absolutely not to kill them. When torturing them it is necessary to examine their state of health first and necessary to examine the whip. Don't greedily want to kill them. Politics is very important whereas torture is secondary. Thus the question of doing politics takes the lead at all times. Even when

their husbands, their children were either put to work at the age of seven or given away to the barren wives of party functionaries, so as to be brought up in the mould of fanatical warriors of the revolution. Pol Pot was a thorough man.

Bonfires were made of the books from universities and schools, as wretched, maltreated citizens were forced to chant as the works of civilisation perished in the flames. There were 'hate-ins', when people were whipped before pictures of members of the old regime. It was a nightmare world, sinister and hopeless, for the Cambodian people were literally isolated from the world. There was no postal service, no diplomatic ties with any country, no telephones and no travel; it was truly a nation lost to the world.

questioning it is always necessary to do constant propaganda.

TORTURE WITHOUT REASON

'At the same time it is necessary to avoid any question of hesitancy or half-heartedness, of not daring to do torture, which makes it impossible to get answers to our questions from our enemies, which slows down and delays our work. In sum, whether doing propaganda or torturing or bringing up questions to ask them or accusing them of something, it is necessary to hold steadfastly to a stance of not being half-hearted or hesitant. We must be absolute. Only thus can we work to good effect. We torture them but forget to give the reason first. Only then do they become totally helpless.' The notorious Chinese water torture, crucifictions and suffocations with a plastic bag were three among numerous torture methods practiced by the evil men of the Khmer Rouge.

The S21 facility, from which the document took its name, was the most infamous institution in the whole of Cambodia. Based in the north-east of the country, at least thirty thousand victims of the regime died there. Only seven prisoners are known to have survived – prisoners kept alive because they had administrative skills necessary to their overlords in the running of the dreadful place.

Torture was only one instrument of fear brandished over the heads of the cowed populace. The frequency with which people were executed was another. Many times, inmates in the new country camps were caught eating the flesh of their dead comrades in their desperation for food. The penalty for this was a horrible death of being buried up to the neck in mud and left to starve and thirst while ants and other creatures gnawed at the victim. Then the heads were cut off and stuck on pikes around the settlement with the words painted on a sign hanging from the neck: 'I am a traitor of the revolution!'

Dith Pran, a Cambodian interpreter for American journalist, Sydney Schanberg, emerged from the years of slaughter as a witness to the horrors of Pol Pot's reign. His own experiences, including his threatened execution, were chronicled in the film 'The Killing Fields', in which the torment

of the Cambodian people was, for the first time, starkly revealed to the world. Pran's journey from his civilised childhood to a prison camp, where he pretended to be illiterate in order to survive, was a harrowing tale that reduced audiences to tears of pity. 'Many times,' said Pran, 'I prayed that I was dead rather than having to endure the life that I was forced to live. But some of my family had gotten away to America and it was for them that I carried on living. It was a nightmare time.'

Below: A Khmer Rouge soldier menaces civilians with his gun. The population of Phnom Penh were quickly subdued by the thugs of Pol Pot's army.

STACKS OF SKULLS

Pran was one of the lucky ones who survived the Asian holocaust to be re-united with his family in 1979 in San Francisco. Even now, the mass graves of the unknown, unnamed dead continue to be unearthed in remote corners of the sad country, the skulls stacked against the graves like so many footballs.

It was military muscle and not moral right that, in the end, halted the bloodbath and allowed for some semblance of sanity to return to the blighted land. Britain had, it must be acknowledged, spoken out in 1978 against alleged human rights abuses, after receiving reports, through intermediaries in Thailand, about the reign of terror in Cambodia, but the protest was ignored.

Opposite, top: Peasants feared that they would be forced to join the 'intellectuals' in the labour camps.

Opposite, bellow: Coils of barbed wire marked the Cambodian border with Thailand.

Above: *The fall of Phnom Penh is celebrated by young guerillas of the Khmer Rouge.*

Britain reported to the United Nations Commission on Human Rights, but the hysterical Khmer Rouge representative responded: 'The British Imperialists have no right to speak of the rights of man. The world knows well their barbarous and abject nature. Britain's leaders are living in opulence atop a pile of rotting corpses while the proletariat have only the right to be unemployed, to steal and prostitute.' Regrets were sent from Pol Pot flunkies who said that they were too busy to attend UN enquiries on the allegations to the commission hearings in New York.

In December, 1978, Vietnamese forces, who had been skirmishing for years with the Khmer Rouge over a disputed border region, launched a major offensive with mechanised infantry divisions and full armoured support. The infrastructure of Cambodia had disintegrated so badly by this time, that battlefield reports had to be biked great distances to Khmer Rouge command posts because there were no telephones left in operation.

The Vietnamese, early in 1979, found themselves masters of a blighted land. Pol Pot had fled in his white armoured Mercedes from Phnom Penh, just hours before the Vietnamese troops arrived to liberate the ghostly city. He went scurrying back to his masters in China, glad of the sanctuary, but bitter that they had not come to his aid in resisting the well-armed and determined North Vietnamese onslaught.

'US SURVIVORS REMEMBER OUR FAMILIES BEING TAKEN AWAY, MANY OF THEM, AND OUR FRIENDS BRUTALLY MURDERED.'

Massive amounts of aid flooded into Cambodia as the world realized the full horror of the Khmer Rouge regime and the devastation of the country. The Khmer Rouge were, like the Nazis, particularly methodical when it came to detailing their crimes; investigators found daily logs of shootings, torture, hundreds of photo albums of those to be executed – including those of wives and children of 'intellectuals' liquidated in the earliest days of the terror – and the detailed loggings of the infamous killing fields. These fields, intended to be the basis of the worker's Utopia, a land without money or want, became, instead, the burial pits of a people crushed under the yoke of a cruel tyranny.

Pol Pot seemed to fade into the background but has emerged in recent years to become a major political force vying for power in this embittered region. Like all tyrants, he said that mistakes were made by those under him, that he had faced rebellions on all fronts and that those who died were 'enemies of the state'. In 1981, back in Cambodia, he told a meeting of old friends at a secret location near the Thai border that he was 'too trusting. My policies were sound. Over-zealous regional commanders and sub-district personnel may have mis-interpreted orders. To talk about systematic murder is odious. If we had really killed at that rate, we would have had no one left to fight the Vietnamese. I have been seriously mis-interpreted.'

ANGEL OF DEATH

Misinterpretation on the scale of three million dead – almost twenty-five per cent of the population of the nation – seems too small a word to describe what was done in his name and under his orders. But following Hitler's code, that the bigger the lie, the more people will believe it, Pol Pot has, once again, become a power-player in the region and is able to rally forces in the countryside that continue to believe in him, and are still loyal to him. Now he is a major force once again, only waiting to ride into the country, like some avenging angel of death, to finish off what he started before: his great agrarian revolution.

For Dith Pran and other survivors, the prospect of Pol Pot's return to power, the possibility that he will plunge his tortured land into new depths of depravity, fills them with horror. When the United Nations first announced that the Khmer Rouge would be part of the power-sharing peace process in Cambodia, Pran said: 'I am still shocked when I see the Khmer Rouge flag flying on UN territory. How would you feel if you were Jewish and you saw Hitler's flag flying at the United Nations? Some people went on a fast for three days to protest this, but I did not. I have starved for four years and that is enough for any man.'

There is international lobbying for world governments to have the Cambodian massacres recognized as war crimes in the same way as the Hitlerian genocide of the Jews has been recognised. Yang Sam, of the Cambodian Documentation Commission in New York, is the Cambodian equivalent of Simon Wiesenthal, the Nazi death camp survivor who, from his office in Vienna, devotes his life to tracing and collating evidence against Nazi war criminals. Sam, a survivor of the terror, collects information against the butchers of his own land. He said: 'Those most responsible for the Cambodian genocide – the cabinet members of Pol Pot's regime, the central committee of his Communist party, the Khmer Rouge military commanders whose troops committed so much of the killing, those officials who oversaw, directed and ran the nation-wide network of torture chambers, prison-execution centres and extermination facilities – continue to remain active in Cambodia and international political life. Based in enclaves along the Thai-Cambodian border, they conduct guerilla war seeking to return to power in Phnom Penh. They have not been held accountable for their crime under international law and that is a tragedy of monumental proportions.

'Us survivors remember our families being taken away, many of them, and our friends brutally murdered. We witnessed members of our families and others die of exhaustion from forced marches and slave labour, and from the brutal conditions of life to which the Cambodian people were subjected by the Khmer Rouge.

'We also saw Pol Pot's soldiers destroy our Buddhist temples, end schooling for our children, suppress our culture and eradicate our ethnic minorities. It is difficult for us to understand why the free and democratic nations of the world do not take action against the guilty. Surely this cries out for justice?' But there is no justice here.

WE WITNESSED MEMBERS OF OUR FAMILIES AND OTHERS DIE OF EXHAUSTION FROM FORCED MARCHES AND SLAVE LABOUR.

Below: *The legacy of the Pol Pot years. The skulls of the anonymous dead serve to remind the world of the man's dreadful regime.*

LAMMERDING
Butchery at Oradour

The Nazis were infamous for their brutal reprisals against partisan fighters. But the villagers of Oradour did not die for their brave resistance. They were slaughtered to avenge the greed of a few German officers.

T he tiny hamlet of Oradour-sur-Glane, a village not too far from Limoges in South-Western France existed for close to one thousand years without any more trouble than a bad harvest or blocked drains. Even the conflagration of World War Two had passed by these simple peasant people. Occasionally, they saw German soldiers passing through, or heard the freight trains in the night taking men and supplies to the front after the Allied invasion at Normandy, but to all intents and purposes, the attack that Adolf Hitler had launched against their countrymen had left them relatively unscathed.

Until, on a hot day in June 1944, the soldiers came.

The troops of the 2nd SS Panzer division 'Das Reich' entered Oradour and, in an afternoon of frenzied butchery, massacred its inhabitants. The men were taken away to a barn and shot, the women locked in the church which was then set ablaze with hand grenades. Every building was dynamited, every animal killed, every child rounded up and sent off to concentration camps. In the madness of that hot June day over six hundred of the citizens of Oradour died at the hands of the Nazi butchers. The question constantly asked by historians is – why? The common explanation, accepted down the years, has been that the villagers were punished by the SS because of increased French resistance activity in the region, following the success of the Allied landings. But another theory has surfaced which deserves consideration – the theory that the villagers were not, in fact, meant to die. Instead, they were supposed to turn over large quantities of gold that the Germans – mistakenly – believed was hidden in the sleepy hamlet.

Oradour stands today as a ghost town, preserved as it was after the last explosion and last round had been fired on that day, nearly fifty years ago. The burned-out car from which the town doctor was hauled and executed, still lies abandoned on the cobbled streets. In the burned and charred butcher's shop remain his meat scales, in the house opposite is a broken sewing machine – all artifacts testifying to a close-knit community that was literally wiped from the face of the earth.

It was a hot Saturday afternoon, just four days after the Allies had gained their foothold in France with Operation Overlord, that a company from the Das

ON THAT HOT JUNE DAY, OVER SIX HUNDRED CITIZENS OF ORADOUR DIED AT THE HANDS OF THE NAZI BUTCHERS.

Reich division arrived in Oradour. Many were enjoying the serenity of the day – men fished from the banks of the River Glane, others sipped pastis and played *petanque* at the village café.

The SS men, who rode in on half-tracks, in lorries and on motorcycles, were veterans of the Russian front, men who had fought in the 'war without rules' unleashed by their Führer against Slavic 'inferiors'.

Above: *Some of the villagers were lined up against this wall and shot by the SS. Their bodies were then burned.*

Das Reich division were Waffen SS, the fighting SS elite and had conducted their war with ferocity. By all accounts, they did their grim duty in the East, as they were instructed by their Führer, and were responsible for untold massacres of the civilian population.

The division that arrived in Montauban, France, in 1944, was a lot different from the one that went to war against the Soviet Union in Operation Barbarossa. General Heinz Lammerding, its commanding officer, was highly decorated – but he had

> RETALIATION AGAINST THE FRENCH FOR ACTS OF SABOTAGE WAS SWIFT, BRUTAL AND ARBITRARY.

fight for the swastika. Not unnaturally, the survivors of the Eastern Front regarded themselves as superior in race, attitude and élan to the many other nations that now constituted Das Reich's ranks.

After the Allied onslaught on Normandy, Das Reich was stirred from its days of rest and relaxation, and ordered to begin the long move northwards to the front. And every inch of the way they were targeted by the *Maquis*, the French resistance. With the liberation of their land in sight, and with Allied air superiority ensuring ample

seen the flower of German youth, in the ranks of his division, fall in their thousands. In March 1944, twelve thousand five hundred of the fifteen thousand men that composed this fighting unit were killed and captured on the Russian front in the actions around Cherkassy. The two thousand five hundred survivors, sent to Montauban to become the nucleus of a new division, found themselves surrounded by men of numerous nationalities who had chosen to

Above: *Scene from the post-War trial of twenty-one German soldiers accused of the murders at Oradour.*

supply drops, the French dogged the German advance northwards. Attacks and sabotage had become so commonplace the Germans were stopping to check every piece of horse manure in their pathway in case it was a bomb, for just such a booby trap had claimed the life of three soldiers.

Retaliation against the French for acts of sabotage was swift, brutal and arbitrary. German soldiers of Das Reich division took part in these loathsome reprisals against innocent civilians and they followed the Führer's orders demanding harsh punishment for anyone who raised arms against his armies. The raids on villages and towns became known as *ratissages*, and it became standard practice for the SS men to fill their pockets with plundered loot on these killing missions. Indeed, Lammerding and two officers under him – Major Otto Dickmann and Helmut Kampfe – were also not averse to stockpiling some money for after the War. All three, in late night discussions over the General's finest cognac, were convinced that the War was going to end in the total and utter defeat of Hitler. With such an eventuality in sight, the acquisition of a nest-egg seemed the logical thing to do.

Dickmann was based in St Junien, not far from Oradour, and was guardian of a single, special truck in the divisional transportation corps. He said it contained divisional records and the 'order of battle', or make-up of the formations which comprised the unit. He ordered an Austrian Lieutenant, Bruno Walter, to double the guard on this vehicle.

Dickmann was nervous in St Junien on the night of 9 June, not least because he believed that there were no fewer than two thousand armed resistance *marquisards* in the town, waiting for the slightest opportunity to launch an attack against him, his men or his transport.

THE GOLD BOOTY

But there were no divisional records on board the truck, no order of battle plans. It is believed to have contained more than six million pounds worth of gold – at today's prices. This was the booty that would guarantee Dickmann, Lammerding and Kampfe an easy retirement at the end of the war. They could not send it back to Germany for fear it would be bombed, intercepted or stolen. Besides, the railway network was rapidly disintegrating under Allied air assaults. A third factor – their fear of the disapproval of Heinrich Himmler, chief of the SS, should he learn that they had looted on such a scale – convinced them that they were left with no alternative but to carry their spoils with them into the front line.

The Resistance was aware of the presence of Das Reich division and knew that it was soon to be on the move again, in preparation to deploy its three hundred heavy tanks and thousands of men against the Allies on the beaches of Normandy. The British had warned the Resistance that it feared the Germans could be in the fighting zone within three days; the French were asked to harass their progress every inch of the way. Dickmann and his superiors knew this – hence the tension felt by those guarding the 'special' truck.

On 9 June, at midnight, Dickmann ordered the truck and a detachment of armed SS men to take the first leg of a journey to move the gold northwards. One plan the trio had devised was to store it in the Loire valley region, while they went up to the front line for the battle. Whatever happened, Dickmann had to get the gold out of the Resistance-infested area as quickly as possible. The night he chose to

Below: *Captain Kahn (inset) ordered the massacre. Photographs of victims (main picture) were used as criminal evidence.*

THE YOUNG AND RECKLESS
RESISTANCE MEN, SEEKING
VENGEANCE FOR YEARS OF
NAZI OPPRESSION,
LAUNCHED AN ILL-
PREPARED AMBUSH.

move was one of chaos and madness for the Germans. Although reprisals were still gruesome and swift, the authority of the Nazi occupiers was rapidly breaking down, as the French sensed that their own liberation was close; they realized that the Allied invasion in Normandy was more than a mere feint or a commando raid, and that the Germans' days were finally numbered. Ambushes, stolen petrol supplies, sabotage – the convoys rolling off that night were plagued by Resistance activity. Dickmann was informed, by his intelligence operatives, that a large group of partisans was operating under the cover of the Forêt de Brigueuil – a densely-wooded area outside of St Junien that covered the road to Bellac, the first stop en route that night for the division. He ordered that the special truck take a different route, one that passed near Oradour. It was a route that was to lead to disaster.

A staff car rolled ahead of the truck, and, in front of that, was a squad of heavily armed soldiers in an armoured half-track. According to plan, they would be in Bellac within thirty minutes, but the local Resistance was to mess up that timing. Planning an ambush on another unit fifteen miles away, the *maquisards* were stunned when they saw the headlights of the half-track glinting at the spot where they had hidden their weapons.

Instantly, plans for the scheduled attack were shelved and the Boche heading towards them became the primary target. The young and reckless Resistance men, seeking vengeance for years of Nazi oppression, launched an ill-prepared ambush. Grenades were hurled at the half-track, killing all of the German soldiers aboard, save one, who scrambled to safety down the road, his clothes smoking from the grenade explosions, but otherwise unharmed. The Germans who survived the grenades were cut down by a withering hail of Sten-gun fire levelled at them from the six partisans under the command of a *maquisard* known only as Raoul.

But the enthusiasm of the attackers far outweighed their military skill. Explosions from the half-track, followed by the car and

truck, spewed shrapnel and burning debris everywhere. That, and return fire, accounted for five of Raoul's men. When the shooting was over and the smoke had cleared, he was the only Frenchman left alive to witness the aftermath, illuminated as it was by the burning wrecks of the staff car and the half-track. The truck had not caught fire. Raoul feared that it might be full of wounded Germans, so he lobbed one more 'Gammon' grenade into the vehicle. When there was no sound from within, he pushed aside the charred and smoking

*Right: **Robert Hebras was one of the few survivors, but he was wounded in the attack.***

*Below: **The sad remains of the villagers were mute testament to the Nazi atrocity.***

*Above: **Appalled visitors from other villages came to stare at the devastation.***

tarpaulin, expecting to be confronted with a pile of German corpses. Instead there were wooden boxes, each about the size of a shoe box and each tied down with leather straps. Placing his Sten gun to one side, he used a commando knife to slit the securing straps and open up one of the boxes. It contained gold. Raoul had stumbled on to half a ton of gold.

Risking everything, he hastily removed the gold and dug a shallow trench at the roadside near to the bodies of his dead comrades. One by one, he lowered the thirty-odd boxes into the hole, then covered them with earth. Knowing that if his dead comrades were identified, their families would be murdered by the SS, he poured petrol over each corpse, then over the wreckage in the road, before setting it all ablaze. Then Raoul leapt on his bicycle to ride away from the scene.

When General Otto Lammerding learnt that his *ratissage* loot had been stolen, from under his nose, by the French peasantry he fell into a terrible rage. The half-

RAOUL HAD STUMBLED ON TO HALF A TON OF GOLD.

ton of gold that he intended to use as an escape from the madness of war, to start a new and decent life, had fallen into the hands of the French partisans. He was ordering patrols to rake the countryside for his stolen loot, when he recived the second bad news of the day: Major Kampfe, his compatriot in crime, was reported missing and was presumed to have been captured by the Resistance. Kampfe was a close personal friend and his disappearance fuelled Lammerding's rage to new heights.

LOST PENSION FUND

He used Kampfe's disappearance and the attack on the gold convoy – divisional records to anyone who asked – to delay his progress to the front. He did not want to go blundering into a battle while his pension money was in the hands of these filthy peasants. Lammerding requested his superiors let him deal with the perpetrators of the attack on his convoy, and his wish was granted. He consulted Dickmann in a stormy meeting – attested to after the War by an SS telephonist who heard the row – in which he rebuked him for his decision to send the gold with so few soldiers protecting it, yet requested Dickmann's advice on ways of recovering it.

The Germans suspected that the men who had attacked the convoy the previous night came from the town of Oradour-sur-Glane. Not only was it the hamlet nearest the ambush site, but because an SS man who had been captured by the partisans, then managed to escape them, told Dickmann he was 'certain' that Oradour was one of the places where he had been taken as a prisoner.

Below: *A monument was erected in Oradour to honour the people whose lives had been so brutally taken from them.*

KILLING FOR LOOT

A notorious Nazi called Captain Kahn, who had distinguished himself by his unspeakable brutality in campaigns against partisans and civilians on the Russian front, was chosen to head the *ratissage* against the inhabitants of Oradour. But historians now believe that his troops were not bent on murder when they entered the hamlet – they believe the Germans simply wished to recover the stolen gold. However, when the peasants denied all knowledge of gold, the mindless brutality favoured by Captain Kahn was allowed to find expression in the soldiers' actions. Dickmann and

A LA MEMOIRE DE NOS CHERS MARTYRS

François	Jean	Marie	Marie-Thérèse	Marcelle	Maurice	François	Marthe
LAMAUD	LAMAUD	LAMAUD	LAMAUD	ROBY	ROBY	BRANDY	BRANDY
72 ans	47 ans	47 ans	4 ans	6 ans	12 ans	46 ans	65 ans

Massacrés le 10 Juin 1944

Right: *The Nazis were cruel in their reprisals against the French Resistance, but their actions, such as putting a fifteen-year-old boy before a firing squad, only strengthened the French in their guerilla war against the invaders.*

Lammerding may have wanted to kill the entire village, but he would have preferred to trace his stolen loot.

Kahn's vengeance on the inhabitants of Oradour was as senseless, and as vicious as any massacre committed by German troops on the eastern front. He and his soldiers entered the town when it was crowded with people. Farmworkers, who had been toiling in the fields all morning, had returned for lunch when the first half-tracks clattered up the cobbled street, following the line of the railway that connected this village with others in the area. Citizens were rounded up into the church and barn, while a squad of soldiers, with fixed bayonets, moved through fields and outbuildings, chasing out villagers who had sought refuge there. One soldier, Heinz Barth, had actually been born a Frenchman, but had chosen the uniform of the SS. Now, he brandished a machine pistol as he told terrified villagers: 'You'll see the blood flow today!'

The people of Oradour watched and listened as the two hundred and fifty-four buildings, that made up their village, were destroyed by grenades and satchel charges of plastic explosive. Roger Godfrin, a fifteen-year-old boy, ran for his life. 'I told my two elder sisters to run and hide with me,' he explained later, 'but they refused. I somehow knew what the Boche were going to do to us that day.'

MASSACRE IN CHURCH

A white flare, fired high into the sky, was a signal to Kahn that all the villagers had been rounded up. The killing began. The old and infirm, who had been unable to march to the church, were shot where they lay in their little houses. Anyone who bolted for freedom was cut down by machine guns, positioned to cover the streets and fields leading away from the central village square.

When more than four hundred and fifty women and children were packed into the church, the Germans set off a huge charge of explosives, releasing billowing clouds of black smoke to asphyxiate the victims in the church. Then, the soldiers hurled hand

Above: *Roger Godfrin, the only child to escape the massacre, gives testimony at the military court trial held after the War.*

HE BRANDISHED A MACHINE PISTOL AS HE TOLD TERRIFIED VILLAGERS: 'YOU'LL SEE THE BLOOD FLOW TODAY!'

grenades through the windows; they opened the doors before raking the nave with machine-gun fire. The wooden pews and artifacts caught fire, and the flames consumed most of those trapped in the church, although falling masonry accounted for a number of deaths. Over two hundred men were locked in the barn where they were executed by gunfire. Dickmann, accompanied by two representatives of the hated *Miliciens*, the local militia allied to the Germans, began to question those who had escaped death, demanding they tell him where the gold was hidden. Whenever he met with a denial or ignorance, he shot the person.

In another barn, which had served as execution house to more village men, Jean Darthout was alive, wounded by bullets in his legs. He and three others got away, as did a woman who jumped from a window high above the church altar, although she received five bullet wounds. She hid in a vegetable patch where she was found, close to death, the following day.

THE AFTERMATH

Dickmann, beside himself with rage because the killing and burning had begun before he had had a chance to thoroughly quiz the inhabitants on the whereabouts of the gold, got drunk that afternoon on fine champagne, in the house of a Monsieur Dupic at the farthest end of the village. At seven o'clock that night, as the flames continued to lick at the ruins, Dickmann lurched drunkenly off to his master Lammerding to report that he had failed to find their booty of gold.

Oradour is, today, a ghost town, in ruins, untouched since that dreadful day of destruction. In the little museum that is also a shrine to the dead can be found broken spectacles, love-letters, wine-bottles – the minutae of ordinary peasant life. Many of the victims were burned beyond recognition and are buried in a communal graves in the church and the barns where they were killed. Six hundred and forty-two people died for a hoard of gold about which they knew nothing.

Robin Mackness, a man who once set up the Slumberdown Quilt Company in England, claims he knows what happened to the gold. He wrote a book, 'Oradour –

Above: *The shattered ruins are called the 'Martryd Village' by the French.*

HE SAID THE HISTORIANS WERE WRONG TO ACCEPT THAT ORADOUR DIED AS A MERE ACT OF REVENGE.

Massacre and Aftermath'. It is a book that many leading historians, including a Second World War French Resistance expert, M.R.D. Foot, believe is the true story of the events in Oradour. It details the story of the lost gold for Mackness was involved, quite by chance, in the story of Oradour long after the War was over.

Mackness met Raoul, the French partisan who had buried the gold before fleeing on his bike. In cohorts with business associates in Switzerland, Mackness was smuggling 'black' (illegal) gold across the border from France into Switzerland when he was introduced to Raoul in 1982. The Frenchman told his story, describing the ambush and the reasons why the Germans had selected Oradour as the guilty town. He said the historians were wrong to accept that Oradour died as a mere act of revenge.

Raoul also claimed that he had returned to dig up the hidden gold – stamped with the Nazi *Reichsbank* motif – and that he used some of it to start a business. Now, he wanted to move the remaining loot into a no-questions-asked vault in Switzerland. Mackness says he agreed to help the man, but the mission failed when Mackness was caught by French customs officers. They found twenty thousand pounds worth of the cargo in his car near Lyons in 1982 and he was jailed for twenty-one months.

A SECRET STORY

On his release, Mackness spent years researching Raoul's story and came to the conclusion: 'I don't know exactly what General Lammerding and Major Dickmann said to each other at that meeting on Saturday, 10 June, 1944, but I can guess with some accuracy, because of the story Raoul told me. During my twenty-one months in prison I came to realise that if

Raoul's story were true, and there was nothing to finally persuade me that it wasn't, then he and I were probably the only ones alive who knew the secret story behind the events of that day.

'During Dickmann's meeting with his general, he would have learned that Lammerding knew about the ambush from the soldier who had got away. In the event of anything happening to the special unit, it was probable that survivors were given strict orders to report only to those officers most directly concerned – Majors Dickmann and Kampfe or General Lammerding.'

The principal players in the drama are dead and they never told their story while they lived. But it seems certain now, in the light of Mackness' experiences, that the people of Oradour-sur-Glane were killed for their innocence, because they were ignorant of the loot and could not lead a few greedy men to a stolen pile of gold.

HE AND I WERE PROBABLY THE ONLY ONES ALIVE WHO KNEW THE SECRET STORY BEHIND THE EVENTS OF THAT DAY.

Below: *A wooden cross marks a grave in the churchyard at Oradour.*

WILLIAM CALLEY
The My Lai Massacre

The US army sent untrained rookies to battle in foreign jungles. In some of these soldiers, fear turned to madness and, one dreadful day, the boys of Charlie Company became bloodthirsty barbarians in the village of My Lai.

America went to war in Vietnam in an ideological struggle, a clash between the systems of the West and those of Communism. Young American men marched on to die by the thousand in steamy jungles and snake-infested forests, their blood spilled in unprounounceable places by men with unpronounceable names. But theirs, so said their commanders at the front and the pencil pushers back home, was an honourable cause, fought honourably by the heirs of Patton, MacArthur and Eisenhower. They did not stoop to constructing booby traps of bamboo stakes, smeared with excrement, to cause wounds that immediately became infected, nor did they torture POWs, reducing them to automatons pleading guilt to their 'war crimes' as was the fate of so many Americans captured by the enemy. But any claim to unblemished American morality in Vietnam was cancelled on 16 March, 1968, in a tiny village called My Lai, situated in the Quang Ngai province, on the eastern side of the country where Vietnam bordered on the South China Sea.

On that day, the battle-hardened veterans of Charlie Company, of the American Division's 11th Light Infantry Brigade, entered the undefended coastal plain hamlet and murdered, in cold blood, some five hundred villagers – men, women and babies. In alternating bouts of heated frenzy and cool detachment, the troops of Charlie Company butchered the helpless Vietnamese civilians in an orgy of killing that matched the barbarous acts of the SS in Russia or Poland during the Second World War. Old men were thrown into ditches and bayoneted; pregnant women disembowelled; babies seen crawling away in a paddy field were tossed back on to the heap of corpses from which they had escaped, and were either shot or bayoneted.

The collective madness that engulfed Charlie Company has never been fully understood. Only one man, Lt William Calley, was ever punished for the crime – if three days in a prison can be called punishment. He was released after a presidential review of his case. Over and over again, the men who carried out the massacre, the headquarters' staff in the rear and the American people back home have debated those lethal hours of bloodletting. More than any other episode in that tragic war, My Lai became the symbol of madness, a place that revealed how the strain of war can change decent, respectful, worthy young men into blood-stained barbarians. In the elephant grass and paddy fields around My Lai, the American ideals of truth and justice were cruelly forgotten.

The people of Vietnam were peasant farmers caught up in an horrendous technological war. Napalm, phospherous bombs, Agent Orange defoliant – they had seen the

Opposite: *William Calley Jnr was to play a ghastly role in his country's war against Vietnam.*

Below: *Captain Medina with his lawyer, Lee Bailey, during a court recess.*

Yankees bring these terrible weapons to the placid villages and many were puzzled by the war. What had they done to incur such wrath from the foreigners?

But My Lai – and every other settlement – in the rural areas of Vietnam were seen by the US commanders as guerilla bases for the 'gooks' – the Viet Cong fighters who, with the support of the peasants, managed to stave off the mightiest nation in the world. Frustration, caused by the difficulties of fighting a hidden, secret peasant army, distilled a certain brutality within the American war leaders; they decided to employ scorched earth tactics, the burning and shelling of villages, as a method of driving the enemy into the open. By the time Charlie Company tramped into My Lai, seventy per cent of the villages in the Quang Ngai area had been razed during the scorched earth policy but anyway, in warfare, mercy is not a ready commodity. 'They were dinks,' said one American infantryman at the time. 'They were gooks, spooks, Charlie. They weren't human beings. We never looked at them as being other human beings. To us they became abstract, things that wanted to kill us, so we killed them first. And that went for the youngest son-of-a-bitch to the oldest. That's what Vietnam did to us.'

A HIGH BODY COUNT

Another soldier, Philip Caputo, a Marine, said that, while orders to kill civilians may not have been written down in black and white, the pressure from the Commanding General in Vietnam, William Westmoreland, on front line units to produce 'kills' was felt heavily by each soldier. Caputo said: 'General Westmoreland's strategy of attrition also had an important effect upon our behaviour. Our mission was not to seize positions or win terrain but simply to kill. Victory was a high body count, defeat a low kill ratio, war a matter of arithmetic. The pressure on unit commanders to produce corpses was intense, and they in turn communicated it to their troops. It is not surprising, therefore, that some men acquired a contempt for human life and a predilection for taking it.'

Charlie Company marched into My Lai with such feelings.

> TO US THEY BECAME ABSTRACT, THINGS THAT WANTED TO KILL US, SO WE KILLED THEM FIRST.

Below: *Captain Medina denied most emphatically that he had ordered a massacre of the people of My Lai.*

The company was initially composed of one hundred and fifty young men who were a typical cross section of the American boys who were sent off to fight in Vietnam. In August 1967, while in their training camp in the USA, they were warned that they may be shipped out to Vietnam at any time. For men like William Laws Calley, now a 2nd Lieutenant with the unit, but who had been a drifter in civilian life, the fun was about to start.

During their training at military installations around America, Charlie Company had gained a reputation as an above-average unit. They excelled in infantry tactics, in jungle warfare simulation exercises and in all-round Army expertise. But there were misgivings among some about the lack of discipline in the squad – and the character of some of the men in it. Michael Bernhardt, one of its number, had trained

force. Their target was a VC battalion that had operated in the region for years, despite massive shelling and the dropping of millions of tons of jungle defoliants intended to lay bare their strongholds. Now technology was abandoned, the human element was sent to quell the guerillas, and it came in the shape of Charlie Company, Alpha Company and Bravo Company.

By the middle of February, a pattern of failure and frustration had established itself among the Americans. Whenever these men fanned out to pre-designated areas, hoping to spring traps on the guerilla positions, they found the enemy had been forewarned and had disappeared. The

as a paratrooper only to find himself teamed up in a unit in Charlie Company. From the moment he joined, he had misgivings about the calibre of his fellow soldiers: 'Some of the men in the company were a little unusual. There were some who were cruel. They weren't the bottom of the barrel – they were men who would have been accepted for military service at any time. I wouldn't expect them to murder or torture anybody...'

BAD OPTIONS

Charlie Company landed in 'Nam', as the troops called it, in the second week of December 1967, and their area of operations was in the Quang Ngai province, a region of innumerable villages where the civilian population had been severely decimated by artillery fire and rapid airborne strikes. The peasants were told to deny their homes to the Viet Cong enemy if they wanted to save their own lives and their land. Sadly, these people were unable to refuse when the Communists chose to use their villages as guerilla bases – the guerillas also threatened loss of life and land. The peasants were trapped between the two opposing sides of the jungle war.

On 26 January, 1968, Charlie Company joined other units to forge a strike force of around five hundred men, destined for search-and-destroy missions in 'Indian Country' – the badlands of Quang Ngai where 'gooks' were said to be operating in

Above: *William Calley escorted from court after the guilty verdict. He faced a life sentence.*

Top left: *Attorney Edward MacGill talks to newsmen outside the court.*

bewildered rookies from America were left with nothing but the sounds of their own hearts beating in terror. And in February they began to suffer casualties – a man had half his left side blown away when he stepped on a booby trap. Ron Weber, Lt Calley's radio operator, took a bullet that shattered his kidney when the men of Charlie Company came under a fusillade of sniper fire by a riverbank. He was the first KIA – killed in action – member of the company and it had a profound effect on the men. Calley, leader of the first platoon of Charlie Company, should never have taken his men out into the exposed position that led to Weber's death. This was the first display of his ineptitude as a leader of men.

Daily Mirror

PINKVILLE

❝All of a sudden the GIs just opened fire on the women and children..I couldn't believe what I was seeing❞

5d . Friday, November 21, 1969 ▬ No. 20,499

THE MASSACRE THAT CHILLED THE WORLD

A HORRIFYING story of a massacre by rampaging American troops stunned the world yesterday.

Hundreds of Vietnamese peasants were said to have been murdered in cold blood.

And a cameraman, 28-year-old Ronald Haeberle, produced grim pictures of slaughter in the tiny hamlet of My-Lai, which the troops called Pinkville—because the area was coloured pink on war maps.

The photographs show scenes of murder and other atrocities, and of soldiers throwing fuel into a blazing hut with the bodies of villagers lying nearby.

Cowering

One photograph shows women and children cowering in a doorway and holding their stomachs. All of them were killed, Haeberle claimed.

He said yesterday that he was appalled by the brutality.

"I never saw GIs act like that before," he added.

The chilling story came as a bitter blow to President Richard Nixon's bid to win fresh support for his war policies.

Haeberle said the GIs believed that the villagers were Vietcong sympathisers.

As the troops moved in, guns at

From RALPH CHAMPION in New York

the ready, a man holding two small children in his arms walked towards them.

Haeberle said: "They saw us and were pleading. The little girl was saying 'No, no' in English.

"Then, all of a sudden, there was a burst of fire and they were cut down. One machine-gunner did it—he just opened up.

"There was no reaction from the guy doing the shooting. That's the part that really got me—this little girl pleading and they were just cut down."

That was the beginning of the Massacre of Pinkville — the thirty minutes of killing that left the hamlet destroyed, according to Haeberle.

"A group of people—women, children and babies—were standing around," he said. "The machine gunner was standing in front of them with his ammo-bearer.

"Then he opened up on all those

people in that big circle, and they were trying to run. I don't know how many got out."

There was no mercy for some of those who survived the first hail of bullets, said Haeberle.

GIs went to inspect a pile of bodies. They found one man still alive.

But a soldier "leaned over and finished him off," Haeberle claimed.

"There were two small children, a very young boy and a smaller boy, perhaps four or five years old.

Unarmed

"A guy with an M16 rifle fired at them and the older boy fell over to protect the smaller boy.

"Then they fired six more shots. It was done very businesslike."

Haeberle told of fifteen unarmed Vietnamese who were spotted walking along a dirt road.

"The GIs just opened fire on the women and children," he said.

"Besides that, they were shooting at people with grenade-launchers. I couldn't believe what I was seeing."

Then Haeberle told of his horror as troops found a group of mothers and children. He said:

"A GI grabbed one of the girls and started stripping her. They were keeping the mother away from protecting her daughter."—she must have been around

❝North Vietnam cannot defeat or humiliate the United States. Only Americans can do that❞

President Nixon in a TV and radio report to the nation on Vietnam policy on November 4.

THE SURVIVOR In Vietnam, Do Chuc, 40, who lived through the slaughter, said: "We thought such things were just part of the war."

Continued on Back Page

Above: *The British newspapers carried banner headings about the dreadful war crime.*

'I THINK I PROBABLY SAW PEOPLE BEING TORTURED TO DEATH.'

Unfortunately it would not be his last and his weakness was to prove disastrous.

Calley, 5ft 4ins in height, who volunteered for army duty just days before he was drafted, was perhaps typical of the men the army got, rather than the men they wanted. By the time he was wearing fatigues, anti-war sentiments in the USA were being openly expressed, as draft dodgers fled to Canada, peace marchers burned the American flag and people spat on returning servicemen home on leave from the war zone. In such a climate, the army needed everyone they could get to keep the billion pound-per-month war going. In such a climate William Laws Calley, failed diner cook, car wash attendant, insurance clerk and railway ticket collector, became, when he was twenty-two years old, an officer in the United States Army. It is a proud office.

Patrols through the steamy jungle and paddy fields continued and Charlie Company continued to take casualties. They also took some prisoners, but now the one-hour lectures they had received on the Geneva Convention regarding the treatment of prisoners-of-war were entirely forgotten. The sharp end of war had already eroded their morals. They now, as a matter of course, indulged in the brutal, casual beating of suspects. Fred Widmer, who later came to be called 'Mr Homicide' for his acts in My Lai, recalled in the book 'Four Hours In My Lai', by Michael Bilton and Kevin Sim how decency was lost to the men in Charlie Company. He said: 'The first time I saw something really bad was the point at which we stopped taking prisoners. A couple of shots and they were done. As time went by, things were done, ears were cut off, mutilations.

TESTING THE ENEMY

'One prisoner had his arms tied straight out on a stick... Lit cigarettes were put inside the elastic of the guy's pants and we watched him dance around because they were burning his ass. I think it was a bit of making him talk and a bit of venting our frustration. I don't remember what happened to them. The more it went on the more you didn't trust anyone. You didn't believe anybody because you didn't know who was who, you didn't know who the enemy was.

'As we went on, more and more prisoners would be executed. I would say it was a regular occurrence. I did abuse someone, a *papa san*, a prisoner. I found myself doing the same things that had been going on all along. We cut the beard off him – this was an insult. A *papa san* with a beard is considered as the wise man, and to cut off their beard was a real sign of disrespect to them. You found yourself punching them around, beating them up, trying to get them to talk. I never tortured anyone to death. I think I probably saw people being tortured to death.' It was a sad admission.

The distinction between peasant soldiers and peasant farmers was lost in this dirty war game. In the imagination of the overburdened, terror-stricken soldiers of Charlie Company, the Vietnamese people were all 'gooks'. They all had to die.

THE MISSION

Charlie Company, reduced to one hundred and five men because of sickness, death and injuries, were informed on 15 March, that they were scheduled for a search-and-destroy operation on the following day. The village of My Lai, so Calley and his men were told, was the HQ for the elusive 48th Battalion of the VC that Charlie Company had been trying to find ever since their arrival in Vietnam. The men were told that the civilian population would be evacuated by the time the unit arrived at 7.30am. Anyone remaining would be gooks – VC – and they could deal with them in the way enemy soldiers are treated.

No written notes about the briefing of this operation exist. But the people who took part in it say that every man was under

> 'THIS WAS A TIME FOR US TO GET EVEN. A TIME FOR US TO SETTLE THE SCORE. A TIME FOR REVENGE.'

Below: *Ronald Haeberle, left, was a photographer. Michael Bernhardt (right) was a serving soldier. Both were to give crucial evidence at the My Lai trial.*

no illusions that the drift of the orders was simple: the destruction of all buildings, the slaughter of livestock and the taking of a few prisoners for interrogation. The rest would be consigned to hell. Sergeant Kenneth Hodges remembers his briefing thus: 'This was a time for us to get even. A time for us to settle the score. A time for revenge – when we can get revenge for our fallen comrades. It was clearly explained that there were to be no prisoners. Someone asked if that included the women and the children, and the order was: everyone in the village. They were not sympathetic to the Americans. It was quite clear that no one was to be spared in that village.'

The next day the men, equipped with phosphorus grenades, extra ammunition pouches, mortars and side arms were choppered out on board the green 'Huey' heli-

at the ready. They walked through the paddy fields, moving abreast in lines, and they were shooting. Courts would later be told that women were being cut down by automatic fire before the company had even reached the village.

Once in the village, all sense of American fair play, of decency and humanity, evaporated. The phosphorus grenades were tossed into the straw huts before the villagers were executed at point-blank range with single shots from the men's M.16 rifles. Private Allen Boyce, who, at the subsequent court hearings into the massacre, pleaded the Fifth Amendment on the grounds of self-incrimination, was seen to stab an old man in the chest with a bayonet, then shoot him in the neck. Then he shot another man and threw him down a well. He lobbed a grenade down after him just for good measure.

None of the villagers was armed. From hut to hut Charlie Company moved, grabbing terrified inhabitants by the hair, bellowing 'VC? VC?' at them and then murdering them in cold blood. The shouts

Above: *Survivors of the massacre claimed that they pretended to be dead so that the soldiers would not attack them any further.*

Right: *Ronald Lee Ridenhour witnessed the events. He was so shocked that he informed officials in Washington of the atrocity.*

copters for their appointment with death. The countryside of Vietnam appeared beneath them as a patchwork quilt of greens and browns, with the shadow of their own craft creating eerie silhouettes as they moved across the sky. With them, on the helicopters, were two men who would later be instrumental in confirming events in My Lai – a reporter and a photographer from the Army Information Unit.

THE END OF A VILLAGE

The people of My Lai were following their pattern of traditional village life that morning, as the gunships and troopships approached from the sky and a battery of huge 155mm guns trained their sights upon them. Children played with the pigs in the dirt, the women boiled water on open fires, men drifted off to work in the rice fields. At 7.30 the artillerymen opened fire, sending high explosive and white phosphorus shells into the hamlet. The inhabitants rushed for the crude underground shelters they had hewn for themselves.

Minutes later the barrage lifted and the men from Charlie Company approached the village, weapons fully cocked, grenades

of 'lai dai' – come here – filled the air as the villagers ran away and were mown down from behind. Groups of between twenty-five and forty people, who had huddled in ditches at the side of the road, were hit by bullets fired from the soldiers' automatic weapons.

At one point, Captain Ernest Medina, one of the brigade commanders overseeing operations that day, radioed Lt. Calley to enquire why his men had slowed up in their progress through the village. Calley replied that they had encountered a large group of civilians, some sixty in all. 'Take care of them,' came the reply from Medina. There was no question of asking for clarification of orders; Calley lined them up and from a distance of ten feet shot them dead with a machine gun, aided by two subordinates. Then he grabbed the dead women who had dived on their babies in a frantic gesture at saving their lives, rolled them off and shot the children. Women who made a break for the tree line in the distance were shot at with grenades and machine guns. One man fell when a grenade fired from a rifle penetrated his stomach but did not explode. He was shot through the head moments later.

Another fifty Vietnamese were found in a separate ditch at the far end of the village. Crouching low in the fetid water were old men, old women, young women and babies. Calley screamed at his men to put their M.16s on to full automatic and join him in the execution. Magazine after magazine was pumped into the screaming, writhing mass of humanity. The water in the ditch turned crimson with blood.

Animals fared no better. Pigs and cows were mutilated with bayonets, chickens beheaded. The keening of these animals stayed in some troopers' minds more than the screams of the massacred civilians.

MEN GONE BERSERK

On and on roamed the berserk killing machine that was Charlie Company. Children were despatched with clinical detachment. Widmer, Mr Homicide, killed a boy. 'When I shot him, I was sick to my stomach,' he said. 'Soon as I did it I realised: "My God, what have I done?" ' But there were worse, more heinous acts of depravity than Widmer's. Women were raped and mutilated, corpses beheaded,

some scalped. None of this stomach-churning slaughter affected the appetites of the killers – by mid-morning they had ceased firing and took a lunch break. But the killing was by no means over.

Prisoners who had been taken to a ravine for interrogation were blown away by rifles fired in their mouths. Another hundred civilians were killed in various actions around the village before the company bivouacked for a night when the soft sounds of the jungle were interrupted by the wails of those people who had not been finished off by the death squads. The flames from the burning remains of the villagers' homes lit the night sky.

Dawn revealed the ghastly reality of the previous day's action. Village men who had been working in the fields returned to find their entire families butchered. Weeping, they buried the dead in mass graves, mothers next to fathers, brothers next to sisters, aunts, uncles, cousins. Not one of

Above: *Chief Warrant Officer Hugh Thompson used his helicopter to evacuate wounded women and children from the scene at My Lai.*

'Soon as I did it I realised: "My God, what have I done?" '

these victims had fired a shot in retaliation at these soldiers from a foreign army.

Only one American had been killed by the preparatory artillery barrage.

My Lai had been a victory only for the dark side of war and in the cold light of that day, the US Army began to realise that it had lost forever in Vietnam its status of liberator and defender of freedom. Rumours of a massacre circulated with the speed of a disease among the ranks and soon the brass were being asked awkward questions by the Pentagon. It was only a matter of time before the American nation would know what took place.

Frank Barker, the commanding officer of the task force which mounted the assault on My Lai, and from whom many participants in the massacre say they received their orders to kill civilians, was never able to defend himself – he died three months later in a helicopter crash just as the furore surrounding the slaughter rose to fever pitch. The first the public knew of the mission he led came when a former soldier who was there, and who claimed he had not taken part in the killings, wrote letters describing the My Lai massacre to prominent politicians and government officials in Washington.

WHO GAVE THE ORDERS?

First army, then administration officials began to piece together what had occurred in My Lai. They were given photographs taken by Ron Haeberle, the cameraman included in the mission, who snapped many appalling scenes of the dead. He said, in his statement, that he thought the order to kill women and children must have come from higher up: 'Soldiers just do not start killing civilians in the mass they were doing. This was the first time I have seen something like this. I heard later that the General of the Americal Division praised the task force for the operation, but I take it that he was not told that most of the people killed were unarmed women and children.' His testimony was important.

Stanley Resor, Secretary of State for the army, refused at first to believe the massacre story and the US government assumed that a strategic error had been made, insisting that any civilians who died in My Lai were caught in the cross-fire of a fierce gun battle between Americans and VC troops. However, when Resor received a confidential memo from his staff saying that all indications were of a massacre, he could no longer cover up. Investigators travelled all over Vietnam, South-East Asia and America interviewing the members of the disbanded Charlie Company. They testified with some honesty to their participation in the events of that day.

On 5 June, Calley was recalled to the USA and identified as the man who had thrown the baby back into the ditch. He was formally served notice that he was a

Below: William Calley saluted in proper officer tradition after his trial ended in Fort Benning, Georgia.

DAILY NEWS
NEW YORK'S PICTURE NEWSPAPER ®
FINAL
10¢
Vol. 52. No. 240   Copr. 1971 New York News Inc.   New York, N.Y. 10017, Thursday, April 1, 1971*   WEATHER: Partly cloudy and cool.

CALLEY GETS LIFE TERM

Lt. William L. Calley Jr. salutes as he leaves courthouse at Fort Benning after sentencing.—Stories on page 3 potential suspect in the mass murder enquiry. As it turned out, he became the scapegoat for *all* the men who murdered innocent people that day.

Several officers above him were charged with dereliction of duty and other soldiers charged with murder as the investigation rumbled on. Five were eventually court-martialled, but only Lt Calley was convicted. There was no contrition from him in the dock; he spoke of his duty to kill the Communists, and how he had been a good soldier. It was, perhaps, this refusal to admit that his acts qualified as war crimes that made Calley the symbolic representative of every man who, that day in My Lai, fired a round at an innocent human being.

While some American citizens sported 'Free Calley' stickers on their car bumpers, and anti-war protestors blamed the generals, and not individuals, for what happened, Calley was eventually Found Guilty of a 'speciman' twenty-two murders on 29 March, 1971 and sentenced to hard labour for life. Less than three days later, he was released from prison on the specific instructions of President Nixon and was allowed appeal. He never went back behind bars again, but spent the next three years under house arrest at his spacious apartment in Fort Benning, Georgia, surrounded by the comforts of home, his tropical fish, his dog and other assorted pets.

On 9 November, 1974 he was paroled a free man but was still a victim of war.

The war is long over, the names of the fifty-three thousand Americans who died there etched into the polished granite war memorial in Washington. For Calley, and for the others who were there that day, it is a war that is never over.

NIGHTMARE OF GUILT

Varnado Simpson is typical of the men who went into My Lai that day. Now forty-four, he has attempted suicide three times, seen his son die from a stray bullet – an act that, he believes, was from God as punishment for the massacre – and he gets through each day with endless bottles of pills. 'Yes, I killed. I cut people's ears off. I scalped. Cutting their throats, scalping. Yes, I did that. About twenty-five in all, I guess.

'I have nightmares, I constantly have nightmares of the children. I can go some-

where and see a face that reminds me of the people that I killed. How can you forgive? I can never forgive myself. I don't let anyone get close to me. The loving feeling was killed by My Lai.'

Calley is now a paunched, balding businessman who works at his father-in-law's jewellery store in Columbus, Ohio. He is not on pills, does not need a psychiatrist, has never expressed remorse.

My Lai is never far from his thoughts, but he never, ever speaks of that village. Several years ago he wrote an autobiography in which he attempted justification for the madness that engulfed him and the men under him. He wrote: 'We weren't in My Lai to kill human beings, we were there to kill an ideology that is carried by – I don't know. Pawns. Blobs. Pieces of flesh. And I wasn't in My Lai to destroy intelligent men. I was there to destroy an intangible idea. To destroy Communism. I looked at Communism the way a southerner looks at a negro, supposedly. It's evil. It's bad.'

It is too late for Calley to learn from My Lai but perhaps not too late for mankind.

Above: *'Take care of them' was the chilling command from Captain Edwin Medina as Calley and his men moved through My Lai.*

HOW CAN YOU FORGIVE? I CAN NEVER FORGIVE MYSELF. I DON'T LET ANYONE GET CLOSE TO ME.

STALIN
Crime at Katyn Wood

In the secret heart of the forest, the proud officers of the Polish army were brutally executed. Even their murderers were so shamed by the killings that they denied the facts. But the dreadful truth of Katyn Wood has not remained hidden.

Adolf Hitler, leader of the German Nazi party, sent his emissary Joachim von Ribbentrop to Moscow in August 1939. He wanted a pact with Josef Stalin, bloodthirsty leader of the Soviet peoples. Yet Stalin represented the Slavic races that Hitler had threatened time and time again, in his manic outpourings, to destroy for ever. And Hitler, in Stalin's eyes, was a fascist running dog who persecuted without mercy the Communists. The former champagne salesman, von Ribbentrop, emerged after several days of diplomatic niceties with his Soviet counterpart, foreign minister Vyacheslav Molotov, to proclaim to a stunned world that a new non-aggression pact had been signed between the two former adversaries. This was *Realpolitik* at its most cynical – the conclusion of distasteful business for the mutual benefit of mutual enemies.

The West viewed the Molotov-Ribbentrop Pact as the precursor to an aggressive war of conquest in Western Europe. With the Soviets promising no action if Germany made 'territorial claims' upon her neighbours, strategists saw that Hitler had effectively silenced his biggest, and a potentially lethal, foe without a shot being fired in anger.

But what the West did not know – and would not find out until a month later, when the armies of Hitler launched their attack on Poland that was to start the Second World War – was that 'the pact' contained a secret clause that divided Poland between Hitler and Stalin. Between them, the two great dictators, who despised each other and the systems each represented, had forged a compact to ensure that this independent nation should cease to exist.

Betwixt the two, Poland became a vassal state. Polish Jews were soon earmarked for destruction by the Nazis, while under the Soviets, the intelligentsia and anti-Communist elements were rooted out for 'special treatment' by the NKVD, the forerunner of the KGB, but that concentrated less on espionage and more on mass murder and political suppression.

Opposite: *Josef Stalin, the man of steel. He has more blood on his hands than any other man this century.*

Below: *Polish women weep over their loved ones after the bodies were disinterred.*

Bottom: *German investigators and Russian peasants exhume the vast mass grave.*

One other segment of Polish national life was hated by both sides – the officer corps of the army who were proud, disciplined, fiercely independent men.

It was precisely because they were troublesome to both dictators, that one of the most heinous crimes in wartime history went unsolved for over forty years. In 1940, four thousand Polish officers, from generals to lieutenants, were bound, shot in the back of the head and buried in massive lime pits, surrounded by thick fir trees that made up the forest of Katyn, near Smolensk in western Russia. All the victims had their hands tied to nooses around their necks which tightened when they struggled; all bore the same single-entry head wound testifying to methodical execution by shooting.

For close on five decades the crime at Katyn Wood was not acknowledged or admitted by the perpetrators. The Germans claimed the Russians did it; the Russians that the Germans were the perpetrators. It was not until the demise of the Soviet Union and the release of KGB files that the

Opposite, top: *Molotov, seated, signs a non-aggression pact with Germany.*

Opposite, below: *The Russian admission of responsibility for the massacre at Katyn Wood made headlines all over the world.*

Below: *The villages of Poland were burnt and abandoned as columns of German troops marched through the conquered land.*

truth was out – that the Poles were executed because they were the 'class enemy' of the Soviet people. On 13 April, 1990 Mikhail Gorbachev acknowledged his nation's culpability… forty–seven years after the day that Germany claimed her soldiers in the east had stumbled across the mass graves in the forest.

The events in the clearings of the Katyn Forest during those days of April 1940 make for grim reading. Even now the scars left by the liquidation of these proud warriors remain deep. This is the story of Stalin's massacre of the army allied to Britain – the nation for whom Britain went to war in the first place.

The tale, from being part of the first national army to stand up to Hitler to that degrading execution in the vast mass grave of the Katyn Forest, was a short one for these Polish officers.

IN THESE CAMPS WAS THE BEST OF THE BEST OF POLISH NATIONAL LIFE; EDUCATED, CULTURED, PASSIONATE MEN.

MOLOTOV INFORMED THE POLISH AMBASSADOR: 'THE POLISH STATE CEASES TO EXIST.'

First, Hitler's Stuka dive-bombers and armoured columns brought terror to the civilian population as Operation Case White – the conquest of Poland – began on 1 September. Hitler used a transparently lame excuse for sending his troops across the border; namely, that German soldiers in a frontier post had been killed by marauding Poles. Sixteen days later, with their cities in flames and their armies all but routed, the desperate Poles then had to endure an attack from their eastern neighbour, Russia. Again, it was a flimsy excuse that brought the Red Army pouring over the frontier. In reality, it was the fulfillment of the secret clause in the contemptible Molotov-Ribbentrop Pact.

Stalin camouflaged his military intervention by claiming his soldiers were being sent merely to protect the rights of Byelorussians and Ukrainians, living in Polish territory near the border with the Soviet Union. At 3am on 17 December, hours after Soviet troops, backed up by the death squads of the NKVD, were pouring across the border, Waclaw Grzybowski, the Polish ambassador to Moscow, was summoned to the foreign ministry where he was confronted by Molotov who, shedding all diplomatic niceties, informed him: 'The Polish state ceases to exist. We are aiding you to extricate your people from an unfortunate war in which they have been dragged by unwise leaders and to enable them to live a peaceful life.'

By 5 October, the day the last Polish units ceased fighting, Germany had two-thirds and the Soviet Union one third of Polish territory. Germany took close to six hundred thousand prisoners-of-war; the Red Army captured another two hundred and thirty thousand men. In the wake of the fighting troops came the SS battalions, on the German side, and the NKVD secret police units of Stalin. Both groups were remarkably similar in their initial actions. Round-ups began of intellectuals, university professors, nobles, known radicals, truculent churchmen; anyone who was deemed to pose the smallest threat.

Hitler had used the state as his instrument of repression and murder since he achieved power in 1933, but he was a mere apprentice in the art of massacre compared to Stalin. On his hands was the blood of *tens of millions* of people, murdered across

May, five weeks later. In the previous week the prisoners were rounded up in their camps at Kozelsk, Starobelsk and Ostashkov and taken in batches to railheads to board cattlewagons for unknown destinations. However, the four thousand four hundred Poles from Kozelsk camp were bound for the forest at Katyn.

HOPE OF REPATRIATION

Since their capture, these men had existed on meagre rations and were given few facilities to communicate with their families. During the days that they were herded into trains, they were given a better diet, kindling hope among them that they were

the vast steppes, shot in the cellars of the NKVD prisons, worked to death in the great Gulag archipelago that stretched over the frozen Siberian wastes. Stalin, in his Kremlin office, decreed that the vanquished Poles in the territory he now ruled would, indeed, receive no treatment that had not already been meted out in large measure to his own suffering masses. None could accuse the Man of Steel of inconsistency in his harshness.

Early in November, after a secret edict from Stalin, NKVD units began separating and moving out from a vast string of POW camps the fifteen thousand Polish officers whom they had captured. They were taken to camps set up in old monasteries that had perished under Bolshevism, all of them within Russian territory. In these camps was the best of the best of Polish national life; educated, cultured, passionate men, many of them reservists who had simply abandoned their comfortable lives to put on a uniform and fight for the land they loved.

Only a handful would ever see it again.

The NKVD were preparing for *mokrara rabota* – the agency's slang for bloodletting. For months the NKVD superiors at the prison camps, that held the Poles, had been sending reports back to their Lubyanka masters, suggesting that some of the Polish officers might be transported to Moscow, where they could be assimilated and indoctrinated into the Soviet system. But Josef Stalin had already made up his mind about their fate.

The liquidations at the Katyn Forest began on 3 April and did not end until 13

RUSSIA BLAMES STALIN FOR WIPING OUT 15,000 POLES

50 YEARS ON, KATYN REVEALS THE TERRIBLE SECRET OF ITS 4,254 GRAVES

by OLGA CRAIG

THEY had been told they were going home. Instead, the train taking thousands of Polish prisoners of war across Russia was halted in a remote forest.

The 4,251 officers were ordered out and shot. Their bodies were buried in a mass grave.

The 1941 Katyn massacre was one of the worst outrages of World War Two, but the truth about it stayed an evil secret for 50 years.

It was not until yesterday that the Russians finally admitted Stalin ordered his secret police to slaughter the men and another 10,600 Polish officers whose bodies have never been found.

In an about-turn which stunned the world, Moscow Radio reported the discovery of new archive documents laying the blame firmly at the door of the NKVD, forerunners of the KGB.

Deserted

After the Poles, captured in the Nazi-Soviet partition of their country in 1939, failed to return home, Stalin insisted they had all deserted.

When the mass grave filled with 4,000 bodies was accidentally found during forest clearance in 1943, he blamed the horrific mass slaughter on the Nazi invaders.

The Katyn area had changed hands during the war, controlled first by the Russians, then by the Germans.

Letters

But the Russians held the land in April 1940, the day 4,000 officers at Kozelsk camp were told they were being sent home.

They rushed off letters to loved ones saying they were coming back "via Katyn".

When the train jolted to a halt just outside the western town of Smo-

lensk the officers were still in a celebration mood.

Then the doors were wrenched open and they tumbled blinking into the sunshine.

One by one the bewildered men were dragged into a long line overlooking deep newly-dug trenches.

Side by side they stood, trying to make sense of it all.

An order was shouted and a battery of shots was fired. Four thousand Polish officers were shot in the back of the neck by Russian soldiers.

The remains of another 10,600 officers who were held in camps at Starobelsk and Ostashkov have never been found.

relatives of victims, said it wanted criminal proceedings brought against anyone still alive who was involved.

The Katyn bodies, stacked in layers, were found by the Nazis in April 1943 and immediately used for propaganda against the Allies.

The Soviets always insisted the officers were killed in 1941 by the Nazis after they invaded the Soviet Union.

Historians

After the war, Poland's Communist government continued to echo the Soviet explanation.

But most Poles and Western historians had long concluded that the massacre of "class enemies" was committed by the Soviet secret police on Josef Stalin's order in late April 1940.

As Soviet leader Mikhail Gorbachev's glasnost policies took hold, Soviet and Polish historians joined forces to review Katyn and other

HORROR: Gruesome scene when the grave was found in 1943

IN April - May 1940 394 of the 15, 000 or so Polish officers kept in the three camps were transferred to the Gryazovetsk camp. The larger part, however, were turned over to the NKVD administrations in the Smolensk, Voroshilovgrad and Kalinin regions and never mentioned in NKVD statistical accounts since.

The discovered archival material puts direct responsibility for the atrocities in the Katyn Forest on Beria, Merkulov and their henchmen. The Soviet side, expressing profound regret over the Katyn tragedy, declares that this tragedy is one of the gravest crimes of Stalinism.

TRUTH: The text of the official statement released in Moscow

historical "blank spots".

The Polish side confirmed Soviet responsibility last year, but a promised joint report never appeared.

The Soviets' formal admission of guilt has been timed to coincide with a three-day state visit to

Moscow by Polish President Wojciech Jaruzelski.

Radio Moscow's report, based on an official statement by Soviet news agency Tass, made no attempt to play down the outrage.

It said: "The Soviet side expresses its deep regret over the tragedy and deems it one of the most horrifying Stalinist crimes."

Justice

Accepting responsibility for the atrocity has been one of the conditions for improvement in relations between Poland and the Soviet Union.

Solidarity leader Lech Walesa last night called the Soviet admission "an act of moral justice which has been awaited for a long time".

He said: "It's good that criminals admit their crimes."

Foreign Secretary Douglas Hurd said yesterday: "We must remember the heavy weight of history there is in Russia, the terrible things Stalin did, and the terrible things which were done to Russia during the last war.

"Gradually bits and pieces are coming out, a bit gingerly, as the Katyn story shows.

"But it must be right that it should come out and that they should admit the truth."

But the admission has come 50 years too late for some of the surviving families.

"I regret terribly that my mother could not live until this day," said Wanda Zadroza, whose father was murdered in the forest.

She added: *"But whatever happens now, it is good that the truth will be finally written in our history books."*

Crusade of anguish

A BRITISH officer led the fight for truth.

Sir Frederick Bennett has shared the anguish of widows of the slaughtered Poles. He has seen the letters, now creased and stained with tears, the men wrote to say they were coming home.

Last night the retired major said: "I can't use the word delighted to describe how I feel. Somehow it wouldn't

seem appropriate, but you've no idea how relieved I am."

Former MP Sir Frederick, 71, founded the Katyn Association with top Tory Airey Neave, later killed by an IRA car bomb. Sir Frederick had been approached by Poles he befriended as they fought side by side during the war.

"The letters are tragic," he said, "One soldier jubilantly tells his wife he is being sent

home by train – via Katyn. The Russian admission has boosted Sir Frederick's fight for compensation for the 15 Katyn widows still alive in Britain.

Next Saturday he will unveil a plaque honouring the dead at the Katyn monument in Gunnersbury Cemetery, West London. It says bluntly: "Murdered by Soviet secret police under Stalin's orders."

indeed being repatriated to a new life. Each man received three dried herrings, half-a-pound of bread and some sugar. For some lucky few there was even an issue of Russian cigarettes to treasure.

The NKVD wanted the officers lulled into a state of well-being. Had there been any inkling of what lay in store for them,

Above right: *Red Cross and other officials are shown the grave site by a German officer.*

Above: *German Red Cross workers search for anything to help identify the corpses.*

Right: *Jewellery and military insignia found on one Polish corpse.*

'I AM NOW COMING TO THE CONCLUSION THAT THIS JOURNEY DOES NOT BODE WELL.'

there would have been bloody mutinies from the brave prisoners in the camps.

But once at the railheads, away from the camps and their comrades, the treatment changed immediately. New NKVD men were waiting to board them on the trains, men armed with clubs and dogs and with the vicious, four-sided bayonets issued to the NKVD. Many prisoners were severely, gratuitously beaten as they clambered aboard the trains. Waclaw Kruk, a lieutenant, was one of the officers never to return from Katyn.

A diary was later found near his body in which he wrote down his feelings – feelings that must have been those of all the Poles as they moved out of the camps into the unknown. 'Yesterday a convoy of senior officers left: three generals, twenty to twenty-five colonels and the same number of majors. We were in the best of spirits because of the manner of their departure. Today, my turn came. But at the station we were loaded into prison cars under strict guard. Now we are waiting to depart. Optimistic as I was before, I am now coming to the conclusion that this journey does not bode well.' His diary was found in 1943, near a body tagged 'number 424'.

Another corpse, that of Major Adam Solski, also had a journal near it. Experts who examined it concur that the condemned man wrote the final words less than twenty minutes before he was murdered. It makes sad reading. 'Few minutes before five in the morning: reveille in the prison train. Preparing to get off. We are to go somewhere by car. What next? Five o'clock: ever since dawn the day has run an exceptional course. Departure in prison van with tiny cell-like compartments; horrible. Driven somewhere in the woods, somewhere like a holiday place. Here a detailed search. I was relieved of my watch, which showed 6.30am, asked for my wedding ring. Roubles, belt and pocket knife taken away.'

Journey's end for the soldiers was the Katyn Forest, sloping towards the Dnieper River and not far from the town of Smolensk. Here, gigantic pits had been dug in the sandy soil, within the leafy groves of fir trees and silver birch. Not far from the pits was a building known innocently as The Little Castle of the Dnieper; in reality it was a summer house, a dacha, of the local NKVD and now served as the headquarters of the killing squads who were about to despatch the cream of the Polish army to their deaths.

A SINISTER JOURNEY

The prisoners were taken from the rail cars in what were known as the *chorny voron* – the police buses, which had been a grim feature of Soviet life for years. A glimpse of one of them, in a Soviet street, was enough to send shivers up the back of any innocent observer. These buses were divided into separate steel compartments, each little bigger than a kennel, in which the Polish officers were kept until their turn for execution arrived.

Only one man, a Polish professor, Stanislaw Swianiewicz, saw the killing of his comrades and lived to tell the tale. He was on board one of the trains, but was locked into a compartment by himself, only to be transported to Moscow to face charges of espionage. But he witnessed the scene as his fellow officers were led to their deaths. In the authoritative book 'Katyn' by Allen Paul, the professor was quoted: 'wondered what kind of operation it was. Clearly, my companions were being taken to a place in the vicinity, probably only a few miles away. It was a fine spring day and I wondered why they were not told to march there, as was the usual procedure at camps. The presence of a high-ranking NKVD officer, at what was apparently the simple transferal of several hundred prisoners from one camp to another, could be explained if we were actually going to be handed over to the Germans. But, in such a

Above: *A German officer holds up the decomposing jacket of a murdered Polish officer.*

case, why these extraordinary precautions? Why the fixed bayonets of the escort? I could think of no reasonable explanation. But then, on that brilliant spring day, it never even occurred to me that the operation might entail the execution of my companions.' Such an act was unthinkable.

Execution at the pits was to be cold, methodical, production-line work. Machine guns or grenades could not be used; people would run, there would be survivors, there

WHY THESE EXTRAORDINARY PRECAUTIONS? WHY THE FIXED BAYONETS OF THE ESCORT? I COULD THINK OF NO REASONABLE EXPLANATION.

would be an immediate panic among those prisoners awaiting transport from the train to the execution place. Instead the NKVD agents used 7.65mm Walther German-police issue pistols, considered by handgun experts to be the best pistols of their type in the world. NKVD squads would be waiting with fresh guns to replace those that over-heated in the ceaseless slaughter, others with mounds of ammunition.

Once taken, one by one from the buses, the individual prisoners were bound in a particularly gruesome manner – a manner perfected over the years by the murderers from the NKVD. The victim's hands were first tied behind his back, then a second cord was tied over his head at neck level

> AS THE LAST OF THE SAND WAS BULLDOZED OVER THE GRAVES, THE BUTCHERS PLANTED TINY BIRCH SAPLINGS ON TOP.

Below: Joachim von Ribbentrop announces details of the cynical pact with the Soviet Union to carve up Poland.

with the victim's greatcoat pulled up over it, like a shroud. From the neck the cord was passed down the prisoner's back, looped around the bound hands and tied again at the neck, forcing the arms painfully upwards towards his shoulder blades. Any attempt to lower his arms put pressure on the neck; repeated pressure would result in strangulation.

One by one these brave, noble men were led to the edge of the pits. Many bodies bore the brutal stab-marks of the four-squared NKVD bayonets – proof that, agonizing though their bonds were, they had attempted to struggle for their lives. Each one was despatched with what the Germans called the *Nackenschuss* – a shot through the nape of the neck which caused instant death and limited blood loss. This method had been perfected in countless

> I SENSED A PROPAGANDA EXERCISE. I HATED THE GERMANS. I DID NOT WANT TO BELIEVE THEM.

cellars and execution dens of the NKVD over many years of Stalinist terror.

They fell into the pits and were stacked like cordwood, one on one, in layers of twelve before lime was sprinkled over them and tons of sand bulldozed back over them. But the tons of sand helped to press the corpses down and literally 'mummify' them as the body fluids and blood was squeezed out. The lime failed to work, so when the advancing Germans discovered the graves of Katyn, the thousands of corpses were well preserved.

On and on went the killing. The NKVD butchers fuelled their spirits with massive quantities of vodka consumed in the nearby dacha. Twelve hours a day for six weeks, nothing but the sound of gunshots echoed from those lonely groves until, finally, four thousand one hundred and forty-three victims were dead. As the last of the sand was bulldozed over the graves, the butchers planted tiny birch saplings on top.

The remaining eleven thousand Polish officers, held in other camps were liquidated at killing sites deeper in Russia. Their graves have never been exhumed but there has since been an admission from the now-defunct Soviet Union that all these Polish officers had been annihilated on Stalin's personal orders.

But Katyn was, and remains, the most significant massacre site. It was a known site, yet for decades it was surrounded by lies and duplicity. It justified a deep-rooted hatred of the Soviet state felt by all the people of Poland.

FRIENDS TURN ON EACH OTHER

It was only a matter of time before those arch-enemies, Hitler and Stalin, were to turn on each other. Hitler had written in *Mein Kampf* that *Lebensraum* – living space – in the east was his single greatest goal. On 22 June, 1941 he set out to achieve that with Operation Barbarossa, the attack on the Soviet Union.

Fifteen hundred miles away from Stalingrad, in the dacha where the NKVD executioners planned the killing of the Polish officers, the soldiers in Lt Col Friedrich Ahrens' signal regiment were having a relatively quiet war.

Ahrens and his men had a strange fore-boding about Katyn Wood, the site of the dacha. They heard rumours from the local people about NKVD executions taking place there, and hidden graves. Then, in February 1943, when the German 6th Army was routed at Stalingrad, a wolf unearthed bones in one of the mass grave sites. Ivan Krivozertsev, a local peasant, approached Ahrens and formally informed him of the dark secrets of the forest. NKVD secrecy and planning had not been hidden from the sharp eyes of the peasants.

Below: British prisoners-of-war were taken to the site. The Germans wanted to convince the Allies that the massacre was a Russian act.

the Polish officers had been 'bestially murdered by the Bolsheviks'. The world was stunned into silence, choosing to believe that the report was fabricated by the Nazis. But the Polish government-in-exile, in London, had long harboured suspicions that the Russians had copious amounts of Polish blood on their hands.

On 15 April the Soviets counter-attacked, claiming: 'In launching this monsterous invention the German-Fascist scoundrels did not hesitate at the most unscrupulous and base lies, in their attempts to cover up crimes which, as has now become evident, were perpetrated by themselves. The Hitlerite murders will not escape a just and bloody retribution for their bloody crimes.' Three separate commissions were invited to visit Katyn by the Germans. The first was entirely German, the second composed of scientists and forensic experts from Switzerland, Belgium, Hungary and Bulgaria, and the third was entirely Polish. The evidence was mightily in favour of the German view-point. Although the ammunition was

The Germans prepared to tell the world of the slaughter of the Polish officers, and Dr Gerhard Buhtz, a professor of forensic medicine from a leading German university, was put in charge of the exhumation and examination of the grave pits, which were opened in early March. For ten weeks the stink of rotten flesh and Egyptian tobacco – the Germans smoked it to mask the smell of the dead – mingled with the scents of moss and pine sap as the murdered men were disinterred and laid out. Some prisoners-of-war, American Lt Col John Van Vliet among them, were taken by the Germans to witness the massacre site. He recalled: 'I sensed a propaganda exercise. I hated the Germans. I did not want to believe them. But after seeing the bodies there, piled up like cord-wood, I changed my mind. I told the Allies, after the War, that I thought the Soviets were responsible.'

On 13 April, 1943, at 3.10pm Berlin time, the German radio network officially announced the finding of the graves where

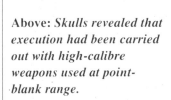

Above: Skulls revealed that execution had been carried out with high-calibre weapons used at point-blank range.

German, records from the manufacturing plants showed it to be batches sold, before the war, to Lithuania only to be siezed later by NKVD police units.

The Soviets claimed that the men were killed by the advancing Germans in 1941 – although not one document with a date later than 6 May, 1940 was ever found on a single corpse. The bayonet thrusts on the bodies were of the four-cornered NKVD type. The fact that there were no insects found in the graves indicated cold weather-burial, not summer as the Soviets claimed – and besides, all the murdered soldiers wore heavy winter clothing.

But their military fight against Hitler had, for the Allied commanders, at that time, a higher priority than a search for justice and truth. Churchill remarked in a cabinet meeting: 'We must not take sides in the Russo-Polish quarrel.' He assured Stalin in a secret communique that he would do his personal best to silence Free Polish newspapers in London over the affair, while he told Wadyslaw Sikorski, the prime minister in exile: 'If they are dead, nothing you can do will bring them back.' President Roosevelt in the White House preferred to believe the Soviet leader's explanation that the murders were committed by the Nazis.

Right: A priest prays at the graveside for the Polish officers, who were denied the blessing of the last rites at their death.

Below: Row upon row of corpses, all tied in the same fashion, were pulled from the mass burial pit.

When the Soviets finally overran the Katyn territory in their great push west-wards, they took the opportunity to cover up the massacre of the Polish officers. The ponderously-named 'Special Commission for Ascertaining and Investigating the Circumstances of the Shooting of Polish Officer Prisoners by the German Invaders in the Katyn Forest' went into overdrive to persuade the world that the murders were the work of the Gestapo and *Einsatzgruppen*. The Soviets stuck to their story that the officers had been murdered a year later than was actually the case – and

as stories of German atrocities throughout the War began to emerge from all over Europe, there were plenty of people willing to believe the Soviets.

By the time the triumphant Red Army rolled into Berlin in May 1945, the myth that the Germans were responsible for Katyn was firmly planted around the world and in the satellite Eastern European nations over which, in Churchill's words, the Kremlin had drawn an 'Iron Curtain'. In Warsaw, the monument to the dead at Katyn blamed the Nazi invaders; at Katyn itself the inscription read: 'To the victims of Fascism. Polish officers shot by the Nazis in 1941.' The Soviets were operating under the maxim that Hitler once used – tell a lie big enough for long enough and it will metamorphose into truth. They denied any reference to the atrocity if it cast suspicion on their forces. Ewa Solska, the daughter of Major Solski whose diary was found on him, wrote 'killed at Katyn' in the box on her university application form which asked for information about her father. She was expelled for giving this information.

Even at Nuremberg, the great post-war trial for the crimes of Nazism, the Soviets were able to bluff the tribunals that Katyn was a Nazi crime. They could not bluff the Polish people, nor the many people around the world who were slowly caming to realise the enormity of Stalin's crimes.

It wasn't until 1990, at a ceremony inside the Kremlin, that Gorbachev, in keeping with the spirit of his Glasnost reforms, handed President Jaruzelski of Poland a box containing NKVD documents and other files, showing that the officers had indeed been murdered by the NKVD. These revealed that the executioners themselves had been 'liquidated' under Stalin's orders, then buried at an unknown grave site somewhere in Russia. Only four hundred prisoners-of-war from the entire Polish officer corps survived, to be taken to Moscow and other Russian cities, where they proved to be willing Communists. Gorbachev labelled the massacre 'one of the gravest crimes of Stalinism'.

Was it all a big mistake on Stalin's part? Some historians believe that his orders may have been 'misinterpreted' by underlings. Stanislaw Mikolajczyk, the successor to Sikorski in London for the Polish government-in-exile, has his view and claims a Soviet bureaucrat secretly gave him the following interpretation of what happened:

A MISSINTERPERATED ORDER

'Early in 1940 the Red Army sent a staff officer to find what Stalin planned to do with the Polish officers. A planned swap in which the officers would be turned over to the Germans in return for thirty thousand Ukrainians had just fallen through. The Ukrainians were Polish Army conscripts captured by Germany the previous September, and were interned in two camps in eastern Poland. The Germans, at first agreed to the exchange but backed out at the last possible moment, telling the Soviets to take the Ukrainians and keep the Poles. Then came rumours in Moscow that the Ukrainian conscripts and the Polish officers would be organised into special units of the Red Army. Senior commanders were aware of such talk but had nothing specific to go on. The staff officer was sent to get Stalin's clarification. The staff officer saw Stalin and briefly explained the problem. Stalin listened patiently. When the staff officer finished, Stalin supplied him with a written order. Such orders were common, often requested by subordinates as a matter of self-protection. In this case. said the informant, Josef Stalin took a sheet of his personal

Above: *The soil in Katyn Wood served to preserve the bodies. This was of considerable help when investigators came to identify bodies and buried papers.*

STALIN TOOK A SHEET OF HIS PERSONAL STATIONERY AND WROTE ONLY ONE WORD ON IT: 'LIQUIDATE'.

---

stationery and wrote only one dreadful word on it: 'Liquidate'.

The staff officer returned the one-word order to his superiors, but they were uncertain what it meant. Did Stalin mean to liquidate the camps or to liquidate the men? He might have meant that the men should be released, sent to other prisons, or to work in the Gulag system. He might also have meant that the men should be shot, or otherwise eliminated. No one knew for sure what the order meant, but no one wanted to risk Stalin's ire by asking him to clarify it. To delay a decision was also risky and could invite retribution. The army took the safe way out and turned the whole matter over to the NKVD. For the NKVD, there was no ambiguity in Stalin's order. It could only mean one thing: that the Poles were to be executed immediately. That is, of course, exactly what happened.'

Many thought Stalin, the Man of Steel would never have had it any other way.

ADOLF HITLER
The Holocaust

Germany was humiliated by defeat after the Great War. Despair gripped the nation. But one man promised to return their pride. All they had to do was build gas chambers and kill, kill, kill. So began the most shocking mass murder in the history of the world.

They met at a place called Wannsee, a charming suburb of Berlin with ornate houses and tree-lined streets that looked out over the lake which gave the area its name. It was 20 January, 1942 and the Reich had reached the zenith of its military victories. The swastika flew over the Russian steppes, over the Balkans and Greece, France, the Low Countries, North Africa, Poland, Norway and Denmark. The wars of conquest had ended in total triumph for Hitler's armies so it was now time to put into effect phase two of his doctrine of Nazism. It was time to implement 'The final solution of the Jewish question in Europe'.

No one who followed the rise of Adolf Hitler and his Nazi party was surprised that he had a diabolical plan to eradicate the Jews. Hitler began his campaign of state terror against the Jews soon after he came to power. He passed the infamous Nuremberg Laws which stripped them of property, valuables, human rights and political power. Then he organized the terror, which culminated in the *Kristallnacht* – 'Night of Broken Glass' – in 1938. This involved the destruction of synagogues and Jewish property throughout Germany during a frenzied night of state-sponsored terror. But Hitler wanted 'a final solution to the Jewish problem' and this was to become a euphemism for mass murder.

That is why at Wannsee, in 1942, SS and Gestapo chiefs, led by Reinhard 'Hangman' Heydrich, gathered at a villa, once owned by a Jewish merchant, to plot the logistics for the collection, transportation and extermination of millions of men, women and children who had no place in the new world order. The men in black and grey uniforms drew up blueprints for the greatest state-sponsored murder in history.

Since the Nazi seizure of power Hitler had experimented with mass-killing techniques at euthanasia laboratories where the mentally ill were killed in gas-vans or by lethal injection. When his armies overran Poland and parts of Russia he walled his Jewish enemies up in medieval-style ghettoes where he allowed starvation and disease to kill the people locked within. In Russia his *Einsatzgruppen* – action squad – SS commandos shot hundreds upon thousands of Jews and other 'undesirables'. But

Opposite: *Adolf Hitler salutes to his followers. Rudolf Hess stands before him.*

Below: *An SA stormtrooper ensures that shoppers follow the order on the sign: 'Do not buy from Jews'.*

Right: Survivors stand in bitter mourning for their lost families at the memorial erected to the victims of the Holocaust.

it was not enough. These methods were cumbersome, slow and inefficient. Hitler was determined to bring some Henry Ford principles into the process of mass murder – a production line of death camps that would dispatch the unfortunates at the greatest speed possible.

Herman Goering, Luftwaffe chief whose first task for the Nazis was setting up the dreaded Gestapo, had Heydrich's orders in a letter, written six months before the Wannsee conference. It read: 'I hereby charge you with making all necessary preparation with regard to organizational and financial matters for bringing about a complete solution of the Jewish problem in the German sphere of influence in Europe.'

Heinrich Himmler, head of the SS; Heydrich, head of the SD, the security arm of the same organisation; Adolf Eichmann, and Ernst Kaltenbrunner, Heydrich's successor after his master was assassinated in Prague in May 1942, can be said to be the architects of the final solution. They built the concentration camp network which spanned all conquered Europe.

Names like Treblinka, Sobibor, Buchenwald, Dachau and Auschwitz – Auschwitz, particularly, the most infamous human abbatoir of them all – have now become household words for evil. In these death factories Jews from all over Europe made a one-way trip to hell. And not only Jews – Gypsies, Poles, Slavs, Russian prisoners-of-war, intellectuals, revolutionaries, homosexuals and artists who did not fit into the racial or political mould were despatched. A new breed of men and

Below: *Former inmates of the death camps show the identity numbers tattooed on their arms by the Nazis.*

Below, right: *A synagogue in ruins after the attacks against Jews during Crystal Night, 9 November, 1938.*

Hoess took a scientific delight in solving the problems of mass murder. Auschwitz, like the other camps, had used mass shootings and hangings to eradicate the inmates, but this was precisely the inefficiency that Hitler and the SS wanted to do away with. Later in 1942 a gas made from prussic acid. that was used to kill rats and mice in German factories, was deployed for the first time against Russian POWs. The Russians were led into a long, sealed room, the walls of which were lined with showers. But the shower faucets were false and the plugholes sealed. And then they heard the rattle of hard crystals dropped on to a wire grating above their heads, before the room filled with a gas, called Zyklon-B, that was released from the crystals. They were all dead within twenty minutes.

At the far south end of the Birkenau camp two massive gas chambers and adjacent crematoriums were built by the inmates themselves. Trains arriving at a railhead were greeted by one Dr Josef Mengele – about whom more will be said later – the SS doctor who became supreme arbiter of life and death within the electrified fences of Auschwitz. With a flick of his riding crop he dictated the fate of the inmates. Those who were to work for the Reich on starvation rations, under the blows of whips and cudgels, marched one way while their elderly parents, sisters brothers, and toddlers walked the other.

women, inconceivable in their cruelty, depraved beyond belief, were recruited to administer these extermination centres.

Such a man was Rudolf Hoess, commandant of Auschwitz where the final solution was to reach remarkable heights of cruel efficiency. Hoess, at his peak, oversaw a complex where men and women lived in filth, were worked like dogs and finally executed when they were no longer of any use to the Reich. Auschwitz, and its annexe camp of Birkenau, where the gas chambers and crematorium were situated, were two miles from the main town of the same name in southern Poland. Every day, in the camps, twelve thousand people died in the gas chambers before being burned in the massive crematorium.

Loudspeakers told the latter group that they were heading off for showers and de-lousing before they were to be re-united with their families in barracks. In fact, they were taken to a long wooden hut where they were told to strip and place all valu-ables in a locker. Then their heads were shaved and the hair collected in giant sacks by other prisoners. Then they were marched in to the giant shower-rooms. But these showers did not flow with water and the naked humiliated prisoners were actu-ally in giant death chambers

BODILY REMAINS

Afterwards, men working for the *Sonderkommando* or special commando squads set up by their SS overlords, entered to disentangle the corpses and remove the gold fillings from their teeth. The bodies were then pushed into the ovens, the ashes raked out and spread over nearby woodland or dumped in the River Vistula.

Cruel and inhuman as the killing machine was, death was often the one thing the living prayed for. The camp culture spawned a sadistic, warped race of guards who took morbid pleasure in the mistreat-ment of their charges. Irma Greese, the 'Blonde Angel of Hell' from Belsen, delighted in flaying women's breasts with a knotted whip. Karl Babor, the camp doctor

Below, left: *Inmates were used to clear away the bodies of their fellow prisoners and feed them into the crematoriums of the death camps.*

Below: *Hitler with his mistress, Eva Braun, relaxes in his mountain retreat at Berchtesgaden.*

of the Gross-Rosen camp, amused himself by burning new-born babies on an open fire. And at Auschwitz there was the infa-mous Dr Mengele, whose smiling face was always there to greet the new arrivals as they arived in stinking cattle wagons.

Mengele was a doctor of medicine who betrayed his Hippocratic oath each and every day, while convincing himself that his scientific research in the camp was carried out on mere 'subhumans'.

His greetings at the train ramp for the Auschwitz arrivals had a dual purpose; he

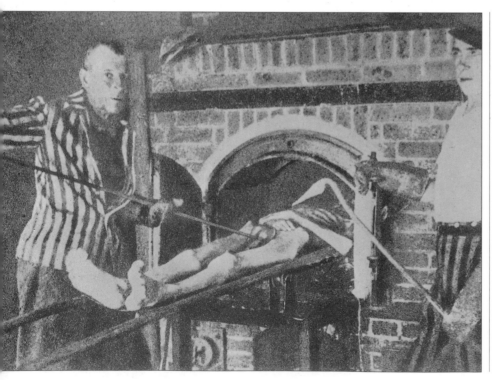

sorted out those who could work for the Reich before their deaths, and he sought blue-eyed twins so he could perform exper-iments aimed at cloning the Nordic super-men which Hitler had decreed were to be the new chosen race. And all the while he salved the shreds of his wicked conscience by claiming that *he* was saving life for the future! Yet all experts concur that on his personal orders alone some four hundred thousand Jews were executed. Prisoners, infected with lice, TB, typhus, typhoid and grotesque medieval-style infections – infections bred by the poor diet and insani-tary conditions which prevailed in the camps – existed in a twilight zone of brutality that could only be eased by death. When they were no longer able to function in the armaments plants and quarries adja-cent to the camps they were eliminated. The gold teeth from the corpses were sent to the Reichsbank in Berlin, their hair was

Left: *Those destined for the concentration camps were packed into cattle trucks for the journey.*

Below: *Grim photographs are both proof of, and constant reminders of, the barbaric slaughter of millions of innocent Europeans in the Nazi camps.*

used to stuff mattresses for troops on the Russian front and the fat from their bodies was processed into soap. Such was the efficiency that Adolf Hitler demanded and got from his loyal servants of evil.

Adolf Eichmann, like Mengele, was a classic product of the twisted logic of Nazism. He saw no evil in what he was doing, believed that he was a 'good soldier' who was only obeying orders. Day after day, as Germany was losing the war on all fronts, this son of an accountant re-routed armaments trains headed for the troops with supplies and rations, and cancelled returning hospital trains, so he could use the rolling stock to clear out the ghettoes of Eastern Europe and thus feed the furnaces at the extermination camps. But he was not flamboyant, more a grey bureaucrat and his cruelty only became public after the collapse of the Reich in May 1945.

During the height of the Holocaust one thousand trains a week were criss-crossing Europe with people destined for the camps. In the middle of 1943 fully a third of all camp inmates assigned to work details died each week. Survival became a matter of co-operating with the SS – by getting a job in a camp clinic, becoming a block captain, seizing any chance to please the SS – anything that might bring a chance of survival. The overwhelming horror of these places was belied by the cynical slogan

Himmler placed above the entrance gates of the camps – *Arbeit Macht Frei* – Work Brings Freedom. It was a bitter lie.

Not the campswere not the only disgrace. As brave German soldiers fought valiantly at places like Stalingrad and Kharkhov, the *Einsatzgruppen* squads were forever besmirching Germany's name with their mass executions. Herman Graebe, a German civilian engineer working on road-building in the Ukraine, witnessed just such

HIMMLER PLACED ABOVE THE ENTRANCE GATES OF THE CAMPS – *ARBEIT MACHT FREI* – WORK BRINGS FREEDOM.

Above: *Allied soldiers guard captured Nazi leaders during the massive war crimes trial held in Nurnberg after the defeat of Nazi Germany*

Right: *Adolf Eichmann was finally captured in the Sixties. He pleaded his cause before a weary Judge Moishe Landau (far right).*

Opposite, far right: *Herman Goering in prison, awaiting sentence, during the war crimes trial.*

'WITHOUT SCREAMING OR WEEPING THESE PEOPLE UNDRESSED, STOOD AROUND IN FAMILY GROUPS, KISSED EACH OTHER, SAID FAREWELLS, AND WAITED FOR THE SIGN FROM THE SS MAN WHO STOOD BESIDE THE PIT.

a scene. He wrote: 'Without screaming or weeping these people undressed, stood around in family groups, kissed each other, said farewells, and waited for the sign from the SS man who stood beside the pit with a whip in his hand. During the fifteen minutes I stood near, I heard no complaint

or plea for mercy. I watched a family... An old woman with snow-white hair was holding a child of about one in her arms, singing to it and tickling it. The child was cooing with delight. The parents were looking on with tears in their eyes. The father was holding the hand of a boy about

ten years old and speaking to him softly; the boy was fighting back tears. The father pointed to the sky, stroked his head and seemed to explain something to him.

'At that moment the SS man at the pit started shouting something to his comrade. The comrade counted off about twenty people and instructed them to go behind the earth mound. Among them was the family I have just mentioned. I well remember a slim girl with black hair who, as she passed me, pointed to herself and said: 'Twenty-three'. I walked around the mound and stood in front of a tremendous grave. People were closely wedged together and lying on top of each other so that only their heads were visible. Nearly all had blood running over their shoulders from their heads. Some were lifting their heads and moving their arms to show that they were still alive. The pit was nearly two-thirds full and I estimated that it contained about one thousand people. I looked at the man who did the shooting. He was an SS man who sat at the edge of the narrow end of the pit, his feet dangling into it. He had a tommy-gun on his knees and was smoking a cigarette. The people, completely naked, went down some steps which were cut in the clay wall of the pit and clambered over the heads of the people lying there, to the place to which the SS man directed them. Some caressed those who were still alive and spoke to them in low voices.'

A DIGNITY IN DEATH

Towards the end of the war the Nazis increased their frantic efforts to wipe out the estimated nine million Jews within the conquered lands. One of Eichmann's greatest coups in the desperate days of 1944, as the Russians were advancing rapidly throughout Eastern Europe, was to get the Hungarians to hand over half of their population of eight hundred thousand Jews. They were all gassed at Auschwitz – an achievement which Eichmann said gave him 'intense satisfaction'.

Most Jews and other Nazi victims went nobly and quietly to their deaths. They had a dignity which mocked the brutality of their tormentors, yet the Nazis liked to crow that the Jews had continually shown their weakness in life's struggle because they did not fight, but meekly submitted to the sword. But in reality, there was nowhere for these tortured people to go if they had escaped, no prospect of victory over well-trained and well-fed guards.

The Nazis did not have it entirely their own way. At Sachsenhausen many guards were killed in an armed breakout and, in 1944, the Jewish Underground in Auschwitz placed explosives in one of the ovens and blew it to smithereens. The most impressive display of defiance came when Hitler ordered the destruction of the Warsaw Ghetto in 1944. Here, the Jews of Poland were housed, but they refused to be taken to the trains and, with smuggled weaponry, killed SS men.

It took half-a-division of SS men with full anti-tank and armour facilities to rout the defenders in four months of bitter fighting. It cost the Jews fifty-six thousand lives and kept valuable German soldiers away from the fight on the front. Such were the twisted values of Nazism – the defenceless Jew always considered more of an enemy than guns, tanks and armed soldiers.

While they may have salved their own consciences about what took place in the death camps, with the excuse that they were 'only obeying orders', the guilty men

In the west, it was the Americans and the British who liberated the Nazi charnel houses of Belsen and Buchenwald.

Josef Kramer, the commandant of Belsen, was puzzled by the fury of the ordinary British squaddies who liberated his fiefdom; could not understand why they were so belligerent towards him. At his

'I DIDN'T FEEL ANYTHING TOWARDS THE PRISONERS. I RECEIVED ORDERS TO KILL THEM AND THAT'S WHAT I DID. SURELY YOU CANNOT EXPECT A SOLDIER IN WARTIME TO DISOBEY AN ORDER?'

Left: *His charm and determination gave Adolf Hitler a terrible power over a nation broken by their defeat in the Great War.*

Below: *A unique picture of Jews arriving from a train at the Czech concentration camp of Terezin.*

knew what awaited them. Auschwitz personnel fled the camp just twenty-four hours before Russian troops arrived to liberate the wretches left inside. The air was still heavy with the sickly-sweet stench of burned human flesh and the crematorium, the one that was still working, had corpses awaiting burning. In a warehouse barracks that the Nazis dubbed 'Canada' because of its vast size, the Russians found a mountain of human hair, gold teeth, underwear, clothing and jewellery – the last destined for the Reichsbank. Hoess had planned to demolish Auschwitz but he left it too late. But Franz Stangl, commandant of Treblinka, managed to destroy his camp. The only testimonies to its existence are the tracks of the railway line, and the deep green hue of the grass over the rich, fertile ground that, in places, is twelve feet thick with human bonemeal.

from Swiss banks the names of wealthy Jewish clients, now used the same good offices of secrecy for their own flight.

REFUGE FOR THE WICKED

South America, where military regimes had long expressed solidarity and sympathy with the Nazi cause, was a favourite destination. Eichmann headed for Argentina; Mengele for Brazil; Joseph Schwammberger, commandant of the concentration camp at Przemysl, to Argentina; Alois Brunner, designer of the mobile gas-wagons and the brains behind the deportation of forty-six thousand Greek Jews to Auschwitz, made it to Damascus where he still lives under Arab protection.

Justice for those left behind was swift; many camp guards were executed within days of liberation. The Nuremberg trials despatched many more, including Kramer and Greese. But it was left to people like Simon Wiesenthal, who lost eighty members of his family in the Holocaust, to become the conscience of the world – to ensure that mankind never forgot what revolting crimes had taken place.

Wiesenthal is an old man now, his shoulders slightly hunched and his hair grey, but his eyes have lost none of their fire. He survived the death camps and has pledged his life to tracking down Nazi war criminals and bringing them to justice. His determination and diligence led to the capture of Eichmann in Argentina and the deportation from South America of Lyons Gestapo chief Klaus Barbie.

Weisenthal's small office in central Vienna is called the Documentation Centre and it is a museum to the memory of the slain. Wiesenthal calculates that as many as fourteen million were claimed by the Nazis in their war of racial purification. From 22 March, 1933, when Dachau, twelve miles from Munich, opened as the Reich's first concentration camp, until the Allies liberated the entire network, Hitler had managed to dispose of over a third of Europe's Jews. Wiesenthal inflates his figures because of the special 'actions' undertaken in Russia, the enormity of which has still to be fully understood.

Even now Weisenthal is still hunting, still ceaselessly bringing to justice those who perpetrated mankind's biggest mass

trial after the war for his crimes at the Natzweiler, Auschwitz and Belsen camps, he told those judging him: 'I didn't feel anything towards the prisoners. I received orders to kill them and that's what I did. Surely you cannot expect a soldier in wartime to disobey an order?'

But Kramer and all the others – Babor of Gross-Rosen, Mengele of Auschwitz, Heinrich 'Gestapo' Mueller, Adolf Eichmann, Franz Stangl of Treblinka – all tried to escape. They knew that their blind obedience to orders would never stand up in a courtroom whose loyalty was not to Adolf Hitler. Using the services of the ODESSA – the Organization of Former Members of the SS – they drew on secret Swiss bank accounts to pay for new identities and lives in distant lands. Much of the money came from the victims whose butchery they had overseen in the camps. It was a final bitter twist of irony that the SS who had tried, without success, to wheedle

Above: *The power-mad, ruthless Herman Goering started the Gestapo to enforce the more ruthless aspects of Nazi rule.*

Opposite, top: *The Nazis sought to whip up anti-semitic feelings with crude caricatures meant to persaude citizens that the Jews were untrustworthy.*

Opposite, below: *Gold was extracted from the teeth of concentration camp victims. The gold was boxed and delivered to the Reichsbank.*

murder. He cannot stop, not while revision-
ist historians and neo-Nazi sympathisers,
now on the rise in Europe and Russia, are
busy denying that the Holocaust with its
death camps ever happened.

Wiesenthal would die a happy man if he
could get Alois Brunner, the committed
Nazi, who, in 1965, said to reporters from a
German newspaper: 'I'm glad! I'm proud
of what I did. If I could have fed more Yids
into the flame I would. I don't regret a
thing – we were only destroying vermin.'

Simon Wiesenthal finds some solace in
the report he will give to the Lord when it
is his time to depart. this life

'We will all be called before the Lord for
judgement,' he said, 'and we will be asked
to give an account of ourselves. One man
will say: "I became a tailor". Another will
say: "I became a doctor". Yet another will
say: "I became a jeweller".

'And I will be able to say: "I did not
forget you…".'

SADDAM HUSSEIN
Genocide of the Kurds

The proud warrior tribes refused to bend before a dictator. So he took his vicious revenge. He sprayed them with terrible chemicals, which brought painful and dreadful death to thousands of Kurdish men, women and children.

Long before the high-tech war visited on his country by the Allied forces during Operation Desert Storm, Iraqi despot Saddam Hussein had waged another, dirtier kind of war within his own borders. His enemy was the fiercely proud Kurdish tribe, the hot-blooded warrior race that, for centuries, has longed for an independent Kurdistan that would span the border between Iraqi and Turkey.

Hussein assembled one of the greatest war machines ever seen, before it was dismantled during the Gulf War. In manpower alone, he had the fifth largest army in the world, plus a formidable array of conventional and chemical weaponry. He needed to ensure that he was the master of the Middle East, but part of his arsenal was developed for a plan every bit as sinister as that hatched by the Nazis. He wanted to wipe out the Kurdish people once and for all. In 1988, before his power was stunted, if not altogether broken by the West, Saddam unleashed his appalling chemical weapons against innocent Kurds, as part of his blueprint for their destruction, killing over four thousand people. Against his arch-enemy Iran, whom he fought for eight futile years, he used mustard gas.

His chemical weapons programme was one of the most advanced in the world. America and the former USSR had long ago curbed production of chemical weapons, which are forbidden under United Nations rulings and the Geneva Convention. The world did not want to repeat the horrors of the First World War

where chemical weapons had been used. But Saddam, who does not yet have nuclear power, realised that massive stockpiles of lethal gas would give him a huge military advantage over his enemies.

The technology has not changed a great deal in the years since the Great War – the poison is still delivered by shell and bomb – but the chemical content has. Saddam developed hydrogen cyanide, a particularly lethal gas which causes death within two seconds when inhaled. He also developed new versions of the nerve gases Tabun and Sarun, pioneered by the Nazis during the Second World War, though never used by them. A very small quantity of either of these gases, will, when it falls on skin, cause a human being to go into convulsions, followed very quickly by death.

THE MEANS OF DESTRUCTION

The technology needed for his gas programme was provided by the Western nations that would one day be arrayed against him. As long as Saddam Hussein was keeping the forces of Islamic fundamentalism on the opposite bank of the Euphrates River, the West was happy to give him the means for mass destruction. Western companies salved their consciences by saying that much of the hardware necessary for the production of chemical warfare was for fertilizer factories

Opposite: *Saddam Hussein, the butcher of Baghdad. He is feared because of his ruthless quest for power in the Middle East.*

Above: *Refugees wend their way to Piranshar in Iran to escape the persecution of Saddam Hussein in Iraq.*

within Iraq, although any scientist knows that it is but a small step from producing fertilizers to poison gas. Some were merely duped. The Phillips Petroleum Company of Bartlesville, Ohio, was one of the American companies whose security system failed it. Phillips, through a Belgian unit, had sold the Iraqis five hundred tons of a complex chemical called thiodiglycol, believing it was for use as a fertilizer. Combined with hydrochloric acid, it makes mustard gas. An understanding of what had been made from their shipment to Saddam hit company executives, when in 1988, they read news reports of Iranian soldiers on a remote battlefield coughing up their lungs, and of corpses covered with horrifying chemical burns.

Germany, Holland and Britain also sold chemical weapon technology and raw materials to Iraq, enabling Saddam to build up stockpiles which sent shivers through his bitterest enemy – Israel. Israel, long before Saddam unleashed his Scud missiles on her cities during the Gulf War, feared a pre-emptive strike with chemical missiles.

When Saddam used his mustard gas on the battlefield, it was in limited quantities and aimed strategically at Iranian command posts and communications centres; rarely was it used against civilians. But in his war against the Kurds he had no such qualms.

The Kurds were, and still are, Saddam Hussein's biggest political problem. They are not impressed by his bellicose speeches, the huge pictures of him that adorn public buildings and stretch over highways; nor do they pay anything other than lip-service to his regime. The Kurds, armed and virtually autonomous in the northern, mountainous region of Iraq were to be taught a tragic, final lesson that they would never be able to forget.

In March 1988, while the war against Iran was still raging, Saddam received reports from his battlefront commanders that Iranian troops, aided by Kurdish guerillas, had seized control of the Kurdish town of Halabja. The town was based near a vital hydro-electric dam. The information that Iranian troops were involved gave Saddam reason to unleash his deadliest poisons on the innocent civilian population. Yet he must have known that there were, in fact, no Iranian troops in the town because they left within hours of taking it.

Above: *A tent city, housing thousands of refugees, has arisen on the Turkish border as people flee the repression of Iraq.*

THE DEADLY CLOUD

The sun was just rising over the mountain peaks when the first shells began to rain down on Halabja. But unlike the high explosives that the citizens had heard falling along the battlefront with Iran, there was only a soft 'plop-plopping' as the shells dropped without detonating. But soon palls of sickly yellow, white and grey gas began to swell and swirl, drifting like fog through the streets, creeping into every nook and cranny. Saddam had uncorked his evil weapons of Tabun, cyanide gas and mustard gas on the townspeople. Chaos and hysteria reigned as panic gripped the

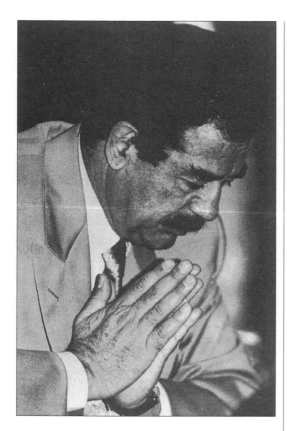

spreads, swelling the internal lining. Many of them had horrible blisters on their necks, chests and thighs, causing huge patches of skin to fall off. Large lesions broke out over their genital areas. They were young and old but they were not soldiers. The youngest I treated was a baby of four months. I could not help but ask what they had done to deserve this.'

Iraq, usually so adept at controlling press coverage within its borders, made the mistake of allowing Western newsmen and foreign relief workers into the area. The pictures of thousands of bodies without any visible wounds whatsoever belied Bagdhad's statement that they had been killed in the cross-fire of shelling between the forces of Iraq and Iran. It was several months before the Iranian leadership admitted to the use of the gas as 'a necessary measure to drive out the Iranian infidels'.

Left: *Hussein may not be a good man, but he is a devout one.*

Below: *Iranian soldiers cower in their trenches during the war against Iraq.*

townsfolk. They ran through the streets, their skin peeling from their faces when the mustard-sulphur clouds hit them. If they ran into Tabun fumes, they were dead within seconds. A shocking photograph recorded a poignant death during this morning of carnage. It shows a mother clutching her dead baby in the main street, both killed as they ran in a frantic attempt to seek cover from the deadly clouds.

By the afternoon the donkeys and goats in the fields were all dead, the vegetation wilted. The sickly smell of rotten onion mixed with burned garlic hung over the air. It was as if someone had gone in with a giant fly spray and snuffed out the life of all the citizens. Only those who had been working in remote fields survived. In all, four thousand men, women and children died on that tragic day in Halabja.

Caglayan Cugen, a Turkish doctor who treated survivors who had burns and respiratory problems, said: 'They talked of seeing these blue canisters from which the gas came. There was an odd odour first and then they remember burning in their eyes, blurring the vision as the eyes smart and itch. There followed uncontrollable bouts of sneezing and vomiting. Their breath shortens in the hours following inhalation of the mustard gas as the inflammation

Above: *Mustard gas killed this woman and her baby during a chemical warfare assault against Kurds in the town of Halabja.*

'DESPITE THE FACT THAT SADDAM HUSSEIN COMMITTED MAJOR ACTS OF GENOCIDE, THE FACT IS, IRAQ GOT AWAY WITH IT.'

A UN official who saw the carnage said: 'The bodies were lying in doorways, in streets, around tables set up for lunch and in cellars where people mistakenly sought shelter from the heavier-than-air gas. Many other corpses were found on the roads leading from the town, where residents had failed to outrun the spreading cloud. The victims seemed to have died quickly, as there were few signs of a struggle. The streets were also littered with the bloated carcasses of cows, dogs, cats, sheep and goats.

A TERRIBLE OUTRAGE

'Some thirty of the victims were flown for treatment at hospitals in the West, which confirmed that several poison gas agents were indeed deployed on the innocent civilians. Iranian doctors I spoke with, who treated those refugees who managed to cross over into their country, said their tests had shown that the gases were mustard, cyanide and nerve gas. The injured suffered from the most appalling burns and their lungs were all but destroyed.'

Western diplomats in Iraq were appalled at the outrage. 'Halabja was inexcuseable in every sense of the word,' said one indignant emissary at the time. 'The use of poison gas against enemy troops is bad enough, but to use it against civilians, and especially your own citizens, is quite unbelieveable.'

Steven Rose, a neurobiologist at Britain's Open University, said: 'Despite the fact that Saddam Hussein committed major acts of genocide, the fact is, Iraq got away with it.' There was no pressure to bring this criminal, a man who clearly and openly violated the rules of war, to justice. No less than six separate United Nations missions went to Iraq before and after the Halabja massacre, each time collecting more information on Iraqi chemical assaults. One team was despatched to the town of Halabja and reported: 'This warns us that the use of chemical weapons against the Kurdish people may become more frequent, even commonplace.'

Saddam was well satisfied with this awesome display of his maniacal power. He had cocked a snook at world opinon, defied

Above: *Western newsmen recorded the murder of Kurds in the streets of Halabja.*

Left: *A frantic and terrified people trekked great distances to reach the safety of Turkey.*

the conventions of the West – which he viewed as weak – and had dealt a stunning blow to his Kurdish enemies. He felt so good about it that he decided to do it again.

TWO BLEEDING NATIONS

In August 1988 the guns finally fell silent in his war with Iran. It had bled the two nations white, ravaged their economies, decimated their populations and cemented the politics of hate for generations to come. But the onset of peace for Saddam meant he could turn more manpower – and more chemical weaponry – against his Kurdish foes.

By the end of August Saddam had moved some sixty thousand troops into the Kurdish region, together with battalions of

'IT IS ONE THING TO BE BLOWN TO PIECES, BUT IT IS ANOTHER TO BE KILLED BY A WEAPON YOU CANNOT HEAR AND CANNOT SEE UNTIL IT IS TOO LATE.'

SEFIKA ALI IS NOW TWENTY-FOUR, BUT HER PRETTY FACE IS WRINKLED LIKE THAT OF A MUCH OLDER WOMAN. THIS IS THE RESULT OF CYANIDE GAS BURNS.

Right: *The presence of their despot cannot be forgotten by the Iraqi people. His image looms on billboards across the country.*

helicopter gunships, tanks and artillery; all effective methods of launching the gas blitz he intended. The first village to die under his onslaught was Butia.

Sefika Ali is now twenty-four, but her pretty face is wrinkled like that of a much older woman. This is the result of cyanide gas burns which happened when her village was wiped out in a gas attack launched from the air. She fled to Turkey with her husband and three children. They were the lucky ones. Left behind were an estimated two thousand neighbours, who suffered the same death as the victims of Halabja. She said: 'I was cooking breakfast for my family when I heard the sound of aircraft. I heard bombs whistling and the next thing I knew was that there was something wrong with my eyes. I started to vomit almost immediately. I knew what was happening. We had heard what had happened at Halabja. My family suffered the same effects. We all drank a lot of milk and then we ran. We ran to get as far away as we could. We know that not many made it out.'

REFUGEES FACING DEATH

In the refugee camps along the Turkish border the hordes of burned, coughing survivors of the latest outrage swelled the hospital tents as medical teams from the West struggled to cope with the aftermath of Saddam's attacks. The refugees were called *Pesh mergas* by the Iraqis – 'Those who face death' – and there were no apologies from Bagdhad for the fate of these victims. It was estimated that along with Butia, two other villages in the Danhuk region of the country were hit, but these suffered few fatalities because the populace were working in far-away fields and strong winds blowing that morning helped disperse the gas away from them.

Kurdish refugees, almost one hundred thousand of them, moved into Turkey, where they were accommodated in insanitary, overcrowded tented camps along the border. Massad Barzani, one of the Kurdish leaders, appealed to the UN to press Iraq not to use any more chemical weapons. He said: 'It is one thing to be blown to pieces, but it is another to be killed by a weapon you cannot hear and cannot see until it is too late. In the name of humanity, the governments of the west must come together to end this nightmare we are suffering. Many women and children who were gassed, but who survived the onslaught were later murdered by Iraqi troops to prevent them from spreading information about what dark deeds were done to them. It is a crime against humanity we are talking about here.'

In September the Reagan administration in America finally woke up to the atrocities, realising that Saddam Hussein was becoming more of a liability than an ally in the region. On 8 September, the State Department said it had obtained proof of the latest outrages and called them abhorrent and unjustifiable. Secretary of State George Shultz met with Iraqi's Minister of State for Foreign Affairs, Saddoun Hammadi, to tell him that the continued use of poison gas would severely affect the future of US - Iraq relations.

Hammadi insisted, despite all the evidence to the contrary, that no civilians had this time been killed by gas. Gwynne Roberts, a British television journalist, had himself collected soil samples from some of the villages he visited in Kurdistan and had them analysed by a laboratory. The laboratory report showed significant traces of mustard gas in the samples.

The anger felt by Shultz and other officials was supported by the American people and there was a popular feeling that maybe America had, after all, been backing the wrong horse in the long struggle between Iran and Iraq. Senator Claiborne Pell, a Democrat from Rhode Island, introduced a bill calling for sanctions against Iraq for what he called its 'anti-Kurdish genocide'. There was a period of an arms embargo after more UN evidence of the chemical atrocities was revealed, but sadly trade soon resumed again.

Below: *The strange dual role played by Saddam Hussein is revealed in this photograph: the militant warrior is also a pious man of God.*

ALFREDO ASTIZ
The Dirty war

The new military government promised to return Argentina to its former glory. Instead, they unleashed a gang of sadists upon the nation – men like Astiz who led a dirty war of murder and torture against his own people.

Between 1976 and 1982 Argentina waged a full-scale war within its own borders. The enemy were classified as those who acted or sympathised with anyone who had a viewpoint other than that espoused by the government. The military junta in power called their reign of terror The Process of National Reorganization. But it was a fancy euphemism for mass murder, whereby people vanished into human slaughterhouses, were tortured there and murdered. Coffee-bar socialists, mothers of radicals, babies of dissidents, long-lost cousins of intellectuals who had once read a Communist pamphlet – these were the victims of this 'Process' known to the rest of the world as the 'Dirty War'. And working within this state terror machine were individuals like Lt Alfredo Astiz.

THE CLEANSING OF SOCIETY

Astiz was a member of the officer corps which took upon itself the burden of 'cleansing' Argentinian society. The military throughout South America has had a long and shameful history of interference in civilian governments but none more so than the Argentinian army. Military rule has dominated Argentina and between 1930 and 1982, the only civilian government to last its full term was that of Juan Peron. For years, after no less than six coups, the men in uniform guided – or rather, misguided – the fortunes of this land rich in minerals, farming and cattle.

When the sophisticated and cosmopolitan citizens of Buenos Aries woke up to the clatter of tank tracks on the cobbled streets of their gracious city on 23 March, 1976 they did not panic; they had, after all, heard and seen it all before.

This time, it was a General Jorge Videla telling the people that massive unemployment, inflation running at eight hundred per cent and a resurgence of left-wing violence had driven the military to grab power. Videla, having seized the radio and

television stations, put it to his people like this: 'Since all constitutional mechanisms have been exhausted, and since the impossibility of recovery through normal processes has been irrefutably demonstrated, the armed forces must put an end to this situation which has burdened the nation. This government will be imbued with a profound national spirit, and will respond only to the most sacred interests of the nation and its inhabitants.'

There was a tone of determination in his voice which made the people of Argentina embrace rather than shrink from military government. Leftist guerillas had, since 1966, been rampant in the countryside, murdering, kidnapping, committing atrocities among the civil population. The country was on an inexorable slide into anarchy as it battled against these guerilla groups, most notably the *Ejercito*

THIS GOVERNMENT WILL BE IMBUED WITH A PROFOUND NATIONAL SPIRIT.

Above: *The Mothers of the Plaza de Mayo defied arrest, torture and even death as they paraded before the junta headquarters in frequent mass demands for the return of their children.*

Opposite: *The raffish, handsome exterior of naval officer, Alfredo Astiz, hid the ugly torturer of the death squads.*

Revolucionarioa del Pueblo – People's Revolutionary Army – and the *Montoneros*. There is a school of thought which says that, had these terrorists not created a climate of fear which brought the army out of its barracks and put the torturers in government, fifteen thousand innocent people might still be alive today. But Videla and his henchmen were welcomed by a tired population who were glad to listen to his ideas on The Process of National Reorganization.

While Videla uttered platitudes and told his own people, and the world at large, that his government would respect human rights, his machinery of terror was being secretly assembled, soon to be unleashed on an unsuspecting population.

The officer corps of the Argentinian armed forces saw themselves as an elite group, imbued with the national spirit as no other body within Argentina. Many proved very happy to oversee the terror required to reorganize their countrymen, but none

Above: *Dagmar Hagelin, a young Swedish woman, disappeared after the junta kidnapped her.*

Opposite, top: *Alfredo Astiz enters the court where he faced charges regarding the disappearance of Dagmar Hagelin.*

Opposite, below: *Ragnar Hagelin stands outside the military court after he was notified of the acquittal of Astiz who was charged with the disappearance of Hagelin's daughter.*

more so than Alfredo Astiz, who was to develop into an infamous torturer, his name forever linked with this shameful period of Argentina's sad history.

THE DEATH SQUADS

Astiz, a handsome naval lieutenant of wealthy parents, drank deeply from the poisoned chalice offered by Videla. He believed the General when he said that the enemies of Argentina were within its own frontiers. With the zeal of a Spanish Inquisition cardinal, Astiz helped enthusiastically in the founding and operation of ESMA, the Navy Mechanics School in Buenos Aries, which was nothing more than a human abbatoir hiding behind the name of an institute of marine engineering.

Thousands of victims of 'The Process' were brought as prisoners to the Navy Mechanics School where they were subjected to the most horrific beatings and torture, then taken out for execution; very few made it back to families and loved ones. It was not only the navy that organized this kind of torture centre; the army, air force and police were also involved, each one vying for glory as they hunted the 'enemy within'. They operated in squads called *patotas* and they each found places to turn into centres of hell, where they dragged the dissidents who, they believed, were destroying the Argentinian way of life and its cultural traditions.

One of the few victims to survive after Astiz and his men had captured her has a horrifying story to tell. Twenty-seven-year-old nursery school teacher Isabel Gamba de Negrotti was pregnant when she was seized at gunpoint by the *patotas* and taken away in a green Ford Falcon car – a make of car that came to be indelibly linked with death – and dumped in the Navy Mechanics School. The young woman described her ordeal: 'They took me to a room after arrival where they kicked me and punched me in the head. Then they undressed me and beat me on the legs, buttocks and shoulders with something made of rubber. This lasted a long time. I fell down several times and they made me stand by supporting myself on a table... While all this was going on they talked to me, insulted me, and asked me about people I didn't know and things I didn't understand.

The junta was going after the children, the students and the trade unionists, the journalists and the teachers – all were swept up in the vortex of terror. Victims were picked up at random and, as these citizens were bundled into the death cars, they would yell out their names and addresses to passers-by who, in turn, would inform families that their relations had joined *los desparecidos* – 'the disappeared'.

Often the military disposed of their victims by pushing bodies, dead or alive, out of helicopters as they flew over rivers. Almost five thousand people are believed to have met their deaths on these 'NN' – 'No-Name' – flights. Others were buried in mass graves on the pampas or in remote corners of country churchyards, buried without name, sacrament or ceremony.

Inside the Navy Mechanics School, Astiz and other torturers preferred even crueller forms of death and practised bizarre forms of torture and sadism against men, women and children.

Many people who came across Astiz compared him to Dr Josef Mengele, the Nazi death camp doctor at Auschwitz. Astiz who was fair-haired and blue-eyed,

'I pleaded with them to leave me alone, otherwise I would lose my baby. I hadn't the strength to speak, the pain was so bad. They started to give me electric shocks on my breasts, the side of my body and under my arms. They kept questioning me. They gave me electric shocks in the vagina and put a pillow over my mouth to stop me screaming. Someone called 'The Colonel' came and said they were going to increase the voltage until I talked, but I didn't know what they wanted me to talk about. They kept throwing water over my body and applying electric shocks all over. Two days later I miscarried.' She survived the ordeal.

Enemies real and imagined were seen everywhere by officers of the junta. Their paranoia is revealed in a telling comment from Fifth Army Corps Commander General Adel Vilas, that he made some months after 'The Process' had started: 'Up to now only the tip of the iceberg has been affected by our war against subversion... it is necessary to destroy the sources which feed, form and indoctrinate the subversive delinquent, and the source is the universities and secondary schools themselves.'

was nicknamed 'the blonde angel' and he revelled in his sadistic work. He was keen from the very beginning of 'The Process' to take on the dirty, murderous tasks that many of his naval comrades refused.

Raul Vilarano, the killer who later confessed to the horrible deeds perpetrated by himself and Astiz, said that he and his cohorts did not work to any pattern at the Navy Mechanics School; rather, they roamed at will, at any hour of the day or night, satisfying whatever grotesque lusts came upon them with any victim they happened upon. Dagmar Hagelin happened to be one of those victims.

Dagmar was arrested on 27 January, 1977. She had Swedish nationality even though she was raised in Argentina, and

Right: *These men of the Junta faced murder charges. Clockwise: Jorge Videla, Emilio Massera, Orlando Agosti, Omar Graffigna, Basilio Lami Dozo, Jorge Anaya, Leopoldo Galtieri, Roberta Viola and, centre, Armando Lambruschini.*

Opposite: *Alfredo Astiz in his role as naval officer signs his surrender to the British during the Falklands War, and in the lower picture, he goes to court as a suspected criminal to face charges of kidnap and murder.*

was a gifted eighteen-year-old classical music student with coffee-table ideas about socialism, but no affiliation with any guerilla groups or other Communist subversives. As she rang the bell at a friend's house two men – a *patota* squad from the Navy Mechanics School – appeared and Dagmar ran, only to be shot down in the street. She was dumped in the boot of a Ford Falcon and driven away. The man who had fired the shot was Astiz.

Unlike other 'no-names' who had disappeared, Dagmar did not come from the poor and powerless. Her father ran a profitable business and was on good terms with the Swedish ambassador but, though he used every influence to trace his daughter, his efforts were to no avail. Dagmar, another innocent among thousands, died in the Navy Mechanics School and her remains have never been found. The Swedish ambassador refused to accept honours from his host country when it came time for him to take up another diplomatic posting – he did not want to give credence to a regime that, he was convinced, murdered young girls.

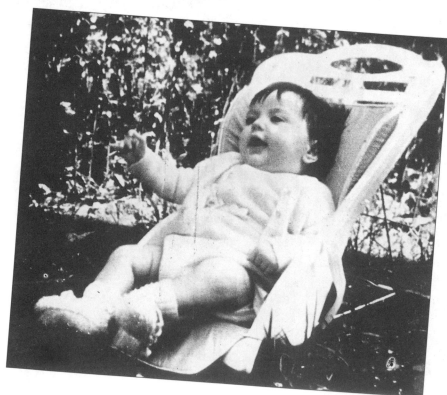

Jacobo Timerman, a Jewish newspaper editor who was deemed sympathetic to the enemies of the state, was tortured by Astiz but he survived to shame the military men with an account of his suffering in the book 'Prisoner Without a Name, Cell Without a Number'. He wrote: 'When electric shocks are applied, all that a man feels is that they're ripping his flesh apart. And he howls. Afterwards, he doesn't feel the blows. Nor does he feel them the next day, when there's no electricity, but only blows. The man spends days confined in a cell without windows, without light, either seated or lying down. The man spends a month without being allowed to wash himself, transported on the floor of an automobile to various places of interrogation, fed badly, smelling bad. The man is left enclosed in a small cell for forty-eight hours, his eyes blindfolded, his hands tied behind him, hearing no voice, seeing no sign of life, having to perform his bodily functions upon himself. And there is not much more. Objectively, nothing more.'

Astiz reached new heights of cynicism and cruelty when he posed as Gustavo Nino, a peasant boy who had lost relatives to the *patotas*. He infiltrated the ranks of the women who came to be called 'The Mothers of the Plaza de Mayo,' the head-scarved women who paraded silently in front of the junta's pink palace with the names of missing loved ones on boards hanging from their necks. These women were the true heroines of the Dirty War, defying truncheons and tear-gas to stage their weekly vigil, a vigil that played a powerful role in bringing the world's atten-

'WHEN ELECTRIC SHOCKS ARE APPLIED, ALL THAT A MAN FEELS IS THAT THEY'RE RIPPING HIS FLESH APART. AND HE HOWLS.'

THESE WOMEN WERE THE TRUE HEROINES OF THE DIRTY WAR, DEFYING TRUNCHEONE AND TEAR GAS TO STAGE THEIR WEEKLY VIGIL IN DEFIANCE OF THE JUNTA

THE MAN SPENDS DAYS CONFINED IN A CELL WITHOUT WINDOWS, WITHOUT LIGHT.

Opposite, top: *A woman weeps at a 'No-Name' cemetery where thousands of Argentinians were dumped in unmarked graves after their murder by the junta.*

Opposite, below: *The baby Clara Anahi Mariani disappeared after her parents were murdered. This baby was either abducted or killed by the junta.*

Left: *The Mothers grew bolder and bolder. They knew they had to attract world attention to their plight if they were to defeat the regime.*

who were waiting with the whips and the electric cattle prods and the flames.

For a time Astiz also worked out of his government's naval bureau in Paris, where he spied on exiled Argentinian human rights groups. After he was rumbled in Paris he headed for South Africa on a naval posting, but was hounded out of the country in 1981 when journalists learned of his unsavoury work at the Mechanics School. His superiors decided to pack him off to the war against Britain in the Falkland Islands in 1982.

THE TORTURER IS FREED

Astiz was captured by Royal Marines and when his name appeared in British newspapers, alarm bells began to ring in the capitals of the world. There were calls for his blood from Stockholm to Paris to the capital of his homeland, where thousands had a righteous claim on his murdering hide. But, under the terms of the Geneva Convention, Astiz was a prisoner-of-war and could not be handed over to foreign powers who suspected him of domestic crimes. He returned home after the war.

In Argentina, the following year, Raul Alfonsin was sworn in as the democratic president, the forty-first in the nation's history. His mandate was not only to steer the country towards democratic reforms, but also to exorcise the evil perpetrated upon his people by the junta. Some of the guilty men were brought to trial – including the suave torturer, Astiz. But he was never punished, never served time in a prison. At his pre-trial hearing his lawyers refused to admit that he had abducted and killed Dagmar – but in a supreme Orwellian twist said that if he had, it did not matter, because he was operating in a 'war time' situation. The military really did believe they were at war with their own people. He is now free in Argentina, a forty-two-year-old man with a wicked past but not a troubled conscience.

A commission was established after the war by the Alfonsin government to probe the terror. It found that the 'final purpose' of the terror was to exterminate the detainees and disfigure the bodies, so they could never be identified. The commission found no common factor to link the victims – they came from every level of

tion to the mass killings taking place in what the West had long regarded as the most 'civilised' of the South American nations. However, when the women's ranks were depleted by arrests, when their homes were raided or set on fire, when more members of their family disappeared, Gustavo Nino was always there to comfort them, never letting on that he had been the one who fed the damning information about their families back to his colleagues,

Above: After the junta fell, Argentinians began to dig up the unmarked graves.

Opposite, top: The military roll their weapons through Buenos Aires.

Opposite, below: Soldiers were seen as heroes before the ignoble Dirty War.

Argentinian society. Almost nine thousand of 'the disappeared' have never been found, despite the fact that more than sixty per cent of those seized were abducted in front of witnesses in public places. Three hundred and forty torture centres were unearthed – centres which, according to the junta, never existed. The commission produced a report fifty thousand pages long but the government failed to bring any of these state murderers to account.

Democracy now rules in Argentina, the dark days of 'The Process' are over. But the men in the olive green uniforms with the dark glasses are still there, lurking, waiting their next chance. Hebe Bonafini hopes they stay hidden. She was one of the founding members of the Mothers of the Plaza de Mayo and lost two sons and a daughter-in-law in the terror. She said: 'The military went to war against people who spoke their own tongue. They never got the right ones anyway, just children, really, no one who was ever a threat. What happened to us must serve as a warning to all people all the time. It can happen anywhere you know, making people disappear. That is the tragedy of it. It can happen to anyone...'.

MAJOR PEIPER
Slaughter in the Snow

Adolf Hitler sneered at the traditions of war and even the most gallant German soldier was corrupted by him, but the heartless massacre of unarmed prisoners-of-war, left to die in the snow, will forever stain the honour of the German army.

By December, 1944, Adolf Hitler had lost his war in Europe but he refused to believe the truth. As the Russians advanced on Germany from the east, determined to vanquish the Germans and punish them for the cruel campaigns of the SS and Gestapo against their people, the Führer concocted one last-gasp scheme aimed at staving off defeat. He underestimated the Russians, and concentrated on the Western Front for he was convinced he could alter the course of the War by smashing the American and British advance. Operating from his 'Wolf's Lair' redoubt in Rastenburg, East Prussia, he was certain that by depriving the advancing armies in Belgium and France of their biggest and most vital supply port – Antwerp – he could slow down the advance, split the armies, starve them into submission, sue for peace and then turn every remaining piece of armour, every aircraft, artillery piece and his men against the Reds.

Any general in the German High Command, who was not a lickspittle or a flunky tried to dissuade Hitler from his scheme. At a time when reserves of men and material should have been preciously conserved, he wanted to waste them on a final, futile mission that everyone else knew would end in failure.

It not only ended in failure, it ended in dishonour as well. A renegade unit of SS troopers forever stained their gallant battle honours with the brutal, cold-blooded slaying of one hundred American troops. They were butchered in the snow, cut down by heavy machine-gun fire under a battle-group commanded by SS Major Joachim Peiper, and their bodies left to be covered by fresh snowfalls. For the Americans, who had seen SS brutality when they had liberated French towns and Nazi labour camps, the massacre made them fight even harder, made them more determined than ever to finish the War and settle the final score with Hitler once and for all. This massacre of one hundred soldiers, in the snow around the Belgian town of Malmedy, was a spur to the American troops in a way that no general's speech or extra training could ever have given them. The Battle of the Bulge in general – and the massacre at Malmedy in particular – served to hasten Fuhrer Adolf Hitler's demise.

THE REICH'S REMAINING HOPE

The German offensive was launched amid great secrecy on 16 December, 1944, in the mountainous, foggy region of the Ardennes Forest in Belgium. General Gerd von Runstedt, acting on Hitler's orders, had gathered together as many serviceable tanks, as much fuel, ammunition and heavy weaponry as he could, and forged them into a force on which every remaining hope of the dying Reich was pinned. There was no lacking the will to win – the Germans remained highly disciplined and supremely ordered – until the very end. But they were exhausted; morale was low.

THERE WAS NO LACKING THE WILL TO WIN – THE GERMANS REMAINED HIGHLY DISCIPLINED AND SUPREMELY ORDERED – UNTIL THE VERY END.

Opposite: *Young American soldiers, including medics, were mown down in the snow. They were unarmed prisoners-of-war.*

Below: *Adolf Hitler ignored his army officers and launched a futile attack against the Allies in 1944.*

IT WAS A GREAT BULGE IN THE ALLIED SECTOR – AND THE FIGHT TO REGAIN IT BECAME KNOWN AS THE BATTLE OF THE BULGE.

Hitler hoped to capitalize on the bad weather that shrouded this region in winter. He knew that the Allied air forces, which now roamed freely over Europe, would be grounded. Counting heavily on speed and surprise, he expected his armoured SS units – SS because he no longer had complete faith in the army, riddled with so many officers involved in the July 1944 plot that almost claimed his life – to be in Antwerp

two thousand three hundred tanks, fifty self-propelled assault guns, and, miraculously, half of the three thousand combat aircraft promised by the chief of the Luftwaffe, Hermann Goering.

When the blow fell on the Allied lines it was shattering. Quite simply, complacent intelligence services of both the American and British armies had totally underestimated the reserves and willpower of the

Above: *This Ardennes landscape shows the harsh weather conditions in Europe when the Allies determined to crush the Germans.*

in a week. He put four armoured divisions of the SS Sixth Army under the command of his old pal Josef Dietrich at the spearhead of this important operation codenamed Autumn Mists.

Another specialist task, fiendishly concocted by Hitler who was forever pushing back the frontiers of conduct in war, was given to his master commando, Otto Skorzeny. Skorzeny, who had rescued Hitler's ally Mussolini in a daring glider operation on a mountaintop the previous year, was instructed to equip three thousand troops with American uniforms and put them behind American lines, thus causing confusion and chaos.

By the time the operation was launched von Rundstedt had scraped together a remarkable force from a nation that had lost nearly four million men since the start of the War. There were thirty divisions, t

enemy facing them. The bad weather had, in fact, grounded Allied air operations, and would continue to do so for the next eight days. The sound of the German preparations for the commencement of the attack was drowned out by the relentless roar of V-1 rockets fired on Antwerp and the city of Liege. At 5.30am two thousand German heavy guns opened up with a storm of fire and steel on the Allied lines.

SS troops penetrated six miles of the line within hours at five different points. It was a great Bulge in the Allied sector – and the fight to regain it became known as the Battle of the Bulge. Hitler chose his élite Black Guard to spearhead the operation to spite the army officer corps. Of all the SS units thrown into the cauldron, none was braver or more decorated than the division which bore the Führer's name – the 1st SS Panzer Division *Liebstandarte* – 'Life

Guard' – Adolf Hitler. And commanding one battle group was the man whose name would always be linked to the infamous incident known as the Malmedy Massacre – Colonel Joachim Peiper.

Peiper was the epitome of gallant German manhood that Hitler adored. At twenty-nine, he was handsome, smart, fluent in three languages, supremely courageous and, unlike many fervent officers,

had never joined the Nazi party. He was also possessed of a sparkling sense of humour, another trait uncommon among his officer comrades. By the time his Panzers shattered the American front line in the Ardennes, Peiper was known personally to his Führer. He had served with incredible bravery in the campaigns in Russia and had developed a reputation as a commando who knew when to obey orders and when to break them.

Among his men he was revered as a 'soldier's soldier' who did not go medal-hunting for the sake of it, although his exploits served to reward him with the Knight's Cross, Germany's highest battlefield honour. And he never left a wounded comrade in the field to be captured by the enemy if he could avoid it. Under Dietrich's command he was heading for Antwerp... but he doubted if he would ever reach it.

Peiper rationalized that if he managed at least to reach the heights over the Meuse River he would have done his duty.

Like all SS formations at this stage of the war, with Germany having suffered over three million dead at the front, the once-strict Adolf Hitler division which once had not allowed foreigners to serve, had been forced to water-down its entry qualifications. *Volkdeutsche*, or ethnic Germans in conquered lands, were absorbed to fill the gaps in the ranks, along with other more racially-dubious candidates that would not have been given a second glance during the heady days of victory. Belgians, Rumanians, Dutchmen, Lithuanians – the turncoat youth of Europe were now being led by Joachim Peiper in this last-chance crusade against the allies.

ADVANCE ON ANTWERP

Peiper commanded five thousand men with a formidable array of Tiger, Royal Tiger and Panther tanks, backed up with anti-aircraft units, self-propelled guns and heavy artillery. His job was to punch a hole in the line and race onwards to seize the Meuse bridgeheads – vital strategically if the mass of German armour was to cross the river to advance on Antwerp.

The initial hours went better than expected, the American line shattered, their mighty air armadas grounded. Panic swept

> PEIPER WAS REVERED AS A 'SOLDIER'S SOLDIER', WHO DID NOT GO MEDAL HUNTING ... AND NEVER LEFT A WOUNDED COMRADE TO BE CAPTURED BY THE ENEMY.

Below: *Joachim Peiper was a brave soldier who had proved himself on the eastern front. Here, he leans over a jeep near Malmedy, the place where he lost his military honour.*

Above: *Passing through woods infested with enemy snipers, weary troops dragged their equipment on sledges.*

Right: *The snow rendered motor vehicles useless. Mules, the traditional heavy transport of war, were brought into the War in 1944.*

weather broke, at any time, his armour would be smashed on the ground by tank-busting fighters. Supply trains got lost or were held up at choked railway junctions and a fourth problem was the countryside; thick woods, and narrow medieval streets in the villages which were not easily navigated by seventy-ton metal monsters. Soon the advance momentum was lost.

HOPELESS TANGLE OF CONFUSION

In the fog of war – aided in part by the confusion created by Skorzeny's American-dressed commando squads – US units found themselves in a hopeless tangle of confusion and disorder the day following the initial assault. One such unit was the 285th Field Artillery Observation Battalion, a relatively inexperienced cadre of men composed mostly of teenagers who knew the business end of a rifle from its stock, but little else. Heading towards the Belgian town of Ligneuville, at a place called the Baugnez crossroads, the unit was trying desperately to link up with the US 7th Armoured Division which it believed had headed in the direction of Viesalm. But the 285th battalion was lost.

The company halted opposite the Bodarwe Café, where an officer enquired of the surly inhabitants if they were headed

the front as the battle-hardened *Liebstandarte* troops proved more than a match for the boys from Nebraska, Omaha and New York. But soon logisitical problems – problems that Peiper knew would make or break the operation – began to pile up. For one thing, he had been told to seize the bridgeheads although the high command knew full well he did not have enough fuel for such a venture. And, if the

in the right direction because many road signs had been switched or simply torn down by Skorzeny's men. But these folk were not the welcoming oppressed villagers that had greeted the Allied advance throughout western Europe. Many of these 'border people' were fiercely pro-German, a traditional alliance that had been forged throughout centuries of shifting frontiers but unchanging causes and aims. The American was met with a mute shrug of the shoulders from the people inside.

As he went out to get his column moving again, the tanks of Kampfgruppe Peiper appeared like black beetles on the horizon. One of the beetles, a half-tracked armoured vehicle barked and a split second later the lead Jeep in the American column vanished in a flash of orange flame and black smoke. Then all the guns of the panzers opened up, one by one, as they crested the ridge and began their clanking crawl towards the scene of chaos and murder before them. The surprised and frightened American soldiers dived for cover in ditches, in a nearby barn, behind haystacks and even in a garden hedge. As soon as the German tanks were upon the shattered column, the cobbled road rang with the metallic clatter of dropped weapons as the Americans raised their hands in surrender and turned themselves over to their S.S. captors.

The Germans rounded the captured men up, frisked them for concealed weapons and pushed the prisoners into a field next to the crossroads. Peiper arrived on the scene, a Schmeisser machine pistol slung over his right shoulder. He ordered several of his men to stand guard on the captured 'Amis' then moved his other men off.

MENACE HUNG HEAVY IN THE AIR

Several of the prisoners began to have doubts for their safety. The guards seemed surly, angry, almost eager for an excuse, perhaps an escape attempt that allowed them to shoot. In the town of Bullingen, which the Germans had just left, they had captured one hundred American prisoners-of-war. Three had broken out, killing an S.S. guard by slitting his throat from ear to ear. Little wonder that a sinister menace hung heavy in that misty, damp air on the afternoon of 17 December, 1944.

'MACHEN ALLE KAPUT,' A VOICE WAS HEARD TO YELL ABOVE THE RACKET OF THE GUNS. 'KILL THEM ALL!'

The Americans sat and smoked in the snow-covered fields, watching glumly as prodigious amounts of enemy armour snaked and struggled to manouvre the tight crossroads along the road to Ligneuville, the route they had intended to take before they were ambushed. Young 2nd Liutenant Virgil Larry felt his throat going dry, as he gazed into the hard-eyes of the young stormtroopers, intoxicated with the flush of their small victory, as they sat atop their mighty panzers. He began to wonder what was going to happen to him and his company. At one point a massive self-propelled 88mm gun stopped in its tracks

Above: *The field of slaughter in Malmedy. Those investigating dishonourable behaviour in the German unit marked the bodies of the murdered Americans with numbers.*

and traversed its menacing barrel directly at the American prisoners sitting quietly in the snow. But an angry German sergeant ordered it to move on with a curse.

Then Peiper himself showed up again, riding on top of a King Tiger tank. With a smile and a wave he yelled out in perfect English: 'See you in Tipperary boys!' and was gone as the Tiger accelerated with a puff of blue diesel smoke belching from its twin rear exhausts. Finally, two armoured vehicles swung around the tight bend at the crossroads and stopped. Rumanian-born Georg Fleps, private first class, a member of the elite German division that would

Below: *Facing the Allies were German veterans of the Russian Front (top picture) The Americans (lower picture) were not daunted. They knew they were on the road to victory.*

have sneered at him in 1940, unbuttoned his holster, withdrew a Luger pistol and jumped to the ground. Walking like a gunslinger, he moved close to the massed ranks of the defenceless prisoners, raised his weapon and fired. An American dropped. He fired again and another dropped. Then the air was rent with the noise of automatic weapons as the heavy machine guns on the armoured vehicles barked in unison and the Americans were

mown down like corn under the relentless onslaught of a combine harvester. '*Machen alle kaput*,' a voice was heard to yell above the racket of the guns. 'Kill them all!'

Virgil Lary saw his driver drop dead, heard the shouts of an officer telling the men to 'stand fast' before he too was shot through the throat and killed. Homer Ford, a military policeman who survived the shooting, later said: 'Men were lying around moaning and crying. I dived under a body and feigned death. The shooting kept going on and on and I felt the blood of one of my buddies running over me.

'Soon the shooting stopped and I heard the Germans coming over. They would say: "Is he breathing?" and would either shoot or hit them with the butt of their guns. The closest they came to me was about ten feet. After they fired at us, I lay stretched out with my hands out and I could feel my blood oozing. I had been hit. I was lying in the snow, and I got wet and started to

shiver, and I was afraid they would see me shivering, but they didn't. I had my head down and they couldn't see, but they were walking around the whole bunch and then they went over toward the road junction. I heard them shoot their pistols right next to me. I could hear them pull the trigger back and then the click. The men were moaning and taking on something terrible. I also heard the rifle butts hit guys' heads and then a terrible squishing sound.'

Samuel Dobyns, a medical orderly who had been recommended for a gallantry award, was one of the unit's few veterans who had been in Europe since D-Day in June. He was lying under the bodies, feigning death like Ford, when he heard the shooting stop and the single pistol shots which indicated that his comrades were being despatched with bullets in the head.

'I didn't want to die like a rabbit,' he said. 'I saw some woods off to the left and suddenly decided to make a run for it. I hadn't got more than twenty yards when I heard a heavy machine gun open up. I felt the slugs rip into me. I took four bullets, I later learned, and my clothes had been shredded by a further eight slugs. I heard Germans coming towards me, their boots crunching in the snow, and I knew they were going to finish me off. But they must have figured I was already dead. They turned around. I saw three or four Germans shoot wounded men who were crying for help. I thought I was the only one left alive.'

SHALL WE MAKE A RUN FOR IT?

Virgil Lary also survived and testified after the war at the trial of the killers: 'After the first machine guns fired, men fell dead and wounded all around me. The firing lasted for about three minutes, maybe a little longer. A man came by me as I lay feigning death and I heard a pistol shot nearby. Then I heard the sound of a new clip being inserted in a pistol and the individual passed me. I heard someone say to someone else: "Have they killed you yet?" He replied: "No not yet... but if the bastards are going to kill me I wish they would come back and get it over with." A bullet had severed my toes and I was in extreme pain and frozen from head to foot. Here and there I heard more raised voices: "Have they gone?" "What shall we do?"

"Is it safe?" "Shall we make a run for it?" Suddenly about fifteen of us decided to make a break for it. We had moved a few yards when rifles cracked, then a machine gun. I managed to clamber over a fence into a wood and ran along a dirt road until I came to a tumbledown shed. There were bundles of sticks inside and I pulled these all over myself. I waited.'

DRUNK WITH BLOOD

A few wounded men managed to crawl across the road to houses of local farmers as the '*Blustrausch*' – 'intoxication of the blood' – continued. But they were mown down before they entered, their bodies mangled by the tracks of the tanks and armoured vehicles of Peiper's rearguard that were now racing to catch up with the forward columns on the road to Ligneuville. Other Americans made it into the Bodarwe Café, but were flushed out by Germans who set it ablaze with flame-throwers. As they ran into the streets with their hands raised high they were mown down by the maddened German soldiers.

Soon silence settled on the field and the SS were gone. All that could be heard as dusk fell were the moans of the wounded and the dying, like the lowing of cattle. It was the most hideous crime ever visited upon American troops in the European theatre of war – one hundred men dead, forty-one alive, many seriously wounded. Soon the Germans in the front line would face the angry retribution of the US forces when they tried to surrender and found their enemy distinctly without mercy.

Word of the massacre sread faster than the bubonic plague through a medieval city. American units in their foxholes that night or billeted in girls' schools and town halls felt a bitterness welling inside them, a determination that turned them from raw troops into that most lethal of battlefield opponents – vengeful soldiers fighting for a cause; in this case, revenge for their murdered comrades. Hal Boyle and Jack Belden of 'Time Magazine' were allowed by the army brass into the crossroads, near the town of Malmedy, to photograph and record what the Germans had done that afternoon. One of the first people they interviewed was Lt Lary who had hobbled painfully from his hiding place. He shook his dismembered toes from his boot, along with the bullet that had severed them, and sobbed: 'We didn't stand a goddamned chance... We just didn't have a chance.' When the story reached the front page of the 'Stars and Stripes', the troops' newspaper, the 328th Infantry Regiment, in the thick of the fighting, received a written order: 'No SS troops or paratroopers will be taken prisoner, but will be shot on sight.'

Peiper's advance, and that of the rest of

Below: *A captured SS trooper was shown more mercy than was given to GIs caught at Malmedy.*

the German attacking force, ground to a halt before the Meuse eight days later. The weather cleared, the Allied air forces pounded the tanks and guns of the Germans into scrap metal and the final attempt by Hitler to hold Europe ended in defeated. Peiper retreated with his men... determined that no comrades should fall into enemy hands for as long as he led and controlled his men.

In the days after the massacre, but before the German surrender, the Judge Advocate's branch of the US army formed a special staff to collect evidence against the murderers at Malmedy. Peiper was captured defending Vienna at the end of the War, when he was an assistant divisional commander. He would pay the price for the crimes of his men at Malmedy, regardless of who had given the orders to open fire. With eight hundred survivors of his unit he was interrogated. Eventually he, the commanding SS General of the operation, Sepp Dietrich and seventy-three others, including

"HAVE THEY GONE?" "WHAT SHALL WE DO?" "IS IT SAFE?" "SHALL WE MAKE A RUN FOR IT?"

the Romanian gunslinger who had fired the first shots into the unarmed American soldiers, stood trial.

The trial took place in Dachau, a fitting setting for retribution, for it was the site of the first concentration camp founded by the Nazis. The trial opened on 16 May, 1946, with chief prosecutor Lt Colonel Burton Ellis saying: 'The troops of the *Liebstabdarte* Adolf Hitler were told to excel in the killing of prisoners-of-war as in fighting. Others were told to make plenty of *rabbatz*, which in SS parlance means to have plenty of fun killing everything that comes in sight. Each defendant was a cog in a giant slaughter machine.'

Several of the prosecution witnesses were German soldiers themselves, sickened by what had taken place at the crossroads near Malmedy. Four enlisted men testified that Peiper had told them to 'give no quarter' in the battle and 'take no prisoners.' Corporal Ernst Kohler told the tribunal: 'We were told to remember the women and children of Germany killed in Allied air attacks and to take no prisoners, nor to show mercy to Belgian civilians.' Lt Heinz Tomhardt said: 'I told my men not to take prisoners.' So the Americans were killed.

There was gripping evidence at the trial from the survivors, men like Lary and Dobyns, who confronted Georg Fleps, the

Above: *The relief of Bastogne, the 'Bastion of the Battered Bastards', spelt the end of the German offensive – and the beginning of the Allied hunt for those responsible for the murders of GIs at Malmedy.*

JUSTICE HAD NOT SERVED THE DEAD OF MALMEDY WELL.

---

man who had first opened fire, and they said: 'This is the man who opened fire into unarmed prisoners-of-war.' As evidence piled on evidence it became clear that Peiper and his men were guilty. Peiper said that he had given no orders for the massacre. Dietrich said that he too had not passed down orders for prisoners to be murdered. But on 16 July, 1946, the dreadful words *'Tod durch erhangen'* – death by hanging – fell upon the ears of the once-gallant soldier, Joachim Peiper. Dietrich was also given the death sentence as were forty-two other German soldiers.

In the end, none was executed. An Atlanta lawyer, William Meade Everett, who had been appointed defence counsel for the Germans at their trial, uncovered evidence that several German confessions of guilt had been extracted by the Americans using the methods that they had gone to war to abolish – namely torture and beatings. Burning matches were inserted under the fingernails of imprisoned SS troopers; several jaws were broken and men burned with cigarettes. It was shameful conduct, worthy of the Gestapo that they had defeated, not officers and men of the US army. Such charges sorely diminished the integrity of the tribunal and Everett, a lawyer with a keen sense of right and wrong, plunged thousands of dollars of his own money into having the cases re-opened.

On 29 July, 1948, a Senate Army Services Commission in Washington was empanelled to review the cases. By 1951 all the death sentences had been commuted and in 1958 Dietrich and Peiper were the last to be released. Justice had not served the dead of Malmedy well.

Joachim Peiper became the butt of many dishonourable accusations, but it seems clear that he was not tainted with any other acts of atrocity during the course of the War. He refused to talk about the old days, and explained his feelings: 'I am sitting on a powder keg. One day someone will come along with another accusation and the powder keg will explode. I'm a fatalist. The world has branded me and my men the scum of the earth. And no one will be able to clear up the Malmedy mess now. Too many lies have been told about it.'

And certainly, the truth died along with those brave men in the pasture next to the Baugnez Crossroads all those years ago.

ASSASSINATION

ASSASSINATION

MURDER AS A POLITICAL
EXPEDIENT PROBABLY
PRE-DATES RECORDED
HISTORY.

Below: *The first celebrity assassination was that of Julius Caesar. He was stabbed to death in 44BC by political opponents who resented the fact that he had declared himself dictator for life.*

What is an assassination? What differentiates it from a random act of murder or a summary execution? Or a killing of domestic passion?

The word assassin derives from the Arabic *hashashin*, literally 'hashish-eaters'. It was used to describe an eleventh-century sect of Shi'ite Muslims, followers of Hasan Ibn al-Sabah, the 'Old Man of the Mountain'. The *hashashin* were centred in Persia at the Castle of Alamut, known as the Eagle's Perch and at one stage, these men, fierce warriors all, held considerable sway throughout the Middle East. They acquired and consolidated their power by the systematic elimination of any opposition.

In the twelfth and thirteenth centuries, the Crusaders crossed swords with the *hashashin*. The French corrupted the word to *assassin* and brought it home with them. It was subsequently adopted throughout northern Europe to describe, in the words of Chambers English Dictionary, 'One who murders by surprise or secret assault, usually for political reasons'.

Assassination, of course, existed long before the eleventh-century and the *hashashin* sect. Murder as a political expedient is mentioned in the Old Testament and probably pre-dates recorded history. The first celebrity assassination was Julius Caesar who was stabbed to death by political opponents in the Senate in 44 BC. His death set a

precedent and the rest of Roman history is littered with political assassinations. The next major figure to be murdered was the mad and corrupt Gaius Caesar, better known as Caligula, who was butchered by members of his own Praetorian Guard in AD 41. Caligula's successor, Claudius, was poisoned by his wife, Agrippina, in AD 54.

AN EMPIRE RULED BY MURDER

After the death of Claudius, assassination unfortunately became the rule rather than the exception in imperial Rome. Many major political figures and twenty subsequent emperors were murdered in the four hundred years that followed.

Many of the emperors of the eastern Roman empire in Constantinople were also victims of assassination. Valens was killed by the Goths in AD 378. He was followed by Flavius Tiberius Mauricius in 602;

Above: *The 'turbulent priest', Thomas à Becket was murdered by the king's soliders at Canterbury Cathedral in 1170.*

Left: *The assassination of Archduke Franz Ferdinand in Sarajevo in 1914 sparked off the beginning of the First World War.*

L'ATTENTAT CONTRE LE ROI DE BULGARIE

Duncan I was killed by MacBeth in 1040 and he in turn was killed by Malcolm III in 1057; and in Denmark, Canute IV was lynched by a mob in 1086.

A KING KILLED WITH A RED-HOT POKER

In England, William Rufus was assassinated while on a hunting trip in 1100. Seventy years later, on Christmas Day 1170, the Archbishop of Canterbury, Thomas à Becket, was butchered in his cathedral by soldiers of the court of King Henry II. In 1327, the deposed King Edward II was the victim of one of history's most barbaric assassinations. He was killed by soldiers who inserted a red-hot poker into his rectum in order to avoid leaving marks on his royal personage. Assassins were less subtle when they dispatched King Richard II in prison in 1399. The fourteen-year-old King Edward V was smothered, along with his younger brother, by order of Richard III in 1483.

There is sometimes a fine line between what constitutes assassination and execution but many would argue that Joan of Arc, heroine of France, was in fact assassinated when when she was burned at the stake in 1431. Four hundred years later, Denis Affre, Archbishop of Paris, was definitely assassinated during a revolt in 1848 and

Above: *King Boris of Bulgaria was one of several European monarchs singled out by would-be assassins. He was one of the lucky ones who escaped death.*

Right:The inept Romanoff rule bred discontent in Russia. Grand-Duke Serge, uncle to the Tzar, was assassinated by bomb-throwing revolutionaries in Moscow, 1905.

Constantine III in 641, Constans II in 668, Justinian II in 711, Anastasius II in 721, Constantine VI who was murdered by order of his own mother in 797; Romanus IV in 1072; Alexius II in 1183; Alexius IV who was murdered by his successor Alexius V, who in turn was thrown to his death from a column in Constantinople by zealous Crusaders in 1204.

Several early Popes were victims of assassination. Pope John VIII was stabbed to death in 882; Steven VI was strangled in 897, as was Benedict VI in 974.

Political murder was not, however, peculiar to the Mediterranean countries. In Norway, King Haakon the Great was murdered in a pigsty by his own soldiers in 995 and two of his successors, Eystein II and Haakon II, were assassinated in 1157 and 1162 respectively. In clannish Scotland, King

ATTENTAT RÉVOLUTIONNAIRE A MOSCOU

Above:_The Kennedys in 1937. Patriarch Joseph is flanked by his sons John (left) who became president only to be assassinated in 1963 and Joseph who died on a bombing mission during the Second World War._

Left: _The White House decked out in mourning for the murdered President Garfield in 1881._

his successor, Archbishop Marie-Domique-Auguste Sibour, was stabbed to death by a mad priest in 1857.

The list of victims of assassination seems endless and political killing appears to be a global phenomenon which is as real today as it was two thousand years ago. In the follow-ing pages we tell the story of some thirty victims whose deaths have altered the course of world history. Most of these are household names yet they are but the tip of the iceberg – assassination has claimed hundreds more who, for the most part, are forgotten and frequently unlamented.

POLITICAL KILLING IS AS REAL TODAY AS IT WAS TWO THOUSAND YEARS AGO.

ABRAHAM LINCOLN

The assassination of Abraham Lincoln was as dramatic as befitted the theatre in which it took place. The murderer, in false beard and make-up, escaped on a black horse but was hunted down and hanged.

Below: *Abraham Lincolm was born in 1809 in Kentucky. He led the Union to victory in the Civil War and emancipated America's slaves in 1863. Although dedicated to reconciling north and south, he had many enemies and was finally assassinated in 1865.*

As Abraham Lincoln sat at his desk in the White House on the morning of Good Friday, 14 April, 1865, he had already been the object of eighty-two assassination plots and attempts on his life. His narrowest escape had come three years earlier, when an assassin's bullet had passed through his stove-pipe hat.

Lincoln seemed resigned to the fact that eventually one of these attempts would be successful. The 'Washington Chronicle" quoted him as saying: 'The only certain way to eliminate all risk to the person of the President, is to imprison him in an iron box where he cannot be made a target for assassins and he cannot perform his duties for the Union.'

Lincoln finished his paperwork at 11am and went into a cabinet meeting which was attended by General Ulysses S. Grant, hero of the Union army. When the meeting was over, Lincoln asked Grant whether he and his wife would care to accompany himself and Mrs Lincoln on a visit to Ford's Theatre to see Laura Keene in Tom Taylor's comedy 'Our American Cousin'. Grant declined, saying that he was due back in New Jersey that evening for a reunion with his sons. Grant had no way of knowing that this family commitment would save his life.

AN IDEAL OPPORTUNITY FOR MURDER

Lincoln's planned visit to Ford's Theatre was a matter of public record and one of those who noted the engagement with particular interest was John Wilkes Booth. Booth, a wealthy, well-respected actor, was a Southerner and no lover of Lincoln and his policies. For some months, Booth and a group of like-minded extremists had been plotting the downfall of Lincoln and his administration. Booth had considered a number of ways by which to achieve this goal, including an elaborate plot to kidnap the President and hold him hostage against the release of Confederate prisoners. Finally, however, he had decided that it would be more effective and dramatic to kill the President along with his Vice

President, Andrew Johnston, and the Secretary of State, William H. Seward.

Lincoln's forthcoming visit to the theatre seemed to provide Booth with the ideal opportunity to implement his plans. On the afternoon of 14 April, he met with his co-conspirators – George A. Atzerodt, Sam Arnold, David Herold and Lewis Paine – at a boarding house owned by Mary Surratt on Washington's 'H' Street.

THREE-WAY MURDER PLOT

The group drank heavily as they discussed their respective roles in the three-way murder plot. Arnold eventually walked out, refusing to have anything to do with murder. In the end, it was agreed that Paine should kill William H. Seward, with Herold's assistance; Atzerodt was assigned to kill the Vice President (in reality, the would-be murderer got very drunk on a pub crawl); and John Wilkes Booth was to assassinate the President himself.

The President and Mrs Lincoln, accompanied by their guests Major Henry Rathbone and his fiancée, Miss Clara Harris, arrived at the theatre shortly after eight o'clock. The first act was already under way, but this was interrupted as the audience of nearly two thousand people stood and the orchestra played 'Hail to the Chief', as the President and his party settled in their box.

At about 9.30pm Booth rode up to the theatre on a hired mare. He was dressed all in black and was disguised with theatrical make-up and a false beard. He was well prepared for the task at hand with a knife in his waistband, two Colt revolvers in his frock coat, and carrying a six-inch Derringer which was loaded and cocked.

John Parker, one of the President's bodyguards, had abandoned his post outside the box and had retired to the bar, as Booth watched the stage and waited for the right moment to strike. Shortly before 10.15, at a point of high comedy on stage, Booth stepped into the President's box and,

Bottom: *Mary Surratt owned the boarding house in Washington where the conspirators met. The court found her guilty and she, too, was hanged.*

Below: *John Wilkes Booth entered the Presidents's box at Ford's Theatre and shot him at point-blank range.*

muttering the words '*Sic semper tyrannis*', fired his Derringer. The $^{7}/_{16}$ lead ball entered the back of Lincoln's skull above his left ear, penetrated the brain and lodged behind his right eye.

Major Rathbone leapt to his feet and tackled Booth, who pulled his knife and slashed the officer's arm to the bone. Booth then leapt from the box and on to the stage. He snagged his spur in the curtain as he went, and crashed to the boards, fracturing his leg just above the ankle. Undeterred, he pushed terrified patrons aside and made his way out of the theatre. He felled the lad who was minding his horse and rode off into the night.

> THE PRESIDENT WAS RUSHED, STILL IN HIS ROCKING CHAIR, FROM THE THEATRE TO A TAILOR'S HOUSE OPPOSITE.

The wounded President was rushed, still in his rocking chair, from the theatre to a tailor's house opposite. The Surgeon General, Dr Stone, was summoned but there was nothing he could do. The President was alive, but very weak, and at 7.20 the following morning, Abraham Lincoln died.

Within minutes of Booth shooting the President, his fellow conspirator, Lewis Paine, was bungling his assassination of the Secretary of State. He had successfully broken into Seward's house and wounded the old man with a knife, but Seward recovered and survived for another eight years after the attack. Atzerodt, who was supposed to be killing the Vice President at the same moment, had lost his nerve, and instead, got very drunk and went on a pub crawl around Washington.

Below: *Soldiers were called out on to the streets to hold back the crowds who came to see Lincoln's funeral cortege and pay their last respects to the President.*

CONSPIRATOR CHOSE SUICIDE RATHER THAN CAPTURE

Some miles from the theatre, Booth met up with Herold. They crossed the Navy Yard Bridge on horseback and headed south into Maryland, seeking refuge with a largely-sympathetic population. Booth had his leg bound up by a friendly doctor and the two continued their eighty–mile ride, re-crossing the river Potomac into the state of Virginia.

Booth and Herold were on the run for eleven days before they were finally tracked down to their hiding place in a tobacco barn near Fort Royal, Virginia. Soldiers surrounded the building and, unable to persuade the two men to surrender, set fire to the barn. Herold finally gave

himself up and, as the flames became more intense, Booth shot himself.

But that was not an end to the matter. Paine, Herold, Atzerodt and Mrs Surratt, were all tried, convicted of conspiracy, and were hanged in the Arsenal grounds. Arnold, though he had played no part in the killing, was sentenced to hard labour for life, as was Dr Samuel Mudd, the physician who attended to Booth's broken leg. Edward Spangler, a scene-shifter at Ford's Theatre, received a sentence of six years for aiding Booth's escape.

And then came the inevitable conspiracy theories. In the years that have elapsed since Lincoln's assassination these have been many and varied. One of the more outlandish suggestions is that Lincoln's death was, in reality, the brain child of the then Secretary of State for War, Edwin Stanton, one of the President's most trusted aides during the Civil War. Evidence to support this and other conspiracy theories is flimsy. The truth is that, like so many assassinations, this was most probably the work of a group of fanatical men, acting in their own self-interest.

The Assassin

JOHN WILKES BOOTH

John Wilkes Booth came from a famous acting family. His father, Junius Brutus Booth, was a tragedian of the London and American stage; and his elder brother Edwin was credited with popularising Shakespeare in America.

As a young man, John was an ardent supporter of the Confederacy and a believer in the right of Southern planters to own slaves. Before the Civil War, he served under Robert E. Lee and stood guard at John Brown's execution. During the War itself, he declared himself a pacifist and returned to the stage but he continued to use his fame, charm and wealth to promote the South as he travelled through the Northern territories. Finally, with the South defeated, he decided propaganda was not enough. It was time for positive action to achieve his aims.

Above: *Four of President Lincoln's assassins were executed on 7 July 1865. They were Mrs Surratt, Lewis Payne, George Atzerott and David Herold. The courts showed no mercy and their accomplices received long sentences.*

THE SURVIVING CONSPIRATORS, INCLUDING MRS SURRATT, WERE ALL TRIED, CONVICTED OF CONSPIRACY AND HANGED.

JOHN F. KENNEDY

Right: The young Democratic Senator John F. Kennedy was elected President of the United States in 1960. He came to office with high hopes and ideals but was assassinated in 1963. Today he is remembered more for the manner of his tragic death than his legislation.

Below: John and Jackie Kennedy were America's golden couple. He was handsome and dashing, she was beautiful and stylish.

The assassination of John F.Kennedy in Dallas, Texas, was a most public murder and so was that of the supposed assassin. However, experts still disagree about who killed the President and why.

The most celebrated assassination of the twentieth century, perhaps the most celebrated assassination of all time, occurred in Dallas, Texas, on 22 November, 1963. The killing of the President of the United States of America, John Fitzgerald Kennedy, has been seen on television and in film, photographed and analysed so often, it has become part of American folklore. No crime in history has been subjected to such scrutiny, yet it remains an enigma. The questions: 'Who killed Jack Kennedy?' 'And why?' have never been satisfactorily answered despite endless attempts to find the truth.

of the car was removed. This was done at the President's insistence, much to the dismay of security men; they feared for Kennedy's safety in right-wing Dallas.

President and Mrs Kennedy took the back of the car, while Governor Connolly and his wife Nellie sat in the front. Secret service men flanked the car on foot as it moved from the airport at snail's pace.

As the presidential motorcade moved through downtown Dallas, it was greeted by an enormous and generally enthusiastic crowd. Kennedy responded to their enthusiasm, waving, smiling and shouting 'Thank you! Thank you!'

"MY GOD, THEY'VE KILLED JACK!"

As the motorcade turned from Main Street into Elm Street, a sudden, 'sharp crack' penetrated the sound of the cheering of the crowd. There was another crack and then a third.

The President clutched his throat, and then his head snapped back as a piece of his skull detached itself. There was blood everywhere. Kennedy slumped forward and Jackie cradled him in her arms, crying out: 'My God, what are they doing? My God, they've killed Jack. They've killed my husband! Jack! Jack!'

The circumstances leading up to the killing are a matter of record. On the morning of Thursday, 22 November, the forty-six-year-old President and his wife Jackie flew into Dallas airport to attend a political rally. They were greeted by the Democratic Governor of Texas, John Connolly, who was to accompany them on their drive through the city of Dallas.

It was just before noon when the President and his party climbed into the presidential limousine. There had been a delay while the bullet-proof Perspex roof

THERE HAD BEEN A FEW MINUTES DELAY WHILE THE BULLET-PROOF PERSPEX ROOF OF THE CAR WAS REMOVED.

THE PRESIDENT CLUTCHED HIS THROAT, AND THEN HIS HEAD SNAPPED BACK AS A PIECE OF HIS SKULL DETACHED ITSELF.

Left: *Jackie Kennedy became America's First Lady of fashion. A stylish dresser, she was best known for her elegant pill-box hats.*

Below: *Joseph and Rose Kennedy with their children. The future president is on the left of the back row.*

Above: The dreadful event was recorded on film, revealing the fear and horror of those close to the scene. The President's wife Jacqueline crawled to safety over the boot of the besieged limousine.

The presidential limousine swung out of the motorcade and accelerated away. Four minutes later it was outside the Parkland Memorial Hospital.

The President was rushed into the casualty department and the futile fight to save his life began. He was given an immediate tracheotomy, blood transfusion and cardiac massage as surgeons worked on his devastating head wound. It was obviously hopeless from the start.

A Roman Catholic priest was called to administer the last rites and, twenty-five minutes after he was shot, John Fitzgerald Kennedy, thirty-fourth President of the United States, was pronounced dead.

Back at the scene of the assassination, chaos reigned. Hysterical Kennedy supporters were screaming and fainting, police and security men were charging about trying to work out just what had happened. Several eyewitnesses pointed up to a multi-storey building overlooking Elm Street. One of them was certain that he had seen a rifle being withdrawn from an upper window immediately after the shooting.

Police swarmed into the building, which housed the Texas School Book Depository. On the sixth floor, they found an open window and, on the floor beneath it, three spent rifle cartridges. Seconds later, they discovered a 6.5 calibre Mannchiler-Carcano riflc, fitted with a telescopic sight, which had been thrown behind a stack of packing cases.

It did not take the authorities long to trace the gun. It had been sold by a Chicago mail order company to one Lee Harvey Oswald, a twenty-four-year-old ex-Marine, social misfit, and employee of the Book Depository. Oswald had been seen leaving the building minutes after the shooting. An all-points bulletin was immediately broadcasted, calling for his arrest.

AT LAST THE ASSASSIN WAS CORNERED

Forty-five minutes after the shooting, Officer J.D. Tippitt happened to be patrolling the area of Dallas where Oswald was known to be living. The officer saw a man answering the description and challenged him. Oswald turned as he heard his name called, pulled a handgun and shot Tippitt dead. Witnesses then saw Oswald run down the street before disappearing into a neighbourhood cinema. The building was surrounded and

Oswald was cornered. He pulled his gun on the arresting officer but it misfired. He was duly arrested and taken down to Dallas Police Headquarters, where he was charged with the murder of Officer Tippitt.

Oswald was questioned at police headquarters for two days, by which time the authorities were convinced that not only had he killed the policeman Tippitt but also

---

Kennedy's Assassin

LEE HARVEY OSWALD

Lee Oswald was born in New Orleans on 18 October, 1939, two months after the death of his father. He spent three years in an orphanage, before being reunited with his mother.

At school, Oswald was a poor student, given to truancy. After completing the ninth grade, at the age of sixteen, he dropped out of school and joined the Marine Corps. In 1959, at the age of twenty, he was released by the Corps on compassionate grounds. He claimed that his mother was dying and needed him to nurse her. In fact, he spent only three days at home with his mother, who was in perfect health, before he travelled to the Soviet Union, where he attempted to establish Soviet citizenship.

He spent almost two years in Russia, during which time he met and married a Russian girl, Marina Nikolaevna Prusakova, and they had a daughter.

In 1961, Oswald returned to New Orleans with his wife and child. A year later, he became involved in an organisation called the Fair Play for Cuba Committee which distributed pro-Castro leaflets and made radio broadcasts on behalf of the Communist regime in Cuba.

In September 1963, Oswald travelled to Mexico City. There he visited the Cuban and Russian embassies in an attempt to obtain visas to visit those two countries. He returned to Dallas, Texas in early October 1963 and obtained a job at the Texas School Book Depository.

The rest is history.

---

that he had assassinated Jack Kennedy, President of the United States.

On Saturday morning, 14 November, it was decided to transfer Oswald to Dallas County jail. Millions of Americans got their first and last glimpse of Kennedy's supposed assassin as police escorted him through the underground car park of the police headquarters.

Suddenly, a burly, middle-aged man pushed his way through the mass of reporters, stuck a revolver in Oswald's ribs and pulled the trigger. Oswald let out a scream of pain and slumped forward.

Oswald was already dead as police half dragged, half carried him back into the police station. Other officers pounced on the gunman. He offered no resistance as he was taken into the police headquarters.

DOING A FAVOUR FOR JACKIE

Oswald's killer was later identified as Jack Rubenstein, better known as Jack Ruby, a Dallas nightclub owner. At the time his only comment about his murderous act was: 'I did it for Jackie.'

Lee Harvey Oswald was dead. Jack Ruby was in jail awaiting trial for his murder. But the world wanted to know what had really happened. Did Lee Harvey Oswald really kill the President? If so, why? Did he act

---

THE GUN HAD BEEN SOLD BY MAIL ORDER TO LEE HARVEY OSWALD, A TWENTY-FOUR-YEAR-OLD EX-MARINE AND SOCIAL MISFIT.

OSWALD TURNED AS HE HEARD HIS NAME CALLED, PULLED A HANDGUN AND SHOT OFFICER TIPPITT DEAD.

Below: *The motorcade had just turned a corner when three shots rang out. There was blood everywhere and President Kennedy slumped forward into his wife's arms.*

Above: *The President was buried on 24 November. With their daughter Caroline at her side, Jackie Kennedy led the mourners at the funeral.*

Left: *Jackie visited her husband's grave at Arlington Cemetery with her brother-in-law Robert, soon himself to become the vicitim of an assassin.*

SUDDENLY, A MAN PUSHED HIS WAY THROUGH THE REPORTERS, STUCK A REVOLVER IN OSWALD'S RIBS AND PULLED THE TRIGGER.

alone? Who was Jack Ruby? What was his motive for killing Oswald? Why did some eyewitnesses say that they heard shots coming from the opposite direction from the Book Depository? Why were the President's wounds inconsistent with the position of the alleged assassin? Was it a conspiracy? Was the Mafia behind it? Were the Cubans behind it? Was the CIA behind it? Just what did happen on that fateful afternoon in Dallas?

Lyndon Johnson, who was sworn in as President within hours of Kennedy's death, immediately announced that he was setting up a special commission to investigate the circumstances surrounding the assassination. The commission was to be headed by Chief Justice Earl Warren and his team included a number of senior Senators, along with Allen Dulles, the former director of the CIA, and John McCloy, an aide to the murdered President.

The Warren Commission report was finally published in September 1964. They had heard five hundred and fifty-two witnesses, received more than three thousand reports from Law Enforcement Agencies which in turn had conducted approximately twenty-six thousand interviews. The evidence filled twenty-six volumes.

In fact, the report said very little. It was vehement in its criticism of the CIA, the FBI and the Dallas police for failing in their duty to protect the President. It also concluded that Kennedy had been killed by Lee Harvey Oswald and that Oswald had acted alone. There was, it said, no evidence of a conspiracy.

There were howls of protest from all quarters. The report was widely denounced as a whitewash, full of omissions and inconsistencies. Rather than silencing conspiracy theories, it spawned countless new ones, some outrageously far-fetched, others frighteningly plausible.

In the twenty years that have elapsed since the President's assassination, there have been more than a hundred books, scores of documentaries, a few feature films, hundreds of scholarly documents, and countless articles on the subject, expounding different versions of what happened on that fateful November day. The reality is that we shall probably never know for certain who killed John F. Kennedy, or why.

San Francisco Chronicle

THE VOICE OF THE WEST

99th YEAR   No. 329   **FINAL HOME EDITION** ★   MONDAY, NOVEMBER 25, 1963   10 CENTS   GArfield 1-1111

Oswald Shot Dead By Dallas 'Avenger'

The Killer Strikes

Single Bullet

Fatal Attack As Police Move Accused Man

A.P. & U.P.

Dallas

Lee Harvey Oswald, accused assassin of President Kennedy, was shot and killed while being transferred from one jail to another yesterday, 48 hours after the death of the President.

He had never wavered in his insistence that he was not the President's killer. He died without saying a word.

The man who shot Oswald, Jack Ruby, 52, bachelor owner of two Dallas night clubs, had stepped swiftly through a mass of police and newsmen at a basement garage ramp in city hall.

He rushed up to Oswald and sent a single pistol bullet into his abdomen.

Oswald dropped unconscious at Ruby's feet, within a cordon of escorting police officers.

At least eight police
See Page 1C, Col. 5

S. F. Stands Still Today To Mourn

JACK DAVIS DEEPLY MOURNS AND

Lee Oswald doubled up as Jack Ruby (with gun) fired the fatal shot

Copyright, 1963, by The Dallas Times-Herald and Photographer Bob Jackson, via UPI Telephoto

---

Oswald's Assassin

JACK RUBY

Jack Ruby was born Jack Rubenstein in 1911. At the time of the Kennedy assassination, he was the proprietor of a dubious nightclub in Dallas. His place was a well known hang-out for criminals of all shapes and sizes and Ruby himself was known to have connections with the sinister Mafia as well as a variety of other organised crime syndicates.

All in all, he was a fairly unsavoury character but, after he shot Lee Harvey Oswald, he found himself elevated to the status of a national hero of sorts. However, the fact that it was widely felt that he had done America a favour by killing Oswald, did not save him from the full might of the law.

Despite having one of the smartest defence attorneys in America, Melvin Belli, Jack Ruby stood trial for the murder of Lee Harvey Oswald and on 14 March, 1964, a Dallas jury gave their verdict on the accused: 'We find the defendant Guilty of murder with malice as charged in the indictment, and assess his punishment as death.'

Belli lambasted the jury in front of national television, calling their verdict a 'violent miscarriage', and promising to lodge an appeal outside Dallas 'where there is justice'.

Belli was true to his word and lodged appeal after appeal. He succeeded in having the sentence commuted to life imprisonment, and he was still fighting for an acquittal when, on 3 January, 1967, Jack Ruby died in prison from a blood clot on his lung.

Above: *Photographer Bob Jackson was standing just feet away and took this extraordinary picture of the murder of Lee Harvey Oswald.*

THE REPORT COMMISSIONED BY THE NEW PRESIDENT, LYNDON JOHNSON SPAWNED COUNTLESS NEW CONSPIRACY THEORIES, SOME OUTRAGEOUSLY FAR-FETCHED, OTHERS FRIGHTENINGLY PLAUSIBLE.

ROBERT KENNEDY

Robert Kennedy knew he was taking a terrible risk when he set out to follow in his murdered brother's footsteps but another assassin struck suddenly, even sooner than anyone predicted.

In June 1968, the Democratic primaries were in full swing, and things were looking good for Robert Fitzgerald Kennedy. To a large section of the American electorate, he was the natural successor to his assassinated older brother. Robert was a handsome and charismatic politician who shared the same personal qualities and the same ideals as Jack. People perceived that there was a certain symmetry, an innate fairness, in the idea that he should be allowed to carry on where Jack Kennedy left off.

Even so, Robert Kennedy was not universally admired. During his terms as United States Attorney General and as a United States senator, he became known as a strong proponent of civil rights legislation, a cause which had alienated him from the far right; and he had used his position to fight against trade union corruption. These two stances earned him some powerful and dangerous enemies.

ROBERT WAS
HEADING TO CERTAIN VICTORY

Kennedy's decision to run for the Democratic nomination was not taken lightly. His family, so long dogged by tragedy, did everything they could to dissuade him. The risk, they said, was simply too great. Robert Kennedy, however, was not a man to be intimidated

and brushed the risks aside. 'Men are not made for safe decisions,' he argued.

For the Kennedy campaign, 4 June, 1968 was a great day. Robert had consolidated his lead over his main Democratic rival, Eugene McCarthy, by winning the primary in California. This brought his total delegate votes to one hundred and ninety-eight and his victory at the final Democratic Presidential Election was a virtual certainty.

On the morning of 5 June, Robert Kennedy washed and dressed in his suite at the Ambassador Hotel in downtown Los Angeles. He had spent a sleepless night but showed no signs of fatigue as he addressed an audience of campaign volunteers.

'On to Chicago', he told his supporters as he marched through the hotel corridors trailed by campaign staff, advisers and a handful of unarmed security guards.

Running a few minutes late, Kennedy decided to take a shortcut to the room where he was due to hold a press conference. The route took him through the hotel kitchens. Kennedy pushed through a set of swing doors and entered a narrow corridor which was teeming with supporters, all anxious to get a glimpse of their hero. No

Far left: *Senator Robert F.Kennedy who was set to follow in his brother's footsteps but was destined instead to join JFK as an assassin's victim at the age of forty-two.*

Above: *Like his own parents, Robert and Ethel Kennedy had a large family. She was expecting their eleventh child when her husband was murdered.*

Right: *Ethel Kennedy and her brother-in-law Edward in front of a bust commemorating Robert Kennedy .*

THE KENNEDYS DID EVERYTHING THEY COULD TO DISSUADE ROBERT FROM RUNNING FOR PRESIDENT: THE RISKS WERE SIMPLY TOO GREAT.

---

one paid any attention to a slight, dark-haired young man who was leaning against an ice-making machine.

Robert Kennedy who was accompanied by his wife Ethel, at this time expecting their eleventh child, paused to shake hands with an admirer.

And then the unthinkable happened.

The young man by the ice-machine rushed forward, pulled a .22 calibre Iver Johnson pistol and fired two shots at

Above: *Both Kennedy brothers were destined to die in front of the world press. The assassin's first bullet tore through Robert Kennedy's shoulder; the second smashed into his skull.*

Kennedy. The first bullet tore through his shoulder; the second smashed into his skull, spilling the young politician's brains on to the linoleum flooring.

The assailant kept firing as an hotel employee, Karl Uecker, tried to wrench the gun from his hand. Three other bystanders were injured before the man was finally pinned to the ground by two of Kennedy's supporters – Rafer Johnson, the Olympic decathlon champion, and Roosevelt 'Rosie' Greer, a massive, professional footballer.

Enraged Kennedy supporters turned into an instant lynch mob, as they fought to get at the gunman. Greer and Johnson kept them at bay. 'Let's not have another Oswald,' Johnson bellowed. After a couple of minutes, the police arrived and led the young man away at gun point. Robert Kennedy was rushed by ambulance to the

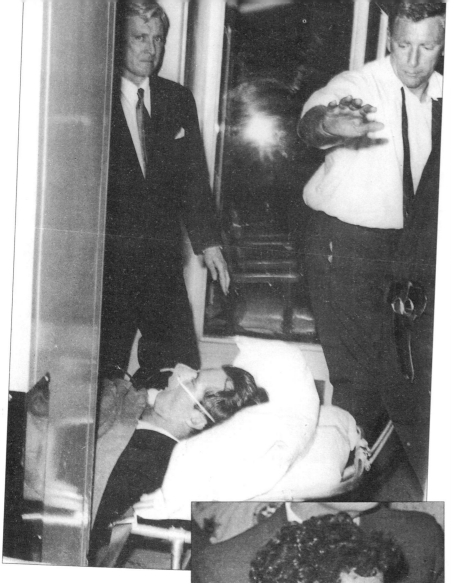

Los Angeles Central Emergency Receiving Station. Dr Victor Boz, who examined him on admission, sadly confessed that, 'Mr Kennedy was virtually dead when he was brought in to the hospital, nonetheless the fight to save him continued.'

Boz administered cardiac massage. 'I was about to put adrenalin into the heart,' he said, 'but as we were working we found we didn't need that. At first he was pulseless, then his pulse came back and we began to hear a heartbeat. Then he began to breathe erratically.'

A team of surgeons, under Dr Henry Cuneo, operated on Kennedy for three hours and forty minutes. After the operation, a medical bulletin was posted that said that his condition was critical and that the next thirty-six hours would prove crucial to the survival of Robert Kennedy.

Top: *Robert Kennedy was rushed to emergency hospital in Los Angeles.*

Above: *Sirhan B.Sirhan, the twenty-four-year-old Palestinian who murdered Robert Kennedy believed this death would advance the Arab cause.*

But, despite the best efforts of the medical staff, Robert Kennedy died at 1.45 on the morning of 6 June, approximately twenty hours after the shooting.

While America mourned the death of Robert Kennedy, the police were questioning his assassin. Twenty-four hours after the shooting, the young man was still refusing to identify himself.

'I wish to remain incognito,' he said.

Police finally managed to trace the Iver Johnson pistol that the assailant had used in the killing, and found it was registered to a twenty-three-year-old Jordanian immigrant, Sirhan B. Sirhan.

Sirhan, who had once been a Kennedy admirer, had been disillusioned by the politician's pro-Israeli stance. Sirhan blamed Israel for making his Palestinian people homeless and had decided that Kennedy must die on or before 5 June, 1968, which marked the first anniversary of the Six Day's War between Israel and the Arab nations.

At his trial, Sirhan entered a plea of insanity but was found sane, convicted of murder and imprisoned for life.

The Assassin

SIRHAN B. SIRHAN

Sirhan Sirhan was a twenty-four-year-old Palestinian who had emigrated to America from Jordan with his family. As a Palestinian, he harboured a deep hatred for Israel and all those who supported Israel's right to exist. In his eyes, they were collectively responsible for making his people stateless.

Robert F. Kennedy was one of those supporters of Israel. Sirhan Sirhan had trailed the Senator for days. On 18 May, 1968, he wrote in his diary: 'RFK must be...be...d...of...disposed of openly. Robert Fitzgerald Kennedy must die... die... die... die... die...'.

His mother blamed his actions on his Palestinian upbringing. Violence and terrorism were a way of life in Jordan. Sirhan's own brother had been killed by a car while escaping gunfire. Violence was the only way the young man knew how to right a perceived wrong.

MURDERS AND NEAR MISSES

The job of American President is possibly the most dangerous in the world – all the security in the world cannot protect him from the determined and demented killers waiting to strike.

Below: President James Garfield had no time to leave his mark on American politics – he was shot dead after less than four months in office.

Below right: Garfield's assassin Charles Guiteau who was still holding the smoking pistol when he was arrested.

The murder of Abraham Lincoln was the first in a constantly growing list of assassination attempts, some successful, some not, on the person of the President of the United States .

Everyone is aware of the terrible events in Dallas on 22 November, 1963, when President John Fitzgerald Kennedy was gunned down (see pages 10-15). Less well known are two earlier Chief Executives who were also shot and killed.

President James Garfield had been in office for less than four months when he was assassinated on 2 July, 1881. Garfield was walking through Washington railway station when he was shot in the back. 'My God! What is this?', he bellowed as he was rushed back to the White House for medical attention.

Garfield's attacker, Charles Guiteau, was still holding a smoking pistol when he was arrested. Guiteau, a member of the ultra-right-wing 'Stalwarts', had petitioned the President for political favours and had been refused. 'I am a Stalwart,' shouted Guiteau, as he was bundled away from the station by lawmen, 'and now Arthur (Garfield's vice-President) is President.'

Left: *President William McKinley photographed just fifteen minutes before he was assassinated on 6 September 1901.*

Below: *A contemporary report of McKinley's murder.*

Guiteau's boast was somewhat premature. In fact, Garfield lived for eleven more weeks before finally dying of blood poisoning, a condition probably caused by the use of unsterile surgical instruments. And, on 20 September, 1881, Chester Alan Arthur did indeed become President of the United States. In the June of the following year, Charles Guiteau, although of dubious sanity, was convicted of Garfield's murder and was hanged.

The year 1901 saw the third assassination of an American President, when William McKinley was shot and killed. McKinley, who had served only six months of his second term in office, is widely credited with having established the United States as a world power. His radical expansionist economic policies had led to the establishment of an empire abroad – Hawaii, Guam, the Philippines and Puerto Rico – that earned him both admirers and enemies. One of the latter was Leon Czolgosz, a Polish anarchist.

THE OUTSTRETCHED HAND HELD A GUN

On 6 September, McKinley was attending the Pan-American exposition in Buffalo. He delivered a speech at the Temple of Music and, after he finished, he mingled with the crowd. Czolgosz approached the President with his hand outstretched as if to greet him. In fact, the hand contained a .38

BUFFALO EXPRESS.
BUFFALO, N.Y., SATURDAY, SEPTEMBER 7, 1901. TEN PAGES.

THE PRESIDENT SHOT AT THE EXPOSITION.

AS THE WOMAN WAS THROWN TO THE GROUND BY SECURITY MEN SHE SCREAMED, 'IT DIDN'T GO OFF...IT DIDN'T GO OFF.'

Right: *President Gerald Ford. In September 1975, two attempts were made on his life, both by women.*

Below: *President Ford with his wife Betty and their family. Mrs Ford gave her name to an addicts' clinic that pioneered radical treatment.*

wrapped in a handkerchief. When he was within a couple of feet of his target, Czolgosz fired twice before being wrestled to the ground and disarmed.

At first, McKinley's wounds were not thought to be serious but his condition gradually deteriorated and eight days later, on 14 September, he died.

Leon Czolgosz was tried and convicted of murder and was executed in the electric chair on 29 October, 1901.

McKinley was succeeded in office by Theodore 'Teddy' Roosevelt who, at forty-two years old, was the youngest ever President of the United States. Despite his youth, Roosevelt was a national figure and a military hero.

Although he was very popular, Roosevelt was not without enemies. He survived two consecutive terms in office (1901-1909) without incident. Then, on 14 October, 1912, he was shot and wounded by one John N. Schrank outside the Gilpatrick Hotel in Milwaukee, Wisconsin. Roosevelt was then in the midst of his campaign to be voted for a third term in the White House on the Progressive ticket. Following the shooting, Roosevelt continued to the Milwaukee Auditorium where he delivered his campaign speech before seeking medical attention. He was to recover from his wounds but he lost the election to William Howard Taft.

The would-be assassin, John Schrank, was judged insane and committed to the Central State Hospital in Wisconsin, where he remained until his death in 1943.

In the autumn of 1951, the White House was being refurbished and the then President, Harry S. Truman was in temporary residence at Blair House on Pennsylvania Avenue, Washington DC. On the afternoon of 1 November, Truman was taking a nap when two Puerto Rican separatists – Oscar Collazo and Griselio Torresola – tried to storm Blair House with a view to assassinating the President. A three-minute gun battle ensued between Presidential guards and the attackers. Torresola and one of the guards were killed during the exchange and Collazo was arrested. At his trial Collazo told the court that he and his companion had bought one-way tickets to Washington, never expecting to survive their mission. He was found Guilty of conspiracy to murder the President of the United States and condemned to die in the electric chair. Truman, however, in a personal act of clemency, had the sentence commuted to life imprisonment.

IF YOU SURVIVE, LIFE MUST GO ON

In September 1975, there were two attempts made on the life of President Gerald Ford. The first happened in Sacramento, California, on 5 September. Ford left the Senator Hotel shortly after

10am and was walking across the Plaza to the Capital Building. He was working the crowd as he went, shaking hands and chatting with supporters. Suddenly a scruffy young woman pushed her way through the crowd, produced a .45 revolver, aimed it at the President's head and pulled the trigger. Nothing happened. As the woman was thrown to the ground by security men, she screamed, 'It didn't go off...It didn't go off.' When police examined the gun later, they found that it was indeed loaded. The would-be assassin was later identified as

Above: *Lynette Fromme pictured as she was led away by security guards after her attempt to kill President Ford failed when her loaded gun did not go off.*

backfire but then we saw a puff of smoke across the street. At first, the President hesitated and looked stunned. Then the secret service hustled him into the car and drove him away sort of hunched down.'

While one group of secret service men were busy spiriting away the shocked President, another was arresting a forty-five-year-old woman who was still holding a .38 automatic. She was Sara Jane Moore, a left-wing activist well known in the San Francisco area. She had recently gained some personal notoriety for her part in the distribution of food to the city's poor, food which had been contributed by Randolph Hearst as part of a ransom deal for the release of his daughter Patty.

Both Miss Moore and Miss Fromme were later tried and convicted of attempting to assassinate the President of the United States and received long custodial sentences.

A TWENTY-YARD WALK INTO DANGER

The most recent assassination attempt against an American President came on 30 March, 1981. At 2.30pm, Ronald Reagan was leaving the Washington Hilton Hotel after addressing a convention of building trade unionists. As he walked the twenty yards from the hotel lobby to his limousine, he waved and smiled at the small crowd who had gathered in the rain to greet him. From behind and to his right, a voice shouted out 'Mr President!' Reagan turned and, as he did so, four shots rang out.

Security men grabbed the seventy-year-old President and bundled him into his car. As they sped away, two more bullets slammed into the body-work of the vehicle.

As a second group of security men forced the would-be assassin, a young man, to the ground, it became clear that other members of the presidential party had been hit by the volley of shots. Jim

twenty-five-year-old Lynette Alice 'Squeaky' Fromme, a member of The Family, a cult founded by convicted mass-murderer Charles Manson.

Such was President Ford's aplomb that, within two hours of the attempt on his life, he delivered an address to the California State Legislature on crime and gun control. Commenting on the assassination bid, he said, 'No way will it prevent or preclude me from contacting the America people... It is just something you have to live with.'

And live with it he did. Less than three weeks after the Sacramento incident, on 21 September, 1975, President Ford was leaving his hotel in Los Angeles when there was another attempt on his life. An eyewitness described the incident: 'He came out of the hotel and everyone was shouting "there he is" and then there was a shot. At first it seemed like some sort of

Brady, the President's Press Secretary, had been hit in the head and was critically injured. A secret service agent and Timothy J. McCarthy, a Washington policeman, had also been shot but, fortunately, their wounds were less serious than Brady's.

Reagan was rushed to the George Washington University Hospital, about a mile from the scene of the shooting. The President walked into the building, supported by two of his staff. There was blood oozing from his left side.

The First Lady, Nancy Reagan, was rushed to the hospital and was taken to see her husband shortly before he went into the operating theatre. 'Honey,' quipped the President, 'I forgot to duck.' Then, turning to the doctors, he grinned and said, 'I hope you guys are Republicans.'

Surgeons operated for an hour to remove a .22 calibre bullet from the President's left lung. It had missed his heart by two inches. One doctor in the medical team commented: 'If that had been a .45 rather than a .22, it would have blown him away.'

Despite his advancing years, the President made a rapid and full recovery. As for the assassin, he was identified as John Hinckley Jnr, a twenty-five-year-old, unemployed disc jockey. He was tried for attempted murder but was found Not Guilty due to insanity. The court ordered him to be committed to a mental institution for an indefinite period.

The Assassin

JOHN HINCKLEY Jnr.

The man who came so close to killing President Ronald Reagan, John Hinckley Jnr, was known to the police. On 9 October, 1980, he had been arrested by airport police in Nashville Tennessee for carrying three hand guns. On that same day, President Jimmy Carter was in town addressing a meeting at the Grand Ole Opry. Hinckley was later released on his own recognisance.

Hinckley was a twenty-five-year-old Yale University drop-out, whose father was chief executive at Vanderbilt Energy Corporation, an oil company in Denver, Colorado. Hinckley Junior was educated at the exclusive Highland Park School in Dallas, Texas, before winning a place at Yale. He quit college during his first semester and went to work as a disc jockey for a country music station in Denver under the name John Warlek.

Friends, family and teachers said that Hinckley had never previously shown any signs of mental instability. When it came to his trial for attempted assassination, however, the court found him to be insane.

Above: *The scene of the attempted assassination of Ronald Reagan on 30 March,1981, outside the Washington Hilton. Heavily armed security men forced John Hinkley Jnr to the ground.*

Far left: *President Reagan and his wife Nancy brought more than just a touch of Hollywood to the White House. In hospital, after he was shot, Reagan said to his wife, 'Honey, I forgot to duck.'*

REAGAN TURNED TO THE DOCTORS AND GRINNED, 'I HOPE YOU GUYS ARE REPUBLICANS.'

LEON TROTSKY

TROTSKY'S WEAPONS WERE HIS PEN AND HIS INTELLECT. BOTH THREATENED AND EMBARRASSED STALIN.

THE MEXICAN COMMUNIST PARTY ORGANISED THEIR OWN ASSASSINATION PLOT AGAINST TROTSKY AND FIREBOMBED HIS VILLA.

Right: *Leon Trotsky's goatee beard and round spectacles were this Russian revolutionary's trademarks. Trotsky organized the Red Army during the 1918-21 civil war but fell out with Stalin and went into exile in 1929.*

Once comrades in arms, Stalin and Trotsky became such enemies that Stalin's hired assassins pursued the exiled intellectual to the ends of the earth.

Leon Trotsky – born Lev Davidovitch Bronstein – was, with Vladimir Ilyich Lenin, co-founder of the Soviet Union. When Lenin died in 1924, a power struggle ensued between Trotsky and Stalin for supreme control of the Communist state. Stalin won and was determined to eliminate his rival completely so Trotsky was forced to flee Russia. He found sanctuary in a succession of countries over the next decade – Turkey, France and Norway

Left: *Trotsky in the happy days of leadership and revolution. He is seen standing at the back of this picture taken at a meeting of international Communists in the Kremlin.*

Below: *Leon and Natalia Trotsky were flanked by police and plain clothesmen when they arrived in Mexico City. This was to be their last place of exile.*

– but each, in turn, found his presence an embarrassment and finally expelled him.

In 1937 Trotsky reached his last asylum, Mexico. By this time, he had long been discredited and vilified in his native Russia and had been sentenced to death in his absence by Marshall Stalin. Stalin claimed that Trotsky was building a power base abroad with offices in every major city in the world, each staffed with espionage agents whose sole purpose was to undermine, and ultimately destroy, the USSR. In reality, Trotsky's weapons were his pen and his intellect. Both threatened and embarrassed Stalin. George Bernard Shaw said of Trotsky's writings: 'When he cuts off his opponent's head, he holds it up to show that there are no brains in it.'

THE NKVD'S CHOSEN ASSASSIN

Stalin charged the NKVD (the Russian secret service) with the task of eliminating his enemy. They had a good track record in this sort of work. During the Twenties and Thirties, literally hundreds of exiled enemies of the Soviet Union had disappeared, been found murdered or appeared to have committed suicide. Even Trotsky's own secretary, Erwin Wolf, had been murdered when he left Norway for Spain and while neither Wolf's death, nor those of countless other dissidents, was ever proved to be the work of the NKVD, there is little doubt that they were responsible.

The NKVD selected Ramon Mercador, alias Frank Jacson, for the task of killing Trotsky. Jacson was the twenty-six-year-

old son of influential Spanish Communist, Caridad Mercador and was a veteran of the Popular Front republican forces and a graduate of the Barcelona school of terrorism. In Moscow, Jacson received training in murder, sabotage, intelligence and guerilla warfare. After his training was completed, he was sent to Paris where, by chance but probably by design, Jacson met an American woman, Sylvia Ageloff, who was in the French capital where she worked as a courier for Leon Trotsky.

Jacson, now calling himself Jacques Mornard, was good looking, charming and plausible and it was not long before he had persuaded Sylvia to marry him. He invented a complete fantasy life for

JACSON INVENTED A COMPLETE FANTASY LIFE FOR HIMSELF, WHICH HIS GULLIBLE FIANCÉE ACCEPTED WITH QUESTION.

himself, which his gullible fiancée accepted without question. And so, when they travelled to New York together, ten days before the outbreak of the Second World War, she believed that she was about to marry a Belgian writer and mountaineer, whose father, an eminent diplomat, had recently died in a car accident. None of this, of course, was true.

HOME-MADE FIRE BOMBS

Jacson and Sylvia flew from New York to Mexico City and Jacson set about infiltrating a group of American Trotskyists. But before he could make much headway, the Mexican Communist Party organized their own assassination plot against Trotsky. On 24 May, 1940, Avadia Viena, Trotsky's villa, was stormed by twenty-four would-be assassins firing machine guns and throwing home-made fire bombs. Despite their numbers and firepower, the operation turned into a complete fiasco and Trotsky, his wife and grandson escaped unhurt.

After the bungled attempt on his life, Trotsky rebuilt his home and, with the help of loyal followers, turned it into a virtual fortress. Among those loyal followers was the sympathetic American, Sylvia Ageloff and, her husband, Frank Jacson.

Trotsky was not impressed with Jacson. He found him boastful, arrogant and conceited but when Jacson asked him to help rewrite an article he was compiling on the Fourth International, Trotsky reluctantly agreed.

The day of 20 August, 1940 was hot in Mexico City but Frank Jacson set off from his apartment to Trotsky's villa dressed in a raincoat and hat. Under the coat he had concealed an alpine ice axe, a hammer and a .45 Estrella automatic.

Jacson arrived at Avadia Viena shortly before 5pm; the electric doors were opened by Trotsky's guards, and Jacson was taken to see the great man, who was in the garden feeding his rabbits. Natalia, Trotsky's wife, commented that it was odd that 'Sylvia's husband' (in fact, the couple never married) should arrive unannounced but Trotsky seemed unconcerned and asked his visitor to stay for dinner.

Jacson declined the invitation but wondered whether Trotsky might take a quick look at the article he had just completed. The two men went to the study together and Trotsky sat behind his desk.

He was within an arm's reach of his Colt revolver, a .25 automatic and an alarm bell that could bring guards to the study in a matter of seconds.

As Trotsky began to read the article, Jacson put his raincoat on the desk, removed the ice axe and smashed it down on Trotsky's skull.

As Jacson prepared to wield the axe for a second time, Trotsky grabbed his arm and bit into the flesh, making him drop the weapon. Trotsky staggered out of the study and into the drawing room. 'Jacson!' he cried. 'See what you have done!' Guards rushed into the drawing room and felled Jacson, just as he was aiming his pistol at Trotsky. 'Impermissible to kill.' Trotsky instructed his guards, 'He must be forced to talk'. With that Trotsky lost consciousness.

The guards obeyed their master's instructions. They did not kill Jacson, but they did give him a terrible beating. Minutes later, both the assassin and his victim were whisked off to the Green Cross hospital in Mexico City. Doctors fought to save Trotsky but the following evening, twenty-six hours after the attack, he died.

Trotsky's body lay in state for five days and during this time, more than thirty thousand people filed past to pay their last respects to the architect of Communist society who had met such a brutal death in exile.

Frank Jacson, alias Ramon Mercador,

> UNDER HIS COAT, HE HAD CONCEALED AN ALPINE ICE AXE, A HAMMER AND A .45 ESTRELLA AUTOMATIC.

Right: *Ramon Mercador, alias Frank Jacson, his head bandaged and unshaven pictured after his arrest for Trotsky's murder.*

Below: *Leon Trotsky unconscious on his death bed after he had the assassin's axe removed from his head. He died twenty-six hours after the attack.*

alias Jacques Mornard, was sentenced to twenty years for Trotsky's murder. He was released from his Mexican prison in March, 1960 and declared a hero of the Soviet Union shortly before his death in Havana, Cuba on 18 October, 1978.

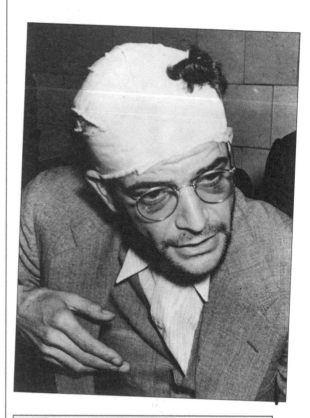

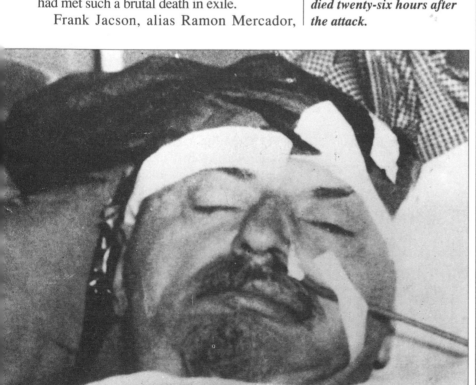

The Assassin

RAMON MERCADOR

Ramon Mercador was born in Spain on 7 February, 1914. His mother, Caridad, was separated from her husband and took young Ramon to France, along with his sister and three brothers. As a teenager, Ramon was sent to a catering school in Lyons, then returned with his family to Barcelona, where he obtained a post as assistant chef at the Ritz hotel.

· Caridad, meanwhile, had been carrying on a long affair with a prominent French Communist and had been converted to the cause. She made a point of indoctrinating her children with Communist ideology. Ramon proved a particulalry receptive pupil and, when it came time to serve the cause, he accepted his assignment without question.

MAHATMA GANDHI

Above: *Mahatma Gandhi, father of Indian independence. In his later years, he gave up western dress and returned to the simple costume of his people.*

Mahatma Gandhi was a revered and charismatic leader. He was also a man of peace who preached tolerance among India's different creeds, yet it was a religious fanatic who gunned him down.

Violence in any form was anathema to Mahatma Gandhi. He argued, pleaded and preached his views for more than thirty years and finally, in 1947, was able to prove the ultimate effectiveness of his non-violent philosophy when his nation achieved peaceful independence from Britain. But, in the wake of that freedom, there came violence on a terrible scale as religious factions vied with each other for control of the sub-continent.

The year 1947 ended in sad disillusion for Gandhi. He continued to preach the immorality and futility of violence, but no one seemed to be listening any more. In January 1948, in a desperate attempt to stop the religious violence, he embarked on a fast unto death. He explained this, saying, 'Death would be glorious deliverance, rather than I should be a helpless witness to the destruction of India, Hinduism, Sikhism and Islam.'

Gandhi's action had the desired effect. Leaders of the religious groups agreed to compromise. Within days of the Mahatma ('wise man') starting his fast, the Hindus delivered an edict: 'We take a pledge that we shall protect the life, property and faith of the Muslims, and the incidents which have happened in Delhi will never happen again.'

On the basis of this promise, Gandhi broke his fast. The inter-factional co-operation did not last long, however, and soon a strong anti-Gandhi movement began to develop. Militant Hindus complained that Gandhi was against members of their religion. Why else, they asked, would he allow such numbers to be butchered in Pakistan? They wanted armed intervention to protect their people but they knew that violence would not be tolerated as long as Gandhi lived. The only solution to their problem was to get rid of him.

THE BOMB EXPLODED A FEW FEET FROM THE MAHATMA

The first attempt on Gandhi's life was on 20 January, 1948, just two days after he ended his fast. He was addressing a prayer meeting at Birla House, his home in Delhi,

Left: *Mourners escorted Gandhi's ashes through the streets of Allahabad.*

Below: *The court where Gandhi's assassins were tried.*

Bottom: *The convicted killer Nathuram Godse who was sentenced to death and hanged.*

when a refugee from the Punjab called Madanlal threw a home-made bomb at him. The device exploded a few feet away from where the Mahatma was standing but he escaped without injury.

The Indian government, understandably alarmed by the incident, urged Gandhi to accept police protection. Gandhi would not hear of it. 'If I am to die by the bullet of a madman,' he said, 'I must do so smiling. God must be in my heart and on my lips. And promise me one thing, should such a thing happen, you are not to shed one tear.'

On the morning of 30 January, 1948, Gandhi rose at 3.30am and started drafting a new constitution for the Congress. He spent the rest of the day working on the document and discussing it with colleagues. Time came for evening prayers and, supported by his niece Abha, he started across the lawn of Birla House.

As usual, there was a crowd to greet him. People rushed forward and jostled for position so that they could touch the Mahatma's feet as he passed. Then, a stranger pushed his way through the crowd. He shoved Abha aside, raised his hands together in a gesture of reverence, and then pulled out a pistol and fired three times.

The assassin was only a matter of two feet from his target. The first two bullets passed straight through Gandhi's frail body. The third lodged in his lung. Ghandi smiled: '*Hey Ram*,' he murmered and then collapsed. The assassin just dropped his

weapon and surrendered. He was, it transpired, Nathuram V. Godse, a young Hindu radical who at the time was working as an editor of a newspaper in Marathi.

It was soon obvious to the authorities that Godse had not acted alone and a massive Hindu conspiracy was uncovered. In all, eight men eventually stood trail for Gandhi's murder: Godse, Narayan Apte, Vishnu Ramrishkhama Karkare, Madan Lal, Gopel Vinayak Godse, Dattalraya Sadashiv Parchure, Shankar Kistayya and Kashmirilal Pahwa.

All the conspirators were found Guilty. Nathuram Godse and Narayan Apte were sentenced to death and hanged at Ambala Jail on 15 November, 1949. The other members of the conspiracy received long prison sentences.

MALCOLM X

Above: *Malcolm X, the one-time criminal who became a respected, articulate and persuasive leader. He formed his own black nationalist party.*

Malcolm X was a dynamic black activist who converted to Islam. An extremist when young, he later led a moderate organization. His changed ideals cost him his life.

Like Dr Martin Luther King, Malcolm X was committed to establishing a fairer American society, where the black man got an even break; and like Dr Martin Luther King, he died for his beliefs at the hands of an assassin. But there the similarity between the two men ends.

Malcolm Little was born into poverty in 1926 and, like so many young, poor blacks, drifted into a life of crime. He spent a total of ten years in various penal institutions, during which time he educated himself, converted to Islam, became politically aware and changed his name to Malcolm X.

In 1961, he joined Elijah Muhammad's Black Muslim movement and soon became their most powerful and effective spokesman. The Black Muslims were an elitist, separatist movement who were lobbying for an autonomous, segregated black nation within the United States, akin to the reservations of the native American Indians. Malcolm X soon became disenchanted with the aims and techniques of the movement. He accused Elijah Muhammad of collusion with the Ku-Klux-Klan in fostering racial unrest to enhance the 'need' for racial segregation.

Malcolm X knew that there must be a better way and, in March 1964, he broke away from the Black Muslims and formed his own rival group, known as the Organisation for Afro-American Unity. The avowed aim of the new group was to form a non-sectarian black nationalist party which would function within the established framework of American political life.

Malcolm X was a charismatic, articulate and persuasive leader, and many of the quarter-million Black Muslim members followed him when he left and rejected Muhammad. To say that there were hard feelings between the two groups would be a masterpiece of understatement.

GUNNED-DOWN IN MID-SPEECH

Malcolm had little doubt that his life was in danger, a fear which was clearly justified on 11 February, 1965, when his home in Queens was fire-bombed. The house had been purchased for him two years earlier by the Black Muslims and, while they denied having anything to do with the attack, there can be little doubt that it was their idea of a repossession order.

A week after the attack, Malcolm X was addressing a rally at the Audubon Ballroom in New York's Harlem. Before he had a chance to start his address, a man in the audience leapt to his feet and yelled, 'Get your hand out of my pocket!' Security guards descended on the heckler, but Malcolm shouted, 'Hold it! Hold it! Let's cool it, brothers.' The guards backed off and the heckler pushed his way towards the stage, produced a sawn-off shotgun from under his coat, aimed and fired it. Then two other men started shooting at Malcolm with

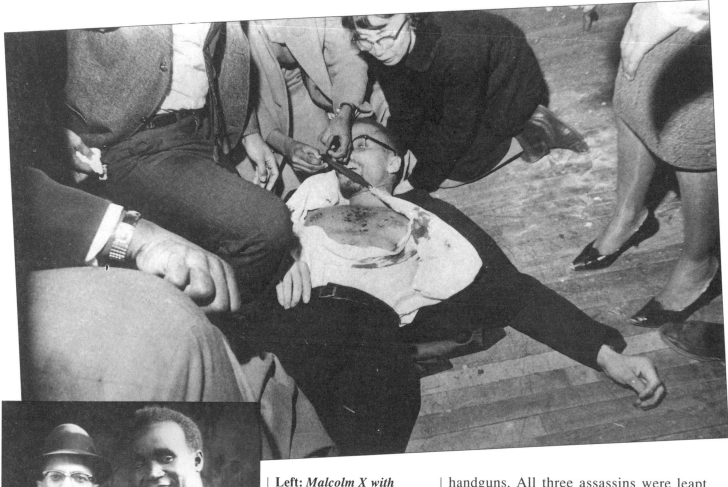

Below: *Malcom X on the floor of the Audubon Ballroom just seconds after he was shot. He was rushed to the nearby Columbia Medical Centre but was dead on arrival.*

Left: *Malcolm X with President Kaunda of Zambia. Malcolm X's crusade for black rights brought him into contact with many leaders of black and Islamic nations.*

'IF THIS WAS DONE BY A BLACK MUSLIM, THEN HE WAS DOING IT ON HIS OWN'.

handguns. All three assassins were leapt upon by Malcolm's security guards.

Within minutes of the shooting, Malcolm X was taken to the Vanderbilt Clinic of the Columbia Medical Centre, but he was declared dead on arrival.

One young black man, Talmage Hayer (real name Thomas Hagen) was arrested on the spot and eventually, police arrested two other young black men – Norman 3X (Norman Butler), and Thomas 15X (Thomas Johnson).

Elijah Muhammad strenuously denied that his Black Muslim organisation had either sanctioned or taken any part in the assassination. A spokesman said: 'If this was done by a Black Muslim, then he was doing it on his own.'

GEORGI MARKOV

Above: *Dissident and broadcaster, forty-nine-year-old Georgi Markov who was murdered in London by agents of the Bulgarian government in 1978.*

Bulgarian broadcaster, Georgi Markov was murdered at a London bus stop with the poisoned tip of an umbrella. This true story is stranger than any spy movie.

If most assassinations are bloody, uncouth affairs, the killing of Georgi Markov was executed with all the perverted subtlety of a James Bond novel.

Georgieu Ivanov Markov, a Bulgarian playwright, fled to England from his Communist homeland in 1969. He settled in London, married an English woman, had a family, and found a job with the BBC World Service.

Markov's broadcasts were beamed to Eastern Europe on a regular basis but, since they were not of an overtly political nature, he had no reason to think that his existence would incur any attention or wrath from the Communist authorities at home. He was wrong.

On Wednesday, 7 September, 1978, Markov was working the evening shift at the BBC studios at Bush House in London's Aldwych. He drove to work from his home in Clapham and, because of parking difficulties in the city, left his car on the South Bank. At 6.30pm, when traffic restrictions ended, he left his office to move his car nearer to Bush House.

A SMALL CUT TO THE BACK OF HIS THIGH

While walking past a bus queue in Aldwych, Markov was prodded in the leg with the tip of an umbrella. The man responsible apologised, hailed a taxi, and disappeared before Markov could challenge him. The man had a thick foreign accent.

Markov had sustained a small cut to the back of his thigh but thought little of it and returned to Bush House to finish his shift. He did some translations, read the 9.30 news and returned home to Clapham at about 10.30pm. He was scheduled to work again at 3am on the Friday morning.

The following day, however, Annabel Markov called Bush House to say that her husband was running a fever and asked for someone to cover his broadcast.

Markov's condition deteriorated rapidly and, at 10.30 on Friday morning, he was admitted to St James' Hospital, Balham. The doctors were baffled by his illness.

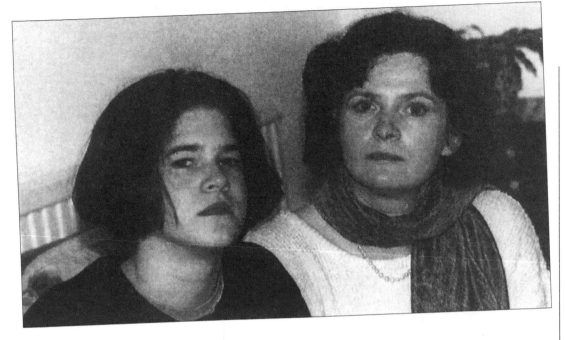

Left: *Mrs Annabel Markov with her daughter Sacha in 1991 when the Bulgarian government finally admitted responsibility for her husband's death.*

Markov told doctors that he thought that he had been deliberately poisoned by a Bulgarian secret agent, wielding an umbrella. Unlikely though this might have seemed to them, they alerted the police but Markov had lapsed into a coma before they could question him. He never regained consciousness before his death.

An immediate post mortem was carried out, but pathologist Dr Rufus Compton was unable to establish the cause of Markov's death. Tissue samples were sent to Scotland Yard's forensic laboratory at Lambeth but they were also baffled. More tissue was then sent to a top-secret chemical defence establishment at Porton Down in Wiltshire. The results of their findings, hardly surprisingly, were never revealed to the public.

By this time, Scotland Yard's anti-terrorist squad, led by Commander James Neville, and officers from MI5 were involved in the investigation. They questioned Markov's friends and associates and found that his life had been threatened six months earlier.

'I HAVE BEEN SENT HERE TO MURDER YOU'

His publisher, David Farrer, told the authorities that Markov had told him that a Bulgarian man had called on him unexpectedly. He had brought an introduction from a German friend of Markov's. The two men apparently had a few drinks together and then the visiting Bulgarian admitted to his host: 'I have been sent here to murder you. But I am not going to do it. I am just going to take the money and go.'

Farrer said that Markov had taken the threat seriously but had thought that it was unlikely that anyone would risk trying to kill him in London.

Mr Peter Fraenkel, head of the BBC's East European Service, confirmed Markov's fears for his safety. He said: 'Georgi was certainly a man worried about the possibility of being kidnapped. He mentioned threats on his life.'

The government was soon convinced that Markov's death-bed allegations were well-founded, and confronted the Bulgarian embassy in London. Predictably, diplomats denied any knowledge of the affair, describing suggestions that their secret police had been somehow involved in the death as 'absurd'.

Despite strenuous police efforts, the man with the umbrella was never found, and the Markov case was effectively closed. It was later discovered that Markov had not, in fact, been killed by some by-product of the chemical warfare industry but by ricin, a highly poisonous derivative of the bean of the castor oil plant, *Ricinus sanguineus*.

One person, however, was not prepared to let the matter rest. Mrs Annabel Markov, Georgi's widow, campaigned for the next fourteen years for a public inquiry into her husband's death. She never got one. It was only in 1991, after the collapse of Bulgaria's Communist regime, that her efforts were finally rewarded. Reluctantly and guardedly, the new regime admitted that their predecessors had indeed assassinated Georgi Markov. Efforts to bring the individual responsible to justice, however, have so far been strenuously resisted.

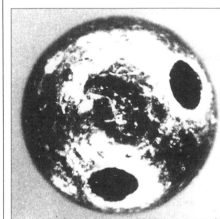

Above: *This tiny platinum ball, shot from a weapon disguised as an umbrella, contained the deadly poison that killed Markov.*

THE POST MORTEM WAS UNABLE TO ESTABLISH THE CAUSE OF DEATH AND SAMPLES WERE SENT TO SCOTLAND YARD'S FORENSIC LABORATORY.

ARCHDUKE FRANZ FERDINAND

Above: *The driver, seeing the flying object, stamped on the accelerator and the grenade bounced off the car.*

When a Balkan revolutionary assassinated Archduke Franz Ferdinand, he hoped to free Bosnia from the grip of the Austro-Hungarian empire. Little did he know that he was really firing the first two shots of the Great War.

Today, as the Balkan states systematically tear themselves apart, one looks back on the assassination of Archduke Franz Ferdinand with a sense of *deja vu*.

In 1914, the whole of Europe was politically unstable and nowhere was this condition more extreme than in the Balkans. Bosnia, annexed by the Austrian Habsburg empire, was demanding autonomy and neighbouring Serbia was fighting to cling to its tenuous independence in the face of Austria's expansionist ambitions.

For decades, Emperor Franz Joseph had managed to maintain a semblance of stability in his vast and disparate empire, largely by pitting rival regions against one another. By 1914, however, Franz Joseph was eighty-four years old, in poor health, and much of his power had been delegated to his heir, Archduke Franz Ferdinand. The Archduke acted as Inspector General of the empire's armed forces and it was in this capacity that he visited Sarajevo in Bosnia in June 1914.

Travelling with his wife, Countess Sophie Chotek, Franz Ferdinand was fully aware of the disdain with which his family's rule was viewed in the region, and must have realised the risks involved in his visit. There were rumours that an assassination was planned. These even reached Jovan Jovanovic, the Serbian Minister to Vienna. Jovanovic passed on the warning but the Archduke dismissed it out of hand and, on 24 June, he and Countess Sophie headed south to the Balkans.

THE YOUNG ASSASSINS

In Sarajevo, a group of young men bent on assassination was making final preparations. The leader of the group was a nineteen-year-old student, Gavrilo Princip, and with him were Nedeljko Cabrinov, and Trifko Grabez, both eighteen.

In the spring of 1914, these three had been at school together in Belgrade, when news reached them of the Archduke's proposed visit to Sarajevo. They had decided on a plan of assassination and to this end had joined *Smrt-ili-Zivot*, a Serbian secret society, headed by Colonel Dragutin Dimitrijevic, better known as Colonel Apis. The society had provided them with revolvers, ammunition, bombs, a modicum of training, and safe passage across the Serbian border into Bosnia. They had also introduced them to another cell of would-be assassins: Danilo Ilic, a twenty-six-year-old student-teacher, and Cvetko Popovic, an eighteen-year-old student.

Franz Ferdinand and his entourage spent the night of 27 June, 1914 at the Hotel Bosnia at Ilidze, some thirty miles south-west of Sarajevo. The Archduke was scheduled to attend a civic reception at the town hall, followed by a sight-seeing tour.

The royal motorcade reached the city shortly after 10am and drove along the Appel Quai, a long boulevard which ran alongside the River Miljacka. The pavements were crowded with onlookers, for the most part supportive, waving their Austrian flags. One onlooker, Nedeljko Cabrinovic, asked a policeman to point out the Archduke's car. When the policeman obliged, Cabrinovic promptly threw a grenade at the car. The driver, seeing the flying object, stamped on the accelerator, and the grenade bounced off the canvas canopy at the rear and exploded under the front wheels of the car behind.

As the Archduke continued on his way, Cabrinovic hurled himself into the River Miljacka but was hauled out and arrested.

The Archduke attended the civic reception, made light of the assassination attempt and insisted on maintaining his planned itinerary. After lunch at the town hall, the royal motorcade set off back down the Appel Quai. Half way down the Quai, however, the driver of the lead car became confused and turned right into Franz Joseph Street.

One of the Bosnian officials yelled at the driver to stop. The whole motorcade ground to a halt and started to reverse back towards the Appel Quai. The Archduke's car stopped outside Moritz Schiller's delicatessen and, by pure chance, Gavrilo Princip was standing in the doorway. After the earlier abortive attempt on the Archduke, Princip had abandoned his post on the Appel Quai but now he found himself standing feet away from his quarry. Princip pulled his Browning revolver and fired two shots. The first bullet hit the Countess Sophie; the second passed through the collar of the Archduke's uniform, severed the jugular vein and lodged in his spine. He lived just long enough to turn to his wife. 'Soferl, Soferl,' he begged 'don't die. Live for my children.' But both Sophie and the Archduke died within minutes.

ONE KILLER OR A CONSPIRACY?

Cabrinovic and Princip were interrogated. Both insisted they were anarchists acting alone but the authorities were convinced a conspiracy lay behind them.

Twenty-five men were eventually arrested and charged with conspiracy. They included Ilic, Grabez and Popovic. All except Ilic were teenagers.

After a week's deliberation, the judge passed sentence. Ilic, an adult, was condemned to death; Princip, Cabrinovic and Grabez received twenty years with hard labour; Popovic thirteen years, but they had in a way been condemned to a living death. Cabrinovic and Grabez died of tuberculosis and malnutrition within two years; Princip, who fired the fatal shots, lasted until 1918; only Popovic survived his prison term.

Above: *The bloodstained dress tunic worn by Archduke Franz Ferdinand of Austria when he was assassinated at Serajevo on 28 June 1914.*

THE FIRST BULLET HIT COUNTESS SOPHIE; THE SECOND SEVERED THE ARCHDUKE'S JUGULAR VEIN AND LODGED IN HIS SPINE.

IN 1914 THE WHOLE OF EUROPE WAS UNSTABLE AND NOWHERE WAS THIS CONDITION MORE EXTREME THAN IN THE BALKANS.

The Assassin

GAVRILO PRINCIP

Gavrilo Princip was born in 1895 to a peasant family in the Grahovo Valley, a remote and historically oppressed region on the Bosnia-Dalmatia border. He was an intelligent young man with jet-black hair, a sallow complexion and startling blue eyes. Princip was a capable student with a formidable knowledge of Serbo-Croat literature and of anarchist and revolutionary texts.

Like many young would-be revolutionaries, he was a serious-minded, earnest young man who spurned alcohol and girls. All his considerable energies were devoted to righting the wrongs in his beloved Bosnia. And the greatest wrong, according to Princip, was the rule of the Habsburg empire.

SPENCER PERCEVAL

Above: *The Right Honourable Spencer Perceval, Prime Minister. This portrait is a contemporary copy of a miniature that belonged to his widow.*

The murder of British Prime Minister Spencer Perceval was far more spectacular than his mediocre political career which was ended by a bullet fired in the Palace of Westminster itself.

Assassination is a very un-British activity and the position of Prime Minister is, compared with that of the President of the United States, relatively safe. There is only one dramatic exception to this – Spencer Perceval.

Perceval became Prime Minister in 1809, when the Duke of Portland resigned due to ill health. Perceval was a compromise candidate for the post. He was not an outstanding politician and his term in office might have been lost in obscurity if it had not been for his dramatic death at the hands of John Bellingham.

Bellingham was an entrepreneur who had extensive business interests in Russia. In 1811, during one of his trips to that country, he was arrested by the Tzarist police, imprisoned and consequently lost both his business and his personal fortune. On his release from prison, Bellingham complained vociferously about his treatment to the British Consul-General in St Petersburg but the official proved singularly unhelpful.

THE BRITISH REFUSED TO LISTEN

Bellingham returned to London an angry and embittered man. He deluged politicians, including Prime Minister Spencer Perceval, with letters demanding action against the Russian authorities. He got short shrift from the British politicians. They said, in essence, that everything that had happened was his own fault because he had not respected Russian laws.

On the afternoon of 11 May, 1812, Bellingham turned up at the House of Commons. He was standing in the Lobby when the Prime Minister arrived at the House from Downing Street. Spencer Perceval, a small thin man, hurried through the Lobby towards the Chamber and, as he did so, John Bellingham, dressed in a snuff coloured coat with metal buttons, stepped from behind a pillar, raised his pistol and fired at point-blank range, hitting the Prime Minister in the chest. Perceval was carried into the Speaker's chambers but he died before a doctor reached him.

By this time, a crowd had gathered in the Lobby. 'Where is the villain who fired?' someone demanded. Bellingham stepped forward and replied, 'I am that unfortunate man.' He was marched off to the cells of the Palace of Westminster.

Bellingham was an old Anglo-Irish settlers' name so conspiracy theories were bandied about but Bellingham himself put a stop to these. 'It's a private injury,' he said. 'I know what I have done. It was a denial of justice on the part of the government.'

It was clear that Bellingham was unbalanced and his trial at the Old Bailey served to define criminal responsibility in law.

In court, Sir James Mansfield successfully argued that the criterion for criminal responsibility in mental cases was this: did the prisoner have, at the time of committing the offense, a sufficient degree of intellectual capacity to distinguish between good and evil. Three decades later, this definition became part of English law when it was included in the McNaughton Rules on criminal sanity, but it did little to help John Bellingham. His plea of insanity was not accepted by the court and, on 18 May, 1812, a mere week after the assassination, he was hanged at Newgate Prison behind the Old Bailey.

Above left: *Bellingham raised his pistol and shot the Prime Minister at point-blank range. Perceval was dead before a doctor could reach him.*

Below: *A carving at the House of Commons showing Spencer Perceval's death .*

ADOLF HITLER

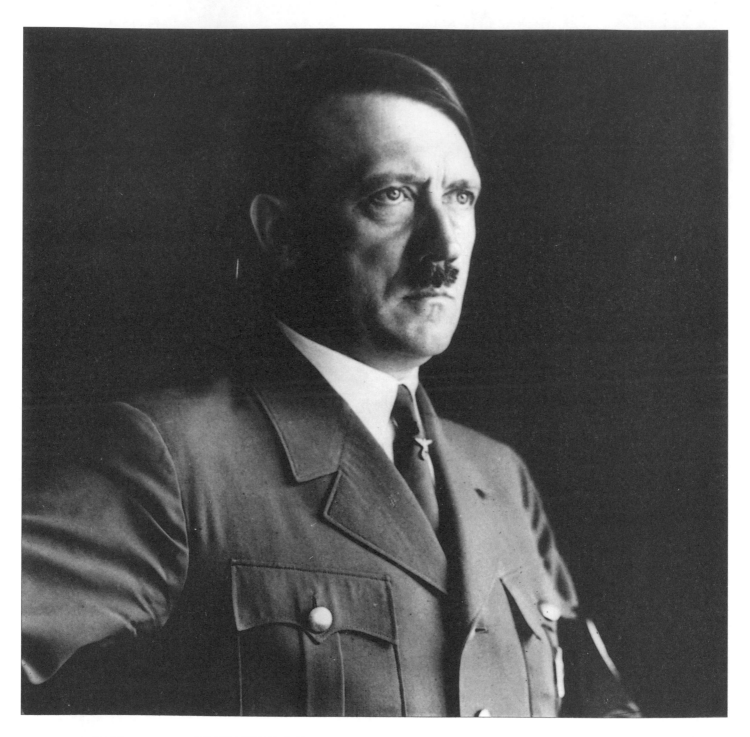

Above: *Adolf Hitler came to power as leader of the Nazi party in 1933 and soon showed his true colours as a brutal dictator.*

Perhaps the bravest German soldiers of the Second World War were those who tried to end Hitler's reign of terror. It was an evil twist of fate that Hitler survived the bomb which killed four of his henchmen.

By the summer of 1944, things were not going well for Hitler's Germany. His armies had suffered disastarous reversals on both the Russian and Italian fronts and on D-Day, 6 June, the Allies landed in France. To most right-minded Germans, there was only one possible outcome to the War, defeat.

There was no question of surrender while the Führer was still in power. Without surrender, Germany faced a catastrophic peace, and so Operation Valkyrie was born. The basic concept was that Hitler, Goering and Himmler should be eliminated and the Resistance should take over in Berlin.

This was not the first time there had been an assassination plot against Hitler by his own Generals – there had been at least six since 1938 – but this was better organised and on a much grander scale.

The concept of Operation Valkyrie dated back to 1943 when a hard-core of senior army officers cemented their allegiance of resistance to Hitler. They included General Ludwig Beck, General Friedrich Olbricht and General Henning von Tresckow. Several less senior officers were gradually introduced into this inner circle, including Colonel Graf von Stauffenberg, an aristocrat and war hero who had lost a hand and an eye while fighting with Rommel in the desert campaign.

A SLAB OF HIGH-EXPLOSIVE AND A TEN-MINUTE FUSE

Von Stauffenberg was the perfect choice to carry out the assassination. He was trusted by the German leader and he had access to regular meetings attended by Hitler and his feared inner advisors. And so the thirty-seven-year-old colonel was equipped with a briefcase containing a dirty shirt, a slab of high-explosive and a ten-minute fuse. His job was to introduce the case to one of the high-level meetings, set the fuse and make himself scarce before the bomb exploded.

THE IDEA WAS THAT HITLER, GOERING AND HIMMLER SHOULD BE ELIMINATED AND THE RESISTANCE SHOULD TAKE OVER BERLIN.

THE COLONEL'S BRIEFCASE CONTAINED A DIRTY SHIRT, A SLAB OF HIGH-EXPLOSIVE AND A TEN-MINUTE FUSE.

Below: *Hitler with (from left) Mussolini, General Jodl who was also injured in the blast, and General Keitel.*

strategic position, activated the fuse and then asked permission to leave for a few minutes. He had an important call coming in from Berlin. Two minutes after the colonel left the room, there was a deafening roar and the ceiling collapsed.

Stauffenberg, who witnessed the blast, was certain that no one could have escaped the building alive. It was a moment of jubilation that caused the soldier to lose his sense of caution. He did not check his impressions or stay to see the job was well done. One moment that cost him and his fellow officers dear. He told another of the

On 11 July, Stauffenberg attended a conference ordered by Hitler at Berchtesgaden. He had his briefcase ready but, finding neither Himmler nor Goering present, he decided to wait for a better opportunity to hit all Hitler's men.

Four days later, the colonel was summoned to Hitler's 'Wolf's Lair' at Rastenberg. Again he took his briefcase, but the meeting was cancelled at the last moment, and re-scheduled for 20 July the following week.

This time Stauffenberg was taking no chances. He armed his adjutant with a second bomb in case his own failed to detonate and, thus equipped, the two rebel officers boarded their Junkers aircraft for the flight to Rastenberg. From there they drove by army staff car, through the maze of checkpoints and mine-fields and electric fences to Hitler's most secret of secret hide-outs, a place that was affectionately known as the 'Wolf's Lair'.

Shortly before noon on that day, Stauffenberg was greeted at the 'Wolf's Lair' by the Chief of Combined Staff, Field Marshall Wilhelm Keitel. Stauffenberg had his briefcase tucked under his artificial arm and Keitel offered to carry it for him as they walked together through the compound to the wooden shed which was being used as a conference room. Stauffenberg refused the courtesy.

Once inside the conference room, Stauffenberg placed the briefcase in a

Top: *The conference room at Rastenberg after the explosion.*

Above: *Top Nazis Huber, Nebe, Himmler, Heydrich and Muller meet after the assassination attempt .*

conspirators, General Erich Fellgiebel, to telephone General Olbricht in Berlin and give him the news that the Führer was dead. When this was done, all communications at the Wolf's Lair were to be severed, lest surviving Nazis attempted to mount their own counter-coup.

Minutes after the explosion, Stauffenberg and his adjutant managed to persuade guards to allow them to drive out of the compound. En route to the airport, they dismantled the back-up bomb and threw it out of the car window. Shortly after one o'clock, the two officers boarded their Junkers and headed back for Berlin, looking forward to playing their part in a Germany without Nazis.

THE MIRACULOUS ESCAPE

In Berlin, Olbricht was already putting Operation Valkyrie into action. Signals were sent to all fronts that Nazi and SS leaders should be arrested; in Berlin, General Beck took over command at the war ministry; and in Paris, Nazi leaders were arrested in large numbers by their own officers.

But Adolf Hitler was not dead. Four men had indeed perished in the blast but the Führer had not been among them. He had staggered from the ruins of the conference room, shocked and bruised but very much alive and very angry.

As soon as news of Hitler's survival reached Berlin, the tables turned on the conspirators who had, by this time, shown their hand. The Führer's revenge was as swift as it was terrible.

That same evening, Stauffenberg and Olbricht were marched into the courtyard of the war ministry, stood against a wall

THAT SAME EVENING, STAUFFENGERG AND OLBRICHT WERE MARCHED INTO THE COURTYARD OF THE WAR MINISTRY AND SHOT.

ONE HUNDRED AND FIFTY ALLEGED CONSPIRATORS WERE EXECUTED, INCLUDING THIRTEEN GENERALS AND TWO AMBASSADORS.

Below: *General Hoose, one of the Operation Valkyrie conspirators, in court on trial for his part in the attempt on Hitler's life.*

and shot. General Beck was allowed to shoot himself.

Elsewhere, in Germany and in the occupied territories of Europe, officers were hounded down. and there were mass arrests. In all, one hundred and fifty alleged conspirators were executed as a result of the assassination attempt, including thirteen generals and two ambassadors. Fifteen other leading figures were given the option of suicide rather than go to trial. Among them was Germany's most popular and respected soldier, Field Marshall Erwin Rommel.

A 'BLOOD THIRSTY GUTTERSNIPE'

These brave men were proud Germans who gave their lives to save their nation from 'blood-thirsty guttersnipe' that was Adolf Hitler. He had taken their country - and, indeed, all Europe - into twelve years of unparelled barbarity, in which thirty million people lost their lives. He had instigated a revolting policy of genocide that was forever to stain his nation's honour.

Never satisfied that all the culprits had been apprehended, Hitler's witch-hunt continued for a long time after the assassination attempt. He never forgot nor forgave his officers for the attempt on his life and his search for the culprits had not ended when the Führer finally took his own life on 30 April, 1945.

CHARLES de GAULLE

The loss of Algeria caused patriotic anger, particularly among army officers who had fought to keep the country as part of France. They determined to kill the man whom they saw as a betrayer to those who had lived and died for Algeria.

In 1960, in wake of terrible bloodshed wreaked by the FLN (*Fronte Liberation Nationale*), France prepared to grant independence to Algeria after one hundred and thirty years of colonial rule.

It was a concession to violence which enraged many senior politicians and most of the military establishment. The French army, particularly the Foreign Legion, saw the decision as a personal affront.

This one divisive issue spawned two secret organisations. The military, inspired by Generals Challe, Zelle, Salan and Jouhaud, formed the *Organisation de l'Armee Secrete* (OAS); and the politicians, led by ex-Prime Minister Georges Bidault and ex-cabinet minster Jacques Soustelle, formed the Council of National Resistance (CNR). The two bodies were separate and autonomous but their aims were the same: the removal and, if necessary, the assassination of President Charles de Gaulle.

In the two years that followed Algerian independence, there were no fewer than six serious attempts on de Gaulle's life.

The first attempt came in May 1961 when a bomb exploded near the President's car while he was driving from Paris to his home at Colombey-les-deux-Eglises. In May the following year, while de Gaulle was touring central France, police uncovered a plot for a sniper to assassinate him as

he walked to mass – this plot may have inspired Frederick Forsyth's novel 'The Day of the Jackal'. A few months later, the President was driving through Pont-sur-Seine, Aube, when another explosion rocked his car. De Gaulle dismissed this attempt as a 'very bad joke'. His lack of humour was evident when the three perpetrators received prison sentences of twenty, fifteen and ten years respectively.

But the most serious, because the most determined, attempt against de Gaulle's life came on 22 August, 1962. Planned with military precision, it involved a hand-picked team of fifteen highly-trained assassins.

At 7.45pm, General de Gaulle, his wife and their son-in-law, Colonel Alain de Boisseau, left the Elysee Palace for the airport at Villacoublay. The presidential motorcade – two black Citroens and four police motorcyclists – headed for the Paris suburb of Petit Clamart.

There, the assassins waited.

Lt Col Jean-Marie Bastien-Thiry was standing nonchalantly by a bus stop, a rolled up copy of the newspaper *France-Soir* in his hand, ready to give the signal for the attack to start. His gunmen were concealed behind parked cars on either side of the avenue.

At 8pm, Bastien-Thiry saw the motorcade approaching. They were travelling at more than sixty miles per hour – much faster than he had anticipated. He waved his paper, and the first gunman fired at the tyres of the presidential car. The car skidded but the driver regained control and drove on. The departing vehicle was peppered with automatic gunfire as it sped away. But de Gaulle was guarded by men who were courageous and efficient.

Above: President de Gaulle in Algeria, where two organisations, angry at his decolonisation policy, determined to assassinate him.

Below: The French remember de Gaulle as the young leader whose wartime work helped in the liberation of Paris.

Inside the car, de Boisseau had pushed the President and his wife to the floor. Soon they were out of range. Nobody was hit.

Back at the scene of the attack, the *gendarmarie* arrived to find the assassins long gone. The officers did, however, discover a stolen car containing many weapons and ammunition.

ROUND-UP OF CONSPIRATORS

There was never any doubt who had been responsible for the attack. The OAS had made no secret of their intention to kill the president and, within forty-eight hours, nine of the fifteen men responsible for the attack had been arrested, including the ring-leader, Bastien-Thiry.

The French government decided the matter should be treated as treason. The nine men appeared at a specially convened court at Fort Vincennes; six others were tried *in absentia*. All fifteen were found guilty. Nine of the men received life sentences, six were condemned to death.

All the death sentences, save one, were later commuted to life imprisonment. That exception was Bastien-Thiry. As he faced the firing squad, the thirty-six-year-old Air Force Colonel was wearing his Knight's Cross of the Legion of Honour, a gallantry award which had been presented to him less than two years earlier by the President of France, Charles de Gaulle.

ANWAR SADAT

Above: *In his white admiral's uniform, President Sadat, a devout Moslem, kneels in prayer.*

He had shared the Nobel Prize for Peace with Menachem Begin but for President Sadat, the price of peace was death.

Anwar As-Sadat was one of that rare breed of politicians, a man of vision, commitment and courage.

Born in the Nile Delta of Egypt on Christmas Day, 1918, Sadat started his life as a professional soldier. After the Second World War, he adapted his military skills to those of the revolutionary fighter and was one of the main figures in the downfall of King Farouk in 1952.

Sadat occupied several key government positions in the Nassar regime and, on Nassar's death in 1973, succeeded him as President of Egypt.

It was obvious from the outset that he was bent on radical change. He dramatically reduced his country's dependence, both financial and military, on the Soviet Union and turned his sights more and more to the United States and the West. He did, however, carry on his predecessor's aggressive stance against the state of Israel and, in October 1973, succeeded in leading his troops across the Suez into Israeli-occupied territory.

CAMP DAVID – A FATAL ACCORD

Yet it was not long before Sadat came to realise the enormous cost, and ultimate futility, of the conflict and his thoughts turned to compromise. He was anxious to build domestic prosperity and he knew this could only be achieved if he could slash his country's massive defence costs by establishing some form of peaceful co-existence with the Israelis.

In November 1977, he did the unthinkable – and in the eyes of Muslim fundamentalists, the unforgiveable – when he accepted an invitation from Israeli Prime Minister, Menachem Begin, to address the the Israeli parliament, the Knesset. This was the first step towards an accord between Egypt and Israel which enraged extremists in both countries. The talks between the two leaders spanned eighteen months, and culminated in March 1979 when Sadat and Begin attended talks at Camp David, Maryland, which had been brokered by US President, Jimmy Carter. The talks were successful and ended with the signing of the Israeli-Egyptian peace treaty, the first such treaty between Israel and an Arab nation.

The two leaders were applauded for their efforts and were jointly awarded the Nobel Peace Prize for their contribution to ending the strife in the Middle East. At home, however, neither leader received total support. Sadat, in particular, was seen throughout the Arab world as a traitor.

Despite the new peace accord, Egypt maintained its tradition of holding an annual celebration to mark their 1973 crossing of the Suez canal and it was at this parade, on 6 October, 1981, that Sadat's enemies finally struck.

Sadat, statesman-like in his black uniform, accompanied by a host of other government officials, senior army officers and visiting dignitaries, sat on a reviewing platform accepting the salute from his military. All eyes were turned skywards watching a flypast by the Egyptian airforce, when an artillery truck drew level with the dais and appeared to stall. Suddenly, an army lieutenant jumped from the back of the lorry, turned, and threw a hand grenade at the president. The missile fell short of its target and exploded. Seconds later, five more blue-bereted soldiers jumped down from the vehicle and opened fire with Kalashnikov sub-machine guns, spraying the stand with bullets.

Sadat rose to his feet as the shooting started and then, hit by a volley of bullets, he collapsed in a pool of blood. Seven other Egyptian officials were killed in that opening salvo, and more than thirty were seriously injured.

The President's bodyguard immediately returned fire. The shooting lasted for at least five minutes and pandemonium reigned as one of the assassins, two soldiers and several innocent bystanders were mown down. The other five assassins including lieutenant, Khaled Ahmed al-Istambouly, were disarmed and arrested.

Anwar Sadat was rushed to a military hospital by helicopter. He was still clinging on to life when he arrived but he died minutes later on the operating table.

SADAT'S IDEAS LIVED ON

Lieutenant Istambouly and his four accomplices stood trial for the assassination,

along with twenty other Egyptians, all of whom were charged with conspiracy. Among the accused were Aboud el Zoumac, an Islamic fundamentalist, who is thought to have masterminded the attack, and Sheik Omar Abdel Rahman, a *mufti* (expert on Koranic law) from Asyud.

Immediately after the attack, a Libyan terrorist group based in Tripoli claimed overall responsibility for the attack and, while it is possible that they aided and abetted the assassins, it is generally considered that Sadat's murder was the work of an extremist Islamic group, the Muslim Brotherhood. Their aim was to reverse the trend of Sadat's government towards westernisation and his tacit acceptance of the state of Israel, by installing a new fundamentalist government with Sheik Rahman at its head.

The assassins' plot to kill the President succeeded but their plan to change the course of Egyptian politics failed. Anwar Sadat was succeeded by his erstwhile Vice President, Hosni Mubarak, a man who was as committed to progress as his mentor.

Above: President Sadat, US President Jimmy Carter and Israeli Prime Minister Menachem Begin preparing to sign the Egypt-Israeli peace treaty on the White House lawn.

Above: A wounded terrorist being dragged away after the killing of President Sadat.

ALDO MORO

Above: *Aldo Moro, leader of the Christian Democratic Party and former Prime Minister of Italy, was kidnapped on his way home from mass. Five members of Moro's staff were killed when his convoy was ambushed in busy Rome traffic.*

Aldo Moro was an honoured and respected politician, but fanatics picked him as a symbol of the system they hated and they killed him.

Shortly after 9am on Sunday, 16 March, 1978, Aldo Moro, former Prime Minister of Italy and leader of the country's Christian Democratic Party, was ambushed on his way home from church in Rome. Moro's car was forced off the road by another car bearing diplomatic licence plates and driven by a man dressed in an airline uniform. A second and third car then pulled up alongside and five men and one woman jumped out and opened fire with Russian-made automatic weapons. They killed Moro's driver, bodyguard and three security men who had been travelling in an escort car. Moro himself was clearly not an assassination target at this point because he was hauled unhurt from his car and whisked away in one of the attacker's vehicles. The attack had lasted no more than three minutes.

Shortly after midday, Signor Moro's kidnappers telephoned various press agencies and identified themselves. It surprised no one that the attack had been the handiwork of a unit of the Red Brigades, a left-wing terrorist organization which had been responsible for countless atrocities in Italy over the previous decade.

A massive search was quickly mounted in which the Italian police were assisted by army units, a West German anti-terrorist squad, and members of the counter-insurgency unit of the British army's SAS.

During the following weeks, as the search continued and scores of known left-wing activists were picked up for questioning, the Red Brigades issued a string of communiques outlining their conditions for Moro's safe release. These were for the most part a mixture of Marxist dogma and outright threats of violence. They said that Signor Moro was being interrogated 'to clarify the imperialist and anti-proletariat policies of the Christian Democrats and to pinpoint precisely the international structures and national affiliations of the imperialist counter-revolutionaries.'

The Italian government made it clear from the start that they were not prepared to negotiate with the kidnappers and this stance initially received all-party support.

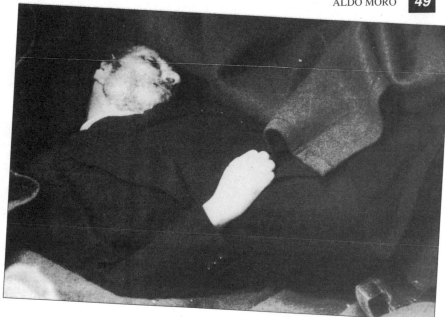

As the weeks passed, the Red Brigades' messages became increasingly menacing and, on 15 April, they issued a statement in which they said that Signor Moro had been tried and found guilty by a 'people's court' and had been sentenced to death. 'The interrogation of Aldo Moro has revealed the evil complicity of his regime,' the communique read. 'It has established the facts and names the real and hidden responsibilities in the bloodiest pages of the history of recent years.' These were stern, but mad, words from the fanatics

Three days later came another communique claiming that Moro had committed suicide and that his body would be found in Lake Duchessa in the Apennine mountains, north of Rome. A massive police search failed to find the body and two days later another communique was issued saying that Moro was, in fact, still alive but that he would be executed in forty-eight hours unless a number of Communist prisoners were released before that deadline.

Meanwhile, the police were closing in. On 18 April, they discovered a Red Brigade hideout on the outskirts of Rome, containing automatic weapons, ammunition, airline uniforms, diplomatic licence plates, and forged documents. They were certain that Moro had been held here until very recently.

The Italian government remained resolute, but other power groups including the Christian Democrats and Moro's family were urging them to find a compromise. A statement from the Christian Democratic Party on 3 May said that in exchange for Moro's safe release the government 'could certainly find some form of generosity and clemency in keeping with the ideals and rules of the constitution.'

The Red Brigades must have been aware of these developments but their patience or, perhaps their nerve, was exhausted. On 5 May, they issued a final communique. 'The battle begun on 16 March with the capture of Aldo Moro has now reached its conclusion ... We have nothing more to say to the Christian Democratic Party, the government or its allies ... The only language which the imperialist lackeys have shown they understand is the language of guns.'

On the same day as this last communique was issued, Moro's wife received a farewell letter from her husband, in which

he wrote with sad conviction, 'They are going to kill me in a little while.'

On 9 May, police had a call from the Red Brigades to say a car bomb had been placed outside the Christian Democratic Party headquarters in Rome. Police sent in a bomb disposal unit but, instead of explosives in the car, they found Aldo Moro. He had been shot eleven times in the head earlier that morning.

On 17 May, the police raided a printing shop in Rome where Red Brigade literature was being prepared. They arrested four men and one woman – Enrico Triaca, Teodoro Spadaccini, Giovanni Lugnini, Antonio Marini and Signora Gabriella Mariani. Other arrests followed and, by the time the trial was finally held in 1982, sixty-three people had been charged with complicity in planning and carrying out the kidnapping and murder of Signor Moro.

Above: *Dressed in a dark suit, Aldo Moro's body was found by police under a blanket in a car boot.*

Below: *In 1979, one year after the Red Brigades' murder of Aldo Moro, demostrators protest at continuing terrorist violence.*

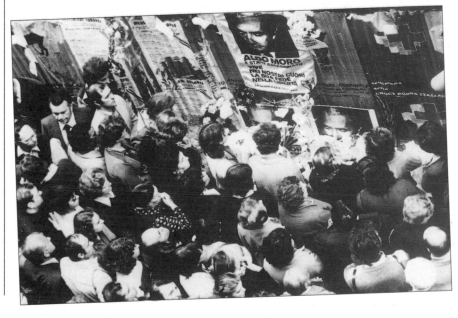

INDIRA GANDHI

Above: *Mrs Indira Gandhi, Prime Minister of India, was a woman of iron will who aroused both passionate loyalty and hatred among her people.*

Indira Gandhi was a feared leader but when she sent the army to sort out a religious dispute, two loyal Sikh bodyguards turned into fanatical assassins.

The Prime Minister of India never has an easy job. The vast sub-continent, with its enormous and diverse population, is rife with problems: poverty, sickness, corruption, ethnic and religious conflicts, and a gargantuan struggle to bring the country into the twentieth century of high technology

In 1984, all these problems faced Indira Gandhi, plus an increasingly militant Sikh population. Reports reached her that Sikh extremists were stockpiling arms and ammunition in the Sikh holy-of-holies, the Golden Temple at Amritsar. This was a doubly alarming situation. Not only did the build-up represent a genuine military threat but the location chosen for their headquarters was also a holy place for many Hindus. Using it as a garrison represented desecration of the worst possible kind. For both political and religious reasons, the extremists had to be confronted and driven out of the temple.

MILITARY SUCCESS

To this end, a military assault on the Golden Temple was mounted – Operation Bluestar. It was a success in strictly military terms because the extremists were dislodged but, as a public relations operation, it was a complete disaster. In his biography of Indira Gandhi, Inder Malhorta describes the Sikhs' outrage at the attack on their holy place: 'To most Sikhs,' he wrote 'the military action against the Golden Temple, during which casualties were heavy and the damage to the holy precincts extensive, was an intolerable desecration of what was, in their eyes, the most hallowed spot on earth. Sikh terrorists, feeding on the community's collective rage, had now vowed revenge. Not a day passed when they did not threaten the Prime Minister, her son and her grandchildren with death.'

The government and Mrs Gandhi herself were in no doubt that her life was in danger. It was suggested that the all-Sikh force, charged with her personal security, should be relieved of their duties but, through trust or arrogance, Mrs Gandhi refused.

On this force of Sikh bodyguards was a sub-inspector called Beant Singh. He had served the Prime Minister for eight years and had accompanied her on several overseas trips. Mrs Gandhi had often expressed her liking and respect for the young officer. What she did not know, however, was that Beant Singh had close links with a group of Sikh extremists, the very same ones who had vowed to avenge the desecration of the Golden Temple. With his unprecedented position of trust and his ready access to the Prime Minister, it is not surprising that Beant Singh was selected by his group as the perfect assassin of Indira Gandhi.

Beant Singh, despite his apparent liking and respect for the Prime Minister as a human being, accepted the assignment. He recruited an accomplice in Satwant Singh, a young police constable recently assigned to the Prime Minster's bodyguard from the Delhi police force.

Indira Gandhi knew that her life was in constant danger. On 30 October, 1984, the day before her assassination, she said: 'I am alive today. Tommorrow I may not be here.

THE GOVERNMENT AND MRS GANDHI WERE IN NO DOUBT THAT HER LIFE WAS IN DANGER.

MRS GANDHI WAS STILL SMILING WHEN BEANT SINGH FIRED HIS .38 THREE TIMES FROM POINT-BLANK RANGE.

Below: *Mrs Gandhi's funeral pyre was set alight in a traditional ceremony on 3 November.*

But every drop of blood in my body will be shed for India.' Brave words they were.

The following morning, 31 October, Mrs Gandhi had one of those rare engagements in her calendar that she anticipated with relish, a television interview with Peter Ustinov. She dressed carefully, selecting a saffron robe which she thought would show up well on television. She also discarded the bullet-proof vest that she normally wore in public because she felt it made her look bulky. It was a small but fatal vanity. Mrs Gandhi walked down the pathway which led from her private residence to her office at Akbar House. She was accompanied by a five-man guard, led by Dinesh Bhatt.

Beant Singh and Satwant Singh were posted some way along the path in the shade of an overhanging bougainvillaea. Mrs Gandhi smiled as she approached the two men. She was still smiling when Beant Singh fired his .38 three times from point-blank range. At the same time Satwant Singh opened fired with Sten gun, spraying Mrs Gandhi's frail body with bullets as it fell.

As the Prime Minister collapsed in a bloody heap, the two assassins were surrounded by members of the Indo-Tibetan Border Police. Beant Singh

Left and above: *Satwant Singh, aged twenty-four, and Kehar Sing, forty-seven, were hanged in New Dehli for their part in the murder of Mrs Indira Gandhi.*

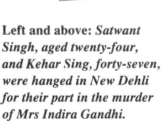

'TOMORROW I MAY NOT BE HERE. BUT EVERY DROP OF BLOOD IN MY BODY WILL BE SHED FOR INDIA.'

shouted at them: *'Maine jo karna tha, kar diya. Ab tum jo marji ai karo'* – 'I have done what I wanted to do. Now do as you please.' The police responded by shooting Beant Singh where he stood. Satwant Singh was also shot but he survived.

As Mrs Gandhi lay dying in the shade of the bouganvillea, Peter Ustinov and his camera crew waited. A production secretary recalled. 'We were ready for her and then it happened. I heard three single shots, and then there was a burst of automatic fire, as if the attackers were making sure of it. I didn't think she had a chance in hell.'

In India as a whole, the reaction to the Prime Minister's death was one of predictable outrage and fury. Much of the anger was directed at the Sikh community. There was widespread rioting and random attacks against Sikhs. The authorities and more moderate members of the Indian nation did their best to protect the innocent but, over the next few weeks, many Sikhs were killed in revenge. The government never learnt who had ordered the death of Indira Gandhi but few believed that the gunmen acted on their own accords.

RAJIV GANDHI

Who could have guessed that the girl offering Rajiv Gandhi a garland was a human bomb? The beautiful young assassin who murdered Indira's last remaining son died for her Tamil cause.

I n May 1991, Rajiv Gandhi was on the come-back trail. He had succeeded his mother, Indira Gandhi, as Prime Minister of India in 1984, shortly after she herself had died in a hail of assassins' bullets. Rajiv had held the post for five years before being ousted from power in 1989. Now he was running for office again and all the indications were that he would be re-elected.

It was a new Rajiv Gandhi that faced the electorate in 1991. In the past, he had been criticised for being arrogant, aloof and out of touch with the common man. He was desperate to shed this image and re-styled himself as the politician of the people; he mixed freely with the electorate, shaking their hands, embracing them, and listening to their concerns.

Shekhar Gupta of 'India Today' described Rajiv's new charismatic approach: 'For a deposed monarch, out to reclaim his kingdom, Rajiv Gandhi could not have asked for a better build-up. Shorn of security, shorn of the aloofness he exhibited in the past, displaying a so-far unknown panache for mixing with the people... People yearn to see him from close, shake his hand, even push him about...'.

IT WAS TO BE A SUICIDE MISSION. TWO YOUNG TAMIL WOMEN WERE RECRUITED TO CARRY OUT THE ASSASSINATION.

Below: *Rajiv Gandhi had re-vamped his public image for the election campaign but the new open approach carried great risks.*

Above: *The barely recognisable body of Rajiv Gandhi after the blast.*

Right: *Rajiv Gandhi's Italian-born wife, Sonia, and their daughter Priyanka (left) and son Rahul at prayer on the first anniversary of Rajiv's death.*

Far right: *Rajiv Gandhi's magnificent funeral procession.*

RUMBLINGS OF DISCONTENT

Gandhi's re-vamped public image certainly won him massive support, but it was not without its attendant risks. India in 1991 was a mess. Dogged by years of incompetent and corrupt government, the exchequer was all but bankrupt. Added to this were the ever-present regional and religious rivalries which had spawned a myriad of radical groups, most notably the Tamil extremist organisation LTTE, which was far from thrilled with the prospect of Rajiv Gandhi's return to power. It saw Rajiv's new relaxed campaigning technique as an opportunity to rid India of the Gandhi dynasty once and for all.

On the morning of 21 May, 1991, Rajiv Gandhi and his entourage drove in a motor-

cade from Madras airport to Sriperumbudur where he was due to address a political rally. The local police and Gandhi's own security men were extremely anxious about the proposed venue for the address, an open-air rostrum. There was nothing to stop the massive crowd from surrounding the dais, of standing within arm's length of the leader and it was, therefore, impossible to guarantee security. But the location was in keeping with Rajiv's new populist image and he over-ruled their objections.

The vulnerability of the venue had not escaped the attention of the LTTE. With plenty of advance warning of the rally, the group decided that it presented an ideal opportunity to assassinate the Prime-Minister-in-waiting. There was nothing subtle about their approach to the job in hand: it was to be a suicide mission. Two young Tamil women, Dhanu (alias Gayarti) and Shubha (alias Shalini), were recruited to carry out the assassination. They were equipped with belts of plastic high-explosives and became, in effect, human bombs.

A DEADLY GIFT

On the morning of 21 May, the assassins mixed freely with the vast crowd which had assembled at Sriperumbudur. As Rajiv Gandhi took the stage, the crowd pushed forward, trying to hang garlands round his

neck or merely to touch him. Dhanu fought her way to the front of the crowd, proffered a garland and bent at Rajiv's feet in an apparent gesture of reverence.

A split second later, one of the young women detonated her bomb, and there was a massive explosion. The blast ripped out Rajiv's intestines, tore open his chest and obliterated his features. Rajiv Gandhi, his assassin and several officials, including Superintendant Iqbal and Sub-Inspector Gupta, all died instantly, as did several bystanders in the crowd. Rajiv's body was flown home in an army transport plane and days later, he was cremated on a mound at Shakti Sthal, a few yards from the spot where his mother had been cremated. The Indian authorities were in no doubt that the LTTE was behind the assassination and they started to round up hundreds of supporters of the organization. Many of the leaders, however, had already fled abroad, while others took their own lives rather than face arrest. A communications expert in Coimbatore blew himself up with gelignite, but most took cyanide to end their lives. However, two of the men suspected of master-minding the operation, Sivarasan and Subha, were traced. The police mounted a raid on the house where the two men lived, but Sivarasan shot himself while Subdha bit into his vial of cyanide.

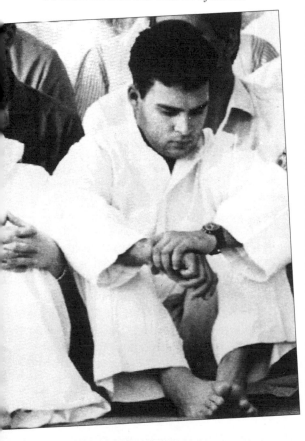

MARGARET THATCHER

The massive IRA bomb that exploded on the night of 12 October, 1984, was meant to change history. Its intended victims were Prime Minister Margaret Thatcher and her Cabinet.

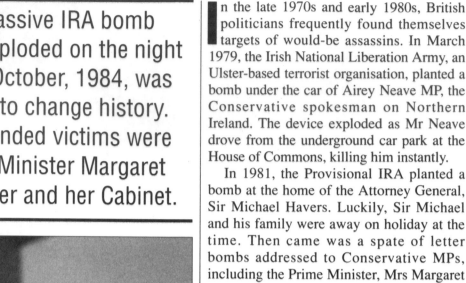

Below: *Margaret Thatcher in her prime as Britain's leader, pictured here at a less explosive Conservative Party Conference held in Bournemouth in 1986.*

In the late 1970s and early 1980s, British politicians frequently found themselves targets of would-be assassins. In March 1979, the Irish National Liberation Army, an Ulster-based terrorist organisation, planted a bomb under the car of Airey Neave MP, the Conservative spokesman on Northern Ireland. The device exploded as Mr Neave drove from the underground car park at the House of Commons, killing him instantly.

In 1981, the Provisional IRA planted a bomb at the home of the Attorney General, Sir Michael Havers. Luckily, Sir Michael and his family were away on holiday at the time. Then came was a spate of letter bombs addressed to Conservative MPs, including the Prime Minister, Mrs Margaret Thatcher. The following year an explosive package was delivered to Mr John Nott, the Secretary of State for Defence. These were all thought to have emanated from the Provisional IRA.

In 1983, it was the Scottish National Liberation Army's turn. They sent incendiary devices to Leon Brittan, the Home Secretary, Norman Tebbit, Secretary of State for Employment, and George Younger, the Secretary of State for Scotland. Only one of these devices actually exploded and no one was hurt.

Later in 1983, bombs were also sent to Michael Heseltine and Mr Tom King, both cabinet ministers at the time. Again these were safely defused.

A DEADLY PLOT

The most audacious and devastating attack against the British political establishment, however, came the following year, 1984. It was intended to wipe out the Prime Minister and her entire government and it almost succeeded. Not since the Gunpowder Plot of 5 November, 1605, has anything on that scale been attempted.

During the second week of October, 1984, the Conservative party was gathered in Brighton for its conference, the annual cheery orgy of self-congratulation masquerading as policy-making. Politicians and the party faithful were lodging in hotels scattered throughout the South Coast resort town. Mrs Thatcher and most of her ministers, however, were all staying at the Grand Hotel, a Victorian pile on the seafront which has often acted as temporary Conservative party headquarters.

At 2.45am, when most of the conference delegates were, as they believed, safe in their beds, there was a massive explosion. The blast literally tore the heart out of the stately Grand Hotel.

The fire brigade and armed police were on the scene in a matter of seconds. Their first concern was the Prime Minister herself. She had been in the Napoleon Suite at the time of the blast, working on a speech. Her bedroom was wrecked and all the windows had been blown out. She herself was unhurt. Escorted from her ruined suite, Mrs Thatcher seemed calm as she commented, 'You read about these things happening but you never believe it will happen to you'.

The adjoining suites, occupied by Sir Geoffrey Howe and Leon Brittan were totally wrecked but miraculously both men escaped uninjured.

Another miraculous escape was visited on Mr Harvey Thomas, the conference organiser and his heavily-pregnant wife. They were blown from the seventh floor to the fifth. 'I was sound asleep,' Thomas said later, 'and I felt a tremendous crashing. I thought it was an earthquake. Then I realised that you don't have earthquakes in Brighton, at least not during the Tory party conference. I almost lost consciousness but not quite. It was freezing cold and water from the hotel tanks was pouring all over us.'

Elsewhere in the hotel, dazed guests scrambled for safety, many through holes in what had once been the walls of their bedrooms, as the emergency services fought their way through fallen masonry in a desperate search for trapped survivors.

It was obvious from the start that there must have been serious casualties, probably fatalities. The rescue given most publicity was that of Norman Tebbit, the Employment Secretary, who had been in a bedroom on an upper floor of the hotel. Firemen found him trapped against a wall above the foyer. It took them four hours to free him before he could be carried on a stretcher, still conscious, through what remained of the hotel lobby and on to the Royal Sussex County Hospital. He

Left: *Firemen searching for survivors in the wreckage of the hotel.*

Below: *Mrs Thatcher with Norman Tebbit who was severely injured in the blast.*

eventually recovered but the bombers left his wife crippled for life.

Around 10am, a fireman said that they had uncovered two pairs of hands, one warm, one cold. As he and colleagues dug away the rubble with their bare hands, they found Mr John Wakeham, the Tory Chief Whip, and his wife Roberta. Mr Wakeham was alive, though seriously injured; his wife was dead.

As the day wore on, the list of casualties grew. Among the dead were Sir Anthony Berry, MP for Enfield and former assistant editor of the Sunday Times newspaper and Mr Eric Taylor, chairman of the North-west Conservative Association. In all, thirty-two people taken to the Royal Sussex Hospital.

No one was in any doubt about who had been responsible for the bombing and therefore it came as no surprise when the Provisional IRA made their announcement later that day. They claimed to have detonated a one-hundred-pound gelignite bomb 'against the British Cabinet and the Tory War-mongers'. The statement, signed P. O'Neill, continued: 'Thatcher will now realise that Britain cannot occupy our country, torture our prisoners and shoot our people in their own streets and get away with it. Today we have been unlucky.'

Less than seven hours after the explosion, Margaret Thatcher walked into the conference hall to a standing ovation. She told her audience: 'We have seen in this country the emergence of an organised revolutionary minority whose real aim is the destruction of democratic parliamentary government...we will never allow terrorism to destroy democracy.'

THE PRIME MINISTER HAD BEEN IN THE NAPOLEON SUITE AT THE TIME OF THE BLAST... HER BEDROOM WAS WRECKED AND ALL THE WINDOWS BLOWN OUT.

'I FELT A TREMENDOUS CRASHING. I THOUGHT IT WAS AN EARTHQUAKE. THEN I REALISED THAT YOU DON'T HAVE EARTHQUAKES IN BRIGHTON.'

THE BRITISH ROYAL FAMILY

British monarchs and their families have, until this age of terrorism, survived relatively unscathed but as the Mountbattens know, no one is immune from the terrible attentions of the IRA.

Below: *The Earl Mountbatten of Burma with the Queen and royal family on the Balcony of Buckingham Palace during the Queen's Silver Jubilee celebrations in 1977.*

Since 1483, when Edward V, the fourteen-year-old King of England, was smothered in the Tower of London, along with his younger brother Richard Plantagenet, no reigning British monarch has died at the hands of an assassin. For centuries this was due more to good luck than good management; and in recent times it is probably due to the fact that the monarchy has ceased to exercise any real political power and, therefore, no longer represents a legitimate target for those wishing to change the status quo.

This is not to say that there have not been attempts on the lives of the royal family but most of these have been carried out by cranks, crackpots and malcontents, rather by than political groups.

Queen Victoria, for example, was attacked or threatened with physical violence on no less than eight occasions during her reign. In 1900, King Edward VII, then Prince of Wales, was attacked while on a trip to Brussels; in 1936, King Edward VIII was shot at by a man with a revolver near Wellington Arch; and in 1939, the Duchess of Kent was the target of a sawn-

off shotgun while leaving her home in Belgrave Square. None of them was injured.

In the past twenty years there have been a handful of isolated attempts against the Queen and her immediate family. The most serious and potentially lethal attack occurred in London on 20 March, 1974, and was aimed at Princess Anne.

Shortly after 8pm, the Princess and Captain Mark Phillips, then her husband, were returning to Buckingham Palace after attending a private showing of a documentary film made by the charity 'Riding for the Disabled' of which the Princess is patron. The couple's chauffeur-driven limousine was travelling along the Mall when a car slewed in front of it, forcing the royal car to a halt.

The driver of the offending vehicle leapt out of his car and fired a volley of shots at the royal limousine. One of the bullets passed between the Princess and her husband, missing both of them by inches. However, the Princess' chauffeur, Alexander Callender, and her personal detective, Inspector James Beaton, were both hit.

A uniformed constable, Michael Hills, on foot-patrol near St James' Palace, heard the shots and ran to the scene. He was shot at and Brian McConnell, a journalist travel-

ling in a cab behind the royal limousine, leapt out of his taxi and made to tackle the would-be assassin but he was shot in the chest. The gunman then fled into the confines of St James' Park.

Soon there were police everywhere, and it was only a matter of minutes before they had cornered and arrested the fugitive. He was taken to Cannon Row Police Station, where he was identified as Ian Ball, an unemployed man of twenty-six.

Police Constable Hills, aged twenty-two, who had a bullet lodged in his liver, and Mr McConnell, forty-six, with a severe chest wound, were both rushed to St George's Hospital, Hyde Park, where both underwent emergency surgery. Alexander Callender, fifty-five, and Detective Inspector Beaton, twenty-six, were taken to Westminster Hospital where their condition was later described as 'serious but satisfactory'.

MESSAGE OF CONCERN

Back in the safety of Buckingham Palace, Princess Anne and Captain Phillips were shaken but unhurt. The Princess made a brief statement: 'We are very thankful to be in one piece. We are deeply concerned about those who got injured, including our chauffeur, Mr Callender, and Inspector Beaton.' Her words had the dignity of a brave woman.

Above: *Prince Charles with Lord Mountbatten at the ceremony to mark the opening of the Earl's home, Broadlands, to the public two months before he was murdered. The Prince and the Earl had always been close and Charles valued the advice of the man he called 'Uncle Dickie'.*

ONE OF THE BULLETS PASSED BETWEEN PRINCESS ANNE AND HER HUSBAND, MISSING BOTH OF THEM BY INCHES.

ON 5 MAY, 1981, A LETTER BOMB ADDRESSED TO THE PRINCE OF WALES, WAS INTERCEPTED AT THE WEST LONDON SORTING OFFICE.

Ian Ball appeared at Bow Street Magistrates Court on the morning of 21 March. There he was charged with the attempted murder of Inspector James Beaton. It was obvious to the court that he was not of sound mind.

The issue was further confused when, the following morning, a letter arrived at Buckingham Palace. Postmarked 21 March, it stated: 'On behalf of the Marxist-Leninist Activist Revolutionary Movement... I would like to take credit for the recent attack on Mr and Mrs M. Phillips... This is

SHOTS RANG OUT AND BURMESE REARED, NEARLY UNSEATING THE QUEEN WHO, ALTHOUGH CLEARLY SHOCKED, CALMED HER MARE AND RODE ON.

EARL MOUNTBATTEN WAS KILLED INSTANTLY BY THE EXPLOSION, AS WERE HIS GRANDSON AND THE BOATMAN.

Left: *Earl Mountbatten of Burma had a long and distinguished career. He will perhaps be best remembered for being the last Viceroy to India.*

Below: *The Mountbatten family on holiday in Ireland in happier times aboard the boat that was later blown up killing the Earl.*

Far right: *Lord Mountbatten's funeral in Westminster Cathedral.*

only the beginning of our campaign, you can expect much more in the coming months... Long Live the Revolution.'

The natural assumption was that Ian Ball had been the instrument of some left-wing extremist group but this was later discounted. The group was apparently trying to gain some perverse kudos from the actions of a madman. Since the attempt on the life of Princess Anne, there have been two other abortive attempts against the Royal family. The first came on 5 May, 1981, when a letter bomb addressed to Prince Charles, the Prince of Wales, was intercepted at the West London sorting office.

Anti-terrorist officers defused the device and described it as 'viable', designed to maim rather than kill. Scotland Yard refused to comment further on the exact nature of the bomb, save that it was contained in a Jiffy bag, similar to those addressed to Mrs Jill Knight, the Conservative MP for Birmingham, Edgbaston, and Mr Barry Porter, Conservative MP for Ellesmere Port.

WITH INTENT TO ALARM

Both these earlier attacks had been the work of the IRA and, since the package addressed to the Prince had been posted in central London within hours of the death of IRA hunger-striker Bobby Sands, it was widely assumed that it originated from the same source.

The press office at Buckingham Palace was quick to praise Steven Mason, aged eighteen, and Russell Davis, nineteen, the postal workers who spotted the package. A spokesman for the Prince said: 'We are very grateful that they were so observant and spotted it so quickly. To my knowledge this is the first time anything like this has been sent to the Royal Family.'

Two months after the letter-bomb affair, the Queen herself came under attack. On 13 June, she was attending the Trooping the Colour. Huge crowds gathered along the Mall as Her Majesty rode past on her black mare, Burmese.

Suddenly six shots rang out, Burmese reared and nearly unseated her rider. The Queen, clearly shocked, calmed the mare and then continued on her way to the parade ground for the ceremony. She showed the same calm her daughter had.

Police and members of the public grabbed the assailant and disarmed him. His weapon was a two-inch Jackal Python starting pistol and it was obvious to officers that the shots he had fired were actually blanks. This by no means mitigated the offence, however, and that same afternoon, Marcus Sarjeant, an unemployed youth from Folkestone, appeared in court and was charged under the Treason Act 1842 of wilfully discharging a gun near the person of the Queen with intent to alarm her.

The most tragic event to befall the Royal family this century, however, came on 27 August, 1979.

Earl Mountbatten of Burma, the Queen's cousin, was on holiday in the quiet fishing village of Mullaghmore, County Sligo. For more than thirty years the Earl had been in the habit of spending his summer holidays at his home in the west of Ireland, and he was well known and well liked there.

On that fateful morning, the Earl and members of his family drove from their home, Classiebawn Castle, to the harbour where their boat, Shadow V, was moored.

Shadow V had barely cleared the harbour mouth when she exploded. An eyewitness described the scene: 'There was a roaring explosion which blew it [the boat] high into the air, smashing it into tiny pieces of wood. Fishing lines, anoraks, plimsolls and bodies were floating in the water.'

Mountbatten was killed instantly by the explosion, as were his grandson, Nicholas, aged fourteen, and Paul Maxwell, a seventeen-year-old boatman. Mountbatten's daughter, Lady Brabourne, and her son Timothy were terribly injured, and her eighty-two-year-old mother-in-law, the Dowager Lady Brabourne, died the following day in hospital.

THE DEATH OF A FRIEND

It came as little surprise when that evening the IRA issued a statement, taking credit for the atrocity. Their justification for killing the old man and his family was, to say the least, vague.

The profound disgust at these callous murders was expressed by a Mullaghmore fisherman: 'He was our friend, not our enemy. He came back here every year. He trusted us. Everyone liked him here and will mourn him greatly.'

BUGSY SIEGEL

Bugsy Siegel's 'company', Murder Inc, was responsible for more than five hundred killings but he is best remembered now as the man who turned the sleepy town of Las Vegas into a gambler's paradise.

Above: *Virginia Hill, Bugsy Siegel's glamorous mistress.*

Right: *Bugsy's twinkling dark eyes and crooked smile concealed a heartless killer.*

IN HOLLYWOOD, BUGSY WAS HOBBNOBBING WITH THE LIKES OF CLARK GABLE, GARY COOPER AND JEAN HARLOW.

Benjamin 'Bugsy' Siegel was the assassin's assassin. More vicious even than Capone, Siegel will probably be best remembered as the man who 'invented' Las Vegas.

Born in New York's Hell's Kitchen, Siegel started off life as just another gangland punk, a numbers runner, thief and breaker-of-legs for local loan sharks. At eighteen, however, he got his start in organised crime as a heroin pusher with Charles 'Lucky' Luciano, and then moved on to Meyer Lansky's bootlegging operation.

Before long, the three young gangsters had formed a syndicate which would last for more than twenty years. Each had his own talent to offer. Luciano was the organiser and fixer; Lansky was the financial wizard; and Siegel was the assassin.

Beneath his charm and dashing good looks, Bugsy was a cold killer, a man who actively enjoyed his job. Unlike Capone, Siegel did not just kill to further his own ends or those of his partners. He offered an assassination service to all-comers, a service which he dubbed Murder Incorporated. In a little under ten years, Bugsy Siegel and Murder Inc is thought to have carried out more than five hundred gangland killings.

In the early days, Siegel restricted his assassinations to gangland figures and petty officials who refused to co-operate with the mob but, in 1936, he became more ambitious and tried to assassinate New York Public Prosecutor, Thomas Dewey. The attempt was unsuccessful and, to avoid investigation, Bugsy moved west to California.

THE DISAPPEARING WITNESS

In Hollywood Bugsy met up with his boyhood friend, actor George Raft, and soon he was accepted by the cream of local society, hobnobbing with the likes of Clark Gable, Gary Cooper and Jean Harlow. He even went so far as having a screen test. Those who saw this particular footage claim that Siegel brought a new meaning to the word 'wooden'.

Despite his glitzy new lifestyle, Siegel was up to his neck in the local rackets – prostitution, extortion and, best of all, illegal gambling. And the killing had not stopped either.

In November 1938, Harry 'Big Greenie' Greenberg, a life-long friend and ex-triggerman for Murder Inc, turned up on Siegel's doorstep. Harry was in trouble. He had recently turned informer and one of the victims of his evidence was none other than Charles 'Lucky' Luciano, Siegel's partner.

Greenberg must have been desperate and very foolish to turn to Bugsy for help. And his stupidity was promptly rewarded by Siegel shooting him. A year later Siegel was indicted for Greenberg's murder but a key witness conveniently disappeared and the case never went to trial.

On his release from jail, Siegel discovered Las Vegas, a broken down town with a population of less than five thousand in the Nevada desert. Nevada was the only state in the Union which allowed gambling. It was a chance for him to make a fortune and go legitimate in one bold and daring move.

Siegel bought a large tract of land outside Las Vegas and began his plan to build the Flamingo, the biggest, gaudiest hotel-casino complex in the world.

CASINO WITH A LOSING STREAK

The initial cost of the project was $1 million, a not inconsiderable sum in 1943 but Siegel managed to persuade Luciano, Lansky and a host of other gangsters to invest in the project but their million didn't go far as the cost of building the Flamingo soon sky-rocketed. There was a war on and materials had to be bought on the black market; building conditions in the desert were dreadful; there was wholesale theft of money and materials at every level; and Siegel himself kept changing the design and details of the building.

The net result was that, when the hotel finally opened on Boxing Day 1946, it had cost $6 million. To get this money, Siegel had double-crossed some of the most dangerous men in the world. And the Flamingo turned out to be that rarest of rare birds, a casino that lost money.

Bugsy Siegel sat in his Beverly Hills home on the evening of 20 June, 1947. Without warning, six shots were fired through the window. The professional assassin, Bugsy 'Blue Eyes' Siegel, was himself assassinated.

No one was ever indicted for the killing of Benjamin Siegel, perhaps because nobody in authority really cared. To their way of thinking, society was was well rid of him.

IN UNDER TEN YEARS, BUGSY SIEGEL AND MURDER INC IS THOUGHT TO HAVE CARRIED OUT MORE THAN FIVE HUNDRED GANGLAND MURDERS.

SIEGEL WILL PROBABLY BE BEST REMEMBERED AS THE MANY WHO 'INVENTED' LAS VEGAS.

Below: *A violent end for a violent man. Bugsy Siegel was gunned down in his Beverly Hills mansion by an unknown assassin.*

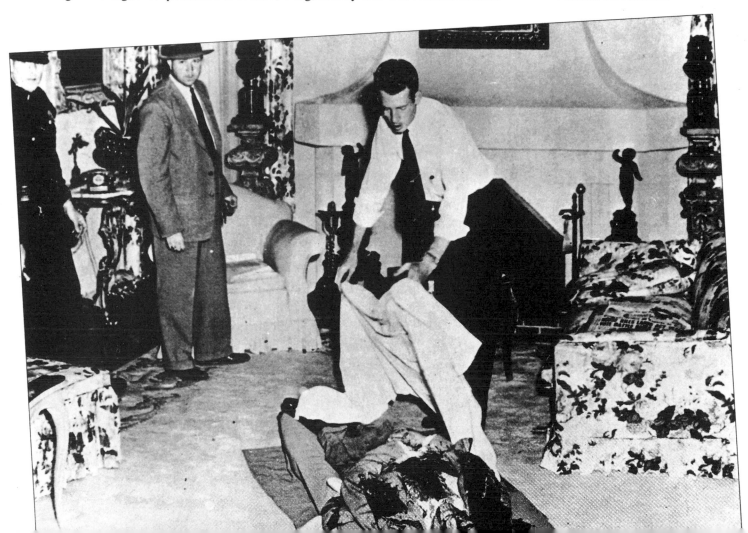

THE ST VALENTINE'S DAY MASSACRE

Above: *Al Capone, caught at last, being led from the Chicago Federal Court after being sentenced to prison for tax evasion. Capone died of syphilis in prison.*

Al Capone's gangster-ridden Chicago has been the setting for hundreds of slick films but there was nothing glamorous about the brutal carnage of the St Valentine's Day massacre.

In the world of organised crime, assassination is part and parcel of everyday life. It is a political and disciplinary expedient which replaces elections, impeachments and demotions; it solves territorial disputes and power struggles; and is an absolute sanction which renders judge and jury redundant, for in gangland there is only the executioner.

The name of Al Capone is synonymous with the establishment of the rule of violence in the American underworld.

Born in Brooklyn in 1899 to Italian parents, Alphonse Capone had killed at least two people before he reached his sixteenth birthday, and by twenty-one he was a lieutenant in New York's notorious Five Points Gang.

In 1919, he was recruited by fellow gangster John Torrio, who controlled the rackets in Chicago's South Side. The North Side of the city, at that time was controlled by another gang, headed by Dion O'Banion, Bugs Moran and Hymie Weiss; and the West Side which was controlled by six Sicilian brothers by the name of Genna. Each of the three groups was looking to expand, but everyone knew that wasn't possible without a war. If there was to be a war, you needed a top assassin and to Torrio's way of thinking, assassins didn't come any better than Al Capone.

Capone's killing career in Chicago started in a modest enough way with the eradication of a small-time crook called Joe Howard. Howard had been stupid enough to hijack two of Torrio's booze trucks. The following evening, he was having a drink in his neighbourhood bar, when Capone walked in with a broad grin on his face.

GANG WARS IN CHICAGO

'Hi, Al,' Joe said, sticking out his hand. Capone responded by shooting him six times. There were at least a dozen witnesses but none of them saw a thing. Or rather, none dared to see.

Capone came to Chicago spoiling for a fight but four years passed before the fragile peace between the three Chicago syndicates finally broke. In late October 1924, the O'Banion gang hijacked some of the Genna brothers' whiskey. The Gennas swore revenge. It was a situation on which Capone was quick to capitalise.

On 4 November, O'Banion was sitting in the back room of his florist shop when he heard customers enter the shop. He went out to confront three people.

Six shots rang out, the last of which exploded in O'Banion's face. By the time the emergency services reached the scene, he was already dead.

In light of the recent feud, the Genna brothers were the most obvious suspects in the assassination but the police were more interested to know Capone's whereabouts at the time of the killing. Naturally he had an unshakeable alibi.

Hymie Weiss, O'Banion's erstwhile partner was equally convinced that Capone had been responsible for his friend's death and promised revenge. Weiss was something of an assassin in his own right. He devised his own method of killing, a technique adopted later by many of his colleagues, in which the potential victim

was seated in the front of the car, with the killer sitting directly behind him. He was then shot in the back of the head. And so the expression 'being taken for a ride' came into modern parlance

ONLY ROOM FOR ONE AT THE TOP

A matter of days after O'Banion's murder, Capone's car was straffed with machine-gun fire but he escaped unhurt. Two weeks later, John Torrio was gunned down by another O'Banion man, Bugs Moran.

Torrio recovered from his injuries but he'd had enough and effectively retired, leaving his Chicago empire in the hands of Capone. Now things changed. Torrio had always acted as a brake on some of Al's excesses but now Al was the boss, and from this time on assassination reigned supreme.

The first to be eliminated were the Genna brothers. Three of them were gunned down within the space of six weeks. The three surviving brothers took their money and beat a hasty retreat to Sicily.

On 11 October 1926, Hymie Weiss was machine-gunned to death on the steps of Chicago's Holy Name Cathedral. His death left only Bugs Moran standing between Capone and his determined ambition to control all Chicago.

The two gangsters met and negotiated territorial boundaries. The peace held for over a year but Capone was merely biding his time, choosing his moment to eliminate his last competitor.

By 1928, Capone was spending much time away from Chicago, usually at his magnificent new home in Palm Beach,

Above: *Al Capone in court in Chicago. If he had not been imprisoned for tax evasion, he surely would have died a violent death.*

Left: *'Machine gun' Jack McGurn who was believed to have taken the leading role in the St Valentine's Day Massacre, although he had an alibi. No one was ever charged with the murders.*

HYMIE WEISS DEVISED HIS OWN METHOD OF KILLING WHICH GAVE US THE EXPRESSION 'BEING TAKEN FOR A RIDE'.

WHEN SHE PUSHED OPEN THE DOOR, SHE SAW SEVEN MEN WERE SPRAWLED ON THE FLOOR, LYING IN A LAKE OF THEIR OWN BLOOD.

THE CHICAGO DAILY NEWS **BLUE STREAK**

THREE CENTS

THURSDAY, FEBRUARY 14, 1929.—FORTY-EIGHT PAGES. □ FINAL EDITION

54TH YEAR—39.

MASSACRE 7 OF MORAN GANG

HAFFA CHANGES HIS MIND; WILL FIGHT PRISON

Owes It to Friends, He Says; Makes Bond, Prepares Appeal.

MAY STAY IN COUNCIL

TWO OF VICTIMS AND SCENE OF LATEST GANGSTER OUTBREAK

KILLING SCENE TOO GRUESOME FOR ONLOOKERS

View of Carnage Proves a Strain on Their Nerves.

IS LIKE A SHAMBLES

VICTIMS ARE LINED AGAINST WALL; ONE VOLLEY KILLS ALL

Assassins Pose as Policemen; Flee in "Squad Car" After Fusillade; Capone Revenge for Murder of Lombardo, Officers Believe.

Seven Moran-O'Banion gangsters were lined up against the wall of a beer-distributing point at 2122 North Clark street at 10.30 o'clock today. Four men, two of them in police uniforms, stood before them, armed with machine guns and sawed-off shot guns. The leader of the execution squad barked an order and the seven fell, six dying at once, the seventh three hours later.

The dead, as identified by the police, were:

GUSENBERG, PETER, notorious gunman for the O'Banion-Weiss-Drucci-Moran mob.

GUSENBERG, FRANK, brother of Peter.

WEINSHANK, AL, north side "alky" peddler.

MAY, JOHN, 1249 West Madison street, a $50-a-week mechanic.

CLARK, JOHN, brother-in-law of George ("Bugs") Moran, leader of the gang.

DAVIS, ARTHUR, west side racketeer.

FOSTER, FRANK, hoodlum.

STAYS GIVEN 2 OF 3 KILLERS DUE TO DIE TONIGHT

Shanks Faces the Electric Chair Alone; Seeks Sanity Test.

1929 FLAPPERS JUST EAT UP VALENTINES

Modern Greetings Take Line of Sandwich; Swains Spend $250,000 Here.

DECIDE TO CUT COOK ADRIFT IN TAX TANGLE

Solons to Rush Laws to Avert Downstate Tieup;

War to Finish Russell's Plan

Above: *The way the St Valentine's Day Massacre was reported in the city where it happened.*

CAPONE'S RULE IN CHICAGO WENT VIRTUALLY UNCHALLENGED, EVEN BY THE AUTHORITIES, MOST OF WHOM WERE ON HIS PAYROLL.

Florida. Moran took advantage of this situation by regularly hijacking Capone liquor shipments. Capone might have been a thousand miles away but he knew exactly what was going on. Over the telephone he instructed his most trusted aid, Jake Guzik, to 'take care' of Bugs Moran. The time and method of the assassination were discussed in minute detail and, on 14 February 1929, Capone made an appointment with a Miami city official to discuss a planning permit. He had good or rather, wicked, reason for arranging a water-tight alibi for himself that particular St Valentine's Day.

At 10.30 on 14 February, as Capone sat with his official in Palm Beach, six of Bugs Moran's men were in a garage in Chicago's North Side, waiting for a truckload of hijacked Canadian whiskey. They were Peter and Frank Gusenberg, Moran's top assassins; James Clark, a Sioux Indian and Moran's brother-in-law; Al Weinshank, his accountant; Adam Heyer, his business

manager; and Johnny May, a safe-cracker. There was also a seventh man in the North Clark Street garage, an optician called Dr Richard Schwimmer, whose presence has never been satisfactorily explained. Moran himself should have been at the garage, but had been delayed.

Shortly after 10.30, Mrs Max Landesman of 2124 North Clark Street heard shots from the adjoining garage. She looked out of her window and saw a man leave and get into a large touring car. From the flat below Mrs Landesman's, Miss Josephine Morin saw two men, apparently under arrest, come out of the garage with their hands up. They were followed by two uniformed police officers. The four men got into a black Cadillac and drove off.

In a fit of ill-advised curiosity, Mrs Landesman hurried over to the garage, pushed open the door and was greeted with a scene of terrible carnage. Seven men were sprawled on the floor, lying in a lake of their own blood. Mrs Landesman ran back to her apartment and telephoned the police.

Bugs Moran himself arrived at the garage fifteen minutes later but, seeing police cars everywhere, presumed there had been a raid and beat a hasty retreat. Later, when he heard about the massacre, he is reported to have said: 'Only Al Capone kills like that!'

The police, too, assumed Capone was responsible. They quickly learned that the man himself was in Florida at the time and contented themselves with picking up one of his top assassins – 'Machine Gun' Jack McGurn. McGurn had an alibi and the police eventually had to release him without charge. In the end, no one was ever charged in connection with the St Valentine's Day massacre. Few dared to confront the murdering gangsters. But no one, including the police, was in any doubt that the mass assassination had been carried out on the orders of Al Capone.

In reality, the assassination had been aimed specifically at Bugs Moran who had escaped but the overall effect was very much the same – Moran was a spent force in the criminal world of Chicago. He had been beaten by a truly ruthless opponent

END OF THE REIGN OF TERROR

Capone returned to the city, convinced that his authority in the city was now absolute but he found that there were still pretenders to his throne, two of his own lieutenants, John Scalise and Albert Anselmi. He invited the two lieutenants to a luncheon in Hammond, Indiana. Capone was half way through the meal when he rounded on the two conspirators: 'I understand you want my job,' he said, 'Well here it is!' and clubbed them to death with a baseball bat.

From this time, Capone's rule in Chicago went virtually unchallenged, even by the authorities whom he bribed anyway. However, Capone's reign of terror was destined to last less than two years. It is ironic that this man of violence was not toppled from power by other, more violent, men but by clerks from the Inland Revenue Service; and his life did not end quickly in a hail of assassin's bullets, but slowly, as tertiary syphilis decayed his brain.

Below: *'A' marks the garage in which seven of Bugs Moran's gang were shot by Capone gunmen.' B' marks the lookout position of Capone's men.*

Bottom: *The grisly scene in the garage into which Mrs Landesman stumbled.*

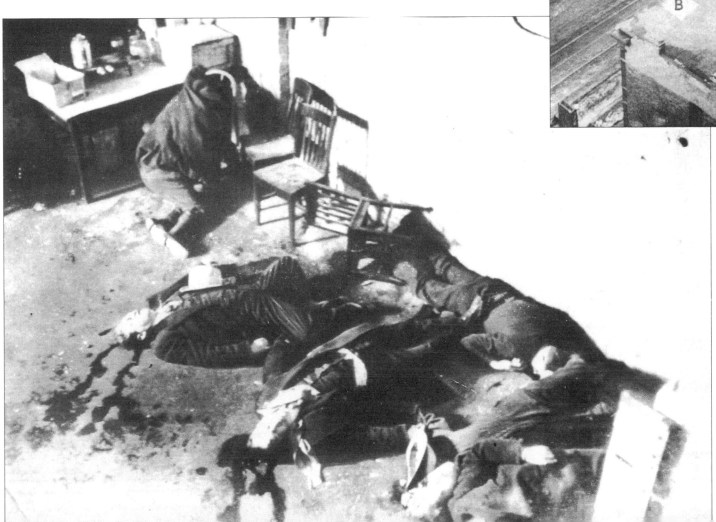

RASPUTIN

He was a powerful, big man with a commanding presence, and Rasputin had few problems in convincing women that they should follow him and his teachings.

Rasputin, the lecherous Siberian monk with the hypnotic gaze, held the Russian court in thrall. Only his death could break his evil spell but killing him was an unbelievably difficult task.

ussia has had more than its fair share of assassinations. Generals, politicians, an entire royal family all came to a violent end as incessant power struggles marked life in this troubled land. Yet the most famous Russian victim of assassination was not of noble birth and held no military rank nor political office. His name was Gregori Efimovitch Rasputin.

Rasputin was born in Siberia in 1871, and he spent the first thirty years of his life in that province. He had no formal education, pursued no known trade, yet he was a legendary figure in his home town of Tyumen, where he was a *staretz*, a wandering holy man, who beguiled everyone who met him, particularly women. Despite the fact that he was married with three children, he was an inveterate lecher. It was said that no women could resist his bold and hypnotic stare.

In order to survive, Rasputin did the rounds of the monasteries where he was given shelter and food. It was in 1905 on a visit to the Monastery of St Michael in Kiev that he was approached by two pilgrims who asked him about his work. Rasputin told them that he could heal the sick by prayer. The pilgrims, the Grand Duchesses Anastasia and Milatza, asked whether he had had any success with haemophilia. When Rasputin assured them that he had, the Russian noblewomen explained that their nephew, Tzarevitch Alexis, fifth child of Tzar Nicholas, was afflicted with the condition. Would he, Rasputin, be prepared to travel with them to St Petersberg and see the child?

A MIRACULOUS RECOVERY

The Romanoff court did not know quite what to make of Rasputin when he arrived in St Petersburg. He was dirty, malodorous and dressed in rags; his hair and beard were matted and unkempt and his fingernails were black. He was crude and uncouth yet his sheer charisma transcended all this; he was taken to the boy Alexis. Rasputin administered various herbs to his patient, then placed his hands on the boy's forehead and prayed. Miraculously, the boy seemed to improve instantly and his improvement became more marked as the days passed. The boy's mother, the Tzarina, was not only grateful to the monk, she was also

falling under his spell. From this time on, Rasputin could do no wrong in her eyes and his influence over her became so profound that, for the next decade, he became the virtual ruler of Russia and was feared by many.

Rasputin managed to maintain his position at court despite his own appalling depravity. He was a drunkard and a lecher who advocated sin as a means of achieving ultimate salvation. His theory was that one must sin in order to be purified by prayer; the greater the sin, the greater the absolution. His devotees, almost all women of high birth, would be encouraged to get drunk, be seduced and indulge in all manner of sexual perversion. When they were sated, they would confess their sins to Rasputin, be absolved, and they were then obliged to start sinning all over again.

Above: *Prince Yussupov was appalled at the power Rasputin extended over the Russian court. The prince saw the murder of the monk as an act of patriotism.*

HIS REPUTATION AS A HEALER WAS LEGENDARY; FOR HOURS SOCIETY WOMEN QUEUED ALONGSIDE BEGGARS TO RECEIVE HIS BLESSINGS.

Rasputin's own conduct was totally outrageous. He was accused of raping a nun, of organising orgies, of frequenting brothels, of cavorting naked through the streets of St Petersburg accompanied by prostitutes, and of keeping eleven concubines under the same roof as his wife and three children.

Above: Rasputin moved in the best society. He was photographed here with (left) Captain Von Lohman of the Ismailovsky Regiment, and Prince Poutiatine.

RASPUTIN COULD DO NO WRONG

Much of Russian society was appalled at Rasputin's behaviour and at the influence he held over the Tzarina, but they didn't dare express this in public. In the Tzarina's eyes, Rasputin could do no wrong and anyone who had the temerity to criticise him was likely to be packed off to Siberia.

As Rasputin's influence at court grew, even the edicts of the Tzar himself were frequently countermanded by him. His reputation as a healer had also reached legendary proportions; for hours society women would queue alongside beggars and the infirm to receive his blessings.

Rasputin was away from court when the First World War broke out. He had taken his son Dimitri back to his native Siberia. While he was there, he was attacked and stabbed by a woman called Guseva. The woman narrowly escaped being lynched and was thrown in prison. She told her inquisitors that she had stabbed the lay monk to avenge all the young Siberian women he had corrupted.

After a period of convalescence, Rasputin returned to St Petersberg and the court. Rasputin's influence would have probably continued unchallenged, had it not been for Prince Felix Yussupov. The Prince, a twenty-seven-year-old Oxford graduate, was married to the Tzar's niece and he was terrified that his young wife might fall under Rasputin's spell. Added to this, he considered Rasputin's influence over the Tzar and Tzarina to be unhealthy, particularly in light of his pro-German stance. All in all, the Prince decided, it was time for Rasputin to go.

There was no way of persuading the Tzarina to get rid of her mentor and so Prince Yussupov and a group of conspirators decided to kill him. They included the Grand Duke Dmitri Pavlovitch, the Tzar's cousin; Dr Stanislaus Lasovert, a Polish physician; and a right-wing politician, Deputy Pourichkevich.

Prince Yussupov organised a party at his home for the evening of 30 December, 1916, and invited Rasputin to attend. Dr Lasovert provided a large quantity of cyanide which was mixed in liberal quantities into six small almond cakes, Rasputin's favourite. The poison was also introduced into a bottle of Madeira wine.

HE WOULD NOT DIE

Rasputin arrived at the party and began to tuck into the cakes. Yussupov watched in astonishment as the monk ate all six then washed them down with the entire bottle of poisoned wine. Rasputin showed no ill effects, got up from the table and started to dance. The hours passed; Rasputin stayed not only alive, but lively.

Prince Yussupov was becoming desperate. Would this man never die? He drew Rasputin's attention to an ivory crucifix that was standing on a cabinet at the end of the room. As the monk bent down to examine the object, the Prince drew his revolver and shot him in the side. Rasputin fell to the floor but, as Yussupov knelt by him, his eyes flashed open and he grabbed his assailant by the throat. The terrified Prince made a dash for the door, pursued by Rasputin on all fours.

Rasputin staggered into the courtyard where he was confronted by Grand Duke Dimitri, who shot him in the chest with his service revolver. Again Rasputin fell. The Prince, wanting to make absolutely sure that he had finished the job, then battered the monk with a steel bar but the terrible eyes continued to stare up at him.

THE SECRET BURIAL

A few minutes after the second shooting, the police arrived. They were dispatched with a tall story and a thousand–rouble bribe, then the conspirators set about disposing of Rasputin's body. They wrapped him in a fur coat, bundled him, still alive, into the back of a car and drove to the River Neva. There they threw the monk into the icy water.

Rasputin's body was discovered three days later, lodged against the pier of a bridge. He was buried secretly in a small

Above and below: *Rasputin surrounded himself with female followers. These photographs, taken in St Petersburg, date from about 1916.*

wooden chapel near the imperial palace. And, while it was widely rumoured that Prince Yussupov and his friends had been responsible for Rasputin's death, there was never a formal inquiry and the Prince never faced prosecution for his actions.

But the monk's power extended beyond the grave. Rasputin had always claimed that, if he died, it would spell the downfall of the Romanoff dynasty. On 18 July, 1918, eighteen months after his death, the entire Russian royal family was assassinated by revolutionaries at Ekaterinburg.

MARTIN LUTHER KING

Above: *Dr Martin Luther King addressing marchers in Selma. He travelled all over the country to spread his message of equality for America's black people.*

KING WAS VIEWED WITH ANYTHING FROM SUSPICION TO DOWNRIGHT HATRED BY MANY WHITES, PARTICULARLY IN THE SOUTH.

James Earl Ray was convicted as the lone rifleman who murdered civil rights activisit Dr King but vital questions about the murder and Ray's accomplices remain unanswered.

The Reverend Dr Martin Luther King was a man of God; he was also the most powerful civil rights activist in America during the 1960s; and he was black. This potent combination guaranteed him more than his fair share of enemies.

Born in Atlanta, Georgia, on 15 January, 1929, King was ordained a minister in 1947 and served as pastor of the Ebenezer Baptist Church in Atlanta. He first came to national attention in connection with the civil rights movement in 1956, when he led a successful boycott of the Montgomery, Alabama bus system.

He was not a fundamentalist Bible-basher, but an educated theologian, devoted to practical Christianity, a man who saw racial segregation as a America's greatest moral and social problem. He was father of the sit-in and was imprisoned several times for his policy of civil disobedience when he broke laws that he considered discriminatory.

On 20 September, 1958, the first attempt was made on King's life when he was seriously injured by a knife-wielding woman in New York. Following his recovery, he organised and led a major civil rights march on Washington DC in support of the Civil Rights Act. In 1964, this Act became law and, in recognition of his non-violent role, King was awarded the Nobel Peace Prize. He was thirty-five and the youngest person ever to be so honoured.

THE ROAD TO MEMPHIS

The Civil Rights Act was law and King had received recognition for his work but his fight against discrimination continued. He achieved a great deal but his non-violent approach was too benign for many black citizens, increasingly impatient with their second-rate status in American life. At the same time, King was viewed with anything from suspicion to down-right hatred by a large proportion of the white population, particularly those in the southern states, to whom white superiority was a God given right, a right which Dr Martin Luther King was trying to usurp.

It was against this background of mounting intolerance that King went to Memphis, Tennessee on 4 April, 1966, to organise a march in support of striking sanitation department workers. King delivered a sermon that morning that suggested that he

was aware of the danger he was in, or at least of his own mortality: 'Every now and then,' he said, 'I guess we all think realistically about that day when we will all be victimised with what is life's final common denominator, that something we call death. We all think about it, and every now and then I think about my own funeral. And I don't think about it in the morbid sense. And every now and then I ask myself what it is that I would want said, and I leave word for you this morning...I won't have any money to leave behind. I won't have the fine and luxurious things to leave behind. But what I do want to do is to leave a committed life behind and that is all I want to say.'

Below: *Friends and colleagues said an emotional farewell to Dr King, who was only thirty-nine years old when he died.*

Bottom: *Martin Luther King and his wife, Coretta, at the head of one of the many civil rights marches he organised.*

THE NEW YORK TIMES

MARTIN LUTHER KING IS SLAIN IN MEMPHIS;
A WHITE IS SUSPECTED; JOHNSON URGES CALM

Above: *Dr King's death was front-page news all over the world. This is how the New York Times reported it.*

KING WAS AWARDED THE NOBEL PEACE PRIZE. AT THIRTY-FIVE, HE WAS THE YOUNGEST MAN EVER TO BE SO HONOURED

Across the road from the comfortable Lorraine Hotel, where Dr King and his wife, Coretta, were staying, stood a $4-a-night flop-house. On the morning of 4 April, a thirty-eight-year-old white man checked in under the name of John Willard.

A GUNMAN AND HIS LUGGAGE

The man had several other aliases, including Eric Stavro Galt and Harvey Lowmyer, but his real name, the name by which the world would come to know him, was James Earl Ray.

Ray arrived at the hotel by car, a white Ford Mustang, and he carried one piece of luggage, a blue canvas bag containing a .30.06 rifle fitted with a telescopic sight. Ray went straight to his room, locked himself in the bathroom and loaded the rifle with dum-dum bullets. Then he adjusted the scope, focusing it at a window of the Lorraine Hotel. The window, some two hundred feet away, belonged to the suite occupied by Dr and Mrs King. Ray sat on the window sill and waited for his quarry to show himself.

After a while, Ray noticed a figure moving about inside the suite but he could not be sure that it was King, nor could he get a clear shot. Then the screen door of the suite slid open and Martin Luther King stepped out on to the small balcony. With time to take care, Ray focused his rifle and fired a single shot; King's head snapped back and he fell to the ground.

Ray waited for a moment to see if his victim showed any sign of life and then, satisfied King was dead, he hurried out of the boarding house, dropped his rifle in an alleyway, jumped into his car and drove off.

Coretta King heard her husband falling and rushed out to the balcony. She found him bleeding and immobile and raised the alarm. The police and ambulance service arrived within minutes but it was too late. Martin Luther King had died instantly from a single bullet wound to the head.

AN ASSASSIN WITH MANY NAMES

Identifying and catching the assassin was a long and complex process. He had checked into the boarding house under the name of Willard, purchased the rifle and ammuni-

MARTIN LUTHER KING. JR.
1929 — 1968
Free at last. Free at last.
Thank God Almighty
I'm Free at last.

tion in the name of Lowmyer and had made his escape in a car registered in the name of Galt. When the FBI finally found a room once rented by Galt, they discovered only one fingerprint. This was identified as the print of a criminal known by the name of James Earl Ray, who was currently on the run from Missouri State Penitentiary where he was meant to be serving a twenty-year sentence for armed robbery.

A massive manhunt took police from Memphis to Toronto where Ray, using the name Ramon George Sneyd, had booked into a boarding house. Then Scotland Yard detectives picked up the trail and informed the FBI that Ray had been in London but that he had since flown on to Portugal.

Portuguese police could find no trace of anyone answering Ray's description and the trail went cold. Then, on 7 June, three months after the killing, a detective at Heathrow Airport stopped a man travelling from Lisbon and asked to see his passport. The Canadian passport, recently issued in Toronto, showed the man's name to be Sneyd. Sneyd was taken to Cannon Row police station. The man's fingerprints were wired to the FBI who confirmed that these were the fingerprints of James Earl Ray.

Ray was extradited to stand trial in Memphis where he pleaded Guilty to

RAY WENT STRAIGHT TO HIS ROOM, LOCKED HIMSELF IN THE BATHROOM AND LOADED THE RIFLE WITH DUM-DUM BULLETS.

PORTUGUESE POLICE COULD FIND NO TRACE OF ANYONE ANSWERING RAY'S DESCRIPTION AND THE TRAIL WENT COLD.

Right: *The face of the man who changed America for ever, and for the better.*

Below: *Dr King's widow, Correta, stands by her husband's crypt as her father-in-law, King Sr, is helped away from his son's memorial service.*

killing Dr King and was sentenced to ninety-nine years imprisonment. But his trial left many questions unanswered. Did he act alone? If so, how did a man of limited intelligence and on the run from prison get hold of a car, a high-powered rifle and ammunition, false documents and enough money to fly half way across the world? By pleading Guilty, Ray avoided answering any of these questions and so they remain unanswered to this day.

The Assassin

JAMES EARL RAY

James Earl Ray was born in 1928 in Atlanta, Georgia. His family, which was extremely poor, had once been a leading light in local society. James Earl Ray's life was a disaster from the start. As a teenager, he had a brief stint with the underworld, then he joined the army, but was thrown out for insubordination and alcoholism. He drifted back into a life of crime and spent the next twenty years in and out of prison.

Ray's innate hatred of blacks was intensified when he learned that his family home had been sold to a black family. Martin Luther King became a symbol of a social injustice which Ray considered to be responsible for his own miserable condition.

POPE JOHN PAUL II

Pope John Paul II's enthusiasm for moving unprotected among his flock allowed him to become the target of an assassin's bullets. Whether by luck or divine intervention, the Pope lived to forgive his would-be killer.

From the beginning of his papacy, Pope John Paul II set out to be more accessible to his people than his predecessors had been. It was a style of leadership which brought him enormous popularity but also one that exposed him to obvious security risks.

On 13 May, 1981, John Paul was travelling through St Peter's Square, Rome, in his open-top car. It was his weekly audience when he blessed the crowd. As the vehicle crawled through thousands of people, the Pope waved and touched the faithful.

At 5.19pm, the car was heading towards the front steps of the Basilica when six shots rang out and the Pope, bleeding profusely, fell forward into the arms of his secretary Don Stanislaw Dziwisz.

POWERFUL BULLETS AND SUPERFICIAL WOUNDS

One eyewitness described the scene: 'I saw two streams of blood. They were clearly visible on the Pope's white silk vestments.' Another said: 'After he fell, he changed his expression with some pain, but the painful expression quickly disappeared and he appeared calm.'

As John Paul was rushed to Gemelli Clinic in Rome, police surrounded the gunman who was still carrying his 9mm Browning automatic weapon.

Meanwhile, the Pope was undergoing a four-and-a-half-hour operation. Despite the massive calibre of the bullets and the proximity of the attacker, none of the bullets had hit any of the Pope's vital organs and his life was never in real danger.

The gunman was soon identified as Mehmed Ali Agca, a twenty-three-year-old right-wing Turkish terrorist, nicknamed the Grey Wolf. Agca had recently escaped from a Turkish jail where he was being held for the murder of Abdi Ipecki, editor of the Turkish daily newspaper *Mulliyet*. However Rome's police found a letter in the boarding

Far left: *Pope John Paul's eagerness to meet his flock, made security a nightmare.*

Below: *Security men rush to the Pope's aid after the shooting as he lay slumped in his Papal car, with blood beginning to seep through his white vestements.*

house in which Agca had been staying. In it, he laid out his plans to kill the Pope 'in order to demonstrate to the world the imperialistic crimes of the Soviet Union and the United States'. Apparently he was protesting against Soviet action in Afganistan and US involvement in El Salvador. For historical reasons, Agca also objected strongly to the Pope's proposed visit to Turkey, saying: 'Western imperialism is planning to dispatch to Turkey, in the guise of a religious leader, the crusader commander, John Paul.'

Agca failed in his mission and the sixty-year-old Pope made a speedy and complete recovery from his wounds. On 22 July, Agca was tried in Rome, convicted of attempted murder and jailed for life.

Two years later, on 27 December, 1983, John Paul visited his attacker in Rome's Rebibbia prison. Agca apparently fell to his knees before the Pope, kissed his hand and begged for his forgiveness. John Paul willingly granted this. He emerged from Agca's cell an hour later, visibly moved, and said, 'I spoke with a brother of ours in whom I have total trust. What we have told each other is a secret between us.'

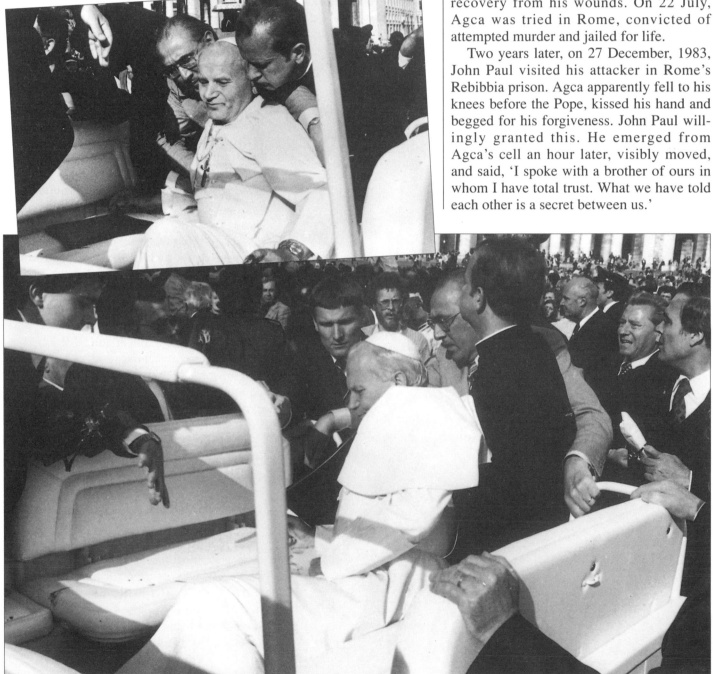

JOHN LENNON

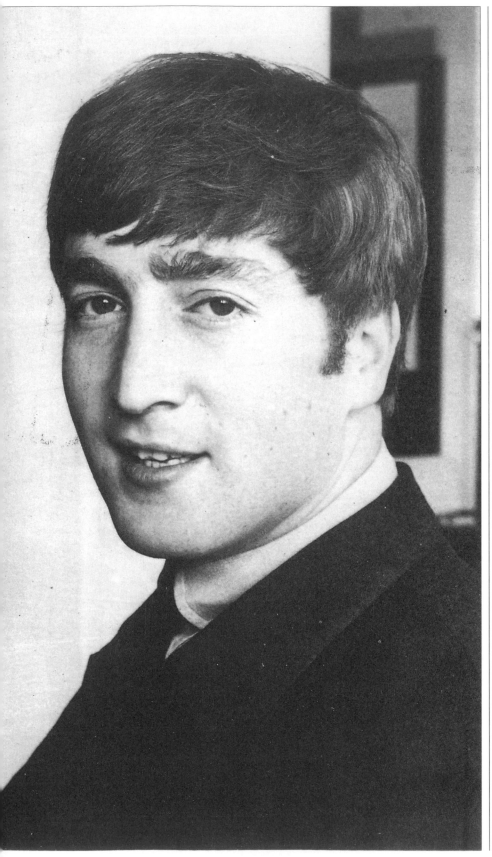

John Lennon believed in peace and love and rock 'n' roll. And so did his millions of fans who found it hard to understand that a lone madman had gunned down their idol for no reason at all.

In the early hours of 9 December, 1980, thousands of people were gathered outside New York's exclusive Dakota apartment building and chanting 'All you need is love'. They were mourning the loss of their idol, John Lennon, who had been gunned down in front of the building.

About 11pm the night before, after he had finished a recording session, Lennon, a founder member and architect of the legendary Beatles, had returned to the Dakota with his wife, Yoko Ono. As they walked towards the forecourt of the building, they heard a man call out, 'Mr Lennon.' Then there was a bang and Lennon staggered back. Yoko turned round to see Mark Chapman, a man who had accosted them earlier in the day, crouching on the pavement pointing a revolver. He fired four more rounds, all of which hit John. Yoko was transfixed, screaming, as her husband somehow managed to stagger into the office of the building's security guard.

'I'm shot', Lennon gasped through the blood that was welling up in his throat. The guard called the police who arrived in less than two minutes. 'I could see he was a goner. He was gasping for breath,' said the thirty-five-year-old police officer who bundled John into the back of a car and sped him to the Roosevelt Hospital, a few blocks away from the Dakota.

The journey took only a few minutes but both of Lennon's lungs had been punctured and he was pronounced dead on arrival at the hospital.

Mark Chapman, the twenty-five-year-old assassin, made no attempt to evade arrest after the shooting. He sat in the security guard's office and calmly read his favourite book, 'Catcher in the Rye', while he waited for the police to take him away.

There was an unprecedented upsurge of grief in America and throughout the world at Lennon's murder. Radio stations played his recordings non-stop for the next twenty-four hours, and more than a quarter of a million letters of sympathy flooded into the Dakota building. Two million records by the Beatles and John Lennon were sold in Britain alone in the following two months. The sadness at Lennon's passing was mixed with disgust and shame that, once again in America, an assassin had found it absurdly simple to approach and kill a famous person.

THE SPOKESMAN FOR A GENERATION

People started to compare the killing with the assassination of President John F. Kennedy in 1963. In some ways, this was not quite as absurd as it sounds, because Lennon was much more than a talented and enormously successful musician. He was, like Kennedy before him, an icon for his generation, a spokesman for their hopes and aspirations. He was an idealist, a poet, a writer and an outspoken proponent of the peace movement. He expressed his beliefs in many of his songs, notably 'Imagine' and, of course, 'All You Need is Love' which his mourners sang as his requiem.

THE END OF A DREAM

Tributes in the American press emphasised how the Beatles had become an integral part of the life of a certain generation of Americans, those who had grown up in the Sixties, now in their twenties and thirties. 'I get a sense of growing up, of finally growing old,' one fan said as he wept with other grieving mourners outside the Dakota building. But President Jimmy Carter summed up the significance of the man, and the universal sense of loss at his death with words that stand as a great obituary to the musician. The President said that John Lennon 'helped create the music and mood of our time. He leaves an extraordinary and permanent legacy. It is especially poignant that John Lennon died of violence, though he had long campaigned for peace.'

Top left: *The headline which brought the news to a shocked British public.*

Above: *Mark Chapman, the man who murdered John Lennon.*

Left: *John Lennon with his second wife, Yoko Ono, during the early and stylish days of their relationship.*

Far Left: *The young Lennon when he was a member of the Beatles.*

Above: *Thousands of mourners gathered at the open-air theatre in Toykyo's Hibiya Park to pay tribute to their dead idol, Lennon.*

Below: *Within hours of Lennon's death, crowds of mourners gathered outside the Dakota building where he had lived and died.*

John Lennon died just as he emerged from a long period of privacy during which he had turned away from his public role and retreated from the world of commercial music. Just hours before Chapman killed him, Lennon had given an interview to a radio reporter, his first in years, to promote his new album 'Double Fantasy'. It was to mark his return to his public life. John told the reporter that this record was intended for people of his generation. 'The people who grew up with me,' he explained, 'I'm saying "Here I am, how are you? How's your relationship going? Wasn't the Seventies a drag, you know? Well here we are, let's make the Eighties great."'

Tragically, John Lennon was not around to help make the Eighties great.

The Assassin

MARK CHAPMAN

Mark Chapman, who was twenty-five years old when he shot John Lennon, grew up in Georgia. Little is known about his background, other than he had an unexceptional middle-class upbringing, was deeply religious, and played the guitar badly. In the mid-Seventies, Chapman moved to Hawaii where he worked as a security guard. His grievance against John Lennon has never been clearly understood but what is certain is that the killing was planned. Chapman borrowed $2,000 to finance his trip to New York with the sole intention of assassination.

At his trial, Chapman gave no clue to his motives, nor did he express any regret for his actions. When invited to speak in his own defence, he simply repeated a passage from J.D. Salinger's 'Catcher in the Rye', the book he was carrying when he shot Lennon.

'I keep picturing all these little kids in this big field of rye – and nobody's around – nobody big I mean – except me, and I'm standing on the edge of some crazy cliff. I mean if they're running and they don't look where they're going, I have to come out from somewhere and catch them, that's all I'd do all day. I'd just be the catcher in the rye, and all.'

Chapman refused to follow his lawyer's advice and plead insanity. In light of this, Judge Dennis Edwards sentenced him to twenty years of life imprisonment, saying 'Mr Chapman is a very dangerous man. He deliberately stalked John Lennon and had no genuine regret for killing a man who was a husband and a father.'